Mastering Income Tax

Mastering Employment Discrimination Law, Second Edition
Paul M. Secunda, Jeffrey M. Hirsch, Joseph A. Seiner

Mastering Environmental Law
Joel A. Mintz, Tracy D. Hester

Mastering Family Law
Janet Leach Richards

Mastering First Amendment Law
John C. Knechtle

Mastering Income Tax, Second Edition
Gail Levin Richmond, Christopher M. Pietruszkiewicz

Mastering Intellectual Property
George W. Kuney, Donna C. Looper

Mastering Labor Law
Paul M. Secunda, Anne Marie Lofaso, Joseph E. Slater, Jeffrey M. Hirsch

Mastering Legal Analysis and Drafting
George W. Kuney, Donna C. Looper

Mastering Legislation, Regulation, and Statutory Interpretation, Third Edition
Linda D. Jellum

**Mastering Negotiable Instruments (UCC Articles 3 and 4) and
Other Payment Systems, Second Edition**
Michael D. Floyd

Mastering Negotiation
Michael R. Fowler

Mastering Partnership Taxation
Stuart Lazar

Mastering Professional Responsibility, Second Edition
Grace M. Giesel

Mastering Property Law, Revised Printing
Darryl C. Wilson, Cynthia Hawkins DeBose

Mastering Sales
Colin P. Marks, Jeremy Kidd

Mastering Secured Transactions: UCC Article 9, Second Edition
Richard H. Nowka

Mastering Tort Law, Second Edition
Russell L. Weaver, Edward C. Martin, Andrew R. Klein,
Paul J. Zwier, II, John H. Bauman

Mastering Trademark and Unfair Competition Law
Lars S. Smith, Llewellyn Joseph Gibbons

Mastering Trusts and Estates
Gail Levin Richmond, Don Castleman

Mastering Income Tax

SECOND EDITION

Gail Levin Richmond

EMERITA PROFESSOR OF LAW
NOVA SOUTHEASTERN UNIVERSITY
SHEPARD BROAD COLLEGE OF LAW

Christopher M. Pietruszkiewicz

FORMER DEAN
STETSON UNIVERSITY COLLEGE OF LAW
PRESIDENT
UNIVERSITY OF EVANSVILLE

CAROLINA ACADEMIC PRESS
Durham, North Carolina

Library of Congress Cataloging in Publication Data

Names: Richmond, Gail Levin, author. | Pietruszkiewicz, Christopher M.,
author.
Title: Mastering income tax / by Gail Levin Richmond, Christopher M.
Pietruszkiewicz.
Description: Second edition. | Durham, North Carolina : Carolina Aca-
demic Press, LLC, [2020] | Series: Carolina Academic Press Mastering
Series | Includes index.
Identifiers: LCCN 2020012987 (print) | LCCN 2020012988 (ebook) | ISBN
9781531016951 (paperback) | ISBN 9781531016968 (ebook)
Subjects: LCSH: Income tax--Law and legislation--United States. | LCGFT:
Textbooks.
Classification: LCC KF6369.85 .P54 2020 (print) | LCC KF6369.85 (ebook) |
DDC 343.7305/2--dc23
LC record available at https://lccn.loc.gov/2020012987
LC ebook record available at https://lccn.loc.gov/2020012988

Carolina Academic Press
700 Kent Street
Durham, NC 27701
Telephone (919) 489-7486
Fax (919) 493-5668
www.cap-press.com

Printed in the United States of America

Contents

Table of Cases

Table of Internal Revenue Code Sections

Table of Regulations

Table of Administrative Authorities

Series Editor's Foreword

The Carolina Academic Press Mastering Series is designed to provide you with a tool that will enable you to easily and efficiently "master" the substance and content of law school courses. Throughout the series, the focus is on quality writing that makes legal concepts understandable. As a result, the series is designed to be easy to read and is not unduly cluttered with footnotes or cites to secondary sources.

In order to facilitate student mastery of topics, the Mastering Series includes a number of pedagogical features designed to improve learning and retention. At the beginning of each chapter, you will find a "Roadmap" that tells you about the chapter and provides you with a sense of the material that you will cover. A "Checkpoint" at the end of each chapter encourages you to stop and review the key concepts, reiterating what you have learned. Throughout the book, key terms are explained and emphasized. Finally, a "Master Checklist" at the end of each book reinforces what you have learned and helps you identify any areas that need review or further study.

We hope that you will enjoy studying with, and learning from, the Mastering Series.

Russell L. Weaver
Professor of Law & Distinguished University Scholar
University of Louisville, Louis D. Brandeis School of Law

Preface

The income tax affects individuals in many ways. First, of course, they must compute the amount they owe (or any refund due to them) on an annual basis. Second, they confront tax consequences when they sell property or make gifts to family members. The attorneys who advise them encounter tax issues in every practice area. If they represent businesses accused of civil or criminal wrongdoing, they try to structure damages and other payments to preserve their deductibility. If they practice matrimonial law, they must understand the tax consequences of property settlements and custody. If they specialize in real property transactions, they regularly encounter the tax consequences of debt restructuring, eminent domain, and like-kind exchanges.

This book covers concepts you are likely to encounter in a basic federal income tax course. These range from the components of taxable income and tax—gross income, exclusions, deductions, and credits—to the rules that govern timing and character of income and deductions. Recognizing that tax must be considered in context, we focus on the most common income and deduction provisions and indicate how they affect taxpayers in various settings. We include numerous examples to illustrate the concepts in addition to citations to relevant authority.

Because it may appear that you must know everything about the income tax to understand any of its provisions, we begin with an overview of how the parts fit together. But our primary focus is on the material in subsequent chapters. We hope you find this book and its structure a useful guide to learning federal income tax.

Gail Levin Richmond
Shepard Broad College of Law
Nova Southeastern University
April 2020

Christopher M. Pietruszkiewicz
University of Evansville
April 2020

Acknowledgments

Christopher Pietruszkiewicz thanks Laralee Garvin, Brian Howsare, Kelly Kromer, Todd Taranto, Erik Vigen, Melissa Grand, Kristen Bell, Sharon Tsai, Emily Brouillette, and Jessica Fehr for their work in checking, updating, and revising the first edition.

Gail Richmond thanks Amy Rojas for her assistance in proofreading portions of the first edition.

Mastering Income Tax

Chapter 1

Introduction

Roadmap
- The federal income tax
- Working with the Code
- Components of the tax computation

A. The Federal Income Tax

The federal income tax raises revenue for government operations, but that is not its only function, nor is it the only federal tax. Most income tax provisions appear in title 26 of the United States Code, usually referred to as the Internal Revenue Code. Some provisions appear in other U.S.C. titles; a few provisions appear only in the Statutes at Large rather than in a U.S.C. title.

The Internal Revenue Code of 1986, as amended, provides the statutory framework. It replaced the 1954 Code, which in turn replaced the 1939 Code and earlier revenue acts. Unless this book refers to a specific codification, references to Code, to I.R.C. §, or simply to §, are to the 1986 Code, as amended.

1. Funding the Government

The federal government can raise revenue by imposing taxes, selling or leasing federal property, or borrowing. It can also impose user fees, such as tolls imposed on drivers. Subjects for taxation include income, transfers (including gratuitous transfers), and ownership. Although this book focuses on income taxes, it includes a brief discussion of the taxes imposed on gratuitous transfers because they might affect the timing of gifts to friends and family members. Taxes on other transfers (sales and use taxes and documentary stamp taxes on transfers of real property) and on ownership (property taxes) are generally imposed by state and local governments rather than the federal government, but the federal government may impose taxes (tariffs) on purchases

3

of goods made in other countries or excise taxes on, for example, gasoline or cigarettes. We ignore those other federal taxes in this book.

Some tax revenues go into the relevant government's general fund, to be used according to appropriations approved by the legislature (Congress, in the case of the federal government). Other taxes may be directed to funds set aside for a particular purpose. For example, gasoline taxes might be directed to improving the highway system, and employment taxes might be used to pay benefits to retirees, fund Medicare and other health-care programs, or aid disabled or unemployed individuals.

2. Tax Base and Rate Structure

Tax computations reflect at least two factors—the tax base and the tax rate(s). The federal income tax computation also reflects marital or other family status and the source of the taxpayer's income.

a. Tax Base

Taxable income is the tax base for computing the federal income tax. It has three major components. First is gross income, a subset of an undefined concept called income. A taxpayer who has no gross income is not subject to the income tax. From gross income, we subtract deductions. We can categorize deductions by where we place them on the tax return or by which aspect of the taxpayer's life (business, investment, or personal) they involve. The discussion in Section C focuses on where deductions are placed—whether they are taken in computing adjusted gross income (AGI) or are deducted from AGI to arrive at taxable income.

b. Rate Structure

A simple income tax might mimic a sales tax—applied at a flat rate no matter how large the tax base and irrespective of the taxpayer's family status. A *proportional* income tax would result in taxpayers who earned more paying a higher tax than, but at the same rate as, taxpayers who earned less. At the other extreme, the tax could mimic the Social Security tax, which—as of 2020—is imposed at a flat rate on earned income, but only up to an annually determined maximum. Because the rate then drops to zero on higher earnings, that tax is *regressive*—individuals who exceed the earnings cap pay no tax on their additional earnings.

With limited exceptions, the federal income tax is neither proportional nor regressive. Instead, it is a *progressive* tax. That term does not mean that the tax leads to progress. It simply means that the tax rates are graduated; they increase at certain income levels. Income within each level is taxed at a rate that is higher than the rate(s) imposed on lower levels of income.

3. Potential Taxpayers

Although the basic income tax course focuses on individuals, your casebook probably includes cases in which the taxpayer is a corporation, trust, or estate. This should not surprise you, as many of the relevant statutes and regulations apply to both individuals and entities. Although this text focuses on the treatment of individuals, we conclude the book with a chapter describing various entities.

Family structure influences the tax computation and rate structure. Individuals who are married and choose to report their income on one return (married, filing jointly) may fare better than two single individuals who are not eligible to file jointly even if they cohabit, but that is not always the case. Certain limits, particularly those involving deductions, may result in a married couple paying more tax than they would as single individuals. We discuss filing status and the effect of family relationships in several chapters.

4. Tax Policy

The problems in your casebook may require computations. They do so to illustrate the outcome; if you read the Code and other authorities correctly, you will arrive at the correct answer (which may simply be "it depends"). But your course probably goes beyond statutory interpretation and computations and considers various policy questions. Topics you may encounter relate to whether married and unmarried taxpayers should be treated differently, whether differences in tax should be based on differences in the source of taxpayers' income rather than differences in the amount of income, whether business deductions should favor acquiring machinery and equipment or paying human employees, and whether realized gains should be indexed for inflation instead of (or in addition to) being taxed at the lower rates applied to net capital gains.

5. Surviving Constant Code Amendments

Throughout this book, we indicate Code provisions that have limited lives, particularly several amended by the Tax Cuts and Jobs Act of 2017 or by legislation enacted during the COVID-19 pandemic. Congress engages in both major tax reform and minor tinkering on a regular basis. Code sections may be added, amended, or repealed, but certain principles remain relevant:

- Taxpayers engaged in a trade or business or an income-producing activity will be treated more generously regarding deductions than taxpayers who are acting in a purely personal capacity.
- Employers will be treated more generously regarding deductions than employees.
- Tax rates will be progressive, although the level of progressivity may change.
- Net capital gains will enjoy lower tax rates or some other advantage.
- Some deductions will be allowed to all taxpayers; other deductions will be allowed only to taxpayers who itemize.
- Taxpayer status (*e.g.*, married, head of household, surviving spouse, unmarried, elderly, dependent) will be relevant.
- Congress will phase some benefits out based on taxpayer income and will provide inflation adjustments for some items.
- Code sections will state general rules and then modify those rules with exceptions and exceptions to the exceptions.
- Income and deductions will have to be assigned to the correct taxpayer and taxable year.
- Transactions between related persons are more likely to be challenged in court or circumscribed by a Code section than transactions between unrelated persons.
- Some deductions will be useable only in a single tax year; if they exceed the taxpayer's income, their benefit is lost. Although other excess deductions will qualify to offset income of other years, the carryover may be limited in duration or indefinite.

B. Working with the Code

In explaining tax concepts, we discuss statutes, regulations, IRS rulings, and judicial decisions. We rarely mention the U.S. Constitution, which authorizes the imposition of taxes. Article I, §8, authorizes Congress to lay and collect taxes. The 16th Amendment authorizes the imposition of an income tax without apportionment among the states.

Constitutional challenges are often brought by tax protesters. Although nonprotester litigation involving constitutional challenges is infrequent, it does occur. In *Northern California Small Business Assistants Inc. v. Commissioner*,

153 T.C. No. 4 (2019), for example, the taxpayer unsuccessfully challenged § 280E (which denies deductions to businesses that "traffic" in controlled substances) as a violation of the 8th Amendment's Excessive Fines clause.

Because the Constitution authorizes Congress to lay and collect taxes, we begin by discussing how to read the Code.

1. The Initial Code Section

When working through a tax problem, you will encounter one or more relevant Code sections. Many of them require you to take several steps. The order that follows is one we suggest, but you may find a different order more useful. First, read the opening subsection; it provides a general rule. Second, continue reading to see if any other subsections (or smaller subdivisions, such as paragraphs or subparagraphs) provide exceptions to that general rule. Often exceptions are added to limit the provision to taxpayers with certain characteristics (*e.g.*, individuals as opposed to corporations or taxpayers engaged in a trade or business as opposed to investors). Third, read on to look for exceptions to the exceptions. As you go through the first three steps, look for language defining terms used in the section. Definitions might appear in a subsection entitled "Definitions" or "Meaning of Terms," but that is not necessarily the case. You can also consult § 7701, which provides definitions that apply throughout the Code. Fourth, if a Code section involves specific dollar amounts, look for subsections providing for inflation adjustments. Fifth, check for language involving effective dates or expiration dates. Because Congress frequently amends the Code, it is important to apply the law in effect when the transaction you are studying occurred.

2. Other Code Sections

Tax problems often involve multiple Code sections. Language in one section may be modified by language in a different section as well as by modifying language in the original section. In addition to helping you determine if a receipt is gross income or an outlay is deductible, those other sections may address determining the relevant taxpayer, the relevant tax year, or the character of the income or deduction (*e.g.*, capital or ordinary).

Although there are exceptions, the Code has a structure you can use to find other relevant sections. Most provisions involving gross income (both specifically included and specifically excluded items) appear in proximity, as do most provisions involving allowable deductions. Additional groupings cover nondeductible items, taxable year and accounting methods, and computation, nonrecognition, and character of gain or loss.

3. Inflation Adjustments, Code Amendments, and Relevant Dates

a. Inflation Adjustments

Some Code sections limit tax benefits based on percentages of income, and others refer to specific dollar amounts; some sections involve both factors. Provisions based on percentages result in different amounts as a taxpayer's income rises or falls. Provisions based only on flat amounts are not affected by changes in a taxpayer's income.

> **Example 1-1.** Aiden had adjusted gross income of $90,000 in 2018 and $100,000 in 2019. I.R.C. § 170(b)(1)(G) let him deduct up to 60% of his AGI for cash gifts to charity. His maximum deduction in 2018 was $54,000; his maximum deduction for 2019 was $60,000.

> **Example 1-2.** Alice placed her home on the market last year. The offer she received was for $225,000 more than she paid for the home eight years ago. She declined the offer and—because of inflation in the housing market—was able to sell the home for a $300,000 profit this year. I.R.C. § 121(b)(1) lets an unmarried taxpayer exclude up to $250,000 of the gain realized on selling a principal residence. That amount was enacted more than 20 years ago and has never been increased to reflect general levels of inflation or inflation specifically in housing markets. If Alice sold her home last year, she would have reported no taxable gain; because she sold it this year, she reports $50,000 of her gain as gross income.

Some Code sections that involve flat amounts also provide formulas for increasing those amounts to reflect changes in the cost of living. We refer to the cost-of-living formulas as inflation adjustments and use the inflation-adjusted amounts in effect on January 1, 2020. Many of those amounts will increase in 2021 and later years. Because those adjustments occur annually, we do not cite to the revenue procedures announcing the new amounts. When working with a Code section that lists a flat deduction or exclusion, check later in that section to see if it includes an inflation adjustment.

> **Example 1-3.** Arthur took the standard deduction instead of itemizing in 2019 and 2020. I.R.C. § 63(c)(7)(A)(ii) gives an unmarried individual

a $12,000 standard deduction for 2018 through 2025. Because §63(c)(7)(B) increases this amount to reflect inflation, Arthur's standard deduction for 2020 ($12,400) was larger than his 2019 deduction ($12,200).

b. Code Amendments and Effective Dates

Congress regularly amends the Code. Some amendments involve extensive changes, as occurred with the Tax Cuts and Jobs Act of 2017. Other amendments, often covering only a few sections, may be included in legislation primarily focused on other matters. Still other provisions appear in Technical Corrections Acts, which are often necessary to fix glitches in an earlier act's language. Constant change frustrates practitioners (and their clients) as much as it does law students because it makes planning more difficult. When determining the tax consequences applied to an event, check the effective date of any relevant Code section.

c. Expiration Dates

Although Congress can amend Code sections anytime, certain provisions include expiration dates. Example 1-3 illustrates one such provision. Unless Congress extends the version currently in effect, the standard deduction will revert to its pre-2018 version in 2026. Congress often postpones expiration dates by enacting "extender" legislation. Extender legislation does not necessarily cover every expiring provision.

Several provisions enacted in the Tax Cuts and Jobs Act of 2017 have expiration dates, but others do not. We focus on legislation in effect in 2020 but may cover the pre-2017 Act legislation as part of our explanations.

Several Code sections expired at the end of 2019 or even earlier. Some had previously expired and been extended, sometimes multiple times, and sometimes by retroactive legislation. Some were extended through December 2020 by the Further Consolidated Appropriations Act, 2020, Pub. L. No. 116-94. It is likely that those sections (and perhaps other expired provisions) will be extended again, either in their current form or with amendments. The staff of the Joint Committee on Taxation (jct.gov) annually publishes a list of Code sections due to expire over a multi-year period; JCX-1-20 covers provisions set to expire in 2020 through 2029.

Commentators often criticize Congress for enacting provisions with expiration dates and then extending those dates rather than permanently retaining or eliminating the provisions. Taxpayers find planning more difficult when they don't know if a particular provision will still be the law in the future. In addition, because extenders often apply retroactively, they benefit taxpayers who may have acted without relying on the provision being reinstated.

4. IRS and Judicial Interpretations

The Code sections you find may not answer all your questions. In that case, you might read regulations, IRS rulings, and judicial decisions covering those sections. Your casebook probably cites to numerous regulations and includes the text of selected IRS rulings and judicial decisions. When reading judicial decisions, keep the year in mind. Decisions issued for the 1939 Code may still be accurate representations of the law, but the Code sections they cite to follow a different numbering system than the system used in the 1954 and 1986 Codes. Your casebook editor may have substituted the current Code section number for the number in use when the case was decided, but that may not be the case.

a. IRS Guidance

Although Congress enacts the governing statutes, the executive branch is responsible for enforcing them. Section 7805 authorizes the Secretary to "prescribe all needful rules and regulations for the enforcement of [the Code]." The Secretary referred to is the Secretary of the Treasury. The Treasury Department is an agency within the executive branch. One of its subdivisions, the IRS, drafts regulations, which the Treasury Department issues pursuant to § 7805 or to the authority contained in other Code sections.

Regulations issued pursuant to § 7805 are general authority regulations. They are often called interpretive or interpretative regulations. Regulations issued pursuant to a directive in another Code section are specific authority regulations. They are often called legislative regulations. The distinction is less important since the Supreme Court's decision in *Mayo Foundation for Medical Education and Research v. United States*, 562 U.S. 44 (2011), and we do not distinguish between regulation types in this book.

Regulations can be issued as proposed, temporary, or final regulations. Proposed regulations reflect the Treasury and IRS's initial interpretation of a Code section. They may later be withdrawn, amended, or issued (with or without amendments) as final regulations. Temporary regulations issued since late November 1988 must be finalized (with or without amendments) no more than three years after they are issued; if not finalized, they expire. In addition, a proposed regulation must be issued at the same time. I.R.C. § 7805(e). Proposed regulations do not expire at the end of three years. Final and temporary regulations are published in Code section order in the Code of Federal Regulations. Most tax regulations are in title 26 C.F.R. Regulations are not always current. If the language of a regulation contradicts language in the Code, check to see when the relevant language in each was last amended.

Regulations have three segments—a number that precedes a decimal point; a number that follows that decimal point; and a final number, which follows a hyphen (*e.g.*, 1.162-1 or 1.71-1T). The number preceding the decimal point indicates the appropriate part of title 26 C.F.R. Most income tax regulations begin with 1 because they appear in part 1. The number after the decimal point indicates the Code section being interpreted. The final number does not necessarily indicate anything substantive, but it is useful when citing to particularly long sets of regulations. We refer to final regulations as Regulation or Reg.; proposed regulations as Proposed Regulation or Prop. Reg.; and temporary regulations—which include a T in their number—as Temporary Regulation or Temp. Reg. When you cite regulations in articles or briefs, add Treasury or Treas. before Regulation or Reg. to differentiate these regulations from regulations issued by other federal agencies.

The IRS issues published guidance on substantive tax issues by issuing revenue rulings. These include a set of facts and legal conclusions. The facts often reflect an issue that taxpayers commonly encounter. Revenue procedures provide guidance on procedural issues. We cite these items as Rev. Rul. and Rev. Proc. The IRS also issues less formal published guidance—notices and announcements. Revenue rulings, revenue procedures, notices, and announcements appear in the weekly Internal Revenue Bulletin (I.R.B.). The IRS compiled the weekly Bulletins into semiannual Cumulative Bulletins (C.B.), but it stopped publishing the C.B. after 2008-2 C.B.

The IRS also issues private letter rulings (PLRs). PLRs resemble revenue rulings, but they are issued to a specific, unnamed taxpayer. Other taxpayers can read them but cannot cite them as precedent for substantive tax issues. Other forms of IRS guidance include technical advice memoranda (TAMs), which provide opinions on issues raised in an audit, various forms of advice from the Chief Counsel's office (CCAs), and actions on decisions (AODs). AODs and notices of acquiescence (acq.) or nonacquiescence (nonacq.) indicate if the IRS will continue litigating an issue after a court rules against its position. The IRS website (irs.gov) also includes tax-return-oriented publications and FAQ sections.

b. Judicial Action

Our tax system relies on self-assessment (taxpayer-prepared tax returns). Compliance is encouraged through tax withholding, information returns that permit the IRS to verify that taxpayers are reporting the proper amount of income, and the possibility of an audit. If the IRS and the taxpayer disagree about the amount of tax due, they try to resolve their dispute through administrative processes. A taxpayer who cannot resolve her differences with the IRS at the administrative level may decide to litigate in an appropriate judicial forum.

Litigation. Taxpayers may litigate in three different forums, the Tax Court, the Court of Federal Claims, and federal district court. The Tax Court and the Court of Federal Claims have national jurisdiction; the appropriate district court reflects the taxpayer's residence. Jury trials are available only in district court.

In Tax Court, the taxpayer may litigate without first paying the proposed liability. The Court of Federal Claims or a district court has jurisdiction only if she pays the proposed liability in full, timely files a claim for refund, and timely files a petition. Because she is not required to pay the proposed deficiency before litigating in Tax Court, most tax cases are litigated there.

Although the Tax Court has national jurisdiction, precedent that would bind a district court also binds the Tax Court for cases filed in that district. That is because an adverse decision of the Tax Court is appealed to the circuit court that would hear an appeal from a district court decision. The Tax Court applies the "law of the circuit" even if it would hold differently in the absence of circuit precedent. *Golsen v. Commissioner*, 54 T.C. 742 (1970). Appeals from the Court of Federal Claims are to the Federal Circuit. An appeal from any circuit is to the U.S. Supreme Court.

The Tax Court issues several types of opinions. The government publishes regular Tax Court decisions (also called division opinions), which are cited T.C. Those decisions often involve disputes over what the Code or other authority means. Memorandum decisions generally involve disputes over how the law applies to a set of facts. Although the Tax Court makes memorandum decisions available on its website, it does not issue them in bound volumes. We cite to memorandum decisions by year and number, *e.g.*, T.C. Memo. 2020-3; some publishers use other numbering systems (*e.g.*, T.C.M.). Both regular and memorandum decisions can be appealed to the circuit court covering the taxpayer's jurisdiction. A taxpayer can bring cases involving $50,000 or less in liability in the Tax Court's small case division. The summary opinion issued in a small case cannot be appealed or cited as precedent.

The Tax Court was preceded by the Board of Tax Appeals. A citation that includes B.T.A. is a citation to a case litigated in that tribunal before it became the Tax Court in 1942.

Although taxpayers living in different jurisdictions may be involved in the same transaction, they do not have to take the same route through the courts. For example, one taxpayer may pay the tax and litigate in district court, and the other may file in Tax Court without paying the tax. A taxpayer who lives in a circuit with an adverse appellate precedent may choose to litigate in the Court of Federal Claims, which is not bound by the law of her circuit.

> **Example 1-4.** Alexis resides in Louisiana. Barb resides in Pennsylvania. Each was audited for the same issue and could not reach agreement with the IRS. Alexis filed a petition in Tax Court. After an adverse decision, she appealed to the Court of Appeals for the Fifth Circuit based on her Louisiana residence. Barb paid the proposed liability and filed a petition in the District Court for the Middle District of Pennsylvania. After an adverse decision, Barb appealed to the Court of Appeals for the Third Circuit based on her Pennsylvania residence. Each of them could instead have paid the tax, filed a petition in the Court of Federal Claims, and appealed an adverse decision to the Court of Appeals for the Federal Circuit.

The case name indicates litigation that began in Tax Court if it includes *Commissioner*. If it instead includes *United States*, the litigation began in either a district court or the Court of Federal Claims. Earlier decisions used the name of government officials rather than Commissioner; *Helvering* is an example.

The discussion above ignores federal bankruptcy courts, which can also decide tax issues. Appeals from those courts may go to a district court, to a bankruptcy appellate panel, or to a circuit court. This book does not include any bankruptcy court decisions.

5. Interpretive Doctrines

IRS guidance and judicial decisions may refer to interpretive doctrines guiding their decision. Most of these doctrines are not part of the Code. In fact, some of them are used to change the tax results of a transaction whose form follows statutory language. The doctrines described below are among those you may encounter.

One such doctrine involves determining whether a transaction's form accurately reflects its substance. For example, a taxpayer who owns a business may claim that amounts she paid her child to work were deductible compensation for services rendered when they appear more in the nature of a nondeductible gift. The step transaction doctrine collapses multiple steps when it appears that some steps were added to secure a tax result that the parties would not have achieved by directly reaching the end result. A third doctrine, later codified as §7701(o), requires that a transaction have economic benefit and purpose other than tax savings.

You may also see decisions using two terms of Latin origin. Courts invoke *ejusdem generis* to require a general term to have the same characteristics as the more-specific terms preceding it. For example, the § 165(c)(3) personal casualty loss deduction refers to "fire, storm, shipwreck, other casualty, or theft"; to qualify as an "other casualty," the event must have the same characteristics (*i.e.*, suddenness and unexpectedness) as fire, storm, and shipwreck. Similarly, when the Code lists specific items but does not list others (and fails to say "includes"), a court may refuse to treat the unlisted items the same as those Congress listed. The court relies on *expressio unius, exclusio alterius* (stating one excludes others that are not stated) in that situation.

Two other doctrines relate to the difference between inclusions (a gross income concept) and deductions. Courts interpret gross income expansively; they hold that Congress intended to exercise its taxing power to the fullest extent. The taxpayer has the burden of establishing that an item should be excluded. Courts use a different rule in determining whether a taxpayer can claim a deduction. They state that deductions are a matter of legislative grace; the taxpayer has the burden of establishing her right to take a claimed deduction.

C. Components of the Tax Computation

The income tax applies to taxable income. We begin with relevant receipts (gross income). We then determine which outlays (deductions) are used in computing an intermediate step (adjusted gross income) and which are deducted from adjusted gross income and may require the taxpayer to itemize. After we subtract deductions and reach taxable income, we compute the tax. We reduce the tax by any credits to which we are entitled. As you deal with the Code's general rules, exceptions to those rules, and exceptions to the exceptions, keep this general schematic in mind:

	Gross Income
Minus	Above-the-Line Deductions
Equals	Adjusted Gross Income (AGI)
Minus	Qualified Business Income Deduction
Minus	Standard Deduction OR Itemized Deductions
Equals	Taxable Income
Times	Relevant Tax Rate(s)
Equals	Tax Liability Before Credits
Minus	Tax Credits
Equals	Net Tax Liability (or Tax Refund)

1. Gross Income

The Code describes gross income expansively. Gross income means "all income from whatever source derived." I.R.C. §61(a). That section specifically lists 14 items, including compensation for services, gross income from business, gains derived from dealings in property, interest, rents, and royalties. The list is not exclusive. Gross income potentially includes *every* financial benefit received, not merely those listed.

Section 61(a) begins with this language: "Except as otherwise provided in [another income tax Code section]." We discuss many of these sections in chapters covering specific items of gross income and exclusions.

Although the schematic above begins with gross income, your casebook may instead begin with "income" because §61(a) states that gross income is *income* from whatever source derived (other than specifically excluded items). A schematic based on income would begin with Income minus Exclusions equals Gross Income.

2. Deductions, Adjusted Gross Income, and Taxable Income

Gross income minus allowable deductions equals taxable income. The Code allows deductions for expenses and losses that affect taxpaying ability. Deductions fall into three categories: trade or business; income-producing; and personal. Adjusted gross income (AGI) is determined by subtracting "above-the-line" deductions from gross income; AGI is the "line." We deduct above-the-line deductions in addition to taking either the standard deduction or itemized deductions. Section 62(a) lists most of the above-the-line deductions, but it does not make any item deductible. It merely determines if an authorized deduction is deducted in computing AGI.

After computing AGI, we deduct either the standard deduction or our itemized deductions. I.R.C. §63. The standard deduction varies based on filing status. Most itemized deductions are for outlays that are not related to business or income-producing activities. These include deductions for state and local taxes, home mortgage interest, charitable contributions, and medical expenses. We may also deduct the §199A deduction for qualified business income. That deduction is unusual in its treatment. Although it is available only to taxpayers who have business income, it is not an above-the-line deduction. Taxpayers can take this deduction whether they take the standard deduction or itemize.

The final deduction would normally be for personal exemptions for the taxpayer, his spouse, and dependents. I.R.C. §151. Although personal exemptions are not deductible in 2018 through 2025, the definition of dependent remains relevant for other provisions we cover in this book.

3. Tax Liability

a. Tax Rates

Ordinary income. Tax liability is determined by applying the tax rate schedules in § 1(j) to taxable income. The rate structure is progressive. Higher amounts of income are subject to higher tax rates, but those higher rates apply only to the additional income. The top rate applied to taxable income is called the marginal tax rate. Each range of income covered by one of the rates is a tax rate bracket. The seven current rates on ordinary income are 10%, 12%, 22%, 24%, 32%, 35%, and 37%.

Each rate applies only to taxable income within its rate bracket. Even if taxable income exceeds $1 billion, part of it is still taxed at the 10% rate. Only amounts in the 37% bracket are taxed at 37%. In 2020, for example, an unmarried individual pays tax at these rates:

> 10% rate on his first $9,875 of taxable income;
> 12% on the next $30,250 (taxable income exceeding $9,875 but not exceeding $40,125);
> 22% on the next $45,400 (taxable income exceeding $40,125 but not exceeding $85,525);
> 24% on the next $77,775 (taxable income exceeding $85,525 but not exceeding $163,300);
> 32% on the next $44,050 (taxable income exceeding $163,300 but not exceeding $207,350);
> 35% on the next $311,050 (taxable income exceeding $207,350 but not exceeding $518,400); and
> 37% on any taxable income exceeding $518,400.

> **Example 1-5.** Betty is unmarried and has 2020 taxable income of $51,000. Her tax (before credits) is 10% of $9,875 ($987.50), plus 12% of $30,250 ($3,630), plus 22% of $10,875 ($2,392.50). That totals $7,010.

Betty is in the 22% marginal tax rate bracket. Because the $7,010 tax is 13.75% of her $51,000 taxable income, her average tax rate (also called effective tax rate) is only 13.75%. Each year the IRS updates the rate brackets to reflect inflation; the 10% rate in 2021 will thus apply to part of the taxable income amount that was subject to the 12% rate in 2020.

Taxpayers do not have to compute their income tax by going through each rate bracket separately. The IRS annually issues tables that collapse the separate steps into one computation.

Net capital gains. The rates applied to net capital gains are 0%, 15%, 20%, 25%, or 28%. The rate that applies reflects the taxpayer's other income and the type of asset sold or exchanged. The three lowest capital gains rates also apply to qualified dividends.

Additional taxes. Higher-income taxpayers face two additional taxes. These taxes raise the effective rates that otherwise apply to taxable income. Both are applied at a flat rate. Neither is indexed for inflation.

The tax imposed by §§ 3101(b)(2) (employees) and 1401(b)(2) (self-employed individuals) is .9% of wages or self-employment income exceeding $250,000 for married taxpayers filing a joint return (lower levels of compensation for other taxpayers). The tax imposed by § 1411 applies to net investment income. The tax is 3.8% of whichever amount is smaller: (1) the net investment income; or (2) the amount by which modified AGI exceeds $250,000 for married taxpayers filing a joint return and surviving spouses (lower modified AGI levels apply to other taxpayers). Because investment income is not subject to Social Security tax, the tax on net investment income reduces some of the disparity between taxpayers who are wage-earners and taxpayers for whom passive investments are a significant source of income.

Phaseouts. The tax rates described above are nominal rates. If a phase-out applies, the effective tax rate is often higher. Rather than increasing nominal tax rates, Congress achieves the same result by phasing out exclusions, deductions, or credits that the taxpayer would otherwise enjoy. Taxpayers who focus only on nominal rates do not realize that they are being taxed at a higher rate on at least part of their income.

Kiddie tax. Because most parents have higher incomes than their children, they might try to reduce the tax rate applied to their investment income by transferring income-producing property to their children. The § 1(g) kiddie tax limits the potential tax savings from this device. It applies only to unearned income. Although it does not apply to a child's earned income, it does apply to unearned income the child receives from investing his earned income.

b. Filing Status

Individuals fall into one of four tax rate categories: (1) married individuals filing joint returns and surviving spouses; (2) heads of households; (3) unmarried individuals (other than surviving spouses and heads of households); and (4) married individuals filing separate returns. I.R.C. § 1(j). For purposes of this chapter, keep these facts in mind: (1) some tax benefits are available to married couples only if they file jointly; (2) taxpayers filing joint returns have joint and several liability unless they qualify for an exception; and (3) some married couples will pay more tax then they would as single individuals (a "marriage penalty"), but others will pay less (a "marriage bonus") because the rate schedule for joint returns is largely based on the rates for two unmarried individuals each earning equal amounts of income.

4. Tax Credits

Because deductions reduce taxable income, their value depends on the marginal tax rate. If a taxpayer in the 24% tax rate bracket takes a $1,000 deduction, his tax is reduced $240. If he is in the 32% tax rate bracket, the reduction is $320. A credit, on the other hand, is a dollar-for-dollar reduction in tax liability. Unless a phase-out applies, a $1,000 credit reduces tax liability by $1,000.

The taxpayer applies nonrefundable and refundable credits after computing his potential tax liability. Refundable credits can produce a refund even if they exceed the pre-credit tax liability. Nonrefundable credits do not, but some of them can be carried forward for use in later tax years. If a taxpayer has both refundable and nonrefundable credits, he applies the nonrefundable credits first. I.R.C. § 6401(b).

> **Example 1-6.** Alfie has a pre-credit tax liability of $500, a nonrefundable tax credit of $700, and a refundable tax credit of $690. The nonrefundable credit reduces his tax liability to zero. The $200 excess nonrefundable credit is lost unless the Code provides for a carryover. Because the nonrefundable tax credit reduced his tax liability to zero, Alfie receives a refund equal to the $690 refundable credit. If Alfie had been required to apply the refundable credit first, he would have lost any benefit from his $700 nonrefundable credit (assuming no carryover provision applied).

Nonrefundable credits include the credit for household and dependent care services, the credit for adoption expenses, the child tax credit (partially refundable), the American opportunity (partially refundable) and lifetime learning credits, and the credit for contributions to retirement savings.

Many refundable credits simply reflect prepayments that exceed the tax otherwise due. These prepayments are for taxes withheld on wages, estimated taxes, and excess Social Security taxes withheld from a taxpayer with multiple employers. The earned income tax credit is a refundable credit that does not reflect a prepayment.

Section 3402 requires employers to withhold taxes from their employees' wages and forward those amounts to the government. Section 31 gives the employee a credit against his tax liability for amounts withheld. Taxpayers who are self-employed, or who receive other income that is not subject to withholding, make quarterly estimated tax payments. Payments of estimated taxes are treated in the same manner as withheld taxes. I.R.C. § 6315.

The combined tax rate for Social Security and Medicare taxes is 15.3% of earned income. If the taxpayer is an employee, his employer withholds half of this amount from his wages and remits it to the government. The employer matches that payment from its own funds. Self-employed individuals pay the full 15.3% on their earnings but receive a deduction for half of their payment. I.R.C. § 164(f). Exclusions for employment tax purposes are not identical to those applied in computing gross income for income tax purposes.

Of the 15.3%, 12.4% represents Social Security taxes and 2.9% represents Medicare taxes. The Medicare tax applies to all earned income that is not specifically excluded from taxation. The Social Security tax applies only to a certain amount of income. The Social Security Administration annually announces the maximum earned income subject to tax. For 2020 compensation, the Social Security tax applies to the first $137,700 of the taxpayer's earned income. If an employee changes jobs, or has more than one job simultaneously, his employers as a group may withhold Social Security tax on amounts greater than the maximum tax base. He treats excess Social Security taxes withheld as a refundable credit.

5. Alternative Minimum Tax

The alternative minimum tax (AMT) is a separate method of determining income tax, devised to ensure that high-income taxpayers pay at least a minimum amount of tax. It eliminates or reduces several tax benefits and differs in other respects from the regular income tax computation. The AMT imposes a tax on a taxpayer's alternative minimum taxable income (AMTI) that exceeds her AMT exemption. AMTI greater than the exemption is referred to as the "taxable excess." The rate is 26% on taxable excess up to $197,900 for 2020 ($98,950 if the taxpayer is married and files a separate return). The tax rate is 28% for any remaining taxable excess. I.R.C. § 55.

The taxpayer pays the AMT only if it exceeds the § 1 income tax. To compute her liability, she makes the adjustments to taxable income described in §§ 56, 57, and 58. Some of these deductions relate to personal expenses. For example, the AMT does not allow the standard deduction, and it reduces or disallows some itemized deductions.

For 2020, the AMT exemption is $72,900 for unmarried taxpayers ($113,400 if married filing jointly or a surviving spouse and $56,700 if married filing separately). The exemption phases out by 25% of the amount by which AMTI exceeds $518,400 for unmarried individuals ($1,036,800 if married filing jointly or a surviving spouse and $518,400 if married filing separately). Various aspects of the AMT computation, including the exemption and the phase-out levels, are adjusted for inflation.

Checkpoints

- The federal income tax is a tool for raising revenue.

- It applies at graduated (progressive) rates to taxable income.

- Most of the relevant statutes appear in the Internal Revenue Code.

- Administrative rulings and judicial decisions are important tools in interpreting the Code.

- Gross income is "income from whatever source derived." It includes financial benefits received that are not excluded by a specific Code section.

- Taxpayers reduce taxable income by taking deductions authorized in the Code.

- The deductions used in computing adjusted gross income (AGI) are often called "above-the-line" deductions.

- Taxable income is AGI reduced by either the applicable standard deduction or itemized deductions and by the qualified business income deduction.

- The marginal tax rate is affected by the amount and type of taxable income and by the taxpayer's filing status.

- Preferential tax rates apply to net capital gains and qualified dividends.

- Phase-outs, the kiddie tax, the alternative minimum tax, and additional taxes assessed against high-income taxpayers may increase the tax otherwise owed.

- Although credits result in a dollar-for-dollar decrease in tax liability, only refundable credits can create a refund that exceeds pre-credit tax liability.

- Many Code sections provide for annual inflation adjustments.

- Some Code sections include expiration dates that Congress may extend instead of allowing the provision to expire.

- Taxpayers file petitions for refund in the Court of Federal Claims or federal district court; they file petitions to challenge proposed deficiencies in the Tax Court. Appeals from the Court of Federal Claims are filed in the Federal Circuit. Appeals from a district court and the Tax Court are filed in the circuit court that hears appeals from that district court.

Chapter 2

Overview of Gross Income

Roadmap

- Introduction
- Receipt of a financial benefit
- Noncash transactions
- Imputed income
- Topics covered in other chapters

A. Introduction

This chapter begins with an overview of gross income. As we indicated in Chapter 1, gross income is a subset of a larger concept called income. In this chapter, we consider definitions and address situations not specifically mentioned in the Code. Although §61(a) provides a non-exclusive list of items included in gross income, it does not address how to value items of gross income, their character, or their timing; nor does it indicate situations in which the recipient is not the appropriate taxpayer. We address those topics in later chapters.

Section 61(a) also indicates that income might not be included in gross income if another Code section excludes it. Unfortunately, no Code section mirrors §61(a) by providing even a partial list of exclusions. Each exclusion has its own Code section.

B. Receipt of a Financial Benefit

Section 61(a) defines gross income as income from whatever source derived that is not excluded by another Code section. Because the Code does not define "income," we rely on judicial and administrative guidance to give the term meaning. As a rule, income means any benefit received that increases the taxpayer's net wealth. Reg. § 1.61-1(a) indicates that gross income can be realized in any form, including money, property, or services. Items that are excluded by other Code sections are called exclusions. Thus, gross income is any benefit received that increases net wealth and is not excluded by a specific Code provision.

An arguably more accurate measurement of income is the Haig-Simons definition: consumption during the year plus change in net worth. For example, a taxpayer whose net worth increased by $10,000 and who spent $30,000 would have income of $40,000 for the year. If we computed taxable income using that definition, we would have to annually value the taxpayer's assets and liabilities (to determine the change in net worth) and have a reliable mechanism for tracking consumption. Although we do not compute income (and thus taxable income) using the Haig-Simons definition, the IRS does use net worth calculations as an audit technique for determining taxable income. Internal Revenue Manual (IRM) 4.10.4.6.7.

Section 61(a) begins with a reference to "gross income." That term's meaning has long been the subject of debate—and often litigation. Even if we agree an item should eventually be included, we may be unsure which taxable year is the appropriate year for reporting. We may also be unsure whether the taxpayer who received the benefit is the taxpayer who should report it as gross income. Finally, we may need to determine if the benefit qualifies for the lower tax rates applied to net capital gain.

1. Statutory Language

Section 61(a) is technically a definition section: it defines gross income. Gross income goes into the computation of taxable income because of another definition section: § 63 defines taxable income as gross income minus various deductions.

Section 61(a) has several features that are relevant to a discussion of gross income. The easiest feature to understand is its list of gross income items. There are currently 14 such items, none of which should surprise you. They are compensation for services, gross income from business, gains derived from dealings in property, interest, rents, royalties, dividends, annuities, income from life insurance and endowment contracts, pensions, income from discharge of indebtedness, distributive share of partnership income, income in respect of a decedent, and income from an interest in an estate or trust.

Before reaching that list, we encounter prefatory language: "Except as otherwise provided in this subtitle, gross income means all income from whatever source derived ...." That language indicates that this list governs unless we find a Code section that prevents a listed item from being included. The sentence continues by saying "including (but not limited to) [those 14 items]." In other words, an item can be included in gross income even if it is not one of the listed items, and both listed and unlisted items can be excluded from gross income if another Code section so provides.

Section 61(b) provides additional guidance by referring to groups of sections that cover items specifically included in gross income (beginning with § 71) and items specifically excluded from gross income (beginning with § 101). Those groupings are helpful, but they can be misleading. Some exclusions are covered in the first group of sections, as exceptions to those sections' general rules; likewise, some inclusions are covered in the second group of sections, also as exceptions to general rules.

Neither § 61(a) nor those other sections address three other matters we will consider in later chapters: to whom the income should be taxed; when the income should be taxed; and whether the income qualifies for the lower rates available for net capital gains.

2. Undeniable Accessions to Wealth

Your common sense should help you through a gross income analysis. Likely, if someone ends up wealthier than she began, she has gross income. *Commissioner v. Glenshaw Glass Co.*, 348 U.S. 426, 431 (1955), held that punitive damages were included in gross income. The taxpayer unsuccessfully argued that the damages should be excluded because they were not gain derived from its capital, labor, or both but were imposed to punish the wrongdoer. The Court used a phrase that is regularly cited in controversies over whether an item constitutes gross income: "Here we have instances of undeniable accessions to wealth, clearly realized, and over which the taxpayers have complete dominion." In general, the source and type of income is not important. The benefit is gross income unless the Code specifically excludes it. The fact that § 61(a) does not mention damages does not change the outcome.

3. Treasure Trove and Bargain Purchases

Treasure trove is found wealth. The taxpayer receives a windfall, often without any effort on her part. It is gross income when she reduces it to her undisputed possession. It is irrelevant that no Code section expressly taxes treasure trove. What is important is that no Code section expressly excludes it. Gross income is interpreted expansively because Congress is exerting the full measure of its power to tax.

What if the taxpayer finds a second item inside property he purchased? In *Cesarini v. United States*, 296 F. Supp. 3 (N.D. Ohio 1969), the taxpayers purchased a used piano at auction. Several years later, they discovered money inside it. In addition to deciding that the found money was gross income, the court had to determine *when* it was gross income. Its choices were the year the taxpayers purchased the piano or the year they found the money. This choice mattered because the statute of limitations was closed for the earlier year. The court held that the treasure trove was gross income when it was "reduced to undisputed possession." This holding made sense — if they had disposed of the piano before finding the money, they could not recover it from the new owners.

Cesarini involved U.S. currency, but its rule applies to other found property. Reg. § 1.61-14(a) includes treasure trove in gross income using its value in U.S. currency.

> **Example 2-1.** In 2015, Bob purchased a vacant lot for $10,000. In 2020, he decided to start a garden and began digging on his property. He discovered a chest filled with gold jewelry. Bob has 2020 gross income equal to the value of the jewelry he found.

Windfalls are not limited to found property. They can also occur in a different context — the taxpayer buys property that turns out to be worth more than she paid for it. If the purchase was an arm's-length transaction, she does not have gross income.

> **Example 2-2.** Aleta bought a painting for $5 at a garage sale. Six months later, she discovered it was a lost masterpiece worth $2 million. Although she made an extraordinarily good deal at the garage sale, she did not have gross income when she discovered the painting's true value. She purchased a painting, and that is all she received. If she sells the painting for its $2 million value, her gain is gross income.

4. The Realization Principle

We can also use Example 2-2 to consider the realization principle. If Aleta is fortunate, her painting will continue to increase in value. Even if we initially exclude its $2 million actual value until she sells it, what about any future increases in its value? Instead of having taxpayers revalue their property every year and report increases and decreases in value, § 1001 provides for computing and reporting gains (and losses) *realized*. The realization principle lets taxpayers defer reporting gain until they have disposed of the property. This principle works to the taxpayer's benefit because she can sell her loss property and deduct the realized loss immediately while continuing to hold her appreciated property and avoid reporting her unrealized gain. The benefit is enhanced by the § 1014 basis rules that apply to her heirs if she holds her appreciated property until she dies, and the heirs sell the property.

5. Promotional Programs

Promotional programs raise several issues. A merchant that advertises its product for a $2 discount is not making a gift to potential customers. Rather, it is trying to induce them to purchase its product. Because it is available to anyone who buys the product, the discount is effectively a temporary price change and is not included in the customer's gross income. The same tax treatment applies to taxpayers who use coupons, take advantage of buy-one/get-one-free promotions, or keep product samples received in the mail. But taxpayers do have gross income if they receive product samples and then claim charitable contribution deductions for donating them to charity. *See Haverly v. United States*, 513 F.2d 224 (7th Cir. 1975).

Frequent flier miles and similar benefits taxpayers use to obtain free or upgraded tickets or hotel rooms present both theoretical and practical problems. Taxpayers could argue that airlines and hotel chains are really offering a variation on the buy-one/get-one-free offer used by retailers. By spending a set number of dollars or flying a set number of miles, they qualify for free or upgraded tickets or rooms. On the other hand, many taxpayers earn their miles through deductible business travel but use them for nondeductible personal travel. That use should result in gross income. However, the lack of uniformity in ticket and room prices creates valuation problems. In addition, taxpayers often earn these miles over a multi-year period, which results in timing problems. Given the complexity involved (and the popularity of these programs), the IRS announced that it would not treat receiving or using frequent flier miles (or similar benefits) as gross income unless they were converted to cash. Announcement 2002-18, 2002-1 C.B. 621. At least one court had already treated such a conversion as gross income. At that point, there could be no argument as to value or timing, and the taxpayer had dominion over the cash received. *Charley v. Commissioner*, 91 F.3d 72 (9th Cir. 1996).

6. Borrowing

Section 61(a) includes income from discharge of indebtedness in gross income, but it does not mention obtaining the initial loan. Taxpayers do not have gross income when they borrow money. Because the obligation to repay the lender offsets the loan proceeds, the borrower does not increase his net wealth. Of course, if he never intended to repay the loan, he has gross income when he "borrows" the funds; this is really a theft (another item not mentioned in § 61(a)) and not a loan. If he originally intended to repay the loan, but fails to do so, he may have gross income when the loan is canceled.

> **Example 2-3.** Bonnie embezzled $20,000 from her employer. She has $20,000 of gross income even though she realized the money from illegal activity. Reg. § 1.61-14(a); *James v. United States*, 366 U.S. 213 (1961).

> **Example 2-4.** Ada borrowed $30,000 from the XYZ Bank. Because of financial problems, she could not repay the loan. She has gross income of $30,000 when the loan is canceled unless one of the § 108 exclusions applies.

C. Noncash Transactions

Wages, salaries, commissions, and compensation in any form (money, other property, or even services) received in return for services are gross income. Reg. §§ 1.61-1(a), 1.61-2(a)(1). If services are paid for in property, the service provider has gross income equal to the value of the property received. Likewise, if services are provided in exchange for other services, the service provider includes the value of the services received in his gross income. Reg. § 1.61-2(d). This rule extends beyond transfers from an employer to an employee. It also applies to barter exchanges between independent contractors.

> **Example 2-5.** Andy's house needed painting. Brian needed a caterer for a party he was hosting. Andy agreed to cater Brian's party "for free," and Brian agreed to paint Andy's house "for free." Andy would normally charge $3,000 for a catering job. Even though no money changes hands, both taxpayers have gross income. If this is an arm's-length transaction, the value of the services exchanged is presumed to be equal. They each have gross income of $3,000.

If you have trouble conceptualizing the receipt of property in exchange for services, you might consider a two-step imaginary transaction. Assume that the taxpayer received money in exchange for his services and then used the money to purchase the property he received. This method will work unless a Code section specifically treats the receipt of money differently from the receipt of other property or services.

Although barter transactions in a commercial setting are taxable, we tend to ignore informal exchanges between family members, close friends, or neighbors. Grandmother might take care of Son's children after school, while Son shovels snow off her walkway each winter and mows her lawn in the summer. Consider the administrative difficulty involved in monitoring and valuing these arrangements.

D. Imputed Income

Imputed income is income from producing, using, or consuming your own property, goods, or services. From a policy perspective, imputed income is income. Nevertheless, it is excluded from gross income, in part because of administrative difficulties.

> **Example 2-6.** Basil, a criminal defense lawyer, received a speeding ticket. He decided to contest the ticket and represented himself in court. Basil does not have gross income for the value of the services he performed in representing himself.

The same concept applies to using your own property without paying rent. For example, a taxpayer who owns and occupies a building does not have gross income equal to the rent he avoids paying. On the other hand, if he lives rent-free in someone else's property, he has gross income unless the owner is letting him do so as a gift.

> **Example 2-7.** AB Corporation owns an office building and occupies one floor as its corporate offices. AB does not pay itself rent; all other tenants pay rent of $6,000 per month. AB's gross income does not include imputed income from its rent-free use of its building.

> **Example 2-8.** AB's bank indicated that it needed more assets before the bank would continue making loans to it. AB's shareholders, Alvin and Bella, transferred their personal residence to AB to satisfy the bank's request. They continued to live in the house but paid no rent. Even though they are its only shareholders, AB is a separate legal and taxpaying entity, distinct from its shareholders. Alvin and Bella include the rental value of the house in their gross income. *See Dean v. Commissioner*, 187 F.2d 1019 (3d Cir. 1951).

Because we do not generally tax imputed income, Basil (Example 2-6) had no gross income from rendering services to himself even though he might have netted a larger amount by spending his time representing paying clients and hiring a different lawyer to contest his speeding ticket. We usually focus on what the taxpayer did, not on what he could have done. The imputed interest provisions discussed later in this book are an exception to that rule.

From an economic standpoint, a taxpayer who occupies his own property may be better off after taxes than a taxpayer who invests his funds and lives in rented property. The owner-occupant does not treat the rental value of his home as gross income, and he can deduct his mortgage interest and property taxes. The investor is taxed on his investment earnings and cannot deduct the rent he pays. The difference in after-tax consequences results in taxpayers with similar economic income paying different amounts of tax.

E. Topics Covered in Other Chapters

This chapter introduced the broad scope of gross income. Once we determine that a taxpayer received a financial benefit, we must consider other issues. Does any Code section specifically include or exclude that benefit? When is it included in gross income? Is the person who received it always the appropriate taxpayer? Do any special tax rates apply to it? Is it affected by the taxpayer's other income or her marital status? Does it matter if the taxpayer was dealing with a related party? Later chapters consider these questions.

Checkpoints

- Gross income involves "undeniable accessions to wealth, clearly realized, and over which the taxpayers have complete dominion."

- Items of financial benefit are included in gross income unless a Code section excludes them.

- A taxpayer who finds treasure trove includes its value in gross income when he reduces it to his undisputed possession.

- A taxpayer who makes a bargain purchase does not have gross income merely because the property is worth more than she paid for it.

- A taxpayer who borrows money does not have gross income because he has an obligation to repay the lender.

- The realization principle lets taxpayers defer reporting gains until they dispose of the property.

- If services are performed in exchange for other services or for property, gross income includes the value of the services or property received.

- Imputed income is the value of using or consuming your own property, goods, or services. Gross income does not usually include imputed income.

- If we include an item in gross income, we must also determine which taxpayer reports the income, when he reports it, and what tax rates apply.

Chapter 3

Income from Performing Services

Roadmap

- Compensation for services
- Employee achievement awards
- Compensation subject to a substantial risk of forfeiture
- Health care
- Group-term life insurance
- Education
- Children and other dependents
- Meals and lodging
- Section 132
- Miscellaneous employment-related exclusions
- Cafeteria plans

A. Compensation for Services

1. Employee's Gross Income

Gross income includes compensation for services, including fees, commissions, fringe benefits, and similar items. All those items are economic benefits to the service provider. I.R.C. §61(a)(1).

A service provider may have an ownership interest in her employer, which can affect how we treat payments she receives. Although a service provider may be the payor's employee or may be an independent contractor offering her services to more than one potential recipient, we usually refer to "employees" in this chapter.

Throughout this chapter, keep three facts in mind. First, an employee can exclude compensation as gross income only if a specific Code section excludes the item received. Second, an employee's tax consequences are not necessarily consistent with her employer's consequences. An employee may be taxed on (or be able to exclude) the value of what she receives, while an employer's deduction is usually based on its cost. In addition, an employer may be able to deduct amounts that the employee excludes, but it is possible that the employee can exclude items that the employer cannot deduct or that the employee has gross income even though the employer receives no deduction. The employee's tax consequences are covered by Code sections defining gross income. The employer's tax consequences are covered by Code sections providing for and limiting deductions. Third, the treatment of compensation-related payments can change over time. The treatment of unemployment compensation illustrates how Congress changes the Code in reaction to economic events. Until 1986, individuals who lost their jobs could exclude at least a portion of their unemployment benefits, which are funded from taxes paid by employers and are thus a form of compensation for services rendered. Congress then changed that rule and included all unemployment compensation in gross income. I.R.C. §85. During a recent economic downturn, however, it reinstated a partial exclusion; that exclusion applied only in 2009 through 2014.

Compensation for services is usually received in cash, but that is not always the case. Unlike wages and salaries, most fringe benefits are not paid in cash. Instead, the employer provides an item of property or a service for free or at a reduced cost. The employer and the employee consider these benefits part of the compensation package. The employee reports the value of the benefit as gross income unless one of the exclusions covered in this chapter applies. The net effect is the same as if he received cash and used it to purchase the fringe benefit item.

An employee need not directly receive money or other property to realize an economic benefit; even an indirect benefit can be gross income. If the employer pays its employee's federal income taxes, the employee has gross income. *Old Colony Trust Co. v. Commissioner*, 279 U.S. 716 (1929). Because she is relieved from paying the tax, she effectively increases her wealth.

> **Example 3-1.** Audrey is the president of ABC Company. Her salary is $200,000, and her federal income tax is $50,000. If ABC pays her income tax, she has $50,000 of additional gross income. This is true whether ABC pays her taxes directly or reimburses her if she pays them.

In this context, ABC is "grossing up" its employee's salary by the tax she owed on that income. In *Old Colony Trust Co.*, the taxpayer argued that this would result in a never-ending cycle: each time the tax was added to the employee's gross income, it would trigger an additional tax that the employer would have to pay and add to the employee's gross income. Because the government had so far included only the initial tax payment in the employee's gross income, the Court did not address that issue.

Grossing up is not merely a theoretical concept. In the fringe benefit context, an employer might gross up salaries for employees with domestic partners covered by the employer's health plan. The gross income exclusion for those plans applies to payments covering the employee, the employee's spouse, the employee's children who are under age 27, and the employee's dependents. An employee who covers a non-dependent domestic partner reports the value of the benefit as gross income.

2. Fringe Benefits

Most of the benefits discussed in this chapter are excluded from gross income. As you review them, keep the distinction between cost and value in mind. If a benefit is provided in cash, the employer deducts the amount paid. The employee's tax consequences — gross income or exclusion — are based on that amount. If a benefit takes a different form, the employee's tax consequences reflect the value of the benefit received.

Exclusions for fringe benefits have been criticized for reducing the overall amount on which tax is paid. The tax base is further eroded by benefits that apply to the employee's spouse or other relatives. Other criticisms focus on horizontal equity. Employees with identical overall compensation report different taxable incomes if one receives only cash compensation while the other receives a combination of cash and excluded fringe benefits.

> Example 3-2. Agnes received two employment offers, each worth $46,000 before taxes. Employer A will pay $45,000 and give her free use of an on-premises gym. Employer B will pay $46,000. Agnes currently pays $1,000 per year for a nondeductible health club membership, which she would drop if she accepts A's offer. Because § 132(j)(4) provides an exclusion for employer-provided gyms, she is taxed on $45,000 if she accepts A's offer and on $46,000 if she accepts B's offer.

Because some fringe benefits are covered by more than one Code section, they add to the Code's complexity. Fringe benefits may also affect employment taxes and Social Security benefits. The formula for those benefits reflects the amount of an employee's covered compensation; some excluded fringe benefits reduce that amount. Employees who prefer paying lower employment taxes may regret that decision when they retire and receive lower Social Security benefits. Although income tax courses focus on the income tax, employment taxes are also relevant in practice.

3. Employer's Deduction

Employers can deduct reasonable compensation for services rendered. I.R.C. § 162(a)(1). Both stated salary and fringe benefits go into determining reasonableness. Employers who offer fringe benefits must consider other factors. First, nondiscrimination rules apply to many benefits. Second, some benefits must be limited to the actual employee, while others can be made available to members of the employee's family. Third, valuation is important when statutory limits apply to noncash benefits. Fourth, some benefits are not deductible even though the employee's compensation is reasonable. Finally, although not discussed in this text, the rules for employee-owners may differ from the rules for other employees.

B. Employee Achievement Awards

1. Requirements

Section 74(c) authorizes a limited exclusion for employee achievement awards described in § 274(j). The employee excludes the award if it meets four requirements. First, it must recognize either length of service or safety achievement. No employee can receive an award that qualifies as a length of service award in his first five years of employment or more often than every five years. I.R.C. § 274(j)(4)(B). No more than 10% of an employer's employees can receive qualifying safety achievement awards in any taxable year. Awards made to an employee who is a manager, administrator, clerical employee, or other professional cannot qualify as safety achievement awards. Those employees are subtracted from the total employee count in making the 10% computation. I.R.C. § 274(j)(4)(C). If the employer makes awards to more than 10% of its employees, the awards made before it exceeds that limit may still qualify. Prop. Reg. § 1.274-8(d)(3). The employer can ignore awards that qualify as de minimis fringe benefits in computing eligibility for employee achievement awards.

Second, the award must be made in tangible personal property. Cash or cash equivalents, gift cards, gift coupons, gift certificates, vacations, meals, lodging, event tickets, stocks and bonds, and interests in real property do not qualify. The employer can provide a gift certificate that lets employees select an award from a limited array of qualifying items. I.R.C. § 274(j)(3)(A)(ii). Third, it must be made as part of a meaningful ceremony. Fourth, it must be made under conditions and circumstances that make it unlikely that it is disguised compensation. An example of disguised compensation involves an award of property worth significantly more than the employer's cost and significantly more than the dollar limitations discussed below. Prop. Reg. § 1.74-2(c), Example 2.

2. Amount Excluded

Section 74(c)(1) excludes the award's value only if the employer's cost does not exceed the maximum amount specified in § 274(j). Because the award's value and the employer's cost may differ, this distinction is important. The general rule in § 274(j)(2)(A) lets an employer deduct no more than $400 per year with respect to any employee. If the employer's *cost* is $400 or less, the employee can exclude the *value* of the award even if it exceeds $400. The only exception is that provided in the proposed regulations for situations involving disguised compensation.

> **Example 3-3.** Every year, Armand awards a bicycle to each 10-year employee, including Ben. Armand received a discount for multiple purchases and paid $380 for each bicycle. The bicycles normally sell at retail for $410 each. Even though he received a bicycle worth more than $400, Ben has no gross income.

> **Example 3-4.** Assume instead that Armand paid $450 for each bicycle; they normally sell at retail for $480 each. Unfortunately, an improved model became available shortly before the awards ceremony, and the bicycle was worth only $370 when Ben received it. Because Armand paid more than $400, Ben has some gross income.

If the employer has a written plan that does not discriminate in favor of highly compensated employees, and its average cost for awards does not exceed $400, its awards are qualified plan awards. I.R.C. § 274(j)(3)(B). In that case, it can deduct up to $1,600 for some awards, and the employees who receive them can exclude a greater amount. I.R.C. § 274(j)(2)(B). An employer cannot count nominal awards in determining whether its average award cost is $400 or less.

> **Example 3-5.** Anderson has a written plan providing for length of service achievement awards made the year after his employees complete

5, 10, 15, 20, etc., years of service. He spends an average of $75 for each 5-year employee, $150 for each 10-year employee, $300 for each 15-year employee, and $600 for each 20-year and up employee. Each year, he computes the average he spent on all awards. If he averages $400 or less, he can deduct the $600 awards in full, and employees who receive them can exclude their value. Employees whose awards cost $400 or less exclude their awards even if the other employees do not qualify for the full exclusion.

Example 3-6. Anderson instead spends an average of $5 for each 5-year employee, $15 for each 10-year employee, $30 for each 15-year employee, and $900 for each 20-year and up employee. Although the average cost for all employees may be $400 or less, the awards made at the lower levels are nominal in amount. Anderson's average cost will be deemed to be $900. Employees who have worked 20 years or more will not qualify for a full exclusion.

If the employer's cost exceeds the statutory limit, the employee includes part of the value in gross income and excludes the remaining value. He is taxed on the *greater* of two amounts. The first amount is the portion of the employer's *cost* that could not be deducted. This amount cannot exceed the property's value. The second amount is the amount by which the award's *value* exceeds the amount the employer could deduct. I.R.C. § 74(c)(2).

Example 3-7. In Example 3-4, Armand paid $450 for bicycles that were worth only $370 at the time of the awards ceremony. Armand did not have a qualified plan, so his maximum deduction for any employee is $400. Ben received one of these awards. Because the bicycle's $370 value is less than the $400 maximum deduction, Ben's gross income equals the difference between Armand's $450 cost and $400. Ben reports $50 of gross income and excludes $320.

Example 3-8. Assume that the market value declined even more drastically, and the bicycles were worth only $40 at the time of the awards ceremony. The $50 difference between Armand's cost and the maximum deduction exceeds the value of the bicycle. In that case, Ben reports gross income of only $40.

Example 3-9. Assume instead that the market value of the bicycles was $475 at the time of the ceremony. In this case, Ben reports $75 of gross income even though only $50 of Armand's cost was disallowed as a deduction. The $75 represents the amount by which the bicycle's value exceeded Armand's allowable deduction. Ben excludes the remaining $400 of the bicycle's value.

3. De Minimis Fringe Benefits

Section 74(c)(4) contains a cross-reference to the exclusion for de minimis fringe benefits. The proposed regulations indicate that "under appropriate circumstances, a traditional retirement award will be treated as a de minimis fringe" covered by § 132(e). Those awards are not subject to the dollar limitations in §§ 74(c) and 274(j).

4. Employer Payments for Its Own Benefit

Reg. § 1.74-1(a)(1) specifically applies the rules of § 74 to "any prizes and awards from an employer to an employee in recognition of some achievement in connection with his employment." If an employer sends outstanding employees to conventions or other events, we consider the relevant facts to determine the tax consequences. For example, in *McCann v. United States*, 696 F.2d 1386 (Fed. Cir. 1983), an employer held an annual sales seminar for employees who met sales targets. Spouses attended, seminar locations offered significant entertainment opportunities, there were few employment-related activities, and employees who did not accept the trip suffered no penalties. The employee had gross income equal to the value of the trip. By contrast, the employee had no gross income in *McDonell v. Commissioner*, T.C. Memo. 1967-18. He was selected in a drawing to accompany prize winners to Hawaii; while there, he had to perform significant duties for the employer's benefit.

C. Compensation Subject to a Substantial Risk of Forfeiture

1. Scope of Section 83

The discussion in the preceding section assumed that the employee was under no obligation to return an item of compensation, but that is not always the case. Section 83 applies to compensation that is subject to a condition: the item is not transferable and it is subject to a substantial risk of forfeiture. The service provider might receive it without making any payment, or he may make a payment in addition to rendering services. The service provider can be either an employee or an independent contractor. Reg. § 1.83-1(a)(1). The service recipient can be an individual or an entity.

Section 83 applies if the service recipient transfers property to *any* other person. I.R.C. § 83(a). Even if the person receiving property is not the service provider, the initial tax consequences affect the actual service provider. I.R.C. § 83(a) (flush language).

Section 83 governs the timing, amount, and character of the service provider's gross income. It also governs the service recipient's tax consequences. The discussion in this section focuses on service providers receiving corporate stock that is subject to a substantial risk of forfeiture. Although we use the terms employer and employee instead of service recipient and service provider, remember that this section also applies to service providers who are independent contractors.

For purposes of § 83, property is treated as transferred if the employee acquires a beneficial ownership interest in it. Reg. § 1.83-3(a)(1)–(7). An option to acquire property is not a beneficial interest in the underlying property. In addition, an event that *must* occur — such as a requirement that the property be returned no matter why the employment ends — may preclude treatment as a transfer. In these and similar situations, the regulations focus on whether the employee is subject to the benefits and risks of beneficial ownership.

The discussion below ignores the § 83(i) qualified stock provisions added by the Tax Cuts and Jobs Act of 2017. Those rules apply to certain employer stock acquired pursuant to an option or settlement of a restricted stock unit. The provisions are elective.

2. Transfers Covered

Section 83 applies if the property transferred is subject to a substantial risk of forfeiture *and* is not transferable. The first term is usually more important because it is unlikely that the rights of a transferee will exceed the rights held by the employee. If property is subject to a substantial risk of forfeiture and is not transferable, it is "substantially nonvested." Property that is not subject to a substantial risk of forfeiture *or* that is transferable is "substantially vested." Reg. § 1.83-3(b).

Property is subject to a substantial risk of forfeiture if the transferee's rights to full enjoyment are conditioned on the performance of substantial future services by any person. I.R.C. § 83(c)(1). The condition imposed can be that the employee provide services or refrain from providing services. The enjoyment of the property can be conditioned on the occurrence of a condition related to a purpose of the transfer. Reg. § 1.83-3(c)(1). For example, the employee could forfeit the property unless the employer's profits increase by at least 3% a year for the next five years. The condition encourages him to render substantial services so that his employer meets that goal and he can retain the property.

Reg. § 1.83-3(c)(2) lists conditions that qualify as substantial risks of forfeiture and conditions that do not qualify. A requirement that the employee return the property if he is discharged for cause or commits a crime is not a substantial risk of forfeiture. The Tax Court held that the regulation applies to termination for serious misconduct which, like criminal misconduct, is highly unlikely to occur. *Austin v. Commissioner,* 141 T.C. 551 (2013). The agreement involved listed three types of termination for cause. One was dishonesty, fraud, and similar acts; the other two related to performance of his duties and following the employer's policies. Because the court held that the regulation did not apply to the latter provisions, the transfer was subject to a substantial risk of forfeiture.

A requirement that he return the property if he accepts employment with a competitor qualifies only if the facts and circumstances indicate there is a substantial risk of forfeiture occurring. Relevant factors include his age, health, skill, and likelihood of obtaining such employment and the employer's practice of enforcing such conditions in the past.

Section 83 does not apply to every service requirement. The services to be performed must be substantial. Reg. § 1.83-3(c)(2) indicates that the regularity of the performance of services and the amount of time spent in that performance are relevant factors.

Property is transferable if a transferee's rights would not be subject to a substantial risk of forfeiture. I.R.C. § 83(c)(2). If the employee can transfer the property, but the transferee takes it subject to the risk of forfeiture, it is not transferable. If the transferee would not forfeit the property, but the employee would be liable for damages, the property is treated as transferable. Reg. § 1.83-1(f), Example 2.

> **Example 3-10.** XYZ Corporation transferred 100 shares of its stock to Angus. If he resigns in the next three years, he forfeits the stock. If he transfers the stock to another person, the transferee is subject to the forfeiture condition. The stock is substantially nonvested.

An employee who receives stock in a publicly traded corporation covered by § 16(b) of the Securities Exchange Act of 1934 might be subject to a lawsuit if he sells the stock at a profit within six months after acquiring it. Section 83(c)(3) provides that stock is considered substantially nonvested if sale at a profit could give rise to such a lawsuit. This rule applies even if the stock is otherwise substantially vested.

3. Employee Does Not Elect Immediate Gross Income

When the employee receives substantially nonvested property, § 83(a) covers his tax consequences unless he makes the election discussed in the next subsection. If the property never becomes substantially vested, he may never have gross income. If the property becomes substantially vested, he reports compensation income equal to the difference between the property's value on the earliest date his rights become substantially vested and any amount he paid for it. The amount included in gross income, increased by any amount he paid for the property, becomes his basis. His holding period begins when the property is substantially vested, not when it is initially transferred to him. I.R.C. § 83(f).

In determining the gross income from substantial vesting, we consider nonlapse restrictions that affect the property's value. I.R.C. § 83(d). We ignore restrictions that will lapse. For example, a forfeiture condition requiring future services is a lapse restriction if it is limited in time or by some other event. Reg. § 1.83-3(i).

Reg. § 1.83-3(h) defines a nonlapse restriction as a permanent restriction which by its terms will never lapse. It requires any holder of the property to sell it (or offer to sell it) at a price determined by a formula. Reg. § 1.83-5(c) includes examples of nonlapse restrictions based on formula prices for selling stock to the issuing corporation: selling at book value or selling at a multiple of earnings per share that approximates the multiple at the time the stock was originally transferred. If the nonlapse restriction sets a formula price for selling the property, its value is that formula price.

> **Example 3-11.** ABC Corporation transferred stock to Alvin in Year 1. He made no payment for it and would forfeit it if he left ABC's employment before Year 5. After the stock was substantially vested, he could sell it only to ABC. ABC would pay 10 times its earnings per share; that was its value when the transfer occurred. Alvin did not include the transfer in gross income in Year 1. In Year 5, when the stock was substantially vested, ABC's earnings were $5 per share and its shares traded for $150 per share. Because a nonlapse restriction applied, Alvin's gross income was only $50 per share.

A restriction is not a nonlapse restriction if it requires the employee to sell to a particular person at fair market value (as opposed to at a formula). In addition, limitations based on state or federal securities registration requirements are not nonlapse restrictions. Reg. § 1.83-3(h) (flush language).

Even if the property never becomes substantially vested, the employee might transfer it. If he realizes gain or loss, the amount and character depend on the type of disposition. If he sells it in an arm's-length transaction, he reports compensation income equal to the excess of any amount realized over any amount he paid for the property. Reg. § 1.83-1(b)(1). If he transfers the property and receives substantially nonvested property in return, he does not recognize gain. The new property is covered by § 83 in place of the original property. Reg. § 1.83-1(b)(3). If the sale is not at arm's-length, he reports compensation income equal to the lesser of (1) the value of the substantially nonvested property transferred reduced by the amount he paid for it or (2) the consideration received. Reg. § 1.83-1(c).

If he forfeits substantially nonvested property, he reports ordinary gain or loss. Gain or loss is the difference between any amount he receives when he forfeits it and any amount he paid when it was transferred to him. Reg. § 1.83-1(b)(2). Both amounts might be zero. If he dies while the property is substantially nonvested, income reported on the property's disposition is income in respect of a decedent. Any income under § 83 is taxed to the appropriate recipient, as provided in § 691. Reg. § 1.83-1(d). If he forfeits property because of a lapse restriction after it becomes substantially vested, he is likely to realize a loss. The loss attributable to including the property's value in his income is an ordinary loss. Ordinary loss treatment is available only to the employee, not to a subsequent transferee. Reg. § 1.83-1(e).

The employee may receive dividends from transferred stock. Dividends received before the stock is substantially vested are gross income from compensation, not gross income from dividends. Reg. § 1.83-1(a)(1) (flush language).

4. Employee Elects Immediate Gross Income

Section 83(b) applies if the employee elects to report the substantially nonvested property as gross income in the year it is transferred to him. His gross income equals the excess of the property's value over any amount he pays for it. As discussed above, that value reflects only restrictions that will never lapse. He can make the election even if he pays an amount equal to the property's value when it is transferred. Reg. § 1.83-2(a).

His gross income is compensation for services rendered. The amount included in gross income, increased by any amount he paid for the property, becomes his basis. His holding period begins just after the date the property is transferred even though it remains substantially nonvested. Reg. § 1.83-4(a).

There are potential benefits in making the § 83(b) election. If the property later becomes substantially vested, the employee does not report additional gross income. His compensation income, basis, and holding period were determined when he made the election. If he later sells the property, he computes gain or loss by comparing the amount realized on the disposition to his adjusted basis. If the property is a capital asset, he qualifies for capital gain or loss treatment.

If he forfeits the property before it becomes substantially vested, he cannot deduct the income he reported when he made the election. I.R.C. § 83(b)(1) (flush language). His loss is the difference between any amount he receives on the forfeiture and any amount he paid when he acquired the property. Reg. § 1.83-2(a). Both amounts might be zero. If the property is a capital asset, the loss is a capital loss because the forfeiture is treated as a sale or exchange.

After making the election, the employee is treated as the owner even though the property is substantially nonvested. He reports dividends received as dividends, not as additional compensation.

5. Employer's Tax Consequences

The employer generally takes a deduction under § 162 because the transfer is an ordinary and necessary business expense. It takes that deduction in the taxable year in which the employee reports gross income. I.R.C. § 83(h). If the employee elects to report gross income while the property is substantially nonvested, the employer takes its deduction in that year. If the employee does not report gross income until the property is substantially vested, the employer waits until that later year to deduct any expense. If the employee never reports gross income because he did not make the election, and forfeits the property before satisfying the conditions, the employer takes no deduction. If the employee and employer have different taxable years, the taxable year used by the employer is the taxable year in which (or with which) the employee's year ends.

> **Example 3-12.** DEF Corporation reports taxable income using a fiscal year ending on November 30. It transferred property to Alicia on September 1, 2019. She must return the property if DEF's profits do not increase by 4% in each of the next five years. She elected to report the value of the property immediately and reported the income on her 2019 tax return. DEF reports its deduction for its taxable year ending November 30, 2020. Alicia's 2019 taxable year ends during DEF's 2020 fiscal year.

The employer deducts the amount the employee reported as gross income. If it had a basis for the property transferred, it reports gain or loss for that property unless the property was its own stock. Reg. § 1.83-6(b). If the property was its own stock, it does not report gain or loss because § 1032 provides that corporations do not recognize gain or loss when they transfer their stock in exchange for money or other property; that includes transfers made as compensation for services. Reg. § 1.1032-1(a).

If the transfer is treated as a capital expenditure, the employer treats the amount computed above as a nondeductible capital expenditure instead of as deductible compensation; it adjusts basis accordingly. This rule also applies to transfers that constitute deferred expenses or amounts properly includible in the value of its inventory. Reg. § 1.83-6(a)(4).

If the employee later forfeits the property, the employer reports the amount it previously deducted as gross income in the year the forfeiture occurs. If the amount was a capital expenditure or was allocable to inventory, the employer increases its gross income by the amount it included in basis or that reduced gross income. Reg. § 1.83-6(c).

D. Health Care

Section 106(a) lets employees exclude employer-provided coverage under an accident or health plan. Allowable benefits go beyond providing insurance to cover expenses qualifying as medical care. An employer's plan can also provide disability payments and payments for loss of use of a bodily structure or function. This section applies only to funding the benefit. When an employee becomes ill, injured, or disabled, the tax consequences of employer-provided health and accident benefits are governed by § 105.

E. Group-Term Life Insurance

Section 101(a) excludes the proceeds of a life insurance policy paid by reason of the death of the insured. It applies even if the employer paid the premiums on that policy. If the employee can designate the beneficiary who will receive the death benefit, the premiums are compensation and should be gross income.

Section 79(a) provides a partial exclusion for those premiums. The employee has no gross income if the policy's death benefit is $50,000 or less. If the benefit exceeds $50,000, she includes only the premium the employer pays for "excess" insurance coverage. The exclusion is available if the policy provides benefits that § 101(a) would exclude, is offered to a group of employees, and provides insurance based on a formula (*e.g.*, compensation, age, or years of service). Reg. § 1.79-1(a). Section 79(d) contains extensive nondiscrimination provisions. The exclusion applies only to a group-term policy. If the policy is whole life, employer-paid premiums are gross income to the employee.

Example 3-13. Beneficent pays for group-term life insurance for each employee. The death benefit equals the employee's annual salary, and each employee can select the beneficiary. Angie's salary is $250,000. The $200,000 excess death benefit is 80% of the $250,000 total benefit. Her gross income includes 80% of the premiums Beneficent is deemed to pay for the policy.

Example 3-14. Beneficent instead pays the premium for $60,000 of coverage and Angie pays the premium for the other $190,000. Angie is taxed only on the premium Beneficent is deemed to pay for $10,000 of insurance.

The employee's gross income is based on the amount the employer is *deemed to pay*. We compute that amount using the tables in Reg. § 1.79-3. Reflecting the requirements of § 79(c), the table amounts increase at five-year age intervals. This approach reflects the fact that the risk of death increases with age, which results in a higher premium.

Example 3-15. Angie is 28 years old. The regulations assign a cost of six cents per month for each $1,000 of coverage for employees between 25 and 29 years old. If Beneficent paid for $60,000 of coverage, Angie includes $7.20 in gross income ($0.06 per month multiplied by 12 months and multiplied by 10 units of $1,000). Her gross income does not reflect Beneficent's *actual cost* for the policy.

Employees who purchase their own life insurance cannot deduct the premiums. They are nondeductible personal, living, or family expenses or expenses to produce tax-exempt income. I.R.C. §§ 262, 265. Section 79 thus converts a nondeductible outlay into an excluded employee benefit.

F. Education

1. Potential Exclusions

Section 127(a) excludes up to $5,250 per year for amounts received under an educational assistance program. The employer must have a written plan, give reasonable notice to eligible employees, not discriminate in favor of highly compensated employees regarding eligibility, and not require the employee to forgo taxable remuneration to use plan benefits. I.R.C. § 127(b). It can require a minimum grade or successful completion of the course. I.R.C. § 127(c)(5)(B).

Plan benefits can cover tuition, fees, books, supplies, and equipment. They cannot cover tools and supplies that the employee can keep, meals, lodging, or transportation, or education involving sports, games, or hobbies. I.R.C. § 127(c)(1). Between March 28 and December 31, 2020, payments can even cover principal and interest on an employee's student loans. Some ineligible benefits may still qualify for exclusion as § 117 scholarships or as deductible § 162 trade or business expenses. I.R.C. § 127(c)(6).

> **Example 3-16.** Adrianna's employer has an educational assistance program that covers up to $5,250 of tuition each year for any employee. A separate program pays key employees, including Adrianna, $500 per course for each grade of A. That payment discriminates in favor of highly compensated employees. Adrianna paid tuition of $4,000 and earned two grades of A. She excludes $4,000 of the $5,000 her employer paid her. The additional $1,000 is gross income.

The general provisions governing scholarships are covered in Chapter 10. That discussion includes the § 117(d) exclusion for qualified tuition reductions that an educational organization provides to its employees and to individuals treated as employees. The rules in § 132(h), discussed in this chapter, determine who is treated as an employee. The exclusion generally applies only to education below the graduate level. I.R.C. § 117(d)(2). But graduate students who are engaged in teaching or research activities may also qualify. I.R.C. § 117(d)(5). This exclusion is subject to nondiscrimination rules.

Educational expense reimbursements might also qualify as a working condition fringe benefit. I.R.C. § 132(a)(3). The reimbursement is excluded only if the employee could have deducted the expense himself as a business expense or as a depreciation expense. I.R.C. § 132(d). This exclusion has no nondiscrimination requirements or dollar limits.

The overlap between §§ 117, 127, and 132 illustrates the importance of reading all relevant guidance. Section 132(l) provides that § 132 does not apply if the tax treatment of a fringe benefit is expressly provided for in another section, but it provides exceptions for de minimis fringe benefits and for moving expense reimbursement fringe benefits. Although § 132(l) seems to prevent an employee from treating education costs as a working condition fringe if his employer was an educational organization and the tuition is for undergraduate education or if his employer offers an educational assistance program, that reading may be overly restrictive. First, § 132(j)(8) provides that amounts that cannot be excluded under § 127 may qualify for exclusion under § 132 as a working condition fringe. Second, Reg. § 1.132-1(f) includes this language:

[B]ecause section 117(d) applies to tuition reductions, the exclusions under section 132 do not apply to free or discounted tuition provided to an employee by an organization operated by the employer, whether the tuition is for study at or below the graduate level. Of course, if the amounts paid by the employer are for education relating to the employee's trade or business of being an employee of the employer so that, if the employee paid for the education, the amount paid could be deducted under section 162, the costs of the education may be eligible for exclusion as a working condition fringe.

2. Comparison of Exclusions

Sections 127 and 132(a)(3) apply to all employers; § 117(d) applies only to educational organizations. The § 127 exclusion cannot exceed $5,250 per year; no dollar limit applies to the other two exclusions. Only the actual employee can use §§ 127 and 132(a)(3); the employee's spouse and dependent children may qualify for the § 117(d) exclusion. Section 127 can be used for undergraduate and graduate education; § 117(d) is generally limited to undergraduate education; § 132 rarely applies to undergraduate education because an initial degree is generally obtained to meet the minimum requirements for *entering* a trade or business and thus would not be deductible by the employee. Education that qualifies under § 132(a)(3) must be job-related; the other two exclusions do not have a job-related condition.

3. Other Benefits for Education Costs

Several benefits for education are covered in other chapters. Exclusions are available for qualified scholarships, certain discharged educational debt, and using U.S. government bonds, qualified tuition programs, and Coverdell education savings accounts to pay educational expenses. There are also deductions and credits allowed for qualifying education expenses.

G. Children and Other Dependents

1. Dependent Care Assistance Programs

In *Smith v. Commissioner*, 40 B.T.A. 1038 (1939), the Board of Tax Appeals held that outlays for child care were not ordinary and necessary business expenses even if they enabled a taxpayer to work outside the home. Instead, the outlays were nondeductible personal, living, or family expenses. The Code now includes the § 129 exclusion for employer-provided benefits and the § 21 credit for outlays made from a taxpayer's own funds.

Section 129 excludes benefits received from employer-provided dependent care assistance programs. The employer must have a written plan that does not discriminate in favor of highly compensated employees, and the maximum exclusion is $5,000 per year ($2,500 if the employee is married but filing a separate return). If the employee's (or his spouse's) earned income is less than $5,000, the maximum exclusion is reduced to that lower amount unless the spouse is a student or is incapable of self-care.

Many of the rules governing the exclusion for dependent care assistance benefits are found in § 21, which governs the credit for household and dependent care costs the employee pays from her own funds. Payments qualify only if made for an individual who is under the age of 13 or who is incapable of self-care. In addition, certain types of care, such as overnight camp, do not qualify.

One difference between the two sections relates to number of individuals receiving care. The exclusion cannot exceed $5,000 no matter how many individuals receive care. The maximum amount used in computing the credit is $3,000 if there is one individual receiving care and $6,000 if there is more than one. An employee who receives benefits from an employer plan reduces that maximum by any excluded benefits. I.R.C. § 21(c). A second difference relates to the effect of a taxpayer's income. Because the exclusion reduces a taxpayer's gross income and taxable income, taxpayers in a higher marginal tax rate bracket receive a greater tax benefit than do taxpayers in a lower bracket. The credit percentage, on the other hand, begins at 35% and declines to 20% as the taxpayer's adjusted gross income (AGI) rises. I.R.C. § 21(a). Thus, a lower-income taxpayer might benefit more from the credit than from the exclusion.

An employer can provide dependent care assistance benefits in addition to its employees' normal compensation. Alternatively, it can let employees reduce their normal compensation and divert the funds to a flexible spending plan. Prop. Reg. § 1.125-5(h), (i). The plan reimburses employees for qualified outlays.

If the employer offers a salary reduction plan, employees must consider their marginal tax rate and AGI in deciding between the credit and the exclusion. The marginal tax rate is used to value the exclusion; the AGI affects the employee's dependent care credit percentage.

Example 3-17. Bram's employer lets employees reduce their salaries by up to $5,000 per year to pay for dependent care expenses. Bram spent $3,000 on qualified dependent care expenses. If he reduced his salary by $3,000 to pay for these expenses, his savings is $3,000 multiplied by his marginal tax rate (anywhere from 10% to 37%). If he did not reduce his salary, and instead took a credit for his outlays, his tax savings will range from 20% to 35% of $3,000.

Example 3-18. If Bram has more than one dependent and had dependent care outlays of $6,000, his decision is more complicated. He could take salary reduction of $5,000 and take a credit based on the remaining $1,000. He could take no salary reduction and take a credit based on the entire $6,000. Without knowing his tax rate and his eligibility for other tax benefits, we cannot determine his best option.

2. Adoption Assistance Programs

Section 137 excludes employer-provided adoption assistance benefits. There is a maximum per-adoption limit on this benefit. I.R.C. § 137(b)(1), (f). The inflation-adjusted limit for 2020 is $14,300. The exclusion is generally limited to the actual adoption expenses—reasonable and necessary adoption fees, court costs, attorney fees, and other expenses directly related to the adoption. I.R.C. § 23(d). The maximum exclusion is available for adopting a special-needs child even if actual outlays are lower. I.R.C. § 137(a)(2). Many of the rules governing this exclusion are found in § 23, which governs the credit for adoption costs paid by the adoptive parent from his own funds.

Eligibility phases out as income increases; the phase-out begins at modified AGI of $214,520 in 2020. Married individuals must file joint returns to qualify for either the exclusion or the credit. No benefits are available to taxpayers who adopt their spouse's child, are involved in surrogacy arrangements, or who adopt a child over 18 unless the child is physically or mentally incapable of self-care.

An employer can provide adoption assistance benefits in addition to its employees' normal compensation. Alternatively, it can let its employees reduce their normal compensation and divert the funds to a flexible spending plan. Prop. Reg. § 1.125-5(h), (j). The plan reimburses employees for qualified outlays. An employee who receives excluded benefits may also take the credit for out-of-pocket expenses that exceed the excluded amount. He does not reduce the maximum credit by the excluded amount.

H. Meals and Lodging

1. Section 119

Section 119(a) excludes the value of meals and lodging provided to the employee, his spouse, and his dependents. Meals and lodging must be provided on the employer's business premises for the convenience of the employer. Lodging must also be required as a condition of employment. These terms are defined in the regulations or in judicial opinions.

Before § 119 was enacted in 1954, administrative rulings and judicial opinions provided a common law convenience of the employer doctrine. For example, *Benaglia v. Commissioner*, 36 B.T.A. 838 (1937), let a hotel manager exclude the value of meals and lodging furnished by his employer. In O.D. 514, 2 C.B. 90 (1920), the IRS excluded supper money paid to an employee who voluntarily performed extra labor after normal business hours.

The employer's business premises are defined as the employee's place of employment. Reg. § 1.119-1(c). Some judicial decisions have approved premises where the employee conducts substantial work or premises adjacent to his place of business. In *Lindeman v. Commissioner*, 60 T.C. 609 (1973), for example, the hotel manager lived across the street in a house provided by his employer. He did some of his work there, and he occasionally entertained business guests. The court distinguished a Sixth Circuit decision in which the house was "two short blocks" away. *Commissioner v. Anderson*, 371 F.2d 59 (6th Cir. 1966). It noted that the Sixth Circuit did not conclude that the living quarters were an integral part of the business property. In most cases, the "condition of employment" test will be more important than the "employer's business premises" test.

Meals are furnished for the convenience of the employer if there is a substantial noncompensatory business reason for providing them. If so, they are excluded even if the employer also has a compensatory reason for providing them. The determination is based on the relevant facts and circumstances. Reg. § 1.119-1(a)(2). Meals furnished during the employee's working hours qualify if he must be available for emergency calls during his meal period. The employer must show that such emergencies have occurred or are reasonably likely to occur. Meals qualify if the employer's business requires restricting employees to a short meal period, and the employee could not be expected to eat elsewhere during that period. The employer's peak workload might, for example, occur during the meal period. Even if the meal period is longer, meals qualify if the employee could not otherwise secure proper meals within a reasonable meal period. For example, there may not be enough restaurants nearby. Reg. § 1.119-1(a)(2)(ii)(a)–(c).

If the employer charges an employee for meals only if she eats them, meals are not furnished for the convenience of the employer. If it deducts a meal charge even if she does not accept the meal, there are two potential outcomes. Even if the meal is not furnished for the convenience of the employer, she excludes the amount deducted from her pay from her gross income. I.R.C.

§ 119(b)(3). If the meal is not provided for the convenience of the employer, she includes its *value* in her gross income. Reg. § 1.119-1(a)(3).

> **Example 3-19.** Big Company charges each employee $6 a day for lunch. It deducts this amount from the employee's salary even if she doesn't eat in the company cafeteria. A restaurant would charge $9 for a comparable meal. Agatha eats there every day because she prefers to stay in the building. Beth eats there every day because she is on call for emergencies. Each excludes $6 per day for the meal charge. Agatha, but not Beth, also includes $9 per day because she does not qualify for the exclusion. The net effect on Agatha's gross income is a $3 per day increase; the net effect on Beth's gross income is a $6 per day decrease.

What if the employer provides something other than an actual meal? In *Commissioner v. Kowalski*, 434 U.S. 77 (1977), the Supreme Court held the exclusion did not apply to cash allowances that state troopers could use to eat at restaurants along their assigned route. In *Jacob v. United States*, 493 F.2d 1294 (3d Cir. 1974), the Third Circuit let the taxpayer exclude groceries that he received from his employer's commissary. He used the groceries to prepare meals he and his family ate in their home (which *was* on the employer's business premises). Although the *Jacob* opinion cited favorably to pre-*Kowalski* decisions in which lower courts had excluded trooper meal allowances, the *Kowalski* opinion did not mention *Jacob*. The *Jacob* decision may have continuing viability based on one distinction between it and *Kowalski*. We assume Dr. Jacob did not bring groceries home unless he planned to use them. The troopers in *Kowalski* received the meal allowance even if they skipped the meal and used the money for other purposes. However, the IRS has indicated that it follows *Jacob* only in the Third Circuit. PLR 9126063

In TAM 201903017, the IRS held that § 119 did not apply to employer-provided meals or snacks but that employees could exclude the value of snacks as § 132(e)(1) de minimis fringe benefits. The TAM includes an extensive analysis of the employer's rationales for providing the meals and reasons why those rationales were insufficient. Reflecting changes in meal consumption patterns, the TAM indicates that "meal delivery options should be considered when evaluating other business reasons proffered by employers as support for providing meals for the 'convenience of the employer' ...."

Reg. § 1.119-1(b) lists three tests for lodging—employer's business premises, convenience of the employer, and required to accept the lodging as a condition of employment—but discusses only the third test. Merely telling the employee that he must live on the premises is not sufficient to satisfy the condition of employment test. The lodging must be provided "to enable him properly to perform the duties of his employment." The regulations indicate that the test is satisfied by an employee who is always on call or who could not perform the services required of him unless lodging was provided. PLR 9126063 illustrates how the IRS interprets this requirement. It held that prison wardens and kennel supervisors who were provided lodging satisfied the test. It did not decide whether other employees who received lodging met the test but did note that they rarely, if ever, responded to emergencies. In addition to prison wardens, employees who are likely to meet the condition of employment test include apartment managers who are on call to make repairs, dormitory resident advisors, and employees working on cruise ships.

Section 119(d) excludes the value of qualified campus lodging provided to employees of an educational institution. Lodging must be (1) located on or in the proximity of the campus and (2) furnished to the employee, his spouse, and his dependents by (or on behalf of) the educational institution. Although this exclusion may help institutions in high-cost areas attract faculty members who could not otherwise afford to live near campus, it is an example of the Code's favoring one occupation over others. The exclusion is limited by a formula in § 119(d)(2). An employee who pays less in rent than the formula amount reports the difference as gross income unless she qualifies under the general § 119(a) rule for lodging. A university president could qualify for a full exclusion if she regularly uses her residence for receptions and other university business; a faculty member would be limited to the formula provided in § 119(d).

2. Parsonage Allowance

Section 107 excludes the rental value of housing (and housing allowances) provided a minister of the gospel as an identified part of his compensation. Reg. § 1.107-1(b). If the congregation provides an allowance instead of providing a home, the exclusion cannot exceed the amount that he uses to rent or provide a home. It is also limited to the fair rental value of the home, including furnishings and utilities. Outlays for food do not qualify as costs of providing a home. Reg. § 1.107-1(c). The exclusion appears to be limited to one house at a time. *Commissioner v. Driscoll*, 669 F.3d 1309 (11th Cir. 2012).

An individual qualifies if the services he performs are those which are ordinarily the duties of a minister. Reg. § 1.107-1(a). The regulations include the performance of sacerdotal functions, the conduct of religious worship, the administration and maintenance of religious organizations and their integral agencies, and the performance of teaching and administrative duties at theological seminaries. The exclusion applies regardless of religious affiliation. *See* Rev. Rul. 78-301, 1978-2 C.B. 103 (Jewish cantor).

Ministers who own the home for which they receive an allowance can deduct mortgage interest and property taxes despite the general rule of §265(a)(1), which disallows deductions for expenses allocable to tax-exempt income. Section 265(a)(6) lets individuals receiving parsonage allowances or military housing allowances deduct these expenses.

This exclusion's constitutionality has been challenged several times as favoring religious messages over secular messages. *See Gaylor v. Mnuchin*, 919 F.3d 420 (7th Cir. 2019).

3. Employer Cafeteria

Section 132(e)(2) treats an employer-operated eating facility as a de minimis fringe benefit. Employees who purchase meals for a reduced price do not report the discount as gross income. The employer must derive revenue from the facility that normally equals or exceeds its direct operating costs. These are the cost of food and beverages and the cost of labor performed on the premises. Reg. §1.132-7(b). The facility must be located on or near its business premises. It can own the premises or lease them; it can operate the facility itself or contract with another person to operate it. The meals must be provided during, or immediately before or after, the employee's workday. The facility must operate on a nondiscriminatory basis. Reg. §1.132-7(a)(ii).

This exclusion differs from the exclusion for meals provided for the convenience of the employer because it does not require a noncompensatory purpose. If the eating facility is used by employees who meet the §119 tests for meals provided for the convenience of the employer, they are treated as paying the direct costs of their meals even if they receive them for free. They do not prevent the facility from being a de minimis fringe for other employees.

I. Section 132

Before Congress enacted §132, many employers provided benefits that were not specifically excluded; they relied on old rulings (such as the ruling mentioned above regarding supper money) or simply analogized new benefits to benefits covered by an exclusion. Unless an audit revealed the practice, the benefit escaped taxation. Section 132 initially limited the exclusion for so-called nonstatutory fringe benefits to four generic categories: no-additional-cost service; qualified employee discount; working condition fringe; and de minimis fringe. It later added other categories.

1. No-Additional-Cost Service Benefits

a. General Rule

Section 132(a)(1) excludes no-additional-cost service benefits. These benefits are often called excess capacity benefits because the employee is not displacing a paying customer. As its title indicates, this exclusion is limited to services; it is not available for a company's products. Qualified services can be provided for free or at a discount.

Section 132(b) has two requirements. First, the service must be offered for sale to customers in the line of business in which the employee performs services. I.R.C. § 132(b)(1). If an employer is engaged in only one line of business, all employees can qualify. But if it operates multiple lines of business — e.g., an inter-city charter bus service and an airport shuttle service — many employees are likely to work in only one of them. Because company executives and other "central office" staff are likely to perform services directly benefiting each line of business, they can be treated as working in each line. Reg. § 1.132-4(a)(1)(iv). The regulations include several special rules, including rules that grandfather past practices by specified industries.

The second requirement relates to the employer's costs. The benefit does not qualify unless the employer incurs no substantial additional cost in providing it. For this purpose, forgone revenue is treated as a cost. We ignore payments made by the employee in determining whether the employer incurs substantial additional cost. I.R.C. § 132(b)(2). The exclusion does not apply if, for example, an airline lets employees reserve seats; the reservation could prevent a paying customer from booking those seats. Reg. § 1.132-2(c).

The regulations list three types of business that are included in the definition of excess capacity services: hotel accommodations; transportation; and telephone. Reg. § 1.132-2(a)(2). Because the regulation uses the term "include," other services could qualify. But the regulations limit service-intensive companies' ability to provide qualifying benefits. Reg. § 1.132-2(a)(5)(ii) differentiates between services requiring a substantial amount of time and services that are merely incidental to the primary service. It requires the employer to consider the cost of labor even if the services are provided outside normal business hours or in down time.

b. Qualifying as an Employee

Both no-additional-cost service and qualified employee discount fringe benefits define employee broadly. In addition to actual employees, their spouses, and dependent children, § 132(h) includes former employees who retired or left because of disability. It also includes surviving spouses of employees who died while working or after retiring. A child is dependent if he meets the definition of a dependent in § 152(f)(1) or, if both parents are deceased, is under age 25.

Additional categories may qualify for exclusions. First, if the employer provides air transportation, parents of employees, including retired and disabled former employees, are also treated as employees. I.R.C. § 132(h)(3). Second, reciprocal arrangements between employers qualify. I.R.C. § 132(i). Employees of one employer can use services provided by a second employer if they have a written agreement and neither employer incurs substantial additional cost in providing the services. The services still must qualify as no-additional-cost services, including meeting the line of business requirement.

c. Limitations

The no-additional-cost service fringe and the qualified employee discount fringe are subject to nondiscrimination requirements. I.R.C. § 132(j)(1). If non-highly compensated employees are not offered the benefit (or offered it on less favorable terms), the regulations disqualify the highly compensated employees from excluding even the limited benefit available to the other employees. Classifications based on seniority, full-time versus part-time employment, or job description are acceptable unless they are discriminatory as applied. Reg. § 1.132-8(d). Reg. § 1.132-8(c)(2) lets employers limit a benefit based on first-come, first-served or on seniority if they provide equal notice to all employees.

2. Qualified Employee Discounts

Section 132(a)(2) excludes any price reduction for goods or services that meets the requirements of a qualified employee discount. It applies if the employee can acquire the product or service for less than the price at which it is offered to customers, determined at the time of the sale. I.R.C. § 132(c); Reg. § 1.132-3(b)(2). The benefit must be provided in the line of the employer's business for which the employee works, and it must meet nondiscrimination requirements. Those requirements are discussed above in connection with no-additional-cost service benefits. Section 132(h) makes the discount available to most of the individuals (e.g., spouse and dependent children) who qualify for no-additional-cost service benefits, but the exclusion does not apply to reciprocal arrangements.

As noted in the discussion of no-additional-cost service benefits, the regulations governing the treatment of discriminatory benefits may disallow the entire exclusion if the employer provides an "excess" benefit to its highly compensated employees. Reg. § 1.132-8(a)(2)(i).

Example 3-20. Employer offers a 10% discount to non-highly compensated employees and a 15% discount to highly compensated employees. The entire 15% discount is gross income to any highly compensated employee who takes advantage of it.

The qualified discount for products is limited to the employer's gross profit percentage. I.R.C. § 132(c)(1)(A). If the employer sells the item to its employee for less than cost, the employee includes the excess discount in gross income; the permissible discount is still excluded. Because the employer determines its gross profit percentage based on its aggregate sales, a discount for a particular item may exceed its profit on that item and still qualify for the exclusion.

The gross profit percentage is computed by subtracting the employer's aggregate cost from its aggregate sales price and then dividing by the aggregate sales price. The determination is generally based on the prior year's sales and is done separately for each line of business if the employer has more than one. I.R.C. § 132(c)(2); Reg. § 1.132-3(c)(1)(ii). For example, an employer that paid $500,000 for products it sold last year for $800,000 has a gross profit percentage of 37.5% (($800,000 minus $500,000)/$800,000). It could offer its employees excluded discounts of up to 37.5% this year.

The employee cannot exclude discounts on real property and any tangible or intangible property of a kind normally held for investment. It is irrelevant whether the employee planned to hold the item for investment. Reg. § 1.132-3(a)(2)(ii).

Excluded discounts for services are limited to 20% of the normal price for the service. I.R.C. § 132(c)(1)(B). Any excess discount is included in gross income. The employer's profit margin is not considered when services are provided at a discount.

3. Working Condition Fringe Benefits

Section 132(a)(3) excludes working condition fringe benefits. These are amounts that the employee could have deducted as a business expense or through depreciation if she had paid them herself. I.R.C. § 132(d). If she is engaged in more than one trade or business, the expenses must relate to the business of the employer providing the benefit. Reg. § 1.132-5(a)(2).

The exclusion is usually preferable to a deduction because most unreimbursed employee business expenses were subject to deduction limits before the Tax Cuts and Jobs Act of 2017 and are not deductible at all in 2018 through 2025. Although nondeductibility is ignored for purposes of the exclusion, substantiation rules are not. If the employee would have been subject to § 274 substantiation rules if she made the outlay herself, the employer must require substantiation. Reg. § 1.132-5(a)(1)(ii). An employer that provides funds in advance must have a procedure for verifying the employee's outlay and must require the return of unexpended funds. Reg. § 1.132-5(a)(1)(v).

Items that are likely to qualify include professional association dues and subscriptions to professional journals. Employer-provided cell phones provided for noncompensatory business reasons also qualify. Notice 2011-72, 2011-38 I.R.B. 407. If an employee's educational expenses meet the tests of Reg. § 1.162-5, employer payments for those costs qualify as working condition fringes. Section 132(a)(3) is not subject to the $5,250 per year limitation that applies to the § 127 exclusion for employer-provided educational assistance programs. Section 132(j)(8) excludes amounts that do not qualify under § 127 if they qualify as working condition fringe benefits.

It is unlikely that every employee will incur deductible business expenses. Not surprisingly, then, these fringe benefits are not subject to nondiscrimination requirements. In addition, the definition of employee does not include her spouse or dependent children.

Section 132 specifically mentions only two items in connection with working condition fringes: qualified automobile demonstration use and, indirectly, employer-provided education benefits. Reg. § 1.132-5 provides qualification and valuation rules for other benefits that might qualify. These include employer-provided vehicles; chauffeur services; employer-provided aircraft; transportation and other costs attributable to bona fide business-oriented security concerns; products provided for testing outside the workplace; and payments for expenses of volunteers.

4. De Minimis Fringe Benefits

Section 132(a)(4) excludes de minimis fringe benefits. A benefit is de minimis if its value "is (after taking into account the frequency with which similar fringes are provided by the employer to the employer's employees) so small as to make accounting for it unreasonable or administratively impracticable." I.R.C. § 132(e)(1). The benefit can be property or services.

Employer-provided eating facilities qualify as de minimis fringes if they meet the requirements of § 132(e)(2), including nondiscrimination requirements. Reg. § 1.132-6(f). Other de minimis benefits are not subject to nondiscrimination requirements.

Reg. § 1.132-6(e)(1) provides several examples of de minimis fringe benefits. It lists such benefits as occasional typing of personal letters by a company secretary, occasional cocktail parties, group meals, or picnics for employees and their guests, and traditional birthday or holiday gifts of property (not cash) with a low fair market value. The regulations also cover the exclusion previously allowed by O.D. 514, 2 C.B. 90 (1920): occasional meals, meal money, or local transportation for an employee who works overtime. Reg. § 1.132-6(d)(2). Items that do not qualify include season tickets to various events, memberships in country clubs or athletic clubs, and group-term life insurance provided on the life of the employee's spouse or child. Reg. § 1.132-6(e)(2).

Except for the occasional meal money or transit fares mentioned above, cash benefits do not qualify. Nor do benefits provided through gift certificates or credit cards. Reg. § 1.132-6(c). In TAM 200437030, for example, the IRS ruled that $35 holiday gift coupons that were redeemable at local grocery stores could not qualify. The employer had previously provided ham, turkey, or gift baskets worth approximately $35 but switched to certificates because of employees' religious convictions or dietary concerns. It was not administratively impractical to account for gift certificates with a fixed value.

5. Qualified Transportation Fringe Benefits

Section 132(a)(5) excludes qualified transportation fringe benefits. It covers transportation in a commuter highway vehicle in connection with travel between the employee's residence and place of employment, transit passes, qualified parking, and (before 2018 and after 2025) qualified bicycle commuting reimbursements. I.R.C. § 132(f)(1). The employer can provide these benefits directly or provide cash reimbursements. An employer that provides reimbursements must have a substantiation procedure. Reg. § 1.132-9(b), Q&A-16(c).

A vehicle is a commuter highway vehicle if it seats at least six passengers in addition to the driver. The employer must reasonably expect that at least 80% of the mileage use will be for transporting employees in connection with travel between their homes and their employment. It must expect that the number of passengers will be at least half of the passenger seating capacity. I.R.C. § 132(f)(5)(B). Section 132(f)(5)(D) allows a vehicle operated *for* the employer to qualify.

A transit pass entitles the holder to travel free or at a reduced price on mass transit facilities. Alternatively, it can entitle him to use transportation provided by someone who transports customers for hire in a commuter highway vehicle. I.R.C. § 132(f)(5)(A). The employer can reimburse employees for transit passes only if it cannot reasonably obtain a voucher or other item to give the employee to exchange for a pass. I.R.C. § 132(f)(3). For example, the voucher provider's minimum purchase requirement may exceed the amount needed for the number of employees. Reg. § 1.132-9(b), Q&A-16(b).

An employer can provide parking on or near its business premises. It can also provide parking on or near a location (other than the employee's residence) from which the employee commutes to work using a transit pass, in a commuter highway vehicle, or by carpool. I.R.C. § 132(f)(5)(C).

Congress added the exclusion for bicycle commuting beginning in 2009. It lets the employer reimburse the employee for reasonable expenses of purchasing a bicycle and improvements, repairing it, and storing it. The employee qualifies only for months in which she regularly uses the bicycle for a substantial portion of her travel between her residence and place of employment. I.R.C. § 132(f)(5)(F). The regulations discussed above do not specifically address bicycle commuting expenses, which were added to the Code after the current regulations were issued and are not eligible for exclusion in 2018 through 2025. I.R.C. § 132(f)(8). When this exclusion was available, it was limited to $20 per month and had no inflation adjustment.

Transportation fringe benefits are subject to separate dollar limits, each of which applies on a monthly basis. The 2020 inflation-adjusted exclusion for transportation in a commuter vehicle and transit passes is $270 per month; the exclusion limit for qualified parking is also $270 per month.

An employer can provide more than one qualified transportation fringe benefit. Reg. § 1.132-9(b), Q&A-1(b). Although a cafeteria plan cannot include benefits covered by § 132, the employee will not have constructive receipt if the employer offers a choice between qualified transportation fringe benefits and taxable compensation. I.R.C. § 132(f)(4).

Commuting between home and work is generally considered a nondeductible personal expense. Reg. § 1.262-1(b)(5). Section 132(f) thus lets an employee exclude benefits for expenses that she could not deduct if she paid them herself.

> **Example 3-21.** Amelia drives to work and pays $200 a month to park her car. She cannot deduct that cost because it is commuting. If her employer provides free parking worth $200 per month, she does not report gross income. She has effectively received a tax-free salary increase. If her employer instead lets her reduce her salary by $200 a month, which it uses to pay for her parking, she is no worse off before taxes than when she paid for her own parking. She is better off after taxes because her gross income is reduced by $200 per month and she no longer pays for nondeductible parking.

6. Other Section 132 Benefits

Section 217 lets an employee deduct certain costs associated with moving to take a new job or a first job. Section 132(a)(6) provides an exclusion if the employer pays for or reimburses moving expenses that the employee could have deducted if she paid them herself. I.R.C. § 132(g). For 2018 through 2025, only active duty members of the military qualify for the deduction and the exclusion.

Section 132(a)(7) excludes qualified retirement planning services fringe benefits. This benefit could not separately qualify as a working condition fringe benefit because retirement planning is not an expense of carrying on the employee's trade or business. The exclusion does not apply unless the employer maintains a qualified plan for retirement savings; the plan must meet nondiscrimination rules. I.R.C. § 132(m).

Section 132(a)(8) excludes a qualified military base realignment and closure fringe benefit. The benefit covers payments to members of the military to compensate for losses sustained on selling a home on or near a military base when there is a base closure or realignment or a permanent reassignment to a new duty station. It applies within a limited range of purchase and sale dates. I.R.C. § 132(n).

Section 132(j)(4) covers on-premises athletic facilities provided to employees. The exclusion applies to a gym or other athletic facility located on the employer's premises. Substantially all the use must be by employees, their spouses, and dependent children. The premises can be owned or leased, the employer can operate the facility itself or contract the operation to another person, and a group of employers can jointly operate (or contract for the operation of) a facility. This benefit is not subject to nondiscrimination rules. Reg. § 1.132-1(e).

J. Miscellaneous Employment-Related Exclusions

Other employment-related exclusions include worker's compensation benefits for physical injury or sickness (§ 104(a)(1)); compensation received by military personnel for service in a combat zone or for a period of hospitalization for wounds or injury incurred during that service (§ 112); and other benefits provided members of the military (§ 134). Employees also benefit if an employer operates a qualified retirement program. The employee has no gross income until she receives distributions. Those are likely to occur in retirement, when she may be in a lower tax rate bracket.

Social Security benefits are funded equally by employer contributions, which are excluded from the employee's gross income, and employee contributions, which are not deductible in computing the employee's taxable income. When the employee retires, § 86 determines what portion of the benefits she can exclude. If her income is small enough, she excludes the full amount received even though part is attributable to employer contributions she excluded from gross income. Even if her income is much higher, gross income does not exceed 85% of her benefits. I.R.C. §86(a)(2).

K. Cafeteria Plans

Before Congress enacted §125, the IRS argued that an employee who could choose between excluded benefits and cash had gross income no matter which she chose. It argued that she had constructively received the cash. Section 125(a) provides that an employee who participates in a cafeteria plan does not have gross income solely because of having that choice. She has gross income only to the extent she selects permitted taxable benefits.

A cafeteria plan is a written plan that offers a choice between qualified benefits and permitted taxable benefits. I.R.C. §125(d)(1). It must offer at least one qualified benefit and one permitted taxable benefit. Prop. Reg. §1.125-1(a)(1). Although the Code lists only cash as an option to qualified benefits, the regulations use the broader term "permitted taxable benefits." Section 125 provides rules to prevent the plan from discriminating in favor of highly compensated participants.

A cafeteria plan can be used to fund excluded fringe benefits. Premiums to purchase group-term life insurance greater than $50,000 can be funded through a plan. Dependent care assistance benefits and adoption benefits also qualify. I.R.C. §125(f); Prop. Reg. §1.125-1(a)(3). It cannot be used to fund benefits excluded by §§106(b) (Archer medical savings accounts), 117 (qualified scholarships), 127 (educational assistance programs), or 132 (nonstatutory fringe benefits). Section 106(b) provides separate rules letting an employer offer an employee a choice between contributions to an Archer MSA or to another health plan.

Some benefits are subject to limits. For example, health flexible spending arrangements cannot be included in a cafeteria plan unless the plan limits employee salary reductions to an inflation-adjusted maximum amount per year ($2,750 in 2020). I.R.C. §125(i).

Although cafeteria plans and flexible spending arrangements or accounts are frequently referred to interchangeably, there are differences. In a cafeteria plan, the employer offers a choice of benefits. A flexible spending arrangement provides for reimbursements of specified incurred expenses. A cafeteria plan can include three types of flexible spending arrangements funded with an employee's pre-tax compensation: dependent care assistance; adoption assistance; and medical reimbursements. Prop. Reg. §1.125-5(h). An employee lowers her income taxes by funding a flexible spending account because she pays her expenses with pre-tax dollars instead of dollars that have already been taxed. These plans have a potential risk, however. Any funds the employee fails to use by the plan deadline revert to the employer. She cannot reduce the amount of salary placed in the account merely because she realizes she selected too high an amount.

> **Example 3-22.** Anita's employer lets employees reduce their salaries by up to $2,750 to fund medical benefits. Anita reduced her salary by $1,500; her employer placed the $1,500 in a flexible spending arrangement that will reimburse her for up to $1,500 of medical expenses. If her marginal tax rate is 24%, reducing her salary by $1,500 reduces her income tax by $360. But if she spends only $1,000 on her medical care this year, she forfeits the other $500. In that case, she forfeits $140 more than her tax savings. To break even, she must spend at least $1,140 of the $1,500 she placed in the plan.

The IRS originally required that forfeiture occur at the end of the plan year, thus giving employees 12 months to use the funds contributed that year. It now allows a grace period of up to two months and 15 days following the end of the plan year. Prop. Reg. § 1.125-1(e). Employers can instead let employees carry up to $500 of unused funds over for a full year. Notice 2013-71, 2013-47 I.R.B. 532. The plan cannot include both the grace period and the full-year carryover.

Checkpoints

- Gross income includes the receipt of wages, salaries, commissions, and fringe benefits. It also includes unemployment compensation.

- Compensation can be made in property or other benefits; it is not limited to the receipt of money.

- Section 83 applies if property transferred to a service provider is subject to a substantial risk of forfeiture if he fails to render the required services or other conditions are not satisfied.

- The service provider does not have gross income until the property is substantially vested. His gross income from compensation is the property's value when it becomes substantially vested, reduced by any amount he pays for it.

- The service provider can instead elect to report gross income when the property is transferred to him. His gross income is the property's value at the transfer date, reduced by any amount he pays. His holding period begins then, and subsequent appreciation is not compensation income. If he later forfeits the property, he cannot deduct the amount previously included in income.

- The service recipient cannot take a deduction for transferring the property until the service provider includes its value in gross income.

- If a fringe benefit is excluded, the employee reports no gross income even if the employer can deduct the cost of providing it.

- Most excluded fringe benefits include nondiscrimination rules to prevent employers from limiting them to highly compensated employees.

- Excluded fringe benefits are available for health care, group-term life insurance, education expenses, adoption expenses, dependent care expenses, and certain meals and lodging expenses. There are also generic fringe benefits, such as no-additional-cost service and qualified employee discounts.

- Some benefits are covered by multiple Code sections, which adds to complexity employees face in computing their taxes.

- Employers can offer a cafeteria plan, which lets employees choose between permitted taxable benefits and excluded benefits.

- A flexible spending arrangement lets employees pay for certain expenses through salary reduction. They forfeit any unspent funds.

Chapter 4

Gratuitous Transfers; Transfers Between Spouses and Former Spouses

---

Roadmap

- Gifts and transfers treated as gifts
- Bequests, devises, and inheritances
- Donative transfers involving income
- The transferee's basis
- The transferor's tax consequences

A. Gifts and Transfers Treated as Gifts

1. Definition

Section 102(a) excludes money or other property acquired by gift. The Code and regulations do not define the term gift. When taxpayers and the IRS dispute whether a transfer qualifies, courts often quote language used by the Supreme Court 60 years ago. Citing its statements in earlier cases, the Court characterized a gift as an item transferred with a "detached and disinterested generosity ... out of affection, respect, admiration, charity or like impulses." *Commissioner v. Duberstein*, 363 U.S. 278, 285 (1960). It also stated that the decision "must be based ultimately on the application of the fact-finding tribunal's experience with the mainsprings of human conduct to the totality of the facts in each case." *Id.* at 289. Because most tax litigation is conducted in Tax Court, a judge is usually the factfinder.

A transfer does not qualify as a gift merely because it is made voluntarily. Even calling the transferor "the donor" does not guarantee the recipient can exclude it. In determining whether a transfer is a gift or some other type of event, the transferor's intent is often the most relevant factor.

> **Example 4-1.** Based on her celebrity status, Alina received a gift bag worth more than $100,000 for attending the Oscars. The items she received are not gifts; the companies that included their products did not act out of detached and disinterested generosity. Alina has gross income equal to the value of the contents.

A transfer does not qualify for exclusion if it is made under any moral or legal obligation. It also fails to qualify if the transferor anticipates a future economic benefit or is compensating the transferee for past services. For this reason, service providers include tips received in gross income.

As noted in *Duberstein*, the determination of whether a transfer is a gift is based on the experience of the trier of fact. Factual determinations are rarely disturbed on appeal because the trier of fact is in the best position to judge the credibility of any testimony. Occasionally, however, an appellate court will reverse the factfinder's decision. In *Olk v. United States*, 536 F.2d 876 (9th Cir. 1976), for example, the district court held that "tokes" a craps dealer received from gamblers were received out of detached and disinterested generosity. Gamblers had no obligation to make these payments, and some winners voluntarily shared their winnings with other gamblers. But a dealer who did not place tokes in a common pool for sharing by the other dealers would be terminated. The appellate court included the tokes in gross income.

Most transfers by and between family and friends are gifts that are excluded from gross income. In *Duberstein*, the IRS argued for a bright line test—that only transfers of property made for personal reasons, as distinguished from business reasons, should be excluded. Although the Supreme Court rejected this construction in favor of the "detached and disinterested generosity" test, Congress later enacted § 102(c) to cover transfers from an employer to an employee.

2. Transfers in an Employment Setting

If an employee receives an item that is not required by her employment contract, she might think it is a gift rather than compensation, but it is hard to qualify for the exclusion for gifts in the employment context. Payments by an employer to an employee are usually compensation for services. Section 102(c) provides that § 102(a) does not apply to any amount transferred by (or for) an employer to (or for the benefit of) an employee. Unless another exclusion section applies, the employee has gross income.

Example 4-2. XYZ Corporation gave its employee Adela a holiday bonus of $3,000. The $3,000 is gross income. Section 102(c) prevents her from treating it as a gift. She would have the same result if XYZ gave her a three-day ski trip to Aspen, valued at $3,000.

Although § 102(a) does not apply, an employee can exclude a transfer if it qualifies under another exclusion provision. Some transfers might qualify as de minimis fringe benefits or as employee achievement awards.

Section 102(c) does not apply to transfers from one employee to another. In that situation, the relevant facts and circumstances determine whether the transfer is a gift. It also does not apply to transfers to business associates who are not the transferor's employees. The *Duberstein* decision involved such a transfer. Section 274(b)(1), however, provides a significant limitation. The transferor's business expense deduction cannot exceed $25 per donee per year if the donee can exclude the transfer only under § 102. The transferor must either forgo deducting more than $25 or make it clear to the recipient that the transfer is not a § 102 gift. Section 274(b)(1) was enacted in 1962, after the events in *Duberstein*. It has not been adjusted for inflation.

Even if § 102(c) does not apply, a transfer is not a gift unless the facts and circumstances indicate detached and disinterested generosity. For example, in *Goodwin v. United States*, 67 F.3d 149 (8th Cir. 1995), a minister was taxed on "gifts" he received from members of his congregation on "special occasion days." Although the members gave anonymously and the church was his actual employer, church leaders collected the funds in a "routinized, highly structured program," and the funds were substantial in relation to his actual salary. The Tax Court reached the same result for blue envelopes in *Felton v. Commissioner*, T.C. Memo. 2018-168. Reverend Felton's parishioners used different colored envelopes for their offerings. Blue envelopes were for unsolicited donations, parishioners received them only if they asked for them, and they were told that amounts put in blue envelopes were not tax-deductible donations. One factor in the court's decision was the high amount of blue envelope funds, particularly in relation to his parsonage allowance and his salary.

If an employee is also the employer's family member, we use a facts-and-circumstances test to determine the capacity in which she received the transfer. The transfer is excluded by § 102(a) if it was given with detached and disinterested generosity because she was a family member. It is included in gross income if it was on account of the employment relationship. Prop. Reg. § 1.102-1(f)(2) provides that § 102(c) does not apply to an extraordinary transfer to an employee who is the natural object of the transferor's bounty. The purpose of the transfer must be substantially attributed to the family relationship rather than to the employment relationship.

Important considerations include whether she received the "gift" in the employment setting, such as at an office function or party, and whether she received the same item that other employees received. In those circumstances, § 102(c) probably applies. On the other hand, if she received a gift outside of the work context or received an item that was significantly different in character and value from what other employees received, facts and circumstances would suggest that it should be excluded from gross income.

3. Transfers Between Spouses and Former Spouses

Property transfers between spouses are governed by § 1041 instead of by the Code sections governing sales or gifts. This section provides uniformity and recognizes a marital unit for most purposes as one economic entity. That section also applies to transfers between former spouses that are "incident to a divorce." That term is defined, and examples provided, in Chapter 17. Section 1041 does not apply to property transfers made before marriage, even if made pursuant to a prenuptial agreement. It is also inapplicable if the transferee spouse is a nonresident alien. I.R.C. § 1041(d).

Section 1041(b)(1) treats the transferee as receiving the property by gift. As a result, § 102(a) excludes its value from her gross income. Gift treatment applies even if she provided consideration. She treats the transfer as a gift even if she paid the transferor the property's value. Even if the transfer is incident to a divorce, the lack of detached and disinterested generosity is irrelevant.

B. Bequests, Devises, and Inheritances

In addition to excluding gifts from gross income, § 102(a) also excludes the value of property acquired by bequest, devise, or inheritance. Reg. § 1.102-1(a) indicates that the exclusion applies to property received under a will or under statutes of descent and distribution. Many jurisdictions use the term devise for all gifts made in a will. Others distinguish between bequests (transfers of personal, movable property) and devises (transfers of real, immovable property). Statutes of descent and distribution are often called intestacy statutes; they govern the disposition of probate property that is not covered by a will provision.

State law determines whether an individual is an heir, devisee, legatee, or beneficiary and the extent of that individual's rights. Federal law determines his tax consequences. If the property qualifies as a bequest, devise, or inheritance, he has no gross income.

Section 102(a) can even apply to property received following a will contest. The amount received through a judgment or settlement is in lieu of what the recipient might have received by bequest, devise, or inheritance. *Lyeth v. Hoey*, 305 U.S. 188 (1938).

Section 102(a) does not apply if the transfer is made in return for services. In the case of transfers at death, those services are usually past services, but it is possible that the transfer could be for anticipated future services (*e.g.*, caring for the decedent's pet). The fact that the transfer was provided for in a will is not controlling if the facts and circumstances indicate a compensatory motive. *Wolder v. Commissioner*, 493 F.2d 608 (2d Cir. 1974). In such circumstances, the form of the payment (bequest, devise, or inheritance) is disregarded in favor of its substance (compensation for services).

> **Example 4-3.** Amy painted a portrait of Brenda but did not charge her usual $10,000 fee. Instead of paying Amy, Brenda revised her will to devise $10,000 to Amy. This sum is attributable to the previously performed services and is included in Amy's gross income. The result is the same if Brenda devised Amy a necklace worth $10,000.

A transfer can be compensatory even if there is no traditional employment relationship. In one case, a couple agreed not to marry because the man had a "mental problem about marriage." In exchange for the woman's "stay[ing] with him without marriage," he promised that he would leave her everything when he died. In his will, he devised his property to his brother and sister. The woman sued for the value of wifely services, and the parties settled for more than $900,000. The Tax Court held that the settlement was not an excluded gift or bequest. The award was based on *quantum meruit* and not on the testator's sentiments of affection, respect, and admiration. *Green v. Commissioner*, T.C. Memo. 1987-503.

C. Donative Transfers Involving Income

1. Income Generated by Gifted Property

Although property received as a gift, bequest, devise, or inheritance is excluded from gross income, the exclusion does not apply to income generated by that property. I.R.C. § 102(b)(1).

> **Example 4-4.** Arthur gave his son Bram $200 as an excluded gift. Bram acquired a $200 certificate of deposit and received $10 of interest when the certificate matured. Bram must report the $10 interest as gross income.

2. Gift of Income Produced by Property

If the donor transferred the income an item of property produces, the form of the transfer is relevant. The outcome is affected by whether the donor transferred the income-producing property or retained it and merely transferred the income.

If a donor transfers property to a trustee to pay the income to one beneficiary and eventually distribute the principal to another beneficiary, the income beneficiary reports the income received as gross income. He is also taxed if he is entitled to receive the income for a fixed period and then receive the principal. Although he received the right to income as a gift or bequest, § 102(b)(2) applies. It provides that § 102(a) does not exclude gifts, bequests, devises, and inheritances of income from property.

> **Example 4-5.** In his will, Anton devised the income from the rental of his ranch to his son, Blake. After Anton died, Blake began receiving the rental income. He includes the rental income in his gross income.

If the donor retains the underlying property and makes a gift of income as it is earned, the results are different. The donor is taxed on the income based on assignment of income principles. The donee does not report gross income. Reg. § 1.102-1(e).

Although § 102(a) does not exclude these transfers, it is possible another exclusion section will apply. In Example 4-4, Bram could have purchased a bond issued by a local government instead of purchasing a certificate of deposit. Section 103 excludes interest received on state and local obligations from the recipient's gross income.

3. Income in Respect of a Decedent

A beneficiary may receive money or other property that a third party owed the decedent. The payment could represent unpaid salary. It could also represent a survivor's contractual right to retirement benefits funded by the decedent or the decedent's employer. The beneficiary steps into the decedent's shoes with respect to such payments, which are referred to as income in respect of a decedent. I.R.C. §691. They are her gross income to the extent they would have been gross income if received by the decedent.

D. The Transferee's Basis

The recipient may sell the property he received. Because gains are included in gross income (and some losses are deductible), he must be able to determine if the sale results in gain or loss. If he received the property by gift, bequest, devise, or inheritance, he did not purchase the property for adequate consideration. As a result, he has little or no investment (§1012 cost basis) to offset against the selling price. His basis is instead governed by §1014 (bequest, devise, or inheritance) or §1015 (inter vivos gift). If he received it as a transfer from a spouse, or from a former spouse incident to a divorce, it does not matter if he provided adequate consideration; §1041 governs his basis.

1. Property Acquired by Inter Vivos Gift

a. General Rule

Section 1015(a) begins with a general rule: the donee takes the donor's basis in the property. Although the term carryover basis is frequently used, the Code refers to this as transferred basis; the donor's basis is transferred to the donee. I.R.C. §7701(a)(43). When the general rule applies, the donee uses the donor's basis for computing gain or loss on a subsequent sale. If the donor received the property by gift, the donee's basis computation begins with the basis of the last preceding owner who did not acquire it by gift.

> **Example 4-6.** Andrew transferred land worth $60,000 to his daughter Bree. He originally paid $35,000 to acquire it. She takes the property with his $35,000 basis. If she later sells the land to Curt for $65,000, she realizes a gain of $30,000. If the land instead declined in value after she received it, and she sells it to Curt for $32,000, she realizes a loss of $3,000.

Although the donor's basis becomes the donee's original basis, it is not necessarily her final basis. She increases her basis by improvements and reduces it by any deductions she takes for depreciation. She also increases her basis by the donor's gift tax attributable to appreciation above his adjusted basis. I.R.C. § 1015(d)(6). Because the gift tax exemption currently exceeds $11 million, this discussion ignores any gift tax adjustment.

If the donee takes the donor's basis, she also takes his holding period for the property. That is relevant to the capital gain and loss computations later in this book. If the donor took depreciation deductions, the donee takes that prior depreciation into account in determining potential depreciation recapture. She does not take his *purpose* for holding the property. For example, property that the donor used in a trade or business becomes personal-use property in the hands of a donee who uses it for personal purposes.

b. Exception for Donor's Unrealized Loss

Section 1015(a) applies a different rule if the property's value at the time of the gift is less than the donor's basis. In that case, the donee's basis for determining loss is that lower value. This rule prevents donors from transferring a potential loss deduction to a taxpayer in a higher rate bracket. It does not prevent the donee from deducting *any* loss; it simply prevents her from deducting a decline in value that occurred before she received the property. In this situation, she takes one basis for gain (donor's basis) and a lower basis for loss (value on the date of the gift).

> **Example 4-7.** Abe transferred land worth $25,000 to his daughter Beth. He originally paid $40,000 to acquire it. Beth takes the property with his $40,000 basis, but only for the purpose of calculating gain. If she later sells the land to Cal for $45,000, she realizes a gain of $5,000.

> **Example 4-8.** Assume instead that the land declined in value after Abe transferred it to Beth. Because its value was less than his adjusted basis when he gave her the land, her basis for determining loss is $25,000. If she later sells the land to Cal for $20,000, she realizes a loss of only $5,000, the difference between the $20,000 amount realized and her $25,000 basis for computing loss.

We use the lower basis for loss only if two conditions are satisfied. First, the property must be worth less than the donor's basis when the transfer occurs. Second, the donee must dispose of the property at a loss. Unless both conditions are satisfied, or the situation described in the next paragraph applies, the donee uses the donor's basis to compute both gain and loss.

Loss property might increase in value after the gift—but not above the donor's basis. The basis for loss would result in a gain, while the basis for gain would result in a loss. In that case, the donee reports neither gain nor loss on the sale. Reg. § 1.1015-1(a)(2).

> **Example 4-9.** Assume that Beth later sells the land to Cal for $30,000. For purposes of calculating gain, her adjusted basis is $40,000. When she compares that amount to her $30,000 amount realized, she has a $10,000 loss. For purposes of calculating loss, her adjusted basis is $25,000. When she compares that amount to her $30,000 amount realized, she has a gain of $5,000. Her basis for gain results in a loss; her basis for loss results in a gain. Beth has neither gain nor loss when she sells the land for $30,000.

c. Part Gift/Part Sale Transfers

A taxpayer may sell property to a family member or to a charity for less than its actual value. Because she could have received more consideration, she shows donative intent. But, because she receives some consideration, there is also a realization event. And, in the charitable setting, there is a potential charitable contribution deduction.

If the transfer is to a family member, it is a transfer that is in part a gift and in part a sale ("part gift/part sale"). Its tax consequences are discussed in this section. If the transferee is a charity, it is a bargain sale to a charitable organization, and the rules discussed in Chapter 13 apply. I.R.C. §§ 170(e)(2), 1011(b).

When a part gift/part sale occurs, Reg. § 1.1001-1(e) governs the transferor's tax consequences. She reports gain only if the amount realized exceeds her adjusted basis for the entire property transferred. She does not sustain a loss even if the amount realized is less than her adjusted basis. Reg. § 1.1015-4(a) governs the transferee's tax consequences. His initial basis is whichever of two amounts is greater: the transferor's adjusted basis or the amount he paid her for the property.

> **Example 4-10.** Angela transferred property worth $120,000 to her son Brad. Her adjusted basis for it was $80,000. Brad paid her $30,000. Angela does not have a gain because her amount realized was less than her basis. She also has no loss even though the $30,000 amount realized was less than her basis. Reg. § 1.1001-1(e). She made a gift of $90,000, the excess of the property's $120,000 value over her amount realized. Brad's initial basis is $80,000 because that exceeds his $30,000 payment.

Example 4-11. If Brad instead paid Angela $85,000, she realizes a $5,000 gain. She made a gift of $35,000, the excess of the property's $120,000 value over her amount realized. Brad's initial basis is $85,000 because that exceeds Angela's adjusted basis.

The property described in the examples above was worth more than the transferor's basis at the time of the transfer. If the property is worth less than her basis, the transferee is governed by both the part gift/part sale rules and the loss limitation rules described in the preceding subsection. His basis for loss cannot exceed the fair market value of the property at the date of the gift. Reg. § 1.1015-4(a) (flush language).

Example 4-12. Alisa transferred property worth $120,000 to her son Basil. Her adjusted basis for it was $180,000. Basil paid her $30,000. She does not have a gain because her amount realized was less than her basis. She also has no loss even though her amount realized was less than her basis. Reg. § 1.1001-1(e). She made a gift of $90,000, the excess of the property's $120,000 value over her amount realized. Basil's initial basis *for gain* is $180,000 because that exceeds his $30,000 payment. Because Alisa's adjusted basis exceeded the property's value at the time of the transfer, the § 1015(a) loss limitation applies. Basil's initial basis *for loss* cannot exceed the $120,000 value of the property on the date of the gift.

Do not confuse these transactions with losses covered by § 267(a)(1). That provision disallows otherwise deductible losses on sales or exchanges between related parties. In a part gift/part sale transaction, the transferor is voluntarily accepting less than the property's actual value. Because she is not treated as sustaining a loss, there is no loss for § 267(a)(1) to disallow.

2. Property Acquired from a Decedent

The property's value when the decedent dies is the most significant factor in determining the recipient's basis. Section 1014(b) defines "property acquired from a decedent" quite broadly. In addition to property received by bequest, devise, or inheritance, it includes property received from a trust the decedent established before his death if he retained certain powers over (or interests in) it. It also includes the surviving spouse's share of community property and the value of certain property received by right of survivorship. It does not include property representing a right to income the decedent did not receive before death. In that case, the § 691 income in respect of a decedent rules apply. I.R.C. § 1014(c).

Section 1014(a) provides rules for determining basis when property is acquired from a decedent. Section 1014(a)(1) provides the general rule: the recipient's basis is the value of the property on the date of the decedent's death. If the executor elects an alternate valuation date—namely six months after the decedent's death—the recipient's basis is the value on that alternate date (or earlier date of disposition for property disposed of during the six-month period). I.R.C. § 1014(a)(2).

When the recipient takes a fair market value basis in appreciated property, we say that he has a "stepped-up" basis. His basis is stepped up from the decedent's basis to the value of the property on the date of death (or alternate valuation date). Unfortunately, this rule also works in reverse: if the property's value declined while the decedent owned it, the recipient takes a "stepped-down" basis. In addition to these general rules, § 1014(a) includes special rules covering real estate used in business or farming and property subject to conservation easements. This discussion ignores those rules.

> **Example 4-13.** Angie purchased a painting for $10,000 and shares of stock for $18,000. She devised the painting to her daughter Betsy and the stock to her son Buddy. Each asset was worth $17,000 on the date she died, and her executor valued the estate as of that date. Betsy's basis for the painting is $17,000. Neither Angie nor Betsy will ever pay income tax on the $7,000 increase in value that occurred before Angie died. Buddy's basis for the stock is $17,000. Neither Angie nor Buddy will ever be able to deduct the $1,000 decline in value that occurred before Angie died.

Section 1014(e) prevents a basis step-up for certain transfers of property that a decedent received by gift within one year of his death. It targets taxpayers who transfer appreciated property to individuals with a short life expectancy because they expect to later receive that property back with a stepped-up basis. If the original donor (or her spouse) acquires the property from the decedent, § 1014(a) does not apply. Instead she takes the basis that the decedent had in the property immediately prior to his death. That basis would be the original donor's pre-transfer basis (because the decedent took that basis under § 1015(a) when he received the inter vivos gift of appreciated property). By imposing a bright-line test, Congress limited taxpayers' ability to use a prearranged transfer and retransfer to obtain a stepped-up basis.

> **Example 4-14.** Amelia purchased Blackacre many years ago for $100,000 and it is now worth $500,000. If she sold it, she would realize a $400,000 gain. She transferred Blackacre to her elderly grandfather Baxter as a gift, and he took her basis. He died two months later, and his will

devised Blackacre to Amelia. Because Baxter received Blackacre from
her within one year of his death, and she reacquired it from him when
he died, § 1014(e) prevents Amelia from taking a $500,000 basis. She
instead takes the $100,000 basis that Baxter took when she transferred
Blackacre to him.

Section 1014(e) is arguably both over- and under-inclusive. It does not prevent
the step-up in basis if the decedent-donee lives even a day longer than one year.
It is also ineffective if he devises the property to someone other than the donor
or the donor's spouse. For example, he could devise it to the donor's child. On
the other hand, it would apply even if the donee's life expectancy had been
greater than one year, as might be the case if his death was accidental.

Section 1014(a) gives property owners some planning opportunities. Often,
it may be prudent for them to retain property that has appreciated in value.
Neither they nor their beneficiary ever pays income tax on the unrealized gain.
Owners of property that has lost value have incentives to sell the property
before they die. Otherwise, potential loss deductions are eliminated when the
basis is stepped down at their death.

Gift and estate tax consequences are also relevant. The inflation-adjusted
transfer tax exclusion is $11,580,000 in 2020. Because the exclusion is per-person,
a married couple can transfer double that amount without worrying about gift
or estate tax. Taxpayers whose wealth is within the exclusion can avoid both
income tax on appreciated property and estate tax on its transfer. Their beneficiaries
also avoid income tax on the gain because they receive a stepped-up basis.

Taxpayers who gratuitously receive property from a decedent enjoy other
tax benefits. First, because their basis does not reflect the decedent's basis, they
are not subject to depreciation recapture if the decedent previously depreciated
the property. As a result, any gain they realize on a later sale is likely to qualify
for the lower capital gain rates. Second, for purposes of the capital gain computations, they receive a long-term holding period even if they dispose of the
property within one year after the decedent's death. I.R.C. § 1223(9). Third,
if they inherit literary or artistic works (or other intellectual property) created
by the decedent, they can treat them as capital assets because they are not using
the creator's basis. I.R.C. § 1221(a)(3)(C).

3. Property Acquired from a Spouse or Former Spouse

As discussed above, § 1041(b)(1) treats the transferee spouse or former
spouse as receiving the property by gift. Section 1041(b)(2) provides that the

transferee's initial basis for the property is the same as the transferor's adjusted basis for the property. This rule mirrors the basis provisions for transfers by gift, but with one major exception—the loss limitation rule in § 1015(a) does not apply. Even if the transferor's basis exceeds the value of the property when the transfer occurs, the recipient uses the transferor's basis for both gain and loss instead of having a separate basis for each. I.R.C. § 1015(e).

Section 1041(a) is a nonrecognition provision for the transferor. Although he does not recognize gain or loss, the gain or loss potential does not permanently disappear. Instead, it is transferred to the transferee, to be recognized if she later sells the property. She takes the transferor's adjusted basis, bears the burden of any deferred gain, and may benefit from any deferred loss. Because we ignore consideration when we compute the recipient's basis, § 1041(b)(2) could result in unexpected consequences for a recipient-purchaser.

> **Example 4-15.** Amos sold land to his wife Bonnie for its $100,000 value. He originally paid $60,000 to acquire the land. He does not recognize his $40,000 realized gain. Even though Bonnie paid $100,000 to acquire the land, her initial basis is only $60,000 because she takes his basis for the land.

> **Example 4-16.** Pursuant to their divorce agreement, Art sold land to his ex-wife Bev for its $25,000 value. He originally paid $40,000 to acquire the land. He does not recognize his $15,000 loss. Bev takes his $40,000 basis for calculating any future gain or loss.

If the property is transferred to a trust instead of outright, an exception applies. Section 1041(a) does not apply if the sum of the liabilities assumed and the liabilities to which the property is subject exceeds the transferor's adjusted basis. In that case, the transferor recognizes that excess as gain. The transferee's basis is increased by the transferor's gain recognized so that it is not taxed a second time when the property is sold. I.R.C. § 1041(e). This exception to nonrecognition applies only to transfers in trust. If one spouse transfers encumbered property directly to his spouse, he recognizes no gain even if the liabilities exceed his basis, and her basis is not increased by that excess. Temp. Reg. § 1.1041-1T(d), Q&A-12.

When the recipient spouse takes the transferor spouse's basis, she also takes his holding period for the property. That is relevant to her capital gain and loss computations. If he took depreciation deductions, she takes that prior depreciation into account in determining potential depreciation recapture. She does not take his *purpose* for holding the property. For example, property that the transferor used in a trade or business becomes personal-use property in the hands of a recipient who uses it for personal purposes.

E. The Transferor's Tax Consequences

Gratuitous transfers do not usually affect the donor's income tax. This is true even if the property's value changed while she owned it. A purely gratuitous transaction is not treated as a realization event. If she receives some compensation, the part gift/part sale rules or the bargain sale to charity rules apply. If the amount of money — or the value of other property — transferred is large enough, she might be subject to gift tax, estate tax, or both. Those taxes are covered in courses focusing on transfer taxes.

If the transfer is between spouses, or between former spouses incident to a divorce, the transferor generally recognizes no gain or loss. It is irrelevant whether the transferee provided any consideration for the property transferred.

Checkpoints

- Amounts received as gifts, bequests, devises, or inheritances are excluded from gross income.

- The exclusion does not apply to income produced by the gifted property, to gifts of income, or to income in respect of a decedent.

- A gift involves detached and disinterested generosity or affection, respect, admiration, charity, or like impulses.

- Gifts from employers are usually included in the employee's gross income. It is irrelevant that they are not required by the employee's contract.

- Transfers to spouses, and to former spouses if incident to a divorce, are excluded from the recipient's gross income. The lack of detached, disinterested motives of generosity is irrelevant.

- The donee of an inter vivos gift generally takes the donor's basis when computing gain or loss on a subsequent sale.

- If the donor's basis exceeds the property's value on the date of the gift, the donee uses that lower value solely for computing loss. He uses the donor's basis for computing gain.

- If a donor receives consideration that is less than the property's value, the transfer is a part gift/part sale transaction. She realizes gain only if the consideration exceeds her total basis. She does not realize a loss. The recipient's basis is the greater of the donor's adjusted basis or the amount he paid her.

- Property transfers between spouses (or between former spouses incident to a divorce) do not result in recognized gain or loss for the transferor. The recipient takes the transferor's basis.

- If property is received by bequest, devise, or inheritance, the recipient's basis is usually the property's value on the date of the transferor's death (or six months later).

Chapter 5

Gain and Loss: Basis and Amount Realized

A. Introduction

We begin this chapter with the computation of gain or loss in the most basic situation: the taxpayer purchased property or manufactured property and later sold it. He may be disposing of a single item, such as a home or investment land, or he may be selling inventory. We then address gain or loss computations in other situations. These include acquiring property using debt, in a taxable transaction that is not a purchase, or in a nonrecognition transaction. The previous chapter addressed acquiring property from an inter vivos donor, from a spouse (or a former spouse incident to a divorce), and from a decedent.

For most property, gain or loss reflects the taxpayer's ability to recover his investment in property. Because he may hold property for several years before transferring it, we must determine his initial investment, any improvements he made, and any depreciation or partial losses he deducted.

B. General Rules and Terminology

1. Computing Gain or Loss

Section 61(a) includes two provisions involving gains and gross income. Section 61(a)(2), gross income derived from business, applies to a taxpayer who regularly sells inventory he manufactured for sale or purchased for resale. Rather than compute gain or loss on each item sold, he computes a gross profit that compares his total sales revenue to his total cost of goods sold. He uses inventory accounting methods to compute that cost.

This chapter focuses on the second provision. Section 61(a)(3) includes gains derived from dealings in property. To understand its application, we consider Code sections governing the computation of gain (or, if the taxpayer is unfortunate, loss). Section 1001(a) defines gain from the sale or other disposition of property as the excess of the amount realized over the property's adjusted basis for determining gain. Conversely, loss from the sale or other disposition of property is the excess of the adjusted basis for determining loss over the amount realized. In most situations, the basis for gain and the basis for loss are identical. But that is not always the case. If the two amounts differ, basis for gain exceeds basis for loss.

A mere change in value does not trigger gain or loss computations. There must be a realization event, usually a sale or other disposition of property, to trigger § 1001(a).

> **Example 5-1.** Arvin purchased common stock in BCD Corporation for $10,000 on March 1, 2019. On April 3, 2020, the value of his BCD stock was $13,000. He has no gross income, even though his stock appreciated in value, because no realization event occurred. If he sold the stock for $13,000, he realized a $3,000 gain.

When § 1001 applies, we consider amount realized, adjusted basis, gain (or loss) realized, gain or loss recognized, and character of gain or loss. The discussion below ignores selling expenses, which reduce gain (or increase loss). They are not separately deducted as expenses.

2. Amount Realized

The amount realized from a sale or other disposition is the sum of any money plus the fair market value of any other property received. I.R.C. § 1001(b). When computing the amount realized, we use the value of the property received, not the value of the property sold. The definition of amount realized covers transactions in which the transferor receives only money, only other property, or a combination of money and other property. Debt relief is also considered in computing amount realized.

Convertible virtual currencies (*e.g.*, Bitcoin) are treated as property rather than as money in computing amount realized. Notice 2014-21, 2014-16 I.R.B. 938. A taxpayer who receives convertible virtual currency in exchange for property includes its value in his amount realized. If he later uses that currency to pay for other property or services, he will realize gain or loss if its value has changed.

3. Cost Basis

In describing gain or loss realized, § 1001(a) refers to the adjusted basis provided in § 1011. Section 1011 is a referral section. It provides for taking the taxpayer's basis and adjusting it as provided in § 1016, and it provides that basis is determined by § 1012 or other applicable Code sections. Although the Code does not use these modifiers, those provisions define *initial, original,* or *unadjusted* basis for the property.

In this section, we focus on § 1012. Later in this chapter, we consider basis provisions that apply to property received in other contexts. Because § 1012 is our primary focus, we cite to it rather than to § 1011 when referring to initial basis. Keep in mind, however, that it is § 1011 that instructs us to make basis adjustments.

Section 1012(a) provides that the basis of property is its cost. Thus far, the gain (or loss) realized from the sale or disposition of property is the amount realized, as determined under § 1001(b), minus the basis, as determined under § 1012 (with adjustments provided in § 1016).

> Example 5-2. Al purchased land for $40,000 to use as a business parking lot. His cost basis is $40,000. Two months later, he changed his mind and sold the lot for $42,000. His amount realized is $42,000. His gain realized is $2,000.

Assumptions about the order in which a taxpayer sells non-inventory property are generally unnecessary, but there is one major exception. A taxpayer may purchase shares of stock or other securities over a period of time rather than in a single transaction. He may hold shares of one or more corporations, or he may hold shares in a regulated investment company (RIC) that owns stock issued by many corporations. He may also acquire shares by participating in a dividend reinvestment plan. Participants in those plans acquire additional whole or fractional shares instead of receiving cash dividends. Shares in the same corporation or RIC are fungible; each share is worth the same amount no matter when it was purchased. So how do we determine the basis and holding period when he sells some of his holdings?

If he sells only part of his shares, we must determine his basis for the shares sold. Reg. § 1.1012-1(c)(1) provides a general rule. If he cannot adequately identify the lot from which he sold the stock, he is treated as selling the shares in the order in which he acquired them. If he does not have the actual stock certificates, he makes adequate identification by specifying to his broker which shares he is selling (and receiving a confirmation within a reasonable time). A taxpayer who acquired stock using a dividend reinvestment plan can use any identification method that would be acceptable for shares held in a RIC. I.R.C. § 1012(d). He can elect to use an average basis method for those shares. If he does not instruct the plan that he is doing so, he must use the plan's default method of determining basis. Reg. § 1.1012-1(e).

4. Adjustments to Basis

Section 1016(a) adjusts basis for "expenditures, receipts, losses, or other items, properly chargeable to capital account." It also adjusts basis for "exhaustion, wear and tear, obsolescence, amortization, and depletion." The discussion below focuses on capital expenditures and depreciation.

The original basis is increased by capital expenditures. These are outlays described in the improvement regulations. Reg. § 1.263(a)-3. Depreciation is the most common basis reduction. The reference in § 1016(a)(2) to adjustments for exhaustion, wear and tear, and obsolescence reflects language in § 167 authorizing a depreciation deduction. This deduction is available only for property used in a trade or business or held for the production of income. It allocates both original basis and improvements over the asset's life. Note that the example below ignores opportunities discussed in Chapter 12 to deduct the entire cost in the year the taxpayer placed the property in service.

> **Example 5-3.** Amanda purchased a delivery truck for $40,000 and depreciated its cost over its five-year life. By the end of that period, she will have deducted $40,000 and her adjusted basis will be zero. If she later spends $18,000 to enclose the truck's delivery area, she has made a capital expenditure, which increases the adjusted basis by $18,000. She recovers that outlay through depreciation deductions using the same useful life she uses to depreciate the truck. I.R.C. § 168(i)(6).

5. Gain or Loss Realized and Recognized

The taxpayer realizes a gain if the amount realized exceeds the adjusted basis. He realizes a loss if the adjusted basis exceeds the amount realized. I.R.C. § 1001(a).

> **Example 5-4.** Four years ago, Avery paid $15,000 to purchase property for his business. Two years ago, he spent $6,000 for improvements. During the time he owned the property, he deducted depreciation for the original property — and the improvements — of $8,000. This year, he sold the property for its $16,000 value. His amount realized is $16,000. His adjusted basis of $13,000 has three components: his original cost basis of $15,000; an increase of $6,000 for the improvements; and a decrease of $8,000 for the depreciation he deducted. His gain realized is $3,000.

Section 1001(a) does not tell us if the realized gain or loss is recognized. A gain is recognized when it is taken into account in computing gross income. A loss is recognized when it is taken into account in computing taxable income.

Section 1001(c) provides a general rule: we recognize the entire amount of gain or loss realized. That rule is subject to exceptions, as indicated by its introductory phrase: "Except as otherwise provided in this subtitle." In some cases, the gain or loss is not recognized at all or is only partially recognized. Common nonrecognition provisions include like-kind exchanges governed by § 1031 and transfers to a spouse or former spouse governed by § 1041.

Although nonrecognition technically applies to any gain or loss that is not currently used in computing taxable income, practitioners distinguish between transactions that postpone tax consequences and transactions that never affect taxable income. They use "nonrecognition" for transactions whose tax consequences are postponed to a later date, usually when another disposition occurs. They refer to Code sections covering transactions that will never affect taxable income as exclusion and nondeductibility provisions. When an exclusion provision applies, the gain is never taxed. The same is true with respect to losses. If no Code section makes a loss deductible, nonrecognition provisions are irrelevant because there is no loss deduction to postpone.

6. Character of Gain or Loss

Gains and losses may be ordinary, capital, or § 1231 gains and losses. Lower tax rates apply to net capital gains, which may reflect not only capital gains and losses but also § 1231 gains and losses.

C. Transactions Involving Debt

1. Cost

A taxpayer may purchase property by paying part of the cost immediately and financing the remainder. In that situation, we could determine her basis by counting only the amount she initially paid and increasing it each year as she repaid the loan. If that were the rule, she would recompute her cost basis every year. If the property was depreciable, her depreciation computation would also change every year.

Because we assume that she will pay the amount borrowed—to avoid having the property repossessed—we simplify the basis computation by including the debt in her original basis. In other words, her basis includes both her initial payment and any amount borrowed (from the seller or from a third party) to purchase the property (or make improvements). Because the amount borrowed is included in her original basis, she does not increase her basis as she repays the loan.

Acquisition debt is included in the taxpayer's basis even if she is not the original borrower. A taxpayer who acquires mortgaged property and assumes the mortgage—or takes the property subject to the mortgage—includes that debt in her basis.

> **Example 5-5.** Art purchased an apartment building with funds borrowed from ABC Bank. When it was worth $500,000, he sold it to Beth. She paid him $50,000 in cash and assumed his $450,000 mortgage debt. Beth's cost basis for the building is $500,000—the $450,000 debt she assumed plus the $50,000 she paid Art.

Ordinarily, the purchaser's basis is the value of the property acquired. When a nonrecourse loan is involved, the purchaser may be tempted to artificially inflate basis by promising to pay more than the property is actually worth. His goal is to increase his initial basis, so that he can take larger depreciation deductions. He plans to forfeit the property or restructure the "debt" in the future. There is a limit to his ability to do this. The court disallowed the depreciation deductions in *Estate of Franklin v. Commissioner*, 544 F.2d 1045 (9th Cir. 1976), noting that "the purchase price exceeds a demonstrably reasonable estimate of the fair market value" of the property being acquired with nonrecourse debt.

When property is encumbered *after* the taxpayer acquires it, it is important to focus on what she does with the borrowed funds. If she borrows against her equity to make an improvement to that property, she increases her adjusted basis for that property. But if she uses the debt proceeds to acquire or improve a completely different asset—or uses them to pay expenses—she does not increase the basis of the original asset.

> **Example 5-6.** Ava purchased land several years ago for $100,000. It is currently worth $140,000. She borrowed $18,000, using the land as security for the loan. She spent $10,000 to landscape it, $5,000 to purchase office furniture, and $3,000 to pay vacation expenses. She increases her basis for the land by only $10,000. She takes a $5,000 cost basis for the office furniture. It is irrelevant that she borrowed against her equity in the land to fund that purchase. The remaining $3,000 does not affect the basis of any asset. She used those funds to pay expenses rather than to acquire or improve an asset.

2. Amount Realized

Section 1001(b) lists money and other property as components of the amount realized. But debt relief also gives the transferor a financial benefit. Unless the computation of amount realized takes debt relief into account, his gain is understated (or his loss is overstated). Reg. § 1.1001-2(a)(1) provides a general rule: the amount realized includes the amount of liabilities from which he is discharged.

The type of debt may be relevant if it exceeds the value of the property. With a nonrecourse mortgage, a lender's only option if the debtor defaults is to take the encumbered property. A recourse mortgage, by contrast, lets the lender seek repayment from the debtor's other assets if the encumbered property is worth less than the amount he is owed.

When property is transferred subject to a nonrecourse mortgage, the amount realized includes the amount of the mortgage, even if it exceeds the value of the property transferred. *Commissioner v. Tufts*, 461 U.S. 300 (1983). In *Crane v. Commissioner*, 331 U.S. 1 (1947), the Supreme Court held that a taxpayer who sells property encumbered by a nonrecourse mortgage includes the unpaid balance of the mortgage in computing the amount realized. In that case, the Court, in footnote 37, expressly withheld a determination of whether that rule applied if the value of the property transferred was less than the balance of the debt. In *Tufts*, it held that the transferor realizes the amount of the nonrecourse mortgage even if it exceeds the value of the property transferred. Reg. § 1.1001-2(c), Example (7), illustrates this situation.

> **Example 5-7.** Andy owns property that has a value of $10,000 and an adjusted basis of $11,000. He financed the purchase with a nonrecourse mortgage in favor of First Bank. If he transfers the property to the

bank when the mortgage balance is $15,000, his amount realized is $15,000. Because the entire amount of the nonrecourse debt is treated as his amount realized, Andy realizes a gain of $4,000 on transferring the property to his creditor and extinguishing his debt.

When recourse debt is involved, and the property value exceeds the amount of debt, the amount realized includes the full amount of the debt the purchaser agrees to pay. This is true even though the lender does not release the seller from liability. Reg. § 1.1001-2(a)(4)(ii). If the recourse debt exceeds the property's value, the tax consequences differ from those described above for nonrecourse debt. If the lender cancels any of the excess debt, the canceled amount is governed by the § 108 debt discharge rules. The amount of debt included in the amount realized does not exceed the property's value. Reg. § 1.1001-2(a)(2). Reg. § 1.1001-2(c), Example 8, illustrates this situation.

> **Example 5-8.** Axel owns property that has a value of $10,000 and an adjusted basis of $11,000. He financed the purchase with a recourse mortgage in favor of Last Bank. If he transfers the property to the bank when the mortgage balance is $15,000, and it cancels the entire debt, his amount realized is $10,000. Only the amount of debt equal to the property value is treated as his amount realized. He realizes a loss of $1,000 on transferring the property to his creditor and extinguishing his debt. Unless an exclusion section applies, he also has $5,000 of gross income from discharge of indebtedness.

D. Taxable Transactions Other than Purchases

1. Property Received as a Prize or as Compensation

If a taxpayer wins a prize for competing on a game show, she reports its value as gross income. I.R.C. § 74(a). If she receives compensation in the form of property, and no exclusion section applies, she reports its value as gross income. Reg. § 1.61-2(d). In these cases, the taxpayer does not have an actual "cost" for the property.

If she later sold the property and reported a zero basis, she would be taxed twice on the same income. To avoid that result, she is assigned a "tax cost basis" equal to the amount she reported as gross income when she received the item.

That amount is increased or decreased to reflect any basis adjustments—such as improvements or depreciation—that occur after she acquired the property.

> **Example 5-9.** Alana won a painting worth $5,000 on a game show in Year 1. She reported its $5,000 value as gross income. She sold it for $6,000 in Year 5. She reports a gain of $1,000 in Year 5. Although she has no actual cost for the painting, she has a cost for tax purposes of $5,000. In effect, she is treated as winning $5,000 cash and using it to purchase the painting.

2. Property Transferred in Exchange for Services

If property is transferred in exchange for services, the transferor's amount realized is the fair market value of those services. It does not matter that § 1001(b) lists only money or other property in its definition of amount realized. *International Freighting Corp., Inc. v. Commissioner*, 135 F.2d 310 (2d Cir. 1943).

> **Example 5-10.** Burr paid Al 150 shares of ABC stock for performing services worth $25,000. Burr had a $16,000 basis for the stock, which was then worth $25,000. When he transferred the stock to Al, Burr had an amount realized of $25,000, which represented the value of the services received. As a result, he had a gain realized of $9,000. Al includes the $25,000 value in gross income, and Burr deducts $25,000 compensation for services rendered. On these facts, Burr reports both gross income ($9,000 gain realized) and an expense deduction ($25,000 compensation paid). He reports these transactions separately because his gain may qualify for the lower tax rates applied to net capital gains. Al takes a $25,000 tax cost basis for the stock.

3. Property Received in an Exchange

In Section B, we indicated that the amount realized in an exchange includes the value of the property received, not the value of the property relinquished. That discussion ignored any problems in valuing the property received. It also ignored the taxpayer's initial basis for that property. Determining that basis is necessary for potential depreciation deductions and for computing gain or loss on a later sale.

In some instances, the value of property received can be difficult to determine. Value is readily determined for publicly traded stock and merchandise offered for sale to customers. It is harder to determine for real estate and collectibles, because it depends on anticipated rates of return, location, and such subjective factors as consumer preferences.

The decision in *Philadelphia Park Amusement Co. v. United States*, 126 F. Supp. 184 (Ct. Cl. 1954), is often cited for the relevant valuation rules when there is an arm's-length exchange. First, the taxpayer's cost basis for property received in a taxable exchange is its value when the exchange occurs. Second, if the value of that property cannot be determined, his cost basis for it is the value of the property he relinquished. In the unlikely event that we cannot determine the value of either property, the basis of the property he relinquished carries over to the property he received.

The *Philadelphia Park* facts may appear daunting because of the nature and number of transactions, but there are only five relevant events. First, the taxpayer received a 50-year franchise to operate a passenger railway. Second, it spent $381,000 to build a bridge used by its streetcars. Third, it transferred the bridge to the city that granted the franchise and received a 10-year extension of the franchise. After that transfer, its franchise had 15 years to run, and it no longer owned the bridge. Presumably, it should have computed gain or loss on the bridge when this event occurred. It would also need to determine its cost basis for the 10-year extension. This became important when the fourth and fifth events occurred. It deducted depreciation expense for the 10-year franchise extension, and it deducted a loss when it relinquished the franchise three years before its term ended. Although the court's opinion focused on its cost basis for the franchise extension, it impliedly considered its amount realized on relinquishing the bridge to obtain the extension.

> **Example 5-11.** Alisa purchased a building for $300,000 several years ago. She properly deducted depreciation of $120,000, leaving her with an adjusted basis of $180,000. She exchanged her building for publicly traded shares of ABC Corporation stock worth $200,000. She reports $200,000, the value of the ABC shares, as her amount realized. She realizes gain of $20,000 on exchanging her building and has a $200,000 cost basis for the ABC shares she received.

> **Example 5-12.** Assume that Alisa executed the exchange agreement on January 15, with a closing date of February 15. On February 15, the ABC shares were worth $203,000. In that case, she reports an amount realized of $203,000 because that is the value of what she received. The value on the date she signed the contract is irrelevant. The value of the building on February 15 is also irrelevant unless the contract provided for equalizing any change in values that occurred between January 15 and February 15. She realizes a $23,000 gain on

exchanging her building and has a $203,000 cost basis for the ABC shares she received.

Example 5-13. Aimee owned publicly traded shares of AFJ Corporation stock. Brody developed a process for desalting sea water and has applied for a patent. Aimee agreed to acquire the patent application in exchange for shares of AFJ. She consulted several engineers, who agreed that Brody had a greater than 50% chance of obtaining a patent, and that the commercial value of his invention ranged from zero (no patent) to $500,000. Even if the patent was worth $500,000, it would take several years before that amount was received. Aimee and Brody agreed that 1,000 shares of AFJ, then worth $225,000, was a fair price for the potential patent rights. Because the value of the patent rights is speculative, and the value of Aimee's stock is readily ascertainable, we use the value of her stock to determine her amount realized. She compares that amount to her basis for the stock in computing gain or loss realized. Because the value of her stock is treated as the value of the rights she received, it also becomes her cost basis for those rights.

Example 5-14. This example is based loosely on the facts in *Philadelphia Park*. Assume that in the years after it constructed a bridge for $381,000, Apex Corporation deducted depreciation of $230,000. That left it with a $151,000 adjusted basis. This year, Apex transferred the bridge to Big City in exchange for a franchise. The value of each property is unknown, and estimates obtained by the parties vary widely. In this case, Apex does not report an amount realized. Instead, it treats its cost of the franchise as being equal to its $151,000 adjusted basis for the bridge.

Example 5-14 is abnormal. As the court said in *Philadelphia Park*, "it is only in rare and extraordinary cases that the value of the property exchanged cannot be ascertained with reasonable accuracy." 126 F. Supp. at 189. Not surprisingly, it remanded the case to the Commissioner to take evidence on the value of the bridge, which the court believed was "subject to more exact measurement" than the value of the franchise. In Chapter 16, we discuss a related topic, the open transaction doctrine and the decision in *Burnet v. Logan*, 283 U.S. 404 (1931).

E. Nonrecognition Transactions

Taxpayers who engage in nonrecognition transactions determine both their realized gain or loss and their recognized gain or loss. Realized gain or loss is computed using the rules discussed earlier in this chapter. The taxpayer compares her amount realized for the property she transferred to her adjusted basis for that property. Most realized gains or losses are reported (recognized) in the year they are realized (with exceptions for gains that are excluded altogether and losses that are not deductible). Some realized gains and losses are deferred because they are subject to a nonrecognition provision. In those situations, to preserve the unrecognized gain or loss, we decrease (for unrecognized gain) or increase (for unrecognized loss) the basis of someone's property. The outcome depends on the type of nonrecognition transaction.

In a § 1031 like-kind exchange, the taxpayer does not recognize gain or loss because he exchanged qualifying real property that he owned for qualifying like-kind real property owned by another taxpayer. As illustrated in Chapter 17, his basis for the property he receives is computed with reference to the basis of the property he transferred. His basis for the replacement property is referred to as an "exchanged basis." I.R.C. § 7701(a)(44).

A taxpayer may instead have a "transferred basis." His basis is computed with reference to the basis his transferor had for that property. As illustrated in Chapter 4, property received from a spouse (or from a former spouse incident to a divorce) takes a transferred basis. I.R.C. § 7701(a)(43).

Checkpoints

- Gain or loss realized is computed by comparing the amount realized to the taxpayer's adjusted basis for the property.

- Adjusted basis is the taxpayer's original basis — usually cost — adjusted for subsequent improvements, depreciation, and other events affecting her investment.

- The taxpayer has a "tax cost" basis for property he wins as a prize or receives in some other taxable transaction.

- The amount realized is not limited to cash. It includes the fair market value of other property received.

- When the taxpayer acquires property with borrowed funds, the debt is included in his cost basis.

- If the taxpayer borrows without recourse, we include the debt in his basis unless it appears that it is significantly inflated and bears no relation to the property's value.

- When encumbered property is sold, the debt assumed by the purchaser is part of the seller's amount realized.

- In some nonrecognition transactions, the transferor's basis shifts to replacement property he receives.

- In other nonrecognition transactions, the transferee takes the transferor's basis for the property.

- The basis rules for nonrecognition transactions preserve the unrecognized gain or loss potential by transferring it to replacement property or to a transferee who receives the original property.

Chapter 6

Excluded Gains

Roadmap

- Sale of a principal residence
- Sale of qualified small business stock

A. Sale of a Principal Residence

Taxpayers who satisfy the requirements of § 121 can permanently exclude gain realized from selling a principal residence. This section is not limited to voluntary sales. In Rev. Rul. 2014-2, 2014-2 I.R.B. 255, for example, the IRS applied it to damages received from a settlement fund established for individuals whose homes were foreclosed because of loan servicing or foreclosure abuse. Although the discussion below focuses primarily on sales, you should consider this exclusion whenever the taxpayer realizes a gain on disposing of a principal residence.

1. Qualifying for the Exclusion

The exclusion has both ownership and use requirements. During the five-year period that ends on the date of sale, the taxpayer must have owned the property for at least two years. In addition, she must have used it as a principal residence for at least two years. I.R.C. § 121(a). The ownership and use periods do not have to coincide. Reg. § 1.121-1(c)(4), Example 3. A principal residence can be a condominium, houseboat, or mobile home. Reg. § 1.121-1(b)(1). For an apartment in a cooperative housing corporation, we apply the ownership requirement to the stock and the use requirement to the apartment. I.R.C. § 121(d)(4).

> Example 6-1. Andrea rented a home in Year 1 and Year 2. She purchased it on January 1 of Year 3. She moved to an apartment in Year 4, and she sold the home in February of Year 5. She used the home as a principal

residence during Years 1, 2, and 3. She owned it in Years 3 and 4 and part of Year 5. She satisfies the ownership and use requirements.

Unless one of the exceptions discussed in this chapter applies, § 121 requires actual ownership for at least two years. A taxpayer who received his home as a gift takes his donor's holding period for the property. I.R.C. § 1015(a). The taxpayer's longer holding period does not help him satisfy the ownership requirement sooner.

> Example 6-2. Albert lived with his parents from the time he was born until they moved to an assisted living facility. At that time, they gifted the home to Albert. He already satisfies the two-year use as a principal residence requirement, but he won't satisfy the ownership requirement until two years after he received the home. He already has a more than one-year holding period for purposes of long-term capital gains, which would matter if he sells the home within a year of receiving it.

The two-year use requirement does not require uninterrupted use. The taxpayer can ignore short, temporary absences in calculating her use. Reg. § 1.121-1(c)(2). Although she cannot ignore indefinite absences, she can still qualify if her *aggregate* use totals at least two years in the five-year period.

The exclusion applies only to the principal residence. If she has more than one residence, we determine the principal residence based on the relevant facts. These include the time spent at each residence, the location of her place of employment, the address she uses for her driver's license, voter registration, tax returns, and correspondence, and the location of her bank, religious organization, and social clubs. Reg. § 1.121-1(b)(2); *Guinan v. United States*, 2003 WL 21224797 (N.D. Ariz. 2003) (residences in three states).

Gates v. Commissioner, 135 T.C. 1 (2010), addressed the principal residence requirement in a different context. The taxpayers decided to enlarge and remodel a home that had been their principal residence for at least two years. On an architect's advice, based in part on building code changes, they instead demolished it and constructed a new home. The new home's foundation perimeter did not correspond to that of the old home, and only about half of the land area overlapped. They sold the new home without ever living in it. Although they could have qualified if they had sold the old residence, the court disallowed the exclusion because they never actually used the new home as their principal residence.

A taxpayer may sell a principal residence separately from adjacent land instead of selling them as a single unit. He can qualify for the exclusion with respect to the separate sale of adjacent land if he owned and used it as part of the principal residence. He must sell the principal residence within two years before or after he sells the land. Reg. § 1.121-1(b)(3). The maximum exclusion applies to the combined gain from the home and the land.

2. Maximum Exclusion

The maximum exclusion is $250,000. I.R.C. § 121(b)(1). If the taxpayer is married and files a joint return, § 121(b)(2)(A) increases the maximum to $500,000. Only one spouse must satisfy the ownership requirement if the couple meets two tests. First, *both* spouses must satisfy the use requirement. Second, the spouse who does not satisfy the ownership requirement must not have excluded gain from selling a principal residence less than two years before this sale. If a married couple does not qualify for the $500,000 maximum exclusion, their exclusion is the sum of their separate available exclusions. I.R.C. § 121(b)(2)(B).

> **Example 6-3.** Arnie and Babs purchased their only home for $150,000 in 1980. They sold it this year for $700,000. Of their $550,000 realized gain, Arnie and Babs exclude $500,000 and report only $50,000 as gross income. Because they both met the use requirement, they qualify for the $500,000 exclusion on a joint return even if the home was titled in only one of their names.

3. Frequency of Using the Exclusion

The exclusion cannot be used more than once in any two-year period. I.R.C. § 121(b)(3). A taxpayer who sells a second principal residence too soon after selling the first residence may benefit by electing not to exclude his gain from the first sale. If he claimed the exclusion for the first sale, he can amend the earlier tax return and include the gain in gross income. The deadline for doing so is three years after the due date for the original tax return. I.R.C. § 121(f); Reg. § 1.121-4(g).

> **Example 6-4.** Alvin purchased Home 1 for $100,000 on January 1 of Year 1 and sold it for $120,000 in Year 4. He initially excluded his $20,000 gain from Year 4 gross income. He purchased and moved into Home 2 on January 10 of Year 3. He paid $150,000 for it and sold it on January 15 of Year 5 for $275,000. None of the relief provisions discussed below apply. Because he sold Home 2 less than two years after selling Home 1, he can exclude the gain on only one of them. He would rather exclude the $125,000 gain on Home 2 than the $20,000

gain on Home 1, so he will amend his Year 4 tax return and report the $20,000 gain as gross income.

4. Relief Provisions

a. Change in Place of Employment, Health, or Unforeseen Circumstances

A taxpayer who sells a principal residence before meeting the ownership or use requirements, or who had sold a different principal residence less than two years earlier, may qualify for a reduced maximum exclusion. The reduced maximum is available if her action was attributable to a change in her place of employment, health, or unforeseen circumstances. I.R.C. § 121(c)(2). The regulations provide safe harbors covering these events. A taxpayer who fails to meet a safe harbor can still qualify based on facts and circumstances. The regulations provide extensive examples. Reg. § 1.121-3.

> **Example 6-5.** Aileen purchased a home for $100,000 on January 1 of Year 1. She sold it for $160,000 on July 1 of Year 2 because her employer transferred her to an office in another state. Because her sale was occasioned by a change in place of employment, she may qualify for a reduced maximum exclusion. The increased distance from the former residence to the new place of employment will be relevant in determining whether she satisfies the safe harbor or must qualify based on the relevant facts and circumstances. Reg. § 1.121-3(c).

> **Example 6-6.** Bob purchased a home for $100,000 on January 1 of Year 1. He sold it for $160,000 on October 1 of Year 2 because he lost his job and could not afford his monthly mortgage payments. He qualifies for a reduced maximum exclusion because his sale was occasioned by unforeseen circumstances. Reg. § 1.121-3(e)(2)(iii)(C).

The reduced maximum is computed based on the period for which the taxpayer met the ownership and use requirements or the period between his first and second sales. That period is the numerator in a ratio, and the required period is the denominator. We can express these in days or in months. Reg. § 1.121-3(g)(1). For example, a taxpayer who sold a home after owning and using it for 15 months qualifies for 15/24 of the maximum exclusion. Alternatively, he can compute the actual number of qualifying days and divide that by 730. The ratio applies to the maximum exclusion, *not* to the taxpayer's gain. As a result, a taxpayer whose actual gain is smaller than the maximum exclusion may end up reporting no gross income.

Example 6-7. In the previous example, Bob owned the home for 21 months. Because his maximum exclusion is $218,750 (21/24 of $250,000), he can exclude his entire $60,000 gain.

Example 6-8. Archer purchased a home for $100,000 six years ago and lived in it continuously. He married Betty last year and immediately added her name to the deed. She developed severe allergies, and her physician recommended moving to another geographic location. They sold the home for a $600,000 gain one year after their wedding. Archer meets both the ownership and use requirements; he can exclude $250,000 of the gain attributable to his half of the property. Betty does not meet either requirement, but the sale was occasioned by her health. She qualifies for the relief provision and can exclude a maximum of $125,000 (12/24) of the gain attributable to her half of the property. Archer and Betty exclude $375,000 of their $600,000 gain.

b. Owner Becomes Incapable of Self-Care

An individual who becomes incapable of self-care and spends time in a facility licensed to provide care for her condition qualifies for a different type of relief from the use requirement. If she used the home as a principal residence for periods that total at least one year during the five years preceding the sale, she can include time spent in the licensed facility in meeting the use requirement. I.R.C. § 121(d)(7). This rule applies even if she moves back and forth between the residence and the facility during the five-year period ending with the sale.

Example 6-9. Audra purchased a home on January 1 of Year 1 and moved in that day. On January 15 of Year 2, she had a stroke and moved into an assisted living facility. Because she hoped to return to her home, she did not offer it for sale until Year 3. She sold the home in March of Year 3, which was more than two years after she purchased it. Because she used the home as a principal residence for periods aggregating at least a year, she can count the time spent in the assisted living facility toward meeting the two-year use requirement. She can exclude up to $250,000 in gain from selling the residence.

Example 6-10. Bree purchased a home on January 1 of Year 1 and moved in that day. On November 1 of Year 1, she had a stroke and moved into an assisted living facility. Because she hoped to return to her home, she did not offer it for sale until Year 3. She sold the home in March of Year 3, which was more than two years after she purchased it. Because she did not use the home as a principal residence for periods aggregating at least a year, she cannot count the time spent in the assisted living facility toward meeting the two-year use requirement. But, because the sale was attributable to her poor health, she may qualify for the reduced maximum exclusion discussed above.

c. Change in Marital Status

Marital dissolutions may involve property transfers from one spouse to another or continued co-ownership of property. If the property is the principal residence, strict adherence to the ownership and use requirements could cause hardship. Section 121(d)(3)(A)–(C) addresses these problems. If one spouse transfers title to the home to the other spouse, the recipient spouse's ownership period includes the period that the transferor spouse owned the property. If the divorce or separation instrument grants one spouse use of the home, but the other spouse still has an ownership interest, the spouse who leaves is treated as using the home as a principal residence during the period in which the other spouse has use of the property. When they do sell the home, perhaps when the youngest child completes high school, each of them can qualify for the exclusion. To satisfy the divorce or separation instrument requirement, there can be a decree of divorce or separate maintenance or a written instrument pursuant to such a decree, a written separation agreement, or a decree requiring payment of spousal support.

Widows and widowers also qualify for relief. First, a widow or widower can include the period during which the deceased spouse owned and used the property in determining his or her own ownership and use periods. I.R.C. § 121(d)(2). Second, if the sale occurs no more than two years after the first spouse's death, the surviving spouse's maximum exclusion can be as high as $500,000 if the spouses could have qualified for the increased exclusion immediately before the first spouse died. I.R.C. § 121(b)(4).

d. Extension of Five-Year Period

Although taxpayers serving in the military are subject to the two-year ownership and use requirements, they do not have to meet those requirements during the five years preceding the sale. They can extend the five-year period for up to 10 years while they are on qualified official extended duty. Relief is also available to members of the Foreign Service and employees of the intelligence community (§ 121(d)(9)) and to taxpayers serving in the Peace Corps (§ 121(d)(12)).

5. Anti-Abuse Provisions

a. Residence Acquired in a Like-Kind Exchange

Taxpayers who acquire a principal residence in a § 1031 like-kind exchange are not eligible for the exclusion during the five years following the exchange. I.R.C. § 121(d)(10). This provision limits their ability to exclude gain that accrued while they owned the other property.

> **Example 6-11.** Barry purchased investment land for $100,000. When it was worth $300,000, he exchanged it for land and a house worth $300,000, which he began renting to a tenant. Barry did not recognize the $200,000 gain he realized on his investment land because he made a like-kind exchange. His new property took the $100,000 adjusted basis of his old property. When the tenant's lease ended, Barry moved into the house and used it as his principal residence. If he could use § 121 after living in the house for two years, he could exclude up to $250,000 of gain on selling it. Arguably, $200,000 of any gain is attributable to the unrecognized gain from the original investment land and not to appreciation of his home. Section 121(d)(10) prevents him from using the exclusion until five years after that exchange.

b. Deducting Depreciation of the Residence

The previous example ignored any deduction for depreciation that Barry took while renting the house to the tenant. Even if he waits five years after the original exchange before selling the home, he cannot exclude any gain that represents depreciation deducted after May 6, 1997. I.R.C. § 121(d)(6). If, for example, he deducted $5,000 during the rental year, and he sold the home at a gain of $240,000 after waiting the five years, he can exclude only $235,000 of the gain.

c. Nonqualified Use of the Residence

Section 121(b)(5) disallows the exclusion for gain attributable to periods of nonqualified use on or after January 1, 2009. A period of nonqualified use is a period in which the taxpayer owns the property but neither he nor his spouse uses it as a principal residence.

The gain allocated to the nonqualified use is computed by dividing the total periods of nonqualified use by the total ownership period. I.R.C. § 121(b)(5)(B). Three exceptions apply. First, any use after the last date on which the property is used as a principal residence is not nonqualified use. Taxpayers who move to a new principal residence before selling the old residence are not penalized.

Second, there are provisions exempting taxpayers who are away from their residence on qualified official extended duty. Third, temporary absences due to change of employment, health conditions, or other unforeseen circumstances are not treated as nonqualified use. Temporary absences cannot exceed a maximum of two years. I.R.C. § 121(b)(5)(C).

> **Example 6-12.** Anna purchased a vacation home on January 1, 2008. On July 1, 2011, she made it her principal residence. She sold it on June 30, 2020, for a gain of $100,000. Although she satisfies both the ownership and use requirements, and her gain does not exceed $250,000, she cannot exclude her entire gain. Her use from January 1, 2009, through June 30, 2011, is nonqualified use. Because her nonqualified use period (30 months) is 20% of her total ownership period (150 months), 20% of her $100,000 gain is gross income. She does not treat her use in 2008 as nonqualified because § 121(b)(5) applies only to nonqualified use after December 31, 2008.

If the taxpayer's nonqualified use involves a trade or business or income-producing activity, he may have taken deductions for depreciation. We make the § 121(b)(5) allocation after we apply the depreciation rules described above. I.R.C. § 121(b)(5)(D).

d. Dual Use of the Residence

Reg. § 1.121-1(e) applies if the taxpayer has a home office or makes other business or income-producing use of the home. In theory, his gain on selling the home should be allocated to each use, but § 121 does not apply that harshly. If the portion of the property used for business is *within* the home, he reports post-1997 depreciation as unrecaptured § 1250 gain, but he does not allocate any of his other gain to the business use.

> **Example 6-13.** Brad purchased a five-room home six years ago. He has always used one room as his principal place of business. Over the six years, he deducted $4,000 in depreciation of that room. This year, he sold the home for a $100,000 gain. He reports $4,000 as unrecaptured § 1250 gain. He excludes the remaining $96,000 even though part of it is allocable to the room used exclusively for business.

If the taxpayer sells property that consists of both the principal residence and a business or rental activity that is not conducted *within* the home, he allocates gain between the sale of the principal residence (excluded from gross income up to the maximum limit) and the sale of the other property (included in gross income). Examples in the regulations include a separate stable and a separate apartment in the same building as the principal residence. If, for example, Brad's office was in a detached structure instead of under the same roof as the rest of his house, he could not exclude gain allocable to the office.

6. Coordination with Other Code Provisions

A taxpayer can postpone recognizing a gain attributable to a compulsory or involuntary conversion if he spends the conversion proceeds on replacement property. I.R.C. § 1033(a)(2). If his principal residence is compulsorily or involuntarily converted, he can apply the exclusion to his gain and to his amount realized. I.R.C. § 121(d)(5). That reduces the amount that he must spend on replacement property if he wants to avoid recognizing the remaining gain.

> **Example 6-14.** Alonzo purchased his home for $100,000 ten years ago. It was destroyed by fire this year, and he received insurance to cover its $800,000 value. He can exclude $250,000 of his $700,000 realized gain. If he wants to postpone taxation of the remaining $450,000 of realized gain, he must spend $550,000 for a new home. This represents the $800,000 insurance proceeds reduced by the $250,000 of excluded gain. If § 121 did not apply, he could postpone recognizing 100% of his gain only by spending the entire $800,000 proceeds on a new home.

A taxpayer who uses a property partly as a principal residence and partly as a business may exchange it for another property that she will also use for both purposes. In that case, she uses the § 121 exclusion for the gain attributable to the principal residence portion and the § 1031 nonrecognition rules for the gain attributable to the business portion. Rev. Proc. 2005-14, 2005-1 C.B. 528.

B. Sale of Qualified Small Business Stock

If a shareholder realizes a gain on a sale or exchange of stock, the gain is generally gross income and usually is capital gain. If the stock is § 1202 qualified small business stock held for more than five years, and it was acquired after enactment of the Creating Small Business Jobs Act of 2010, she may be able to exclude the entire realized gain. I.R.C. § 1202(a)(4).

The excluded gain is the greater of two amounts. The first amount is $10 million reduced by exclusions taken with respect to that corporation's stock in prior years. The second amount is 10 times the aggregate adjusted bases of the corporation's qualified small business stock the taxpayer disposed of during the year. The $10 million amount is halved for married taxpayers who file separate returns. I.R.C. § 1202(b). These limitations apply per issuer, not per taxpayer.

Stock is qualified small business stock for this purpose if it was issued by a qualified small business after the effective date of the Revenue Reconciliation Act of 1993. The shareholder realizing the gain must generally have acquired the stock when it was issued, directly or through an underwriter. She must have done so in exchange for money or other property (not including stock) or as compensation for services. I.R.C. § 1202(c)(1). The corporation must also meet several conditions involving the amount of its assets and the activities in which it engages.

Section 1202 illustrates how important it is to read the section rather than relying on its heading. Although the section heading reads "Partial exclusion," the exclusion has been 100% for stock acquired after the section's 2010 amendment.

Checkpoints

- Taxpayers who sell a principal residence may exclude up to $250,000 of their gain; the maximum is doubled for married taxpayers who file a joint return.

- Taxpayers must own the property and use it as a principal residence for at least two years out of the five years preceding the sale. The exclusion is generally available only once in any two-year period.

- Relief provisions apply if taxpayers cannot meet the qualification rules because of job change, health, or unexpected circumstances. Additional relief provisions apply based on changes in marital status or certain types of employment.

- Anti-abuse rules prevent taxpayers from converting depreciation recapture into excluded gain or from excluding gain that is not attributable to using the property as a principal residence.

- Shareholders who own qualified small business corporation stock can exclude gains from selling their stock.

Chapter 7

Life Insurance and Annuities

Roadmap

- Life insurance terminology
- Excluded life insurance proceeds
- Taxable life insurance proceeds
- Miscellaneous tax consequences of life insurance
- Annuities terminology
- Taxation of annuity payments
- Critiques of tax treatment

A. Life Insurance Terminology

A life insurance policy is a contract between an insurance company and a policy owner (also called a policyholder). The insurer receives premium payments in exchange for its promise to pay certain amounts in the future. Payments made when the insured dies are commonly called the death benefit, face value, or proceeds. The payment due if the policy is canceled is the cash surrender value. In addition to the right to cancel the policy, the owner usually can change the beneficiary and borrow against the cash surrender value.

The beneficiary receives the policy proceeds when the insured person dies. The policy owner, the insured person, and the beneficiary are frequently different people, but that is not required. One person may have two or even all three of these roles. Those roles may affect the tax consequences associated with the insurance policy.

Life insurance is used to provide for future financial needs. Beneficiaries are often family members who rely on the insured for at least some of their support. State law may exempt life insurance payable to beneficiaries (other than the insured's estate) from the claims of his creditors.

Life insurance involves risk-distributing and risk-shifting. *Helvering v. Le Gierse*, 312 U.S. 531 (1941). The insurer sets premiums based on actuarial estimates of life expectancy. Some insureds will die sooner; others will live much longer. They shift the risk of their premature deaths by purchasing insurance. The insurer distributes the risk by issuing a large number of policies. The combined premiums fund death benefits, administrative costs, and the insurer's profit.

The two basic types of policy are term and whole life. Term policies cover a specific term, often as short as one year. The premium charged for the term reflects the risk that the insured will die ("mortality risk"). It also covers the insurer's administrative costs and anticipated profit. Because life expectancy declines as the insured ages, premiums increase each successive term to reflect the increased likelihood of death.

In contrast, whole life policies have level premiums. Premiums paid in the early years exceed the amount needed to cover mortality risk, administrative costs, and profit. The insurer invests the excess payments. In later years, when mortality risk exceeds the premium payment, the insurer applies the previously invested funds (and their earnings) to cover the difference. We use the term "inside build-up" to refer to the invested funds and their earnings.

If a life insurance policy is a "participating" policy, the insurer may distribute excess earnings to its policyholders. Although it may call the distributions dividends, they are not gross income. In this regard, they differ from the common use of the term dividend, which is a taxable distribution to shareholders of a corporation's earnings. Dividends paid with respect to a life insurance policy are a reduction of the premiums paid. They reduce the policyholder's investment in the contract, a concept related to annuities, but they are not amounts received as an annuity. I.R.C. § 72(e)(1)(B).

Insurance companies also market hybrid products, including so-called universal life. Because they allow more flexibility than traditional products, their investment aspects could easily overshadow their insurance features. In response, Congress enacted § 101(f), which applies to flexible premium contracts issued before 1985, and § 7702, which defines life insurance contract and applies to newer policies. This book does not cover those hybrid products.

B. Excluded Life Insurance Proceeds

Although § 61(a)(9) includes income from life insurance contracts in gross income, § 101(a) excludes most life insurance proceeds. It provides a general rule: "gross income does not include amounts received (whether in a single sum or otherwise) under a life insurance contract, if such amounts are paid by reason of the death of the insured." This terminology is important. First, there must be a life insurance contract. Second, the payments must be "by reason of the death of the insured." Finally, although § 101(a) allows payments "in a single sum or otherwise," the full exclusion applies only to the actual death benefit. Any additional amounts are gross income.

The exclusion applies even if the insured's employer paid the premiums. The $50,000 death benefit limitation discussed in Chapter 3 applies to the tax treatment of premiums paid by the employer. I.R.C. § 79. It does not limit the exclusion for the policy proceeds.

The term "paid *by reason of* the death of the insured" is not the same as "paid *after* the death of the insured." The exclusion applies to some payments made before the insured's death. It does not apply to some payments made after his death. As a general rule, however, most payments a beneficiary receives after the insured's death are excluded.

"Accelerated death benefits" qualify for the exclusion if the insured is terminally ill or chronically ill. I.R.C. § 101(g)(1). Qualifying payments can be made by the insurer or by a viatical settlement provider. I.R.C. § 101(g)(2). Viatical settlement providers regularly engage in the business of purchasing or taking assignments of life insurance contracts. Their profit reflects the difference between the amount they pay to acquire the policy, including post-acquisition premiums, and the death benefit they later receive. Although the insured person excludes payments received from the purchaser, the purchaser does not qualify for a full § 101(a) exclusion; it is covered by § 101(a)(3), described in the next section.

The insured is terminally ill if he has an illness or physical condition that is expected to result in death within 24 months after a physician certifies the illness or condition exists. He is chronically ill if he has a condition defined in § 7702B(c), which deals with long-term care insurance. For example, he must be unable to perform at least two activities of daily living without assistance (*e.g.*, eating, dressing, or bathing). I.R.C. § 101(g)(4). Payments to a chronically ill individual qualify only if they are made to cover uninsured costs of qualified long-term care services. I.R.C. § 101(g)(3).

The exclusion for accelerated death benefits does not apply to payments made to someone other than the insured if the recipient had an insurable interest because the insured was a director, officer, or employee of the recipient or because the insured had a financial interest in any of the recipient's businesses. I.R.C. § 101(g)(5). In those situations, the payment would benefit the recipient's business rather than assisting the insured who was suffering a terminal or chronic illness.

The § 101(a) exclusion does not apply to a payment made after the insured's death if that death is not the reason for the payment. For example, a life insurance policy may be used to guarantee payment of the insured's debts. Rev. Rul. 70-254, 1970-1 C.B. 31, illustrates this distinction. As part of a property sale, the seller purchased a life insurance policy on the buyer. When the buyer died, the proceeds were not eligible for the exclusion because they represented "collections of the unpaid balance of the purchase price." In this situation, the seller-beneficiary was treated as if he had actually received payment from the buyer.

C. Taxable Life Insurance Proceeds

1. Transfer for a Valuable Consideration

If the policy is transferred for a valuable consideration, the beneficiary excludes only the sum of the consideration and subsequent premiums paid by the transferee. I.R.C. § 101(a)(2).

> Example 7-1. Anne sold a policy insuring her life to Ben for $21,000. Ben named himself the beneficiary. After the transfer, he paid premiums of $4,000. When Anne died, the insurer paid him the policy's $40,000 face value. He excludes only $25,000.

The transfer for valuable consideration rule has two important exceptions. First, the proceeds are excluded if the transferee's basis in the policy is computed at least in part with reference to the transferor's basis. I.R.C. § 101(a)(2)(A). This might occur if the transfer occurred as part of a divorce settlement.

> Example 7-2. As part of their divorce settlement, Art transferred a whole life policy insuring his life to his ex-wife Bonnie in exchange for $20,000. She named herself the beneficiary. After the transfer, Bonnie paid premiums of $4,000 to the insurer. When Art died, the insurer paid her the policy's $40,000 face value. She excludes the entire $40,000. The transferee takes the transferor's basis if the transfer is between former spouses and incident to their divorce. I.R.C. § 1041(b)(2).

The second exception applies to transfers made to the insured, to his partner, to a partnership in which he is a partner, or to a corporation in which he is a shareholder or officer. I.R.C. § 101(a)(2)(B). This exception facilitates transfers in a business setting. There is an important limitation to remember with respect to transfers to a corporation. Even if the insured is the corporation's most important employee, the full exclusion applies only if he is a shareholder or an officer. If he is neither, the corporation's exclusion is limited to the consideration paid for the policy and any subsequent premiums paid.

The exclusion for transfers for consideration to the insured's partner or partnership, or to a corporation in which he is a shareholder or an officer, applies no matter who makes the transfer. The same is true for transfers made to the insured. However, transfers for consideration *from* an owner qualify for the full exclusion only if the transferee takes the transferor's basis or is one of the permitted recipients listed above. If, for example, an insured's daughter sold a policy to his partner, the partner could exclude any proceeds paid by reason of the death of the insured. If, on the other hand, his partner sold a policy to the insured's daughter, she could exclude only the sum of the consideration and any subsequent premiums she paid.

The Tax Cuts and Jobs Act of 2017 added an exception to these exceptions. The exclusion when the policy is transferred for a valuable consideration does not apply if the transfer is a "reportable policy sale." A reportable policy sale occurs if the person acquiring an interest in the policy for a valuable consideration has no *substantial* family, business, or financial relationship with the insured other than the acquirer's interest in the policy. I.R.C. § 101(a)(3). This provision also applies to indirect acquisitions, such as acquiring an interest in a partnership, trust, or other entity that owns an interest in the policy.

> **Example 7-3.** Mega Corporation has more than one million shareholders. Adam owns less than 1% of Mega's stock. If Mega purchased an interest in Adam's life insurance policy, it could not exclude the full policy proceeds. The transfer would be to a corporation in which Adam was a shareholder, but Mega has no substantial financial relationship with Adam.

Proposed regulations issued in March 2019 indicate that a person can have an interest in a policy without actually owning the policy. An enforceable right to name the beneficiary, for example, is an interest in the policy. Prop. Reg. § 1.101-1(e)(1). Family members are the individual and his great-grandparents, grandparents, parents, and lineal descendants. The definition also includes individuals who are married to, in a domestic partnership with, or in a civil union with any of those individuals. Prop. Reg. § 1.101-1(f)(3).

2. Employer-Owned Life Insurance Contracts

There are good business reasons to insure against the death of a key employee. For example, the company might incur operating losses before it can hire a replacement. Some companies, however, purchased policies covering employees who were not critical to their business success, and they did not cancel policies after employees resigned or retired. Congress determined that this use of company-owned life insurance was an abuse of the exclusion.

Section 101(j) generally limits the employer's exclusion to the premiums or other amounts it paid for the policy. It can exclude the full policy proceeds only if it meets certain conditions. It must give the employee written notice that it plans to insure her life, the maximum face amount of coverage, and that it will be a beneficiary of the proceeds. She must give written consent to being covered by the policy and to coverage being continued after the employment relationship ends. I.R.C. § 101(j)(4). If these requirements are met, the employer can exclude the policy proceeds if the insured was an employee at any time during the 12 months ending on the date of her death or if she was a director or a highly compensated person when the policy was issued. The exclusion also applies if the employer pays the proceeds to a member of the insured's family (using the § 267(c)(4) definition) or to a designated beneficiary who was not the employer. I.R.C. § 101(j)(2)(B).

3. Proceeds Paid at a Date Later than Death

Instead of paying the proceeds in a lump sum, the insurer may pay them in installments that include an interest component. In this situation, the § 101(a) exclusion applies only to the amount that would have been excluded if the beneficiary had received a lump sum. We prorate that amount over the number of installments to determine how much of each payment is excluded. Any payment that exceeds the prorated amount is gross income. I.R.C. § 101(d).

> **Example 7-4.** When Arabella died, her son Burt was entitled to the $100,000 face value of her life insurance policy. He elected to receive $11,000 a year for 10 years. Each year he excludes $10,000 and reports the other $1,000 as gross income.

Note that Reg. § 1.101-4(a)(1)(ii) is obsolete. The additional exclusion for a surviving spouse who takes policy proceeds in installments was repealed in 1986; the regulation was last amended in 1961.

Instead of paying the proceeds in a lump sum immediately after the insured's death, or paying them in installments, the insurer may hold the proceeds and agree to pay interest. The beneficiary includes that interest in gross income. I.R.C. § 101(c). When he receives the policy proceeds, he excludes them from gross income.

D. Miscellaneous Tax Consequences of Life Insurance

1. Sale, Surrender, or Exchange of Policy

The discussion above relates to the income tax consequences of the policy's beneficiary, who receives the proceeds when the insured dies. The discussion in this section covers three additional situations: (1) surrender of the policy to the insurance company; (2) sale of the policy to an unrelated third party; and (3) exchange of the policy for another policy. With respect to the first two alternatives, note the distinctions the IRS applies regarding the identity of the person selling or surrendering the policy. The owner-insured's tax consequences may differ from those of an investor who acquires the policy.

If the owner surrenders a whole life policy and receives its cash surrender value, he is taxed on amounts that exceed his investment in the contract. I.R.C. § 72(e)(5)(A)(ii). If he instead sells the policy to a third party, he computes gain or loss by comparing the consideration received to his adjusted basis in the policy. Gain is more important than loss in this context. Unless the policy is held in a business or investment setting, a loss is not deductible. I.R.C. § 165(c). In addition to computing gain, the owner determines if any of his gain qualifies for the lower tax rates applied to net capital gains.

In 2009, the IRS addressed three situations involving an owner-insured: (1) surrender of a whole life policy to the insurer for its cash surrender value; (2) sale of a whole life policy to an unrelated third party; and (3) sale of a term policy to an unrelated third party. Rev. Rul. 2009-13, 2009-21 I.R.B. 1029. It addressed various tax consequences for a person who purchased a term policy from the insured in Rev. Rul. 2009-14, 2009-21 I.R.B. 1031. Both rulings were affected by an amendment to § 1016 made by the Tax Cuts and Jobs Act of 2017. Section 1016(a)(1)(B) now provides that "no such adjustment shall be made … for mortality, expenses, or other reasonable charges incurred under an annuity or life insurance contract." This change applies to transactions entered into after August 25, 2009.The IRS modified each ruling in Rev. Rul. 2020-5, 2020-9 I.R.B. 454. The discussion below reflects the modified versions of the 2009 rulings.

Actions by the insured. In the first situation, we compare the cash surrender value to the investment (premiums paid) in the policy being surrendered. We do not reduce the owner's investment by amounts allocated to mortality risk. We make our computation on the § 72(e) rules for amounts not received as an annuity. The insured's gain is ordinary income.

In the second situation, as revised, we do not reduce the owner's investment by amounts allocated to mortality risk. We divide his gain into two segments. The first segment equals the excess of the policy's cash surrender value over the total premiums paid. That portion is ordinary income. The remaining gain is capital gain because there was a sale or exchange of the policy. We do not apply § 72(e) because the amount received from the purchaser was not received under a life insurance contract. Instead, we use the § 1001 rules for computing gain or loss. In the third situation, the owner-insured compared his investment in the contract to the selling price and realized a long-term capital loss. The loss is deductible only if § 165(c)(1) or (c)(2) applied.

Actions by the purchaser of a term policy. The purchaser was not related to the insured, would suffer no economic loss when the insured died, and had a profit motive for making the purchase. She named herself the beneficiary. Because the policy was transferred for a valuable consideration, the purchaser-beneficiary can exclude only the sum of the consideration paid and any subsequent premiums she paid. The amount included in gross income is ordinary income. If the purchaser instead sold the policy to another unrelated party, she would report capital gain on the difference between the amounts she had paid and her selling price.

The owner of a life insurance policy can exchange it for another life insurance policy without recognizing gain or loss. I.R.C. § 1035(a)(1). He can also exchange the policy for an annuity contract that will pay him income for life, for an endowment contract that will pay him a lump sum at a specified date, or for a qualified long-term care insurance policy. This is an important benefit if the insured no longer needs life insurance because no family members depend on him for support. If he receives an annuity contract or endowment contract, he reports his gain as he receives payments, using the annuity rules, rather than reporting it all in the year of exchange.

2. Deducting Premiums Paid

As a general rule, policy owners cannot deduct the premiums they pay on life insurance policies. Depending on the relationship between the policy owner, insured, and beneficiary, the payments may be disallowed as a § 262 personal expense, a § 264(a)(1) premium paid in connection with a life insurance contract in which the taxpayer has an interest, or a § 265(a)(1) expense to produce tax-exempt income. On the other hand, an employer who provides life insurance as an employee fringe benefit can deduct those premiums as a § 162(a)(1) business expense.

3. Borrowing Against the Cash Surrender Value

A policy owner can borrow against a whole life policy's cash surrender value. If the cash surrender value exceeds her basis for the policy, the loan might also exceed that basis. Although § 72(e)(4) provides that loans are treated as distributions, and thus are potentially taxable, that rule does not apply to life insurance contracts. I.R.C. § 72(e)(5)(C). Borrowing against the policy's cash surrender value does not result in gross income.

E. Annuities Terminology

An annuity contract is an agreement, generally between an insurance company and another person. The insurer receives an amount of money and promises to make a series of payments pursuant to the contract. Payments may be made for a fixed term or for a person's life. The person receiving the payments is the annuitant. If an annuitant receiving payments dies, and a second person begins receiving payments because the contract required a minimum number of payments, the second person is a beneficiary. Reg. § 1.72-1(e).

Most annuities are issued by insurance companies that pool amounts they receive to cover large groups of annuitants, some of whom will die before their actuarial life expectancy and others of whom will live much longer. Although this chapter refers to the contract issuer as an insurer, taxpayers can also enter into annuity contracts with other entities or even with individuals. For example, a parent might sell property to a child in exchange for the child's promise to pay the parent a fixed amount every month for the rest of the parent's life. This book does not cover those private annuity arrangements.

The person who purchases the annuity may pay for it over a period of time or may buy the annuity with a lump sum payment. In either case, he has transferred funds to an insurer in exchange for a series of future payments rather than investing the funds on his own. Annuity payments may begin as soon as the cost is paid in full or at some future date.

Payments may cover a fixed period, such as 10 years, or may continue for the annuitant's life. An annuity might have one annuitant, or it might be payable jointly to two annuitants (or to the survivor). In other words, the payout period may be based on a single life or on multiple lives. The annuity might guarantee a minimum number of payments. For example, it might be payable for the annuitant's life, but if she dies before receiving eight annual payments, her beneficiary will receive payments through Year 8. The contract may provide for fixed payments over the annuity term, or it may provide for payments that fluctuate based upon the insurer's investment experience.

F. Taxation of Annuity Payments

1. Amounts Received as an Annuity

Section 72(a)(1) provides that amounts received as an annuity are generally gross income. Reg. § 1.72-1(b) defines that term as "amounts which are payable at regular intervals over a period of more than one full year from the date on which they are deemed to begin, provided the total of the amounts so payable or the period for which they are to be paid can be determined as of that date." Reg. § 1.72-2(b)(2) lists three requirements for treating payments as amounts received as an annuity. The payments must be received on or after the annuity starting date. The amounts to be received must be payable in periodic installments at regular intervals over more than a full year from the annuity starting date. The total payments must be determinable based on the terms of the contract, mortality tables, or compound interest computations. Reg. § 1.72-9 includes tables you can use to compute total payments based on life expectancies.

The annuity starting date is the later of (1) the date on which contractual obligations are fixed or (2) the first day of the period which ends on the date of the first annuity payment. Reg. § 1.72-4(b)(1). The periodic payments can be annual or more frequent, but they must be made at regular intervals.

Because the annuity represents a return of the original investment, plus earnings attributable to that investment, we exclude part of each payment from gross income. The amount excluded is determined using the § 72(b) exclusion ratio. The remainder of the annuity payment is ordinary gross income. To compute the exclusion ratio, the taxpayer divides the investment in the contract by her expected return. The investment in the contract is computed in two steps. First, add all the premiums or other payments she made for the contract. Second, subtract any tax-free payment she received before the annuity starting date. I.R.C. § 72(c)(1). Those amounts reduce the annuity cost.

The expected return is determined by multiplying each annuity payment by the number of payments to be received. If the payments are for a fixed term, that term establishes the number of payments. If the payments are for the annuitant's "life," the actuarial tables provide a "multiple" that represents the number of payments. The tables currently in use are unisex in nature; the tables in effect for investments made through June 30, 1986, were based on gender-specific life expectancies. Separate tables cover annuities based on a single life and annuities based on two lives. Reg. § 1.72-9.

> **Example 7-5.** Andre paid Alpha Insurer $90,000. He will receive annuity payments of $10,000 per year for the next 12 years. His investment in the contract is $90,000; his expected return is $120,000. He applies the exclusion ratio of $90,000/$120,000 (75%) to each payment. He excludes $7,500 of each payment; the remaining $2,500 is gross income.

> **Example 7-6.** Becky paid Alpha Insurer $90,000. She will receive annuity payments of $5,000 per year for life beginning at age 65. She can expect to receive 20 annual payments of $5,000 (Reg. § 1.72-9, Table V). Her investment in the contract is $90,000; her expected return is $100,000. She applies the exclusion ratio of 90% to each payment. She excludes $4,500 of each payment; the remaining $500 is gross income.

> **Example 7-7.** Al and Betsy paid Alpha Insurer $90,450. They will receive annuity payments of $3,000 per year while at least one of them is alive. Payments will begin when Al is 50 and Betsy is 48. They can expect to receive 40.2 annual payments of $3,000 (Reg. § 1.72-9, Table VI); their expected return is $120,600. They apply the exclusion ratio of 75% to each payment. They exclude $2,250 of each payment; the remaining $750 is gross income.

If an annuity provides payments for life, an annuitant who outlives her actuarial life expectancy keeps receiving payments even though she has recovered her investment tax-free. When that event occurs, each payment is fully included in her gross income. I.R.C. § 72(b)(2).

> **Example 7-8.** In Example 7-6, Becky purchased an annuity that would pay her $5,000 a year for life. At the time she purchased the contract, her life expectancy was 20 years. She was still alive at the end of the 20-year period. Beginning in Year 21, each $5,000 payment she receives is gross income.

Another annuitant may die before recovering her investment in the contract. This occurs if the amounts she previously excluded are less than her investment in the contract. The amount used for this purpose is the tax-free amount, *not* the total amount received. I.R.C. § 72(b)(4). If payments cease, the unrecovered investment is deductible on her final tax return. I.R.C. § 72(b)(3).

> **Example 7-9.** Assume Becky died after receiving 19 payments. Although the $95,000 she received exceeded her $90,000 investment, only 90%

of those payments ($85,500) had been excluded from her gross income. She did not recover the remaining $4,500 of her investment because she died before receiving the 20th payment. The tax return filed for the year she died shows a $4,500 loss deduction.

If the taxpayer has a variable annuity contract, the payments each year are based on the performance of stocks and other securities in which the insurer has invested. Because it is technically impossible to determine the amount the annuitant will receive, we allocate the investment in the contract over the annuity term (fixed or life expectancy) to compute the amount of each payment that is excluded. Reg. §§ 1.72-2(b)(3), 1.72-4(d)(3).

2. Other Amounts Received Under the Contract

The rules discussed above apply only to amounts received as an annuity. Amounts received before the annuity starting date, and amounts received at irregular intervals are not amounts received as an annuity. Amounts received after the annuity starting date, but not received as an annuity, are gross income. I.R.C. § 72(e)(2)(A). Amounts received before the annuity starting date are allocated between the investment in the contract and income. I.R.C. § 72(e)(2)(B). Any amount received is gross income to the extent it does not exceed the excess of the contract's cash value over the investment in the contract. I.R.C. § 72(e)(3). The exclusion ratio used for amounts received as an annuity does not apply.

3. Borrowing Against the Investment in the Contract

Taxpayers who borrow against their investment in an annuity contract are subject to § 72(e)(2)(B), discussed in the preceding paragraph. I.R.C. § 72(e)(4)(A). Their obligation to repay the loan is ignored. They report the loan, up to the excess of the contract's cash value over their investment in the contract, as gross income.

4. Exchanging an Annuity Policy

The nonrecognition rules applied to insurance policies also apply to annuity contracts. A taxpayer who exchanges an annuity contract does not recognize gain or loss on exchanging it for another annuity contract or for a qualified long-term care insurance contract. I.R.C. § 1035(a)(3). Note that annuity contracts offer fewer nonrecognition options than do life insurance contracts.

5. Penalties for Early Withdrawals

Annuities are usually viewed as vehicles for retirement savings. In fact, many retirement plans meet the definition of annuity because they provide for a series of payments. To deter taxpayers from disinvesting funds, § 72(q) provides a 10% penalty for premature distributions from annuity contracts, and § 72(t) provides a 10% penalty for premature distributions from qualified retirement plans. Distributions made after the taxpayer reaches age 59.5 are not considered premature. Numerous other exceptions apply to the penalty provisions.

G. Critiques of Tax Treatment

1. Life Insurance

The exclusion for life insurance proceeds has been criticized for providing a tax-free substitute for the taxable compensation the insured would have earned if she had lived. In rebuttal, others argue that individuals who purchase insurance provide a financial cushion for their families, thus helping them avoid or limit their use of tax-free public assistance.

A related criticism involves employer-provided, group-term life insurance. If the policy's face value is $50,000 or less, the employee reports no gross income when the employer pays the premium. When the employee dies, his beneficiaries exclude the policy proceeds because they are paid by reason of the death of the insured. As a result, employer-funded amounts that are arguably salary replacements escape income taxation even though the employer deducts the premium as a business expense.

Another criticism relates to inside build-up on whole life policies. At any given age, the initial premium for a term policy, which covers mortality risk, is lower than that for a whole life policy, which invests the excess to cover future premiums. Income earned on the inside build-up is not included in the policy owner's gross income unless she sells or surrenders the policy and receives more than her basis. If the proceeds are paid when she dies, they are generally excluded from the beneficiary's gross income. If the owner instead purchases a term policy and invests the money initially saved from paying lower premiums, the earnings are subject to immediate taxation. Even if the insurer offers a lower rate of return on inside build-up, the tax consequences may favor whole life.

Example 7-10. Amara can purchase a one-year term life insurance policy for a premium of $400; each year the premium will increase. Alternatively, she can purchase a whole life policy for $1,000 a year; the premium will not increase. If she purchases the term insurance and invests the $600 cost savings in the stock market, any dividends she receives are gross income. If she purchases the whole life policy, and the insurer invests the $600, she has no gross income currently or when the insurer uses the funds to subsidize her future premium costs.

2. Annuities

Although the inside build-up on annuity contracts is eventually taxed because it is not part of the investment in the contract, the earnings are deferred until the annuitant begins taking payments. If she had invested her savings instead of using them to buy an annuity, her investment earnings would be taxed each year.

Checkpoints

- The proceeds of a life insurance policy are excluded from the beneficiary's gross income if they are paid by reason of the death of the insured.

- The exclusion applies to both term and whole life policies.

- Investment earnings attributable to excess premiums paid for whole life insurance build up on a tax-free basis. The policy owner has no gross income when the insurer applies those earnings to pay premiums.

- The exclusion for proceeds applies to accelerated benefits paid because the insured is terminally or chronically ill.

- The exclusion does not apply, or is limited, if the life insurance policy is transferred for a valuable consideration, if the policy is company-owned life insurance, or if proceeds are payable in installments after the insured's death.

- Disposition of a life insurance policy may result in ordinary income or capital gain, with computations that vary based on the type of policy and identity of the seller. The exchange of one policy for another is a nonrecognition event.

- An annuity is a series of periodic payments made over a fixed term or over a variable term, such as for the annuitant's life.

- The premiums paid for the annuity contract, reduced by any tax-free amounts received before the annuity starting date, are the taxpayer's investment in the contract. The amount he expects to receive is the expected return. The regulations include tables for determining the amount to be received if the payments are "for life."

- The ratio of the investment in the contract to the expected return is the exclusion ratio. The taxpayer excludes that portion of each annuity payment. The rest of the payment is gross income.

- After the taxpayer has fully recovered his investment in the contract on a tax-free basis, all subsequent annuity payments are gross income. If he dies before recovering his investment tax-free, the unrecovered investment is deducted on his final tax return.

Chapter 8

Discharge of Indebtedness

Roadmap

- Tax consequences of borrowing
- Early judicial decisions
- Section 108(a)(1) exclusions
- Other debt discharge exclusions
- Acquisition of debt by related persons
- Property transfers and debt discharge

A. Tax Consequences of Borrowing

The act of borrowing is not treated as the receipt of gross income. Because the taxpayer's receipt of loan proceeds is offset by an obligation to repay, her net worth has not increased and she has no income. If she repays the loan, she takes no deduction; she is merely restored to her pre-loan position. If she does not repay the loan, she has received a benefit (the borrowed funds) that should be gross income. Not surprisingly, §61(a)(11) includes discharge of indebtedness in gross income unless an exclusion provision applies.

Some transactions can be characterized several ways. When someone transfers funds to a relative, or even a close friend, the transfer could be a gift or a loan. The recipient has no gross income under either interpretation. The transferor may call the transfer a loan to avoid reporting it as a gift for gift tax purposes. He may also call it a loan to preserve his ability to deduct a loss if the recipient does not repay him. But the IRS may argue that the substance of the transfer indicated it was a gift and not a loan, particularly if the alleged loan was not memorialized in writing, had no fixed payment schedule, and bore no interest.

Service providers often receive deposits from clients. If the deposit is a pre-payment for services, it should be gross income when received, particularly if the recipient can use those funds without restriction. But if the deposit is made to secure the other party's performance of various terms of the agreement, the recipient can treat the funds as a loan. In *Commissioner v. Indianapolis Power & Light Co.*, 493 U.S. 203 (1990), the Supreme Court treated customer deposits as loans even though the utility was not required to set the funds aside until a customer qualified for a refund or had the funds applied to a utility bill. The customer had no commitment to use electricity and generally had the power to regain the funds. Courts have also reached that result for security deposits paid to landlords and refundable deposits paid to retirement communities. *Highland Farms, Inc. v. Commissioner*, 106 T.C. 237 (1996). The depositor's rights are critical; merely calling an item a deposit does not transform it from prepaid income into a loan.

Initially, embezzlers could treat embezzled funds as loans because they had an obligation to repay the victim. *Commissioner v. Wilcox*, 327 U.S. 404 (1946). If the embezzlement went undetected, they enjoyed a double benefit: they neither repaid the funds nor included them in gross income. In *James v. United States*, 366 U.S. 213 (1961), the Court reversed its holding in *Wilcox*. Embezzlers now have gross income because they do not accept a "consensual" obligation to repay.

On rare occasions, an individual who uses another person's funds can successfully argue for loan treatment. In *Gilbert v. Commissioner*, 552 F.2d 478 (2d Cir. 1977), Mr. Gilbert withdrew corporate funds without authorization. He did, however, take several steps—including informing corporate officers and assigning assets to secure the amount he had taken—that resulted in the court's treating the withdrawal as a loan. On the other hand, an employee's "unilateral intention to pay for the stolen property did not transform a theft into a loan ...." *Collins v. Commissioner*, 3 F.3d 625, 632 (2d Cir. 1993). The Second Circuit distinguished *Gilbert* because Mr. Collins knew he could never repay the amount taken and he had no basis for believing his employer would subsequently ratify his acts.

The outcome in *Gilbert* is unlikely for most unauthorized withdrawals and does not necessarily mean the wrongdoer will never report gross income. He may have income from discharge of indebtedness if he fails to fully repay the withdrawn funds and does not qualify for relief under § 108.

B. Early Judicial Decisions

Although discharge of indebtedness is now covered by statute, early judicial decisions provide a useful background for understanding the Code provisions.

In *United States v. Kirby Lumber Co.*, 284 U.S. 1 (1931), a corporation borrowed money by issuing bonds. Within a year, it purchased some of them in the open market for less than their face value. Thus, although the debtor repaid some of the debt for its value at the time of repayment, that amount was less than the actual amount borrowed. The Supreme Court held that the difference was gross income. Alternate rationales for this holding appear in the same paragraph of its opinion: (1) there was an overall gain or economic benefit; and (2) assets were freed up on its balance sheet.

The taxpayer did not make a clear gain in the transaction described in *Bowers v. Kerbaugh-Empire Co.*, 271 U.S. 170 (1926). It borrowed funds and repaid the amount borrowed but did so in German marks rather than in U.S. dollars. Because marks had declined in value, it was able to purchase the marks needed to repay the debt for less than their value at the time it incurred the debt. The underlying business venture resulted in an overall loss. The Court took this loss into account in holding that the taxpayer did not realize gross income. When it decided *Kirby Lumber*, it distinguished *Kerbaugh-Empire* but did not overrule it.

Two decisions from that era are relevant as precursors to the provisions covering insolvent taxpayers. In *Dallas Transfer & Terminal Warehouse Co. v. Commissioner*, 70 F.2d 95 (5th Cir. 1934), the debtor was insolvent before and after the debt discharge. The court held that it did not have gross income. In *Lakeland Grocery Co. v. Commissioner*, 36 B.T.A. 289 (1937), the Board of Tax Appeals limited the insolvency exclusion. If the taxpayer became solvent as a result of the discharge, it had gross income to the extent it became solvent. Those assets had effectively been freed up.

C. Section 108(a)(1) Exclusions

Because § 108(a)(1) begins by stating that "Gross income does not include," you might assume it excludes certain discharges of indebtedness permanently. In most cases, that is not an accurate description. Instead, it postpones tax consequences. Instead of reporting gross income when the debt is discharged, the taxpayer loses valuable future tax benefits.

Section 108 is a challenging section to read, in part because additional rules governing its various exclusions do not always follow the order of those exclusions. In addition, the exclusions provided in § 108(a)(1) are not the only exclusions § 108 provides. Keep the following general rule in mind. Section 108 lets taxpayers avoid paying tax on certain debt discharges. Avoiding current taxation has a price: the taxpayer must relinquish certain future tax benefits.

1. Bankruptcy and Insolvency

A taxpayer whose debt is discharged in a proceeding covered by title 11 of the United States Code, the Bankruptcy title, does not report the discharge as gross income. I.R.C. § 108(a)(1)(A). The discharge must be granted by the bankruptcy court or be pursuant to a plan it approved. I.R.C. § 108(d)(2). There is no limit on the amount of this exclusion or any requirement that the debtor relinquish all her assets to her creditors.

A taxpayer can exclude debt discharge without going through a bankruptcy proceeding if the discharge occurs when she is insolvent. I.R.C. § 108(a)(1)(B). Section 108(d)(3) defines insolvent to mean that her liabilities exceed the value of her assets immediately before the discharge. The exclusion is limited to the amount of her insolvency. I.R.C. § 108(a)(3). If she remains insolvent after the discharge, the full amount discharged is excluded. If the discharge results in her becoming solvent, she has some gross income unless she qualifies for another exclusion provision.

> **Example 8-1.** Agatha has assets worth $80,000 and liabilities of $95,000. She is insolvent by $15,000. If a creditor discharges $25,000 of her liabilities and takes none of her assets, she ends up with assets worth $80,000 and liabilities of $70,000 and is solvent. Of the $25,000 of debt discharge, only $15,000 qualifies for the insolvency exclusion. The other $10,000, which represents the amount of her post-discharge solvency, is gross income.

The insolvency computation compares the value of a taxpayer's assets to the amount of his liabilities. It does not matter whether he is paying his debts as they come due or whether his debts are secured or unsecured. A worksheet in IRS Publication 4681 contains an extensive list of assets and liabilities that the IRS considers in determining insolvency.

Because this exclusion is limited by the amount of their insolvency, debtors try to have assets omitted—or have debts included—in computing insolvency. For example, they have omitted assets that, by state law, could not be attached to satisfy the claims of creditors. They have included liabilities that were contingent because, for example, they were not the primary obligor. Not surprisingly, the IRS has challenged both actions.

The Tax Court included exempt assets in the computation in *Carlson v. Commissioner*, 116 T.C. 87 (2001). Carlson argued that his fishing permit was exempt from the claims of creditors under Alaska law and should not be used in determining the value of his assets. The court relied on § 108(e)(1) in ruling against him. It limits the insolvency exclusion to that provided in § 108(a)(1)(B). The court held that pre-enactment decisions that ignored exempt assets were no longer good law. Carlson could have used his license (and other assets) to pay his debts. The court reached a different result in *Scheiber v. Commissioner*, T.C. Memo. 2017-32. Because Scheiber had no right to receive a lump sum payment from his pension plan or to assign his future benefits, his assets did not include the plan's value.

Section 108(d)(1) defines indebtedness of the taxpayer as indebtedness for which he is liable and indebtedness subject to which he holds property. It does not specifically cover contingent liabilities, such as those claimed by a guarantor. In *Merkel v. Commissioner*, 109 T.C. 463, 484 (1997), the court held that an obligation could be counted only if, "as of the calculation date, it is more probable than not that he will be called upon to pay that obligation in the amount claimed . . . ." It rejected the taxpayer's argument for a lower standard, which multiplied the contingent liability by a percentage reflecting the probability that he would have to pay it.

2. Other Exclusions

Qualified farm indebtedness. A discharge of qualified farm indebtedness is not gross income. I.R.C. § 108(a)(1)(C). The debt must be incurred directly in connection with operating a trade or business of farming. In addition, at least 50% of the taxpayer's total gross receipts for the three pre-discharge taxable years must have been from the trade or business of farming. In other words, his farming operation cannot have been a minor factor in terms of his gross receipts. I.R.C. § 108(g)(2). Other limitations in § 108(g) restrict the types of creditor and the amount of this exclusion.

Qualified real property business indebtedness. A discharge of qualified real property business indebtedness is not gross income. I.R.C. § 108(a)(1)(D). The debt must be incurred or assumed in connection with real property used in a trade or business, and it must be secured by the property. If it was incurred or assumed after December 31, 1992, it must have been incurred or assumed to acquire, construct, reconstruct, or substantially improve the property. Borrowing against the debtor's equity and using the funds to pay off unrelated debt does not qualify even if the new debt is secured by the real property. This exclusion is elective. I.R.C. § 108(c)(3), (4).

The exclusion cannot exceed the difference between the principal amount of the debt being discharged and the value of the property. If the property is subject to other qualified real property business indebtedness, that other debt offsets the property's value before this computation is made. I.R.C. § 108(c)(2)(A).

> Example 8-2. Alfred owns real property used in his trade or business. It is currently worth $500,000 and is secured by a $520,000 debt that he incurred to purchase it. No more than $20,000 of the debt is eligible

for the qualified real property business indebtedness exclusion. If the property is also secured by a $90,000 debt incurred for a substantial improvement, up to $110,000 of the debt incurred to purchase the property is eligible for the exclusion.

The exclusion cannot exceed the debtor's total basis for all depreciable real property immediately before the discharge. Unlike the first limitation, this limitation ignores the property's value and it counts all his depreciable business real property, not merely the property encumbered by the debt. To prevent abuse, we ignore the basis of property acquired in contemplation of the discharge. I.R.C. § 108(c)(2)(B).

Qualified principal residence indebtedness. If Congress again extends a provision set to expire December 31, 2020, a discharge of qualified principal residence indebtedness will not be gross income. I.R.C. § 108(a)(1)(E). The debt must be incurred or assumed in connection with acquiring, constructing, or substantially improving the taxpayer's principal residence, and it must be secured by the residence. The discharge must be related to a decline in the value of the residence or a decline in her financial condition. It must not be on account of services she renders to the creditor. I.R.C. § 108(h)(2), (3), (5). Section 108(h)(2) limits the amount of qualifying debt to $2 million ($1 million for a married taxpayer filing a separate return). Section 108(h)(4) further limits this exclusion if only part of a discharged loan is qualified principal residence indebtedness.

3. Priority of Exclusions

If a debt is discharged in a bankruptcy proceeding, the bankruptcy exclusion applies even if the taxpayer qualifies for one of the other exclusions. If the debt of an insolvent taxpayer is discharged, and there is no bankruptcy proceeding, the insolvency exclusion takes precedence over the qualified farm indebtedness and qualified real property business indebtedness exclusions. If the debt discharged is qualified principal residence indebtedness, the rules applicable to that exclusion apply unless the taxpayer is insolvent and elects to have the insolvency exclusion apply instead. I.R.C. § 108(a)(2). If the debt is qualified farm indebtedness, it does not qualify for the real property business indebtedness exclusion. I.R.C. § 108(c)(3)(C).

4. Reduction of Tax Attributes

Tax attributes are items that may affect future tax computations. For example, because we compute gain or loss by comparing amount realized to adjusted basis, adjusted basis is a tax attribute. Taxpayers who use a § 108(a)(1) exclusion reduce one or more of their tax attributes, thus reducing their future tax benefits. This section provides an overview of the attribute reduction rules.

Do not confuse tax attributes with ownership attribution. Ownership attribution involves treating taxpayers as owning stock owned by family members or by entities in which they have an interest. The definition of related person covered in Section E is based on the definition in Chapter 14.

Section 108(b) lists the attribute reductions that apply if the taxpayer uses the bankruptcy, insolvency, or qualified farm indebtedness exclusions. As a general rule, these attributes are reduced in the order listed in § 108(b)(2)(A)–(G) and briefly described below. The taxpayer continues through the list of attributes until the reduction equals the amount of excluded debt or she runs out of attributes to reduce.

Net Operating Loss Carryover. If the taxpayer suffered a net operating loss (NOL) for the year of the debt discharge, the NOL deduction is reduced. The reduction also applies to any NOL carried to the year of discharge from another year.

> **Example 8-3.** This year Arielle had more business expenses than total income and suffered a $50,000 NOL. Normally, she could deduct that loss against income from another tax year. She also had $5,000 of debt discharged this year at a time when she was insolvent by at least $5,000. Although she does not report the $5,000 as gross income, she reduces her potential NOL carryover to $45,000.

Tax Credits. Taxpayers may qualify for certain credits that reduce their income tax. Two of these credits, the general business credit and the alternative minimum tax credit, are the next two tax attributes reduced by excluded debt discharge.

Capital Loss Carryover. The next attribute is any net capital loss for the year of the debt discharge and any net capital loss carried to that year from another year.

Basis for Property. The next attribute is the taxpayer's basis for property. That reduction, which is governed by § 1017, is described in more detail below.

Other Tax Attributes. The final two attributes are any passive activity loss (or credit) carryover from the year of the discharge and any carryover to or from the year of the discharge used in computing the foreign tax credit.

Alternative Attribute Reduction. Instead of following the order provided above, taxpayers can elect to reduce their basis for depreciable property, using the § 1017 rules described below. I.R.C. § 108(b)(5).

> **Example 8-4.** Bethany had $150,000 of debt discharged in a bankruptcy proceeding. She was entitled to a $25,000 capital loss carryover and owned property with a basis of $300,000 at all relevant times. This

property was eligible for § 1017 basis reduction. She eliminated her $25,000 capital loss carryover and reduced the basis of her property by the remaining $125,000 of debt discharge. She could instead have elected to retain her capital loss carryover and reduce the basis of her property by $150,000.

Amount of Reduction. Attributes other than credits are reduced by one dollar for every dollar excluded. Credits are reduced by one-third of a dollar for every dollar excluded. I.R.C. § 108(b)(3). Section 108(b)(4) provides ordering rules to use when attributes that may be attributable to more than one year are reduced. For example, if the taxpayer has an NOL for the year of discharge, he reduces it before reducing the NOL for another year that is carried to that year. These ordering rules are important if a carryover is subject to a time limit.

5. Basis Reduction

A taxpayer who excludes a discharge of qualified principal residence indebtedness reduces the basis of that residence. The reduction cannot take the basis below zero. I.R.C. § 108(h)(1).

A taxpayer who excludes a discharge of qualified real property business indebtedness reduces the basis of his depreciable real property. I.R.C. § 108(c)(1). The § 1017 basis reduction rules discussed below apply.

Section 1017(a) applies to three categories: (1) § 108(b)(2)(E) (reduction in property basis after the taxpayer has reduced attributes listed ahead of basis reduction); (2) § 108(b)(5) (election to reduce basis instead of reducing prior attributes); and (3) § 108(c)(1) (reduction in basis following discharge of qualified real property business indebtedness). Section 1017(a) reduces the basis of property the taxpayer holds at the beginning of the year following the year of debt discharge. It does not matter if she owned that property when the discharge occurred.

Although § 1017(a) uses the term "any property," taxpayers cannot select which properties will have their basis reduced. Section 1017(b)(1) authorizes regulations that determine the amount of reduction to be applied and the properties that will have basis reduction. Reg. § 1.1017-1 provides general ordering rules and exceptions. The general rule reduces basis first for property secured by the discharged indebtedness and last for property not used in a trade or business or held for investment. It includes several categories between the two listed here. Section 1017(b) contains three additional sets of rules, which are described briefly below.

The first set of rules applies when the discharge occurs in a bankruptcy proceeding or when the taxpayer is insolvent. If he reduces basis *after* reducing other attributes, such as the NOL deduction, his basis reduction cannot exceed the amount by which the aggregate bases of property he held immediately after the discharge exceeds his aggregate liabilities immediately after the discharge. I.R.C. § 1017(b)(2).

The second set of rules applies if he elects to reduce basis *instead of* first reducing other attributes. These rules also apply to discharges of qualified real property business indebtedness. In these cases, § 1017(b)(3) requires that the basis reduction be made only to depreciable property. A taxpayer who sells real property may elect to treat real property in his inventory as depreciable property for this purpose. As a result, he will report a larger gain on selling his inventory. If the discharge was of qualified real property business indebtedness, the basis reduction can be made only to depreciable *real* property. Inventory cannot be included for this purpose.

The third set of rules applies to a discharge of qualified farm indebtedness when basis is reduced *after* reducing other attributes. The basis reduction can be made only to qualified property and in this order: depreciable property; land used or held for use in farming; and other qualified property. He can elect to treat real property held in inventory as depreciable for this purpose. I.R.C. § 1017(b)(4).

The basis of property that is exempted from the bankruptcy estate by § 522 of title 11 is not reduced. I.R.C. § 1017(c). Section 1017(c) also provides that the basis reductions are not treated as dispositions. If, however, a basis reduction is made to property that is not § 1245 or § 1250 property, that property is treated as § 1245 property and the basis reduction is treated as depreciation. I.R.C. § 1017(d)(1). This rule prevents the taxpayer from later reporting gain attributable to the basis reduction as capital gain.

D. Other Debt Discharge Exclusions

1. Deductible Payments

If the discharged debt was for an amount that the taxpayer could have deducted, the discharge is not gross income. I.R.C. § 108(e)(2). This rule places him in the same after-tax situation as a taxpayer who did pay. The forgone deduction is the attribute he loses.

> **Example 8-5.** Burl rents office space from Landlord for $36,000 per year. Burl paid only $33,000. He could not pay the rent for December because of business reverses, and the landlord discharged the debt. If Burl had paid the final $3,000, he would have been able to deduct it. He does not report the $3,000 discharge as gross income, and his rent deduction is limited to $33,000.

2. Purchase Money Debt Reductions

The reduction of a taxpayer's debt to the seller from whom he acquired property is not gross income. The discharge is treated as a purchase price adjustment, and he reduces his basis accordingly. I.R.C. § 108(e)(5). This provision applies even if there is no dispute about the quality of the property purchased or other factor that justified a price reduction. The debt must arise out of the actual sale, and the creditor must be the seller.

> Example 8-6. Anthony purchased a car from Belinda. He promised to pay $25,000 in annual installments of $5,000 plus interest. Two months after the sale, she agreed to reduce the price (and his debt) to $22,000. The $3,000 debt reduction is not gross income. The debt arose out of the sale of the car, and the seller reduced the debt. His basis for the car is reduced to $22,000. The original transaction is effectively recast as a $22,000 purchase.

> Example 8-7. Amaryllis purchased Greenacre from Bernie for $100,000 and paid cash. She later borrowed $15,000 from him. If he cancels any part of the debt, she cannot treat the cancellation as a purchase price adjustment. The debt did not arise out of the sale of Greenacre.

> Example 8-8. Angus purchased Orangeacre from Brandy for $100,000. He paid $20,000 in cash and borrowed the remaining $80,000 from Friendly Bank. If Friendly later cancels any of the debt, he cannot treat the cancellation as a purchase price adjustment. The debt was not owed to the seller of the property.

The exclusion does not apply to transactions that do not involve the sale of property. For example, the Tax Court has held that a reduction in credit card debt is not covered by § 108(e)(5) because lending money is not a sale of property. *Payne v. Commissioner*, T.C. Memo. 2008-66. Section 108(e)(5) also does not apply to discharges in bankruptcy proceedings or discharges when the taxpayer is insolvent. Taxpayers in those situations use the exclusion rules discussed in Section C.

The exclusion applies only if the discharge would otherwise be included in the debtor's gross income. If it would have been excluded by another Code section, the debtor might not have to reduce her basis for the property.

> Example 8-9. Andrea purchased Blackacre from Dad for $150,000 and agreed to pay the price in installments. She made all payments in a timely manner, but Dad died when she still owed $30,000. In his will,

having acquired the indebtedness. If the related person acquired the debt for less than the amount owed, the debtor has gross income equal to the difference unless one of the § 108 exclusion provisions apply.

F. Property Transfers and Debt Discharge

If a debtor transfers property to a creditor in exchange for debt reduction, the creditor has received a payment. The debtor has income from debt discharge—which may be excludible if § 108 applies—only if the amount canceled exceeds the value of the property transferred. The same rule applies if the debtor renders services, and the creditor reduces her debt by the value of the services. The borrower reports gross income from compensation.

If a borrower cannot afford to continue making loan payments, he may convey the encumbered property to the creditor who has a security interest, or the creditor may acquire it through foreclosure. If the creditor cancels the entire debt, the borrower's tax consequences depend on whether the debt is recourse or nonrecourse. If the debt is recourse, the creditor is not limited to taking the encumbered property. But, by canceling the entire debt, he relinquishes the right to take other property belonging to the borrower. If the debt is nonrecourse, the creditor has no right to seek assets other than the encumbered property.

If the debt is recourse, the regulations treat the transfer as two transactions. The borrower reports gain or loss equal to the difference between the property's value and his adjusted basis. He has debt discharge income—subject to any § 108 exclusions—to the extent the recourse debt exceeds the property's value. Reg. § 1.1001-2(a)(2). The court approved this treatment in *Gehl v. Commissioner*, 50 F.3d 12 (8th Cir. 1995). Gehl had unsuccessfully argued for applying the insolvency exception to the entire transaction.

If the debt is nonrecourse, the regulations treat the transfer as one transaction. The borrower is treated as having sold the property to the creditor for an amount equal to the unpaid debt. The borrower treats that as the amount realized and computes gain or loss. It does not matter that the debt exceeds the value of the property. Reg. § 1.1001-2(b). *See* Reg. § 1.1001-2(c), Examples 7–8. Examples 5-7 and 5-8 in Chapter 5 illustrate the treatment of recourse and nonrecourse debt.

Checkpoints

- A debtor does not have gross income when she borrows money. Because there is an obligation to repay, she does not have an increase in net worth.

- Transactions may be scrutinized to determine whether they are loans or should instead be treated as advance payments, embezzlement proceeds, or gifts.

- Taxpayers who fail to repay a loan have gross income from discharge of indebtedness unless they qualify for an exclusion.

- The § 108 exclusions cover taxpayers who are in bankruptcy proceedings, insolvent, or subject to other listed hardships.

- Most § 108 exclusions are really postponement provisions. Taxpayers reduce tax attributes that could benefit them in the future.

- To prevent abuse, a debtor may be treated as having debt discharge if a related party acquires his debt.

- If encumbered property is transferred to the creditor, the tax consequences depend on whether the debt was recourse or nonrecourse.

Chapter 9

Compensation for Injuries or Sickness

Roadmap

- Introduction
- Damages in general
- Payments covered by Section 104
- Other excluded damage-like payments
- Employer-funded accident and health plans

A. Introduction

This chapter covers compensation for business losses, property damage, and personal injury. Compensation may be paid by a wrongdoer as damages or by an insurance company pursuant to a contract. The taxpayer may have purchased the insurance, or she may have received it as an employer-provided fringe benefit.

As the discussion below indicates, tax consequences depend on the reason for the payment and, in the case of insurance, the identity of the person that purchased the insurance. It may also depend, when damages are involved, on whether there was a judgment or a settlement and on whether the judgment or settlement allocated the damages among the plaintiff's specific claims.

Compensation paid for business losses is usually treated less favorably than compensation for personal injury, and compensation for personal non-physical injury is treated less favorably than compensation for personal physical injury. Compensation attributable to insurance provided by an employer is treated less favorably than compensation attributable to insurance the taxpayer purchases herself. In both business and personal settings, compensation for property damage involves both the amount of compensation and the taxpayer's basis.

B. Damages in General

If a damage award is not an accession to wealth, it is not gross income. If it is an accession to wealth, we consider Code provisions, administrative determinations, and judicial decisions that cover its tax consequences. We focus on the substance of the award rather than relying on the parties' characterization. The nature of the injury, and the facts and circumstances involved, determine whether the award is gross income. The general rule is that damages are gross income if they are a substitute for receipts that would otherwise be taxable.

Injury to property. A taxpayer may suffer harm to land, buildings, equipment, or other items. Unless his property has been fully depreciated (tangible property) or amortized (intangible property), he has an adjusted basis. He compares any damages he receives to that adjusted basis to determine gain or loss. He does not realize a gain unless the amount he realizes exceeds his adjusted basis for computing gain.

> **Example 9-1.** Ashton purchased land for $10,000. Years later, when it was worth $30,000, a tortfeasor destroyed it by dumping chemical waste. If Ashton receives damages of $30,000, the $10,000 that represents his adjusted basis is a return of his investment; it is not gross income. The $20,000 that represents appreciation in the property's value is a realized gain. It is gross income unless he replaces the land as allowed by § 1033 (elective nonrecognition of gains from compulsory or involuntary conversions).

Goodwill is an asset that represents a company's superior earning power. Often the taxpayer has no basis for goodwill because it is attributable to outlays (*e.g.*, advertising and employee training) he deducted in previous years. On the other hand, a taxpayer who purchases an existing business might pay extra for the business goodwill. He takes a cost basis for the goodwill and amortizes it ratably over 15 years. By the end of that period, his basis is zero. I.R.C. § 197. Damages received for the loss of goodwill are gross income only to the extent that they exceed his adjusted basis. *Raytheon Production Corp. v. Commissioner*, 144 F.2d 110 (1st Cir. 1944).

Lost profits. Damages for lost profits are gross income. If the injured party had received the profits as expected, they would have been taxable. The lost profits may arise from actions that reduce the taxpayer's gross income or from actions that increase her expenses.

> **Example 9-2.** Anna sued Brad for breach of contract. Under a court-approved judgment, she received $50,000 for lost profits. The award

is gross income. If Brad had not breached the contract, she would have earned the profits, which would have been gross income.

Punitive damages. Punitive damages received for a business injury are gross income. *Commissioner v. Glenshaw Glass Co.,* 348 U.S. 426 (1955). Punitive damages are also gross income when received for personal injury; this rule is discussed further in the next section.

Interest. Pre-judgment or post-judgment interest that accrues on a court judgment or settlement is also gross income. Using the "in lieu of" analysis discussed above, this result makes sense. Section 61(a)(4) includes interest received in gross income.

C. Payments Covered by Section 104

Section 104(a) excludes amounts received (1) as workmen's compensation for personal injuries or sickness; (2) as damages for personal physical injuries or physical sickness; (3) through accident or health insurance for personal injuries or sickness (except for amounts that are attributable to payments by the taxpayer's employer); (4) for personal injuries or sickness as a result of military or other specified government service; (5) as disability income for injuries sustained as a result of a terrorist or military action; or (6) as payments to dependents of public safety officers whose deaths were attributable to injuries suffered in the line of duty. All six are subject to the exception for previously deducted medical expenses discussed in Subsection 2. The discussion below covers only the first three exclusions.

1. Workmen's Compensation

Section 104(a)(1) excludes amounts received under workmen's compensation for personal injuries or sickness. The exclusion covers monetary awards made to employees who are injured while acting within the course of their employment. It does not cover disability benefits that are not related to an illness or injury. Reg. § 1.104-1(b).

2. Damages for Personal Physical Injuries or Sickness

Section 104(a)(2) excludes damages received for personal physical injuries or physical sickness. The injury need not be defined as a tort by state law, and the statute authorizing the lawsuit does not have to provide for a broad range of remedies. Reg. § 1.104-1(c)(2). The current regulations limit the application of a Supreme Court decision that focused on earlier regulations reflecting tort-type rights. *United States v. Burke*, 504 U.S. 229 (1992). Because *Burke* did not involve physical injury, its result would be the same today (but for different reasons).

The exclusion currently applies only to damages received on account of personal physical injuries or physical sickness. Damages for nonphysical personal injury, such as emotional distress or defamation, are generally included in gross income. Because Congress added "physical" to § 104(a)(2) in 1996, earlier rulings and decisions excluding damages for defamation and other nonphysical personal injuries are no longer good precedents.

> **Example 9-3.** Art successfully sued Bruce for defamation and received $15,000 for emotional distress. The award is gross income. No Code section excludes this type of award in the absence of personal physical injury or physical sickness.

Other than indicating that emotional distress, standing alone, does not qualify as physical injury, § 104(a) does not define physical injury or physical sickness. In PLR 200041022, the IRS indicated that it involved "direct unwanted or uninvited physical contacts resulting in observable bodily harms such as bruises, cuts, swelling, and bleeding." It was willing to presume a physical injury occurred in CCA 200809001, which included the following language:

> Because of the passage of time and because C was a minor when the Tort allegedly occurred, C may have difficulty establishing the extent of his physical injuries. Under these circumstances, it is reasonable for the Service to presume that the settlement compensated C for personal physical injuries, and that all damages for emotional distress were attributable to the physical injuries.

Payments for observable bodily harm are not excluded if the taxpayer voluntarily submitted to the event causing the harm. For example, the taxpayer in *Perez v. Commissioner*, 144 T.C. 51 (2015), could not treat payments she received for allowing her unfertilized eggs to be retrieved. The court treated the payments as compensation for services rendered.

a. Medical Expenses

Because lawsuits often take years to resolve, a plaintiff might incur and deduct uninsured medical expenses many years before he receives damages.

He might also incur such expenses in the year he receives damages. Finally, he might incur additional expenses in a later year. These possibilities have different tax consequences.

The taxpayer cannot exclude the portion of the award attributable to the prior deduction. This rule applies only to the amount the taxpayer deducted, not to the amount he actually paid.

> **Example 9-4.** Anson was injured in an accident in 2019. He paid $25,000 in medical bills that were not covered by insurance. Because of the §213 deduction limitation, he could deduct only $2,000 of his outlays. In 2020, he received compensatory damages that included $25,000 to cover his 2019 medical expenses. His 2020 gross income includes only the $2,000 he deducted in 2019.

The taxpayer excludes amounts received for medical expenses he incurred in the year he receives an award. Because he was compensated for those expenses in the year he paid them, he cannot deduct them.

The taxpayer also excludes amounts received to cover *future* medical expenses. The introductory language of §104(a) applies only to medical expenses deducted in a *prior* year. If he receives an award to cover future expenses, he cannot deduct any future outlays covered by the amount awarded. Rev. Rul. 75-232, 1975-1 C.B. 94. This rule applies only to future expenses related to the award. It does not prevent him from deducting other medical expenses.

> **Example 9-5.** Anson also received $6,000 to cover future medical expenses attributable to the accident. That $6,000 is not included in gross income even if he spends less than $6,000 in the future. The first $6,000 of accident-related medical expenses he incurs in the future is compensated for and cannot be considered in computing his future medical expense deductions.

b. Punitive Damages

A parenthetical in §104(a)(2) indicates that the exclusion does not apply to amounts received as punitive damages. Because punitive damages are imposed to punish the wrongdoer rather than to compensate the victim for physical harm, this limitation makes sense. One limited exception excludes punitive damages from gross income if they are awarded based on a wrongful death claim, and the award of such damages is the only form of recovery in that state based on the law in effect in September 1995. I.R.C. §104(c).

c. Lost Income

Because § 104(a)(2) applies to *all* damages, other than punitive damages, amounts received for lost income are excluded from gross income. This is a statutory exception to the "in lieu of" analysis.

d. Noneconomic Damages

A taxpayer can document or obtain calculated forecasts for medical expenses and lost income. Although pain and suffering, loss of consortium, and similar claims do not involve economic losses, amounts received for these noneconomic damages are excluded if they are attributable to personal physical injuries or physical sickness.

A taxpayer might suffer a physical injury that results in a second taxpayer suffering emotional distress or other nonphysical injury. The legislative history treats the second taxpayer's nonphysical injury as attributable to a physical injury. The IRS approved this treatment in several private letter rulings. *See* PLR 201950004, which involved damages for physical injury and sickness suffered by a child and the parent's resulting emotional distress. The clinic that provided a donor egg had failed to test the donor egg or resulting embryo for genetic mutations.

> **Example 9-6.** Angus sued the driver who injured him in a car accident. His wife Blythe also sued, claiming damages for loss of consortium. Angus and Blythe both qualify for the § 104(a)(2) exclusion.

The flush language of § 104(a) indicates that emotional distress is not considered a physical injury or physical sickness. Damages for emotional distress are excluded in only two situations. First, the taxpayer can exclude damages for emotional distress if they are attributable to a personal physical injury or physical sickness. For example, taxpayers have occasionally succeeded in treating an employer's actions as causing or exacerbating an actual physical sickness. *See Domeny v. Commissioner*, T.C. Memo. 2010-9 (multiple sclerosis); *Parkinson v. Commissioner*, T.C. Memo. 2010-142 (heart attack). Second, he can exclude damages that cover medical care attributable to emotional distress even if there is no physical injury or sickness.

e. Deferred Payments

The exclusion applies to damages received in a lump sum or received in installments. The injured taxpayer may have a choice between taking a lump sum or taking installment payments that total a larger amount. The additional amount represents interest that compensates for the delay in receiving the full amount due. If she takes the lump sum and invests it, interest or other earnings she receives are gross income. If she instead receives her award in installments, the built-in interest is excluded from gross income. This is another instance in which this provision gives a different result than we would reach under an "in lieu of" analysis.

> **Example 9-7.** Anton was injured when he tripped on a broken sidewalk outside a local store. The store owner offered him $40,000 payable immediately or $11,000 a year for four years. He excludes his award no matter which option he selects. The result is the same if he agrees to an increasing payment stream (*e.g.*, $9,000, $10,000, $11,000, $12,000). Rev. Rul. 79-313, 1979-2 C.B. 75.

The IRS does not treat an actual award of interest as favorably as it treats built-in interest. An award of interest to compensate for the time between the wrongdoing and the judgment or settlement may not be covered by § 104(a)(2). *See* PLR 200942017 ("The amount you receive ... for the wrongful death of your [relative] is excludable from your gross income under § 104(a)(2), except for any interest received.").

f. Allocating Damages

Although § 104(a)(2) applies to damages received by suit or agreement, it provides no guidance for allocating damages between taxable and excluded amounts. If the plaintiff wins a judgment that allocates damages, the IRS will probably respect that allocation. The judge or jury heard evidence from both parties regarding liability and damages.

> **Example 9-8.** Ace was injured in a car accident. The jury awarded $200,000 for punitive damages, $50,000 for lost wages, $100,000 for pain and suffering, $50,000 for medical expenses, $75,000 for emotional distress attributable to the accident, and $25,000 for damage to his car. He had not deducted any of the medical expenses in a previous year. He can exclude all but two amounts. The punitive damages are gross income. In addition, the damage to his car is not attributable to a personal physical injury. It is governed by the rules covering amounts received for damage to property. If the $25,000 exceeds the car's adjusted basis, the excess is taxable gain unless he spends at least $25,000 to replace the car and elects nonrecognition for the gain from the involuntary conversion.

There may instead have been (1) an unallocated judgment; (2) an unallocated settlement; or (3) an allocated settlement. If the judgment or settlement does not allocate damages, the taxpayer and the IRS may disagree on the appropriate allocation. They may also disagree even if the settlement allocates damages. The defendant may be more interested in the settlement *amount* than in its *allocation*. In that situation, the allocation discussion is not necessarily between adverse parties. The IRS—which was not a party—may challenge it.

If the damages are not allocated, the injured party's complaint provides evidence for allocating them. But it is not the only evidence available. The IRS considers verifiable amounts more important than speculative amounts. Economic damages (lost wages and medical expenses) are in the first category; pain and suffering, emotional distress, and punitive damages are in the second category. *See* Rev. Rul. 75-230, 1975-1 C.B. 93.

> **Example 9-9.** Allen was injured in a car accident. He sued and asked for $500,000 in damages associated with the accident: $200,000 in punitive damages, $50,000 for lost wages, $100,000 for pain and suffering, $50,000 for medical expenses, $75,000 for emotional distress, and $25,000 for damage to his car. He had not deducted any of the medical expenses in a previous year. Before trial, he settled his lawsuit for $200,000. This is 40% of the amount he initially requested.

If we allocate the settlement pro rata, he receives 40% of each item claimed: $80,000 in punitive damages, $20,000 for lost wages, $40,000 for pain and suffering, $20,000 for medical expenses, $30,000 for emotional distress, and $10,000 for damage to his car. He includes the $80,000 punitive damages in gross income, compares the $10,000 to his basis for the car to determine if he has a gain or loss, and excludes the remaining $110,000.

If we instead focus on the economic damages, we would allocate $50,000 to lost wages, $50,000 to medical expenses, and $25,000 to damage to the car because those items could be verified. Those items total $125,000 of the $200,000 settlement. We might allocate the other $75,000 pro rata among his remaining $375,000 in claims. Because $75,000 is 20% of $375,000, we would allocate $40,000 to punitive damages, $20,000 to pain and suffering, and $15,000 to emotional distress. Another possibility would be to allocate nothing to the punitive damages because he received less than he requested in other damages.

Even if a personal physical injury occurred, the IRS can argue that the settlement includes payments that do not compensate for that injury. For example, in *Amos v. Commissioner*, T.C. Memo. 2003-329, the parties had an unallocated settlement agreement. The court allocated damages between the taxpayer's personal physical injury and his agreement not to defame the wrongdoer (a professional basketball player) or assist the police in pursuing criminal charges against him. It determined that the wrongdoer's dominant motive in making the payments was to compensate Mr. Amos for his physical injuries but that the settlement language indicated that part of the payment was for the agreements rather than for damages.

g. Litigation Expenses

A taxpayer can deduct litigation expenses only if they are allocable to damages included in gross income. Deductible expenses can be considered in computing adjusted gross income only if the taxable damages relate to his business as a self-employed individual or to a claim for damages described in §62(e). I.R.C. §62(a)(1), (20). Those damages cover violations of federal, state, or local laws providing for the enforcement of civil rights or regulating aspects of the employment relationship. Prior to 2018, he could deduct litigation expenses related to other taxable damages only if he itemized his deductions because costs for seeking punitive damages or damages for defamation were miscellaneous itemized deductions. Unless Congress amends or repeals §67(g), miscellaneous itemized deductions are not deductible in 2018 through 2025.

3. Amounts Received Through Accident or Health Insurance

Section 104(a)(3) excludes amounts received through accident or health insurance for personal injuries or sickness. It applies even if the benefits exceed actual medical expenses. It also applies to benefits designed to replace lost income. It does not apply to employer-funded plans.

> **Example 9-10.** Abner was hospitalized for a week. His hospital bill totaled $30,000. He had previously purchased two separate insurance policies—an income replacement policy that paid him $2,000 a week for each week he was hospitalized and a standard health insurance policy that reimbursed him for his medical expenses. He received benefits totaling $32,000. He excludes the entire $32,000 from gross income.

D. Other Excluded Damage-Like Payments

Section 139F excludes civil damages, restitution, or other monetary awards relating to the taxpayer's wrongful incarceration. The person must have been convicted of a "covered offense" (a criminal offense under either federal or state law), have served at least part of a prison sentence related to that offense, and qualify under one of two criteria. She must have been pardoned, granted clemency, or granted amnesty because she was innocent. Alternatively, her conviction must have been reversed or vacated *and* the accusatory instrument was either dismissed or she was found not guilty after a new trial that occurred after her conviction was reversed or vacated. Section 139F would not change the result in *Stadnyk v. Commissioner*, T.C. Memo. 2008-289. Mrs. Stadnyk was arrested, handcuffed, detained, and indicted but did not suffer any physical harm. Her arrest was the result of a bank's error, and she received damages (including damages for emotional distress, humiliation, and damage to reputation) after suing the bank.

Some statutory exclusion provisions have never been added to the U.S. Code. For example, the Ricky Ray Hemophilia Relief Fund Act of 1998, Pub. L. No. 105-369, § 103(h)(1), provides that payments "shall be treated for purposes of the Internal Revenue Code of 1986 as damages described in section 104(a)(2) of such Code." The act was not codified but is a note following 42 U.S.C. § 300c-22.

The IRS has excluded some payments without a specific statutory authority. For example, Notice 2012-12, 2012-6 I.R.B. 365, excludes restitution payments received by victims of human trafficking. Restitution required by the Trafficking Victims Protection Act includes lost income in addition to medical expenses and other damages.

E. Employer-Funded Accident and Health Plans

1. Employer Contributions to Accident and Health Plans

An employee's gross income does not include employer contributions to an accident or health plan. I.R.C. § 106(a). The employer may pay health insurance premiums or establish a fund that makes payments to employees for health care and accidents. That section applies only to *contributions* to a plan, including paying insurance premiums. Section 105 applies when the employee receives *benefits* from the plan.

An employer may let employees reduce their salaries on a pre-tax basis and contribute those amounts to its accident or health plan. Those amounts are treated as employer contributions because the diverted salary is not included in the employee's gross income. The employee forfeits any amounts he does not use within the period discussed in Chapter 3.

An employer may also contribute funds to an employee's health savings account. I.R.C. § 106(d). These plans, which are defined in § 223, provide a continuing source of funds for an employee's medical care. Amounts in the plan carry over for use in future years. The employee reports no gross income when the plan is funded or when he uses plan funds to pay for medical care. The 2020 inflation-adjusted funding limits for such plans are $3,550 for a plan that covers only the employee and $7,100 for a plan providing family coverage. Employees who are over age 55 can make larger contributions. Section 106(b) provides an exclusion for contributions to an employee's Archer medical savings account (§ 220).

2. Benefits Received from an Employer-Funded Plan

Section 104(a)(3) does not apply to accident or health plan benefits attributable to employer contributions that were excluded from the employee's gross income. When she receives benefits from these plans, § 105 governs her tax consequences. It applies to payments received from employer-funded insurance policies and from employer plans that do not involve insurance policies. I.R.C. § 105(e).

Section 105(a) provides a general rule: these amounts are gross income. This rule has two exceptions. Section 105(b) excludes amounts received for medical expenses that the employee did not previously deduct. These benefits can be paid to the employee, her spouse, her dependents, and her child who has not reached age 27. Section 105(c) excludes amounts received for permanent loss or loss of use of a bodily function or based on permanent disfigurement. The amount received must be unrelated to the amount of time that the employee is absent from work.

> **Example 9-11.** Anita was hospitalized for a week. Her hospital bill totaled $30,000. Her employer paid for two policies covering its employees—an income replacement policy that paid her $2,000 a week for each week she was hospitalized and a standard health insurance policy that reimbursed her for medical expenses. She received a total of $32,000 from both policies as a result of her injury. Section 105(b) excludes the $30,000 paid to reimburse her medical expenses. The $2,000 salary continuation payment is gross income.
>
> **Example 9-12.** Addie's doctor amputated two of her fingers after she slammed them in her car door. She received $10,000 from an em-

ployer-funded policy that paid fixed amounts for the loss of a limb. Section 105(c) excludes the $10,000 from her gross income. If the $10,000 had also been based on her time away from work, she could not exclude it.

The examples above highlight differences between benefits received from a plan that is not funded by the employer and benefits attributable to the employer. As illustrated in Example 9-10, a taxpayer who funds his own plan excludes the benefits even if they exceed his medical expenses or replace lost income. His exclusion for employer-provided benefits is limited to actual expenses for medical care and to payments for certain grievous injuries that are not based on the time he is absent from work.

If an employee has her own insurance policy and an employer-funded policy, the IRS allocates the medical expenses between the policies based on the benefits received. Excess benefits attributable to the employer-funded policy are gross income. Excess benefits attributable to the employee-funded policy are excluded. Rev. Rul. 69-154, 1969-1 C.B. 46. The ruling also illustrates the allocation used if a plan is funded by employer contributions and by employee contributions that are not paid on a pre-tax basis.

Section 105 does not exclude benefits for self-employed persons who are treated as employees by § 401(c)(1). In addition, limitations apply to plans that favor highly compensated employees. I.R.C. § 105(g), (h).

Checkpoints

- Damages recovered for lost profits are gross income.

- Damages for loss of property are gross income only to the extent that they exceed the property's adjusted basis.

- If no Code section applies, we consider the nature of the injury and other relevant facts and circumstances to determine if the damages are gross income.

- Section 104(a) excludes amounts received as workmen's compensation, as damages for personal physical injuries or physical sickness, and through accident or health insurance for personal injuries or sickness. Additional exclusions apply for amounts received by members of specified occupations or as a result of specified events.

- Damages for emotional distress are excluded only if the emotional distress is attributable to a personal physical injury or sickness or the damages are paid for medical expenses attributable to emotional distress.

- Punitive damages are not excluded even if there is a personal physical injury or sickness.

- Amounts received through accident or health insurance are excluded unless the plan is funded by the employer. The exclusion applies even if the benefits exceed the taxpayer's expenses.

- Payments to victims of human trafficking, wrongfully convicted prisoners, and hemophiliacs receiving tainted blood are excluded by other provisions.

- Employer contributions to accident or health plans are generally excluded from gross income.

- Amounts received through employer-funded accident or health insurance are generally gross income. The employee can exclude only amounts received to reimburse medical expenses or for certain grievous injuries.

Chapter 10

Miscellaneous Inclusions and Exclusions

Roadmap

- Prizes and other awards
- Scholarships
- Other education benefits
- State and local government activities
- Foreign-source income
- Alimony and child support
- Disaster relief payments
- Additional miscellaneous exclusions

A. Prizes and Other Awards

1. General Rule

Prizes and other awards are generally gross income. I.R.C. § 74(a). A taxpayer who receives a prize or other award confronts two issues. First, does any exclusion provision apply? Second, if the award is taxable, what is the appropriate amount of gross income?

Although often referred to as awards, amounts received as *rewards* are not covered by § 74. Rewards are compensation for services rendered. Reg. § 1.61-2(a)(1); *Campbell v. Commissioner*, 658 F.3d 1255 (11th Cir. 2011) (*qui tam* payment received by a whistleblower).

2. Exceptions

a. Prizes and Awards Directed to Charity

Section 74(b) excludes certain awards directed to charity. The primary reason for the award must be to recognize religious, charitable, scientific, educational, artistic, literary, or civic achievement. In cases litigated under an earlier version of § 74(b), courts routinely held that athletic achievement was not civic achievement. *See Hornung v. Commissioner*, 47 T.C. 428 (1967). The size of the prize is irrelevant. Even Nobel Prizes, which can exceed $1 million, qualify. Prop. Reg. § 1.74-1(b).

The recipient must not have taken any action to enter the contest. I.R.C. § 74(b)(1). In Rev. Rul. 72-163, 1972-1 C.B. 26, the IRS indicated that § 74(b) did not apply to a writer who was invited to apply for a grant that would assist him in writing a future work. It gave two reasons: "the grant to the taxpayer in the instant case is not primarily for past achievements in literary fields and ... his selection was not without action on his part." The recipient must not be required to render substantial future services as a condition of receiving the award. I.R.C. § 74(b)(2). Giving an acceptance speech does not constitute rendering substantial future services.

Section 74(b)(3) requires that the payor transfer the prize to an organization described in § 170(c)(1) or (c)(2) — a governmental unit or qualifying tax-exempt organization. The prize recipient can keep the item for a short time before returning it to the payor for transfer to a qualifying organization. Prop. Reg. § 1.74-1(d). Although she designates the organization that receives the award, she cannot deduct a charitable contribution. Prop. Reg. § 1.74-1(f). That is an appropriate outcome, because she is not reporting the award as gross income. Other than being allowed to select the ultimate recipient, she is treated as if she never received the award.

You might initially assume that this exclusion provides no tax benefit because the recipient can exclude the prize only if she relinquishes it. If she retains the prize, but later donates the same amount to charity, she might think the net effect is the same: her gross income is offset by a charitable gift deduction.

In actuality, § 74(b) benefits recipients who direct their awards to a qualifying organization. The first benefit relates to the limits on charitable deductions. With the exception of gifts made in 2020, the deduction for charitable gifts in cash cannot exceed 60% of a taxpayer's contribution base, which is generally adjusted gross income (AGI). I.R.C. § 170(b)(1)(G). A taxpayer who donates a larger amount can continue deducting the excess, subject to the same rules, but only over a five-year period. If the award is large in relation to her income, deducting the full amount may prove impossible. And, because the gross income is bunched into a single year, she may be subject to a higher than normal tax rate in that year.

> **Example 10-1.** Aurora earns $100,000 a year as a medical researcher. She won the Nobel Prize in medicine in a year other than 2020. Her prize is $1 million. If Aurora keeps the prize money, her gross income is $1,100,000. She can spend the prize money, net of the income tax, on whatever she wishes. Her income tax rate will reach 37% for much of her taxable income, but this is her best option if she doesn't want to make a charitable gift.

> **Example 10-2.** If Aurora accepts the prize, places it in an interest-bearing account, and later donates $1 million to a charity, her gross income is still $1,100,000 and her maximum charitable deduction for the year is $660,000. She can deduct the remaining $340,000 over the next five years, but only to the extent her cash charitable gifts don't exceed 60% of her AGI. If her salary remains $100,000 a year and it is her only income, her maximum charitable deduction in each of the next five years is $60,000, a total of $300,000 for the five-year period. She can never deduct the remaining $40,000.

> **Example 10-3.** If Aurora instead tells the Nobel Prize committee to transfer the funds to a qualifying charity, she does not report the prize as gross income. Her gross income for the year is her $100,000 salary; she does not deduct any of the $1 million transferred to the charity. Her marginal tax rate for the year she wins the prize will be much lower than it would be in the previous examples.

A second advantage of § 74(b) relates to its effect on other deductions. If the award is excluded from gross income, it is also excluded from AGI. As a result, the taxpayer loses a smaller amount of any deduction (*e.g.*, medical expenses) or other tax benefit that is reduced as AGI increases. A taxpayer who does not itemize also benefits, as she can exclude an amount she would not otherwise be able to deduct.

> **Example 10-4.** Roy won a $3,000 award from a state fund designed to recognize scientific teaching excellence in a year other than 2020. He earns $45,000 a year as a chemistry teacher and will not be itemizing his deductions. If he directs his award to a charity, it is excluded from his gross income. If he accepts the award and later donates money to charity, he reports $48,000 of gross income and no deduction.

b. Olympic and Paralympic Prizes

Since 2016, athletes receiving medals or other prizes for performance in Olympic and Paralympic games exclude their awards from gross income. This exclusion benefits athletes who are not self-employed and cannot deduct unreimbursed training expenses and self-employed athletes whose sports involve little or no remuneration. Prize winners whose AGI for the year exceeds $1 million ($500,000 if married but filing a separate return) do not receive this exclusion. I.R.C. § 74(d).

Consider whether this exclusion is justified. Obviously, every exception to a general rule increases the Code's complexity. This exclusion is an exception to the general rule of inclusion in § 74(a), and it has its own exception for high-income taxpayers. Is the once-every-four-years aspect of Olympic competition sufficient justification? If rewarding those who represent the United States is the justification, why not include athletes who win World Cup prizes? And why athletes as opposed to students who win awards (other than excluded scholarships) for academic achievement or for performance at science fairs, spelling bees, or 4-H contests? Section 74(d) returns us to the original version of § 74(b), which excluded awards for certain types of achievement even if the recipient kept the award, but does so with a twist. The original version did not apply to athletic awards; the current version applies *only* to athletic awards (albeit only a limited number of them).

3. Amount of Gross Income

If an award is gross income, the taxpayer reports the amount of money received and the value of any other property or services received. Reg. § 1.74-1(a)(2). Value is normally determined in an arm's-length transaction. That determination may cause problems if a taxpayer wins property that she would never willingly purchase at its list price. The amount that is ultimately included in gross income becomes the taxpayer's basis for the item.

Valuation disputes involve questions of fact. For example, the court in *McCoy v. Commissioner*, 38 T.C. 841 (1962), assigned a $3,900 value to a car the taxpayer won in a sales contest. His employer paid $4,453 for the car, and the taxpayer sold it within 10 days for $3,600. During that period, he drove the car from Jacksonville, Florida, where he received it, to Knoxville, Tennessee, where he lived. The court held that his use was only partially responsible for the car's decline in value.

> **Example 10-5.** Alice appeared on a game show and won an SUV that the show purchased for $24,000. Because she did not want the SUV,

she sold it for $18,000 (the best offer she received). The game show is likely to send her (and the IRS) a Form 1099 indicating that the SUV is worth $24,000. She does not think she should report more than $18,000.

Example 10-6. Assume that Alice litigated the value of the SUV and a court held that its value was $19,000. She has gross income of $19,000 on receiving the SUV. She sustains a $1,000 loss on selling it for $18,000. Because she never used the SUV for personal purposes, her loss may be deductible as a loss incurred in a transaction entered into for profit. I.R.C. § 165(c)(2). Otherwise, it is a nondeductible personal loss.

B. Scholarships

The general rule covering scholarships is a rule of exclusion, and an individual who satisfies two requirements has no gross income. First, the amount received must constitute a "qualified scholarship." Second, the individual must be a candidate for a degree at an educational organization that is defined in § 170(b)(1)(A)(ii). I.R.C. § 117(a).

1. Qualified Scholarships

An award is a qualified scholarship if it is a scholarship or fellowship and covers qualified tuition and related expenses. I.R.C. § 117(b)(1). A scholarship is "an amount paid or allowed to, or for the benefit of, a student, whether an undergraduate or a graduate, to aid such individual in pursuing his studies." Reg. § 1.117-3(a). The definition for fellowship also includes amounts to aid an individual in doing research. Reg. § 1.117-3(c). A 1988 proposal combines the two definitions: "a scholarship or fellowship grant is a cash amount paid or allowed to, or for the benefit of, an individual to aid such individual in the pursuit of study or research." Prop. Reg. § 1.117-6(c)(3).

Section 117(b)(2) defines qualified tuition and related expenses. The first component consists of tuition and fees required for enrollment or attendance at an educational organization. Voluntary fees are not considered qualified tuition. The second component covers fees, books, supplies, and equipment required for courses of instruction at the educational organization. This component involves course requirements rather than overall enrollment requirements. The fees, books, supplies, and equipment must be required of all students enrolled in the course. Prop. Reg. § 1.117-6(c)(2).

Example 10-7. DEF University charges a registration fee of $50 per semester. Students who want to attend athletic events pay a fee of $10 per semester. The registration fee is mandatory; the athletic fee is voluntary. Anna received a scholarship that covered tuition and both fees. The $10 per semester covering the athletic events is gross income.

The exclusion is not available for amounts covering room and board, travel, research, clerical help, and equipment and other expenses that are not required for enrollment or attendance at the organization or in a particular course. Prop. Reg. § 1.117-6(c)(2). Items that are suggested but not required do not qualify. Prop. Reg. § 1.117-6(c)(6), Example 1.

Scholarships can be funded by the school or by donors. The school could directly reduce a student's tuition by the amount of her scholarship award. A charitable foundation might award her a scholarship to cover tuition. It might pay the educational organization directly, or it might give her the funds and let her pay the tuition. Because § 117(b)(1) allows an exclusion if she establishes that she used the funds for qualified items "in accordance with the conditions of the grant," each payment method qualifies for the exclusion.

If she receives an award that she is to use for "her education," she benefits from a presumption in the proposed regulations. Amounts received are excluded unless, under the terms of the award, they cannot be used for qualified tuition and related expenses. Prop. Reg. § 1.117-6(c)(1). She must maintain records that establish the amount used for qualified expenses. Prop. Reg. § 1.117-6(e). Any award that specifically covers room and board or other nonqualified item is not a qualified scholarship even if the school itself awards it.

2. Candidate for Degree

A scholarship is excluded only if the recipient is a candidate for a degree at an educational organization described in § 170(b)(1)(A)(ii). The requirements include maintaining a faculty, curriculum, and regularly enrolled group of students in attendance at the place of instruction. The students can be enrolled as candidates for college degrees, or they can be enrolled in primary or secondary schools. A vocational school can qualify if the program is accredited and the school is authorized by state or federal law. Prop. Reg. § 1.117-6(c)(4). Student status and organization status are separate requirements. An individual who takes classes, but who is not a candidate for a degree, does not qualify. An individual who is a candidate for a degree, but whose educational organization does not meet the § 170 definition, is also ineligible.

3. Payments Related to Employment

An educational organization may require a scholarship recipient to teach or perform research or other services as a condition of receiving the scholarship. In that case, part of the award represents compensation for services and part is a qualified scholarship. With limited exceptions, the compensatory portion is gross income. I.R.C. § 117(c).

> **Example 10-8.** Private University, which charges tuition of $20,000 per semester, awarded Alonzo a $12,000 scholarship for the current semester. As a condition of receiving the scholarship, he must work as a laboratory assistant for five hours a week during the 15-week semester. He will not be separately compensated for this work. Laboratory assistants normally are paid $12 per hour. Of his $12,000 award, $900 is taxable compensation (5 hours per week, multiplied by 15 weeks, multiplied by $12 per hour).

The current regulations provide an exception for situations in which all candidates for the degree are required to perform these services. Reg. § 1.117-2(a)(2). The proposed regulations do not include this exception. Prop. Reg. § 1.117-6(d)(1).

An educational organization may let its employees take courses on a tuition-free or reduced-tuition basis. Alternatively, it may subsidize their attendance at another educational organization. In either case, the employee does not have gross income if the education is below the graduate level. This can include primary or secondary education or education leading to a bachelor's degree. I.R.C. § 117(d)(2). The exclusion for tuition is also available to graduate students who serve as research or teaching assistants. I.R.C. § 117(d)(5).

The educational organization may also offer this tax-free benefit to individuals who are treated as employees using the § 132(h) fringe benefit definition. This provision benefits retired employees, employees' spouses (and surviving spouses of deceased employees), and employees' dependent children. I.R.C. § 117(d)(2). The exclusion is not available for benefits provided to highly compensated employees if the group that is eligible for the benefit is defined in a way that discriminates in favor of those employees. I.R.C. § 117(d)(3).

4. Scholarship Received as a Prize

If an individual receives a qualified scholarship as a prize, § 74(a) provides that § 117 applies rather than § 74. As a result, she can exclude a qualified scholarship even if she entered a contest to win it.

Example 10-9. Amanda entered and won an essay contest her senior year of high school. Her prize was a one-semester scholarship covering tuition at State University. Amanda does not have to render any services to receive the scholarship. Her scholarship is excluded from gross income.

If an employer provides a tuition benefit, § 117 might apply if the employer is an educational organization and the tuition meets the tests described above. Section 117 is not the only provision that authorizes an exclusion for employer-provided educational benefits. Chapter 3 describes two other potential benefits: (1) the exclusion for educational assistance programs; and (2) the exclusion for working condition fringe benefits.

C. Other Education Benefits

Several Code sections discussed elsewhere exclude benefits for education from gross income. These include discharge of student loan debt, scholarships, employer-provided educational assistance programs, and the exclusions discussed below. There are also Code sections allowing deductions or credits for education expenses. These include deductions for tuition as a business expense, interest on education loans, and qualified tuition and related expenses and a credit for educational expenses. The tax consequences of education funding are an example of complexity confronting unsophisticated taxpayers.

1. U.S. Savings Bond Interest

Many taxpayers qualify for a tax benefit associated with U.S. savings bonds issued at a discount. The accrued interest is permanently excluded from gross income if the bond proceeds are used for qualified higher education expenses. I.R.C. § 135(a). Because this benefit applies only in the year of redemption, taxpayers who elect to report the bond interest as it accrues do not benefit from the exclusion. Section 135 applies only to interest on bonds issued after December 31, 1989. The purchaser must be at least 24 years old before the date the bond is issued. I.R.C. § 135(c)(1).

The bond proceeds must be used to pay qualified higher education expenses. These expenses include tuition and fees required for enrollment or attendance at an educational institution described in § 529(e)(5). Qualified expenses also include contributions to a § 529 qualified tuition program or a § 530 Coverdell education savings account. The education expenses can be those of the taxpayer, his spouse, or any other person who qualifies as a dependent for purposes of § 151. I.R.C. § 135(c)(2)(A).

> **Example 10-10.** Adam purchased a U.S. savings bond for $2,500 after attaining age 24. He redeemed it this year for $4,800. He did not report the accrued interest as gross income while he held the bond. Of the $4,800 proceeds, $2,500 is an excluded return of his investment. If he uses all $4,800 for qualified higher education expenses, he reports none of the $2,300 interest as gross income unless he exceeds the income limitations discussed below. If he uses none of the $4,800 for qualified higher education expenses, all $2,300 is gross income.

If the redemption proceeds exceed his payments for qualified higher education expenses, he reports some gross income. His exclusion is based on an "applicable fraction." The numerator is the amount of qualified higher education expenses. The denominator is the bond's redemption proceeds. I.R.C. § 135(b)(1).

> **Example 10-11.** Adam spent $3,600 on qualified higher education expenses in the year he redeemed the bond. His applicable fraction is the $3,600 he spent divided by the $4,800 redemption proceeds (75%). His exclusion is 75% of the $2,300 bond interest. He excludes $1,725 of the interest and includes $575 in gross income.

This exclusion was enacted to aid middle-income and lower-income taxpayers. A taxpayer's ability to use it phases out as his modified adjusted gross income (AGI) increases. I.R.C. § 135(b)(2), (c)(4). The inflation-adjusted phase-out for 2020 begins at modified AGI of $123,550 for joint returns and $82,350 for other returns.

2. Encouraging Saving for Education Expenses

Sections 529 and 530 let a taxpayer save for education expenses on a tax-deferred, and possibly tax-free, basis. While her funds remain in the program, income earned on them is not gross income. If the original fund, augmented by the income growth, is used for qualified expenses, the deferred income is permanently excluded. Neither the taxpayer who establishes the fund, nor the beneficiary who uses it for qualified expenses, reports the earnings as gross income. I.R.C. §§ 529(c)(1), 530(d)(2). Funds not used for qualified expenses are taxed using the § 72 annuity rules.

These plans have other attractive features. Amounts transferred into them qualify for favorable gift tax consequences for the donor-transferor. I.R.C. §§ 529(c)(2), 530(d)(3). If the initial beneficiary does not attend a qualifying school or attends but does not use the entire fund balance, the account can be transferred to a related beneficiary. I.R.C. §§ 529(c)(3)(C), 530(d)(6). Recent amendments have made § 529 plans even more attractive. Section 529(c)(7), added in 2017, treats elementary or secondary school tuition as a qualified higher education expense. This addition applies to public, private, and religious schools. In 2019, Congress added § 529(c)(8) and (9). The first addition lets expenses for fees, books, supplies, and equipment required for participation in certain apprenticeship programs qualify. The second addition treats up to $10,000 of interest and principal paid on qualified education loans as qualified higher education expenses. Payments can be made with respect to loans of the account's designated beneficiary or that beneficiary's sibling.

Section 529 programs are established by a state or a state agency to allow prepaying educational expenses ("prepaid tuition programs") or funding an account designed to meet such expenses ("college savings programs"). Colleges may also establish programs. Distributions can be used for tuition, fees, books, supplies, and equipment required for enrollment or attendance at a qualified educational institution. Room and board expenses are also qualified for students who are enrolled at least half-time. I.R.C. § 529(e)(3). Unlike the exclusions for savings bond interest and for Coverdell education savings accounts, eligibility for § 529 does not phase out as the taxpayer's income rises.

Section 530 Coverdell education savings accounts can be established to pay both qualified higher education expenses and qualified elementary and secondary education expenses. I.R.C. § 530(b)(2). Contributions must be made by the date the beneficiary reaches age 18. I.R.C. § 530(b)(1)(A)(ii). Benefits must be used by the time he reaches age 30. I.R.C. § 530(b)(1)(E). The maximum annual contribution is $2,000. I.R.C. § 530(b)(1)(A)(iii). A taxpayer's eligibility to make contributions phases out as his modified AGI increases. I.R.C. § 530(c)(1).

D. State and Local Government Activities

In addition to collecting taxes, state and local governments engage in various revenue-raising activities. They may operate toll roads or charge for water or garbage collection. Even if revenues exceed expenses, they do not pay federal income tax on these activities. Gross income does not include revenue from operating a public utility or from engaging in any essential government function. I.R.C. § 115.

Debt issued by state and local governments enjoys a tax advantage over debt issued by the U.S. government and by private entities. As a general rule, "gross income does not include interest on any State or local bond." I.R.C. § 103(a). This exclusion lets these governments reduce their borrowing costs. High-income taxpayers purchase the bonds, despite a lower before-tax interest rate, if the after-tax rate of return exceeds the return from taxable bonds.

> **Example 10-12.** If Atiya purchases a $1,000 bond issued by Corporation X with a 6% interest rate, she will receive $60 interest per year. If she is in the 35% federal income tax bracket, her income tax will increase by $21; her after-tax interest will be only $39. If she purchases a $1,000 bond issued by the State of Florida with a 4.2% interest rate, she will receive $42 interest per year. Because this interest is not gross income, her after-tax interest will also be $42. If the bonds are equal in all other aspects, the State of Florida bond is more attractive.

> **Example 10-13.** If Atiya is instead in the 24% marginal tax rate bracket, the tax on the Corporation X bond interest will be only $14.40. She will retain $45.60 after tax. That exceeds the $42 she will receive if she purchases the State of Florida bond. If the bonds are equal in all other aspects, the Corporation X bond is more attractive.

The exclusion applies if the debt is an "obligation" of a state or political subdivision. I.R.C. § 103(c)(1). In other words, interest may qualify even if the obligation is not evidenced by an actual bond or note. The most important factor in determining if the interest is paid on an obligation is whether the debt is issued or incurred pursuant to the government's borrowing power.

The exclusion is subject to three potential exceptions. It is not available for interest from certain private activity bonds, from arbitrage bonds, or from bonds that are not issued in registered form. These limitations reflect abuses Congress intended to limit.

Private activity bonds. The exclusion is supposed to reduce the cost of borrowing for *public* purposes. It is not allowed if the borrowed funds are used for projects that benefit a private entity. I.R.C. § 103(b)(1). But many private projects provide public benefits. For example, if a county lets a corporation use borrowed funds to build a sewage treatment plant, the corporation benefits from the lower interest rate but the county's citizens benefit from cleaner water.

Recognizing this aspect of private projects, § 103(b)(1) applies only to private activity bonds that are not "qualified" bonds. Section 141(e) lists several categories of qualified private activity bonds. These include exempt facility bonds, qualified student loan bonds, and qualified redevelopment bonds.

Arbitrage bonds. Arbitrage is a concept used to describe buying and selling, or borrowing and investing, to take advantage of price or interest rate differentials. A bond is an arbitrage bond if, at the time it is issued, we can reasonably expect that at least part of the bond proceeds will be used to acquire higher yielding investments. I.R.C. § 148(a). In the examples above, the State of Florida issued bonds with a 4.2% interest rate, and Corporation X issued bonds with a 6% interest rate. Given this differential, Florida officials might decide to borrow funds solely for the purpose of buying Corporation X bonds and earning an interest rate profit of 1.8 percentage points. The Florida bonds would be considered arbitrage bonds, and bondholders could not exclude the interest they received. I.R.C. § 103(b)(2). Temporary investments in higher yielding property during a "reasonable temporary period" do not cause a bond to be treated as an arbitrage bond. I.R.C. § 148(c). Statutorily defined minor investments are also allowed. I.R.C. § 148(e).

Bearer bonds. Bonds were once commonly issued in bearer form. When a bond matured, the issuer paid the proceeds to the person who surrendered it; that person was the bearer. Instead of sending interest checks to the bond's owner, it paid the person who surrendered an interest coupon. Bond owners could evade estate and gift taxes when they transferred bonds to another family member if the issuer had no ownership records. They could also avoid § 265(a)(2). That section disallows the interest expense deduction if the taxpayer incurs debt and uses the proceeds to purchase tax-exempt bonds. Since 1982, the § 103(a) exclusion is limited to bonds issued in registered form. I.R.C. §§ 103(b)(3), 149.

E. Foreign-Source Income

A taxpayer can exclude two types of services-related income derived from a foreign source: earned income and employer payments for housing costs. She can elect to exclude either type, neither type, or both types of income. I.R.C. § 911(a).

To qualify, she must have a tax home in a foreign country and meet one of two residence requirements. She can be a U.S. citizen who has been a bona fide resident of at least one foreign country for an uninterrupted period that includes at least one taxable year. Alternatively, she can be a U.S. citizen or resident who was present in one or more foreign countries for at least 330 days in a consecutive 12-month period. I.R.C. §911(d)(1). Note that the first alternative looks to a single taxable year; the second looks to a 12-month period, which can span two taxable years.

The exclusion for earned income applies only to income attributable to services, including wages, salaries, and professional fees. I.R.C. §911(d)(2)(A). It does not apply to pensions and annuities, compensation paid by the United States or one of its agencies, and amounts received after the end of the year following the year in which the services were performed. I.R.C. §911(b)(1). Section 911(d)(6) disallows any deduction, credit, or exclusion that a taxpayer could otherwise use that is allocable to income excluded by §911(a). Deductions that are disallowed when allocable to the foreign source income include business expenses and foreign income taxes. Reg. §1.911-6. The foreign tax credit is disallowed to the extent allocable to excluded income.

The income must be earned from sources within a foreign country. This requirement can give rise to some surprising results. For example, the taxpayer in *LeTourneau v. Commissioner*, T.C. Memo. 2012-45, was a flight attendant who resided in France. She could not exclude earnings attributable to flights in or over the United States or attributable to flights in international airspace. The court denied the latter exclusion based on the regulations, which provide in part: "The term 'foreign country' when used in a geographical sense includes any territory under the sovereignty of a government other than that of the United States." Reg. §1.911-2(h). Taxpayers had similar results in *Rogers v. Commissioner*, 783 F.3d 320 (D.C. Cir. 2015) (international waters), and *Arnett v. Commissioner*, 473 F.3d 790 (7th Cir. 2007) (Antarctica).

There is a maximum, inflation-adjusted exclusion available each year. It is prorated on a daily basis and cannot exceed the taxpayer's earned income. I.R.C. §911(b)(2). Examples in Reg. §1.911-3(f) illustrate the proration.

The maximum exclusion for housing costs paid by an employer is computed using a multi-part formula that reflects actual housing costs, the maximum exclusion allowed for earned income, and days of residence in a foreign country or countries during the year. The IRS can issue regulations providing higher percentage limitations to reflect geographical differences in housing costs. I.R.C. §911(c)(1)–(2). In determining her actual housing costs, the taxpayer includes items such as utilities and insurance but cannot include home mortgage interest or property taxes. She can include the costs of a second foreign residence in which a spouse or dependents reside because of unsafe living conditions in the location of her residence. I.R.C. §911(c)(3).

If her employer does not pay for housing costs, she can deduct the amounts she pays. The deduction cannot exceed the difference between her earned income from foreign sources and the amount excluded by § 911(a). This deduction is taken in computing AGI. I.R.C. § 911(c)(4).

F. Alimony and Child Support

1. Alimony and Separate Maintenance Payments

a. Post-2018 Instruments

The Tax Cuts and Jobs Act of 2017 returned the treatment of alimony and separate maintenance payments to pre-1942 rules. Alimony and separate maintenance payments received pursuant to a post-2018 divorce or separation instrument are excluded from the recipient spouse's gross income. The date of the instrument is critical here. If the parties executed an agreement or a court entered a decree before 2019, the rules discussed below apply. That is true even if the actual divorce occurred after 2018. Parties who amended a pre-2019 instrument after 2018 remain subject to the pre-2019 rules unless the amended instrument expressly provides for applying the post-2018 rules.

b. Pre-2019 Instruments

Section 71(a) includes alimony or separate maintenance payments in the recipient's gross income. Payments qualify if they meet the definition in § 71(b). The parties' subjective belief about a payment's status is irrelevant. It is also irrelevant whether the payment is ordered by a court or meets a state law definition of spousal support. The relevant temporary regulations were promulgated in 1984. They have not been amended to reflect changes to § 71 made in 1985 or the changes affecting post-2018 divorces in 2017.

Section 71(b)(1) begins by stating it includes any payment in cash if the payment meets the requirements of subparagraphs (A) through (D). Payments by check or money order qualify. Payments in other property or by promissory note do not qualify. Payments in the form of services or rent-free use of property also fail to qualify. Temp. Reg. § 1.71-1T(b), Q&A-5.

Section 71(b)(1)(A) has two interrelated requirements. The payment must be received by or on behalf of a spouse, *and* it must be received under a divorce or separation instrument. Both direct payments to the spouse, and indirect payments on her behalf, qualify. Indirect payments include paying rent to the spouse's landlord or paying her mortgage. Temp. Reg. § 1.71-1T(b), Q&A-6.

> **Example 10-14.** Axel and Bev divorced. Pursuant to their divorce decree, Axel pays $150 a month to the dealer who sold Bev her car.

Although these payments are not made directly to Bev, they are made *on her behalf.*

Payments are not made on the other spouse's behalf if the payor financially benefits from them. For example, if the property is titled in his name, mortgage payments are not alimony even if the other spouse occupies the property. The policy behind this rule is straightforward. If he benefits from the payment and deducts it, he receives a double benefit. If the other spouse owns the property, the payor spouse does not benefit when the mortgage is reduced. If the former spouses remain jointly liable for mortgage payments, payments made by one spouse are only partly alimony. They qualify to the extent they cover the other spouse's portion of the liability. Thus, assuming joint liability, the payor spouse can deduct half of the payment as alimony. Rev. Rul. 67-420, 1967-2 C.B. 63.

Similar rules apply when one spouse pays premiums on a life insurance policy insuring his life. If the other spouse owns the policy, the payments satisfy the requirement. If the insured spouse continues to own the policy, the premium payments do not qualify even if the other spouse is the beneficiary. Rev. Rul. 57-125, 1957-1 C.B. 27. The Second Circuit has held that assigning the policy and making the other spouse the irrevocable beneficiary can qualify the payments as alimony. *Stevens v. Commissioner,* 439 F.2d 69 (2d Cir. 1971). Death benefits received by the policy's beneficiary are excluded from her gross income. I.R.C. § 101(a)(1). This rule applies whether or not the premiums are treated as alimony.

Section 71(b)(1)(A) also requires that the payment be made pursuant to a divorce or separation instrument. The instrument must be (1) a decree of divorce or separate maintenance or a written instrument incident to such a decree; (2) a written separation agreement; or (3) a decree ordering support or maintenance payments. I.R.C. § 71(b)(2).

If there is no decree, a court may have to decide whether the parties have a written separation agreement. For example, in *Ewell v. Commissioner,* T.C. Memo. 1996-253, the court held that "the written list of expenses his former spouse gave him, the letters exchanged by the attorneys, and notations petitioner claims he made on checks he issued" were insufficient to show a meeting of the minds. Even if there is a written agreement or decree, voluntary additional payments are not alimony because they are not made pursuant to the instrument.

Section 71(b)(1)(B) let the parties consider their tax consequences in structuring their divorce. They could have decided to treat payments as gross income of the recipient and deductible by the payor, or they could have decided to treat them as excluded by the recipient and not deductible by the payor. If the instrument indicates that the payments are not included in the recipient's gross income and not deductible by the payor, they are not alimony.

If the payor and the recipient are separated under a decree of divorce or separate maintenance, they cannot be members of the same household when the payment is made. I.R.C. § 71(b)(1)(C). The regulations provide a limited exception. A payment made while the payor is preparing to depart the household is deductible if he departs no more than one month later. The spouses can be members of the same household if there is a written separation agreement but no decree. Temp. Reg. § 1.71-1T(b), Q&A-9.

Payments must end when the recipient spouse dies, and there must be no obligation for substitute payments. I.R.C. § 71(b)(1)(D). If substitute payments are required, then even the pre-death payments are not alimony. This provision was designed to discourage the parties from disguising a property settlement as alimony. Property settlement obligations generally do not end when the party receiving payments dies.

> **Example 10-15.** Amanda is obligated under a pre-2019 divorce agreement to make payments to Barney for 12 years. If he dies before the 12-year period ends, she must pay any unpaid amounts to his estate. These payments are not alimony because the decree specifically provides for a substitute payment to Barney's estate. They are not included in his gross income, and she cannot deduct them.

If the parties are still married at year-end, and they file a joint return, the payments do not qualify as alimony. I.R.C. § 71(e).

c. Recapture of Excess Pre-2019 Instrument Payments

To discourage former spouses from structuring property settlements to qualify as alimony payments, Congress enacted the § 71(f) alimony recapture provisions. When these provisions apply, we reverse part of the payor's earlier tax benefits and the recipient's earlier tax detriments. Unless the former spouses execute their divorce or separation instrument before 2019 but delay making the *first* alimony payment until 2019 or later, alimony recapture will not be a factor after 2020. For that reason, we have limited our discussion of this concept.

> **Example 10-16.** Amos would owe Bertha $100,000 as a nondeductible property settlement if they divorced. In 2018, he suggested that he instead pay her $12,000 a year for 10 years as alimony. Although he would pay $20,000 more, the $120,000 total deduction would save him more than $20,000 in taxes over the 10-year period. Because alimony payments cease at the recipient's death, Bertha suggested a payment stream that reduced her risk of dying before she received the full amount. Amos agreed to pay her $50,000 in 2018, $50,000 in 2019,

and $20,000 in 2020. He deducted each payment as he made it; she reported each payment as gross income. They have transformed a property settlement into alimony for tax purposes, but the recapture rules will apply in the third year.

The desire to convert a property settlement into alimony is not the only reason the parties might have front-loaded their payments. Perhaps the payor anticipated reduced income, and lower tax rates, in the near future. Current deductions would reduce his taxes more than future deductions would. Section 71(f) ignores the parties' motives. In any event, the parties could have avoided recapture by limiting the amount of payment reduction between the second and third year and between the average of the second and third years versus the first year. They could also have avoided recapture if they provided for payments that were based on factors beyond the payor's control (*e.g.*, income from professional fees or sales commissions).

2. Child Support

Child support payments are not included in the recipient's gross income even if they meet the §71(b) requirements and there was a pre-2019 divorce or separation instrument. Because they are not included in the recipient's income, the payor spouse cannot deduct them.

> **Example 10-17.** Their pre-2019 divorce decree requires Amelia to pay Bruno $1,000 a month for alimony that meets the definition in §71(b) and another $500 a month for the support of their son Carl. Only $1,000 a month is alimony included in Bruno's gross income and deductible by Amelia; the other $500 is child support. If the decree was entered after 2018, Bruno has no gross income from either payment.

Section 71(c) provides three rules for determining child support. These rules are important for pre-2019 instruments as the payment recipient treats alimony and child support differently.

If the divorce or separation instrument designates a specific amount or a specific portion of a payment as child support, that amount or portion is considered child support. I.R.C. §71(c)(1).

If the instrument does not make a specific designation, we look to §71(c)(2)(A). It applies if the instrument reduces payments when a contingency relating to the child occurs. The Code lists four contingencies: attaining a specified age; marrying; dying; or leaving school. The regulations include additional, non-exclusive examples: attaining a specified income level; leaving the spouse's household; or gaining employment. That section applies even if the instrument does not indicate the payments are for child support and even if the contingency is not certain — or even likely — to occur. Temp. Reg. § 1.71-1T(c), Q&A-17.

> **Example 10-18.** Their divorce decree requires Brian to pay Astrid $1,500 a month. The decree reduces the payment by $500 a month (to $1,000) when their son Chuck graduates from high school. Because payments are reduced by $500 when a contingency related to Chuck occurs, that $500 paid each month is child support. The treatment of the remaining $1,000 depends on when the decree was issued.

Section 71(c)(2)(B) applies when the instrument does not specify an amount (or portion) as child support *and* does not include a contingency related to the child. It treats the amount of any payment reduction as child support if it occurs at a time that can clearly be associated with a contingency of a kind relating to the child. The regulations list only two situations in which payments are presumed to be associated with such a contingency. The two situations involve reductions in payments that occur at certain ages of the child (*e.g.*, 18, 21, or local age of majority when a single reduction is involved) and reductions within a year of certain common ages (when there is more than one child and more than one reduction). Temp. Reg. § 1.71-1T(c), Q&A-18.

G. Disaster Relief Payments

Section 139(a) excludes disaster relief payments related to a qualified disaster. Payments can cover personal, family, living, or funeral expenses. They can also cover expenses to repair or rehabilitate the taxpayer's residence or repair or replace its contents. Payments can be made by a government or government agency to promote the general welfare. They can also be made by a common carrier by reason of death or personal physical injuries. Section 139 does not exclude payments for expenses compensated by insurance or otherwise. Payments can be made to the affected individual or for his benefit. I.R.C. § 139(b). He cannot take a deduction or credit for any amount covered by a § 139 payment. I.R.C. § 139(h).

An event is a qualified disaster if it results from a terroristic or military action; is a federally declared disaster; results from an accident involving a common carrier or other event that is deemed to be catastrophic in nature; or if the government making payments determines that assistance is warranted. I.R.C. § 139(c).

Section 139(g) excludes qualified disaster mitigation payments that are paid pursuant to the Robert T. Stafford Disaster Relief and Emergency Assistance Act or the National Flood Insurance Act. These payments are for hazard mitigation with respect to the recipient's property. They cannot be used to increase the property's basis.

H. Additional Miscellaneous Exclusions

1. Statutory Exclusions

Section 86(a)(1)(A) includes only 50% of Social Security benefits in gross income. A separate computation for lower-income taxpayers may result in an exclusion as high as 100%. I.R.C. § 86(a)(1)(B). Another computation applies to higher-income taxpayers; their exclusion may be as small as 15% of their benefits; the other 85% is gross income. I.R.C. § 86(a)(2). To prevent higher-income taxpayers from reducing their other income by purchasing tax-exempt bonds, § 86(b)(2)(b) includes tax-exempt interest in determining if the taxpayer includes 0%, 50%, or 85% of his Social Security benefits in gross income.

A lessor who receives buildings or improvements when his tenant's lease terminates does not have gross income. I.R.C. § 109. This provision applies only if the improvements were not made as a substitute for rent. This is really a postponement provision because the lessor takes a zero basis for these improvements. I.R.C. § 1019.

Section 131 excludes certain amounts received by foster care providers from a state or political subdivision or a qualified foster care placement agency. The care must be provided in the foster care provider's home. In *Stromme v. Commissioner*, 138 T.C. 213 (2012), the court held that a house did not qualify unless the care provider lived in it. The taxpayers owned two houses, and the house that constituted their principal residence was not the one in which foster care occurred.

Section 136 excludes subsidies that public utility customers receive to purchase or install any energy conservation measure. The property involved must be a dwelling unit as defined in § 280A(f)(1).

Section 139E excludes tribal government benefits paid under a program administered under specified guidelines and that does not discrimination in favor of the tribe's governing body. The benefits must be available to any tribal member (and that member's spouse and dependents) who meets the program guidelines, be for the promotion of general welfare, not be lavish or extravagant, and not be compensation for services.

Exclusions also appear in other U.S. Code titles. For example, title 25 contains several exclusions for funds held for Indian tribes. Benefits due under any law administered by the Veterans Administration are excluded by 38 U.S.C. § 5301(a). The Tax Court held that this exclusion applied to compensation paid to veterans participating in a work therapy program. *Wallace v. Commissioner*, 128 T.C. 132 (2007). The IRS later indicated it would follow *Wallace* and that the benefits qualified for exclusion under § 134, which applies to certain benefits provided members of the military. Rev. Rul. 2007-69, 2007-2 C.B. 1083.

2. General Welfare Exclusion

Both the IRS and courts have invoked the general welfare exclusion with respect to other items. "The Service has consistently held, however, that payments made under governmental programs for the promotion of the general welfare are not includible in an individual recipient's gross income (general welfare exclusion)." Notice 2011-14, 2011-11 I.R.B. 544 (payments made on behalf of financially distressed homeowners under programs designed by state housing finance agencies).

Checkpoints

- Most prizes are included in gross income.

- Prizes received for certain types of achievement are excluded if the recipient did not enter the contest, does not have to render services to receive the prize, and directs that the prize be transferred to a charity or to a government unit.

- Prizes may also be excluded if they are received by Olympic and Paralympic athletes.

- Scholarships received by a candidate for a degree are excluded if they cover tuition and fees required for enrollment at the educational organization or books, fees, and other items required for enrollment in a particular course.

- A scholarship is partially taxable based on the value of any services the recipient is required to perform.

- Educational organizations can provide tax-free tuition benefits — generally limited to tuition below the graduate level — to employees and their family members.

- If a qualified scholarship is received as a prize, the tax consequences are governed by the rules covering scholarships instead of the rules covering prizes.

- Taxpayers who use the proceeds of certain U.S. government savings bonds to pay for college tuition and fees can exclude the interest earned on those bonds.

- Taxpayers may exclude income earned on amounts invested in college savings plans and prepaid tuition programs if they use those funds to pay for tuition, fees, books, supplies, and equipment. Room and board can also be covered if the student attends at least half time. These funds can be used for elementary and secondary education in addition to college education.

- Taxpayers may exclude income earned on amounts invested in Coverdell education savings accounts. These funds can be used for elementary and secondary education in addition to college education.

- State and local governments exclude income derived from public utilities or essential government services.

- Bondholders can exclude interest received from state and local government obligations.

- Taxpayers who live outside the United States may exclude a portion of their foreign earned income and employer-provided housing allowances.

- Alimony received under a post-2018 divorce or separation instrument is not included in the recipient's gross income. Alimony received under an earlier instrument may be included, depending on the terms of the instrument.

- Child support payments are not included in the recipient's gross income.

- Disaster relief payments are not included in the recipient's gross income.

Chapter 11

Overview of Deductions and Credits

Roadmap

- Introduction
- Type of activity
- Tax return placement
- Itemized deductions
- Deductions affected by AGI
- Timing and character of deductions
- Taxpayer status
- Deductions disallowed by the alternative minimum tax
- Credits

A. Introduction

Because taxpayers are not taxed on gross income, we also consider decreases in their wealth. When a taxpayer makes an outlay, commits to making an outlay, or suffers a loss, can he deduct that amount? This chapter introduces categories of deductions and credits discussed in other chapters.

B. Type of Activity

Taxpayers divide their activities into trade or business, income-producing, and personal. An activity's category is not set in stone. An income-producing activity may become a trade or business because the taxpayer increases the frequency or degree of his efforts. A taxpayer may eventually transform a personal "hobby" into a business or an income-producing activity. Alternatively, a business or income-producing activity can later become a hobby if the taxpayer fails to engage in it for profit.

Distinctions between categories are important. Section 162 authorizes deducting trade or business expenses. Section 212 authorizes deducting expenses of income-producing activities. No comparable section authorizes deductions for personal expenses. Section 262 provides that there is no deduction for personal, living, or family expenses unless a specific Code section authorizes the deduction.

The distinction between types of activity is blurred by Code sections that apply to all three categories. It is also blurred by expenses, such as outlays for business meals, with both business and personal aspects. Finally, although an employee is engaged in a trade or business while performing the duties of his employment, his expenses are subject to limits that do not apply to a self-employed taxpayer.

We also categorize losses. A loss may be incurred in a trade or business, in a transaction entered into for profit, or in a purely personal activity. If the taxpayer has a bad debt loss, the distinction is instead between business and nonbusiness.

Finally, the Code authorizes taxpayers to take credits rather than deductions for certain outlays. Because we subtract a credit directly from the tax otherwise due, each dollar of credit is worth a dollar. A deduction on the other hand, affects the computation of taxable income. The value of a deduction depends on the taxpayer's marginal tax rate. Some credits require a business connection. Others are available for purely personal activities.

In addition to Code sections allowing deductions, you must also consider sections that limit those deductions or deny them altogether. Deductions for expenses may be denied or reduced based on public policy, because the personal aspects of an outlay outweigh its connection with a business or income-producing activity, or because the taxpayer used borrowed funds to produce tax-exempt income. Deductions for losses may be denied because a business owner has not put sufficient assets at risk, is not sufficiently active in the business, or is engaged in wagering. Deductions may also be denied because the taxpayer is dealing with a related party.

C. Tax Return Placement

Deductions take two forms: above-the-line and below-the-line. These terms do not appear in the Code. They are an informal method for referring to where a deduction appears on the tax return. Above-the-line deductions are deducted directly from gross income in reaching adjusted gross income (AGI). They are available whether the taxpayer itemizes her other deductions or takes the standard deduction. Section 62 lists deductions that are taken in computing AGI, but it is not a deduction section. A taxpayer determines whether a deduction is allowable in computing AGI only after finding another Code section that authorizes the deduction.

Section 62 lists some trade or business deductions, some income-producing deductions, and even a few personal deductions. Several deductions are described in more than one of its paragraphs. Section 62(a) recognizes this overlap in its flush language: "Nothing in this section shall permit the same item to be deducted more than once."

1. Trade or Business Expenses

Deductions associated with a trade or business—both expenses and losses— are deducted in computing AGI if the taxpayer is self-employed. The §199A deduction, which is based on having qualified business income, is an exception to that rule. That deduction is taken below the line, but it is available even if the taxpayer does not itemize deductions.

Deductions for an employee's trade or business expenses are allowed in computing AGI only if the type of employee or type of expense is specifically listed in §62. Other employee business expenses, including unreimbursed professional or union dues, professional journals, employment-related educational expenses, and depreciation on employment-related equipment, are miscellaneous itemized deductions and not available in 2018 through 2025.

2. Expenses for the Production of Income

Deductions attributable to property held for the production of rents and royalties are deducted in computing AGI. Amounts forfeited to a financial institution for premature withdrawal of funds from a time savings account or certificate of deposit are also deducted in computing AGI. Other expenses related to the production of income are miscellaneous itemized deductions and not available in 2018 through 2025.

3. Losses Related to Sale or Exchange of Property

Losses from the sale or exchange of property are deducted in computing AGI. This includes losses from actual sales or exchanges and losses that are treated as losses from sales or exchanges.

4. Expenses Related to Retirement Income

Contributions to deductible IRAs are deducted in computing AGI. These provisions do not cover amounts paid to an investment advisor for assistance in deciding how to invest. Those payments are miscellaneous itemized deductions and not available in 2018 through 2025.

5. Expenses That Do Not Require a Business or Income-Producing Activity

Outlays for alimony, interest on education loans, certain higher education expenses, and contributions to Archer medical savings accounts and health savings accounts are deducted in computing AGI. The deduction for alimony recapture is also deductible in computing AGI, but the deductions for alimony and alimony recapture are available only for divorce and separation instruments finalized before 2019. The § 215 deduction for alimony paid is available only to the extent § 71 includes the payment in the recipient's gross income. Up to $300 of charitable contributions can be deducted in computing AGI; this provision is currently available only in 2020.

6. Expenses Related to Litigation

A taxpayer who pays attorney fees or court costs deducts them in computing AGI if the action is described in § 62(a)(20), (e). It covers claims for unlawful discrimination and certain other claims based on an extensive list of statutes and several titles of the U.S. Code. Among the claims constituting unlawful discrimination are those for age and disability discrimination. Section 62(a)(21) applies to attorney fees and court costs incurred by individuals who receive whistleblower awards related to violations of federal statutes dealing with tax, securities, or commodities or violations of state false claims acts. The amount deductible in computing AGI for either provision is limited to the amount of the taxpayer's recovery included in his gross income.

If an action is not covered by these subsections, it might still be deducted in computing AGI if another § 62 provision applies. For example, the litigation might be related to a self-employed person's business. If the action is not covered by § 62, deductible attorney fees are likely to be miscellaneous itemized deductions and not available for expenses paid in 2018 through 2025.

Example 11-1. Alvina sued her employer for failing to accommodate a disability. She sued her ex-husband for unpaid alimony. She recovered

$100,000 in each lawsuit and paid her attorney $30,000 for each. She deducts the $30,000 cost of producing the discrimination award in computing AGI. The $30,000 cost of collecting her alimony is a miscellaneous itemized deduction.

7. Miscellaneous Expenses

Other above-the-line deductions are certain expenses of a trust beneficiary or a life tenant and deductions for reforestation expenses and for clean-fuel vehicles.

8. Standard Deduction

Instead of itemized deductions, a taxpayer may take the standard deduction. Taxpayers who take the standard deduction do not have to keep track of itemized deductions or maintain substantiating records. As is true for itemized deductions, taxpayers can take the standard deduction in addition to the deductions available in computing AGI.

9. Personal Exemptions

Before 2018, individuals could deduct personal exemptions for themselves, their spouses, and their dependents. That deduction is scheduled for reinstatement in 2026. Although a taxpayer cannot currently deduct exemptions, the definition of dependent remains important in other contexts. These include determining if a taxpayer can deduct paying another person's medical expenses.

D. Itemized Deductions

When taxpayers refer to itemized deductions, they mean the deductions taken instead of the standard deduction. The currently allowed itemized deductions are for home mortgage interest; investment interest; most state and local (and some foreign) taxes; certain personal casualty and theft losses; charitable contributions; and medical expenses.

The Code headings for the sections authorizing deductions also use the term "itemized." The deductions covered by §§ 161–199A are in Part VI (Itemized Deductions for Individuals and Corporations) of Subchapter B (Computation of Taxable Income). The deductions covered by §§ 211–223 are in Part VII

(Additional Itemized Deductions for Individuals) of Subchapter B. These headings do not use the term itemized to indicate where an item goes on the tax return.

E. Deductions Affected by AGI

AGI affects deductions in two ways. Some deductions are computed using a floor or a ceiling that is based on AGI. Others phase out as AGI rises. When reading a deduction section, look to see if it contains a reference to AGI or modified AGI. Keep in mind that modified AGI is defined differently in different Code sections.

F. Timing and Character of Deductions

Taxable income is computed based on the taxable year, and taxpayers use either the cash or the accrual method. If the deduction is for expenses that are *paid or accrued* or *paid or incurred*, the taxpayer follows her accounting method. Occasionally, a deduction is allowed only for expenses *paid*. Even an accrual-method taxpayer uses the cash method for that item. Finally, some deductions are taken for an *allowance*. That terminology often indicates the deduction is based on a formula.

Each taxable year generally stands on its own. We rarely adjust a prior year's return to reflect later events. We encountered this rule in discussing the exclusion for damages for personal physical injuries. We reduce the current-year exclusion by the earlier medical expense deductions; we do not amend the return for the earlier year. Other chapters cover additional instances in which the events of one year affect the tax consequences of another year. These instances include the tax benefit rule, restoration of amounts received under a claim of right, and various expense and loss carryover provisions.

Deductions for expenses and losses are generally ordinary deductions. If they are capital losses, and exceed the taxpayer's capital gains, they are subject to deduction limits. Deductions for losses are generally capital losses if they result from the sale or exchange of a capital asset or are treated as such. Losses from transactions described in § 1231 may end up being treated as ordinary or as capital; the outcome depends on the relationship between the taxpayer's § 1231 gains and losses.

G. Taxpayer Status

Some deductions require married taxpayers to file joint returns. Other deductions are allowed, but in reduced amounts, if they file separate returns. Taxpayers who are at least age 65 or legally blind can take a larger standard deduction than taxpayers who have neither status, while taxpayers subject to the kiddie tax are likely to have a smaller standard deduction than taxpayers who are not subject to that tax.

H. Deductions Disallowed by the Alternative Minimum Tax

The primary focus of this book is the individual income tax. Chapter 1 briefly discusses a separate tax computation, the alternative minimum tax. The AMT is imposed at only two rates—26% and 28%—on what is referred to as the taxable excess; it applies only if it exceeds the income tax. Several deductions allowed in computing the income tax are not allowed or are treated less favorably in computing the AMT.

I. Credits

A taxpayer can reduce his tax liability by any credits to which he is entitled. Unlike deductions, the value of a credit is not based on the taxpayer's rate bracket; a dollar of credit saves a dollar of tax. The Code provides credits for certain business activity, such as investing in low-income housing. It also provides credits for activity that requires an employment connection, such as the earned income tax credit and the credit for household and dependent care services. Finally, it provides credits for personal activities, such as adopting a child. Some of these credits are refundable—the credit can generate a refund even if it exceeds the tax due. Others are nonrefundable—the credit cannot reduce the tax below zero. Credits are briefly discussed in several chapters.

Checkpoints

- Deductions can be characterized by the type of activity in which the taxpayer is engaged or by where they appear on the tax return.

- Deductions are allowable only if a Code section provides for a deduction.

- Taxpayers take either allowable itemized deductions or the standard deduction. In addition, they can take above-the-line deductions listed in § 62 and a below-the-line deduction for qualified business income.

- Section 62 does not make an outlay deductible; it covers only where an allowable deduction goes on the tax return.

- Some deductions are computed using formulas based on AGI.

- The time for taking a deduction is generally based on the taxpayer's accounting method.

- The character of a deduction (*e.g.*, capital loss) is relevant.

- A taxpayer's marital status affects the amount of certain deductions.

- Credits are a direct offset against the tax otherwise due.

- A refundable credit can result in a refund if it exceeds the tax otherwise due.

Chapter 12

Business and Income-Producing Expenses

Roadmap

- Introduction
- Section 162 requirements
- Section 162 expenses
- Expenses with a business connection
- Significance of employee status
- Section 212 expenses
- Expenses to produce tax-exempt income
- Tax credits

A. Introduction

This chapter focuses on deductions allowed taxpayers who are engaged in a trade or business or an income-producing activity. Most of their deductions are authorized by § 162 (trade or business) or § 212 (income-producing activity). Although both sections are broadly worded, they do not make every activity-related outlay deductible. A deduction is not a constitutional right; it is, instead, "a matter of grace." *Commissioner v. Sullivan*, 356 U.S. 27, 28 (1958).

This chapter also addresses related Code sections and situations in which the taxpayer's status matters. It concludes with a brief discussion of tax credits available to taxpayers engaged in a trade or business or income-producing activity.

B. Section 162 Requirements

Section 162(a) provides a deduction for "all the ordinary and necessary expenses paid or incurred during the taxable year in carrying on any trade or business." The discussion below focuses on those terms.

1. Ordinary and Necessary

To be deductible, a trade or business expense must be "ordinary and necessary." According to the Supreme Court, "what is ordinary, though there must always be a strain of constancy within it, is nonetheless a variable affected by time and place and circumstance. Ordinary in this context does not mean that the payments must be habitual or normal in the sense that the same taxpayer will have to make them often." *Welch v. Helvering*, 290 U.S. 111, 113–14 (1933). An expense is ordinary if it would customarily be made by another business or individual in a similar situation. If it is common within a particular industry, it is "ordinary" even if incurred infrequently.

To meet the necessary prong, the expenditure must be appropriate and helpful. *Welch v. Helvering.* Courts often defer to the taxpayer's business judgment. Although they usually assume that proprietors, partners, and directors act in the best interests of the business, there are limits to their deference. If the taxpayers are related, or the outlay involves elements of personal pleasure, courts give the outlay closer scrutiny. For example, in *Henry v. Commissioner*, 36 T.C. 879, 884 (1961), the court disallowed expenses for the taxpayer's yacht. He was a tax professional who flew a pennant with "1040" on the yacht. The court addressed the business judgment presumption: "But where, as in this case, the expenditures may well have been made to further ends which are primarily personal, this ordinary constraint does not prevail …."

For a creative opinion regarding this requirement, see *Jenkins v. Commissioner*, T.C. Memo. 1983-667, in which Harold Jenkins, who performed as Conway Twitty, reimbursed investors who lost money in his failed restaurant venture, Twitty Burger, Inc. The Tax Court held that the payments were ordinary and necessary business expenses related to his country music business.

Jenkins is distinguishable from *Welch* because Mr. Jenkins had another business (as a singer) that would have been harmed had he not made the payments. Mr. Welch was seeking to enter a business when he made payments to his former employer's creditors. In addition, expectations in Mr. Jenkins's business justified the outlay. For that reason, deductions for repayments had previously been allowed in a less-glamorous setting. In *M. L. Eakes Co., Inc. v. Commissioner*, 686 F.2d 217, 221 (4th Cir. 1982), the taxpayer paid the debts of its bankrupt predecessor, an industrial air-conditioning business. The court distinguished *Welch* based on norms within the business community. The payments were "a practical business necessity for taxpayer in its day-to-day operations and of an ordinary character within the taxpayer's business community."

2. Expenses Versus Capital Expenditures

a. Tangible Assets

Section 162 requires that the outlay be an expense as opposed to a capital expenditure. Section 263(a)(1) disallows deductions for amounts "paid out for new buildings or for permanent improvements or betterments made to increase the value of any property or estate." If a taxpayer's outlay is a capital expenditure, it is added to her basis. She recovers its cost through depreciation or amortization or as an offset to amount realized when she sells the property. The value of treating it as an expense relates to timing. An immediate deduction is worth more to her than a future deduction because she can invest her tax savings sooner.

> Example 12-1. Alma made a $10,000 outlay for her business this year. Because she is in the 24% marginal tax bracket, a $10,000 deduction saves $2,400 in income tax. If she must treat the outlay as a capital expenditure, her deduction and tax savings this year are smaller. Although she may be able to deduct the full $10,000 over a period of years, she prefers the larger immediate tax savings.

Terminology is important. When a capital expenditure is added to the taxpayer's basis for property, it is "capitalized." But it is not necessarily a *capital asset*. To be a capital asset, it must be covered by the definition of capital asset in §1221. For purposes of this chapter, it is safe to assume that business property is not a capital asset although it might receive capital gain treatment because of the §1231 rules discussed in Chapter 19.

Section 263A applies to taxpayers who produce property they will use in a trade or business or hold for profit. It also applies to taxpayers who acquire inventory for resale. Unless one of this section's exceptions applies, these taxpayers must include certain outlays in inventory cost (for items they hold for sale) or basis (for other items they produce). Taxpayers that meet the §448(c) gross receipts test (prior three-year average gross receipts of $25 million or less) are among those exceptions. I.R.C. §263A(i).

Congress enacted §263A in 1986. Previously, the Supreme Court had required a taxpayer to capitalize otherwise-deductible costs used in constructing assets it would use in its business. *Commissioner v. Idaho Power Co.*, 418 U.S. 1 (1974) (depreciation on equipment it used to construct transmission lines, transmission switching stations, and other capital facilities). The regulations issued for § 263A are referred to as the UNICAP regulations.

Acquiring an asset is only step one. The taxpayer might make additional outlays to repair, maintain, or improve it. Repairs and improvements are likely to have different tax consequences. In a 1939 Code ruling, the Tax Court established a distinction between repairs and capital expenditures. If an outlay does not add to the value of property or prolong its expected life, but "merely serve[s] to keep the property in an operating condition," it is a repair, and is deductible as an ordinary and necessary business expense. *Midland Empire Packing Co. v. Commissioner*, 14 T.C. 635 (1950). The regulations issued in 2013 and amended in 2014 are even more specific. Reg. § 1.263(a)-3. They classify outlays as improvements if they constitute betterments or restorations or if they adapt the property to a new or different use. Outlays that do not meet one of these definitions can be deducted immediately; the taxpayer does not have to call them repairs or maintenance.

Betterments include outlays that ameliorate a condition that existed before the property's acquisition (or that arose during its production). *See Mt. Morris Drive-In Theatre Co. v. Commissioner*, 25 T.C. 272 (1955), which involved installing a drainage system to protect against flooding. The taxpayer knew about the drainage problem when it acquired the property. Betterments also include outlays that result in a physical enlargement or material increase in capacity or that are likely to materially increase the property's productivity, efficiency, strength, quality, or output.

Restorations involve replacing a component of the property if the taxpayer previously took its basis into account in computing gain or loss. Returning property that is no longer functional to its ordinarily efficient operating condition is also a restoration. An outlay adapts the property to a new or different use if the adaptation is not consistent with the taxpayer's ordinary use of the property at the time it was originally placed in service.

Note that indirect costs that do not directly benefit the improvement and that are not incurred because of the improvement do not have to be capitalized. But if the property being improved is the taxpayer's principal residence or other personal-use property, she can choose to capitalize repairs and maintenance done at the same time as an improvement. Reg. § 1.263(a)-3(g). This option benefits a taxpayer who later sells personal-use property at a gain, as she could not otherwise deduct amounts treated as repairs or maintenance.

> **Example 12-2.** Arlene added 10,000 square feet of office space by converting an unused attic in her building. The addition is a betterment.

She increases her adjusted basis by the cost of the addition. At the same time, she also replaced a broken window; that outlay is an expense. If the property had instead been Arlene's residence, she could have added the cost of replacing the window to her adjusted basis in addition to adding the cost of the addition.

The improvement regulations are comprehensive and complex, and they include numerous helpful examples. In general, the expenditure is not an improvement if it benefits the property for no more than one taxable year. Longer benefit periods are ignored—and an immediate deduction is allowed—if the outlays satisfy de minimis safe harbors. *See, e.g.*, Reg. § 1.263(a)-3(h)–(i).

Reg. § 1.263(a)-1(f) provides another de minimis safe harbor. Taxpayers who use this safe harbor do not capitalize amounts paid to acquire (Reg. § 1.263(a)-2) or produce (Reg. § 1.263(a)-3) tangible property. Nor can they treat the property as a material or supply covered by the safe harbor provided by Reg. § 1.162-3(a).

b. Intangible Assets

Two Supreme Court decisions are relevant to outlays providing intangible benefits. In *Commissioner v. Lincoln Savings & Loan Association*, 403 U.S. 345 (1971), a savings and loan company had to pay an additional premium to the agency that insured its deposits. The Court required it to capitalize the premium because the outlays created a "separate and distinct asset." In *INDOPCO, Inc. v. Commissioner*, 503 U.S. 79 (1992), it held that capitalization could be required for outlays that produced a long-term benefit even if they did not produce a separate and distinct asset. *INDOPCO* involved payments a company made to advisors who helped it evaluate a takeover offer.

Reg. § 1.263(a)-4 covers the capitalization of intangible assets. Capitalization is required for amounts paid to (1) acquire an intangible; (2) create an intangible; or (3) create or enhance a separate and distinct intangible asset. The last item covers items that are subject to protection under state, federal, or foreign law and that can be transferred separately from a trade or business. Capitalization is also required for outlays that create or enhance a future benefit. Reg. § 1.263(a)-4(b).

As is true for the tangible asset regulations, these regulations are complex and include a variety of exceptions. An important exception relates to advertising and product launch costs, which do not generally require capitalization. Reg. § 1.263(a)-4(l), Example 7. The regulations also include exceptions for de minimis amounts and for certain amounts paid to the taxpayer's employees.

If the taxpayer must capitalize her outlays, she can generally deduct her costs over time through amortization. The regulations also cover intangibles created by prepaying future expenses. Prepayments are discussed in Chapter 16, dealing with accounting methods.

c. Supplies

Regulations for §§ 162 and 263 may apply to the deduction for business supplies that are not held for sale to customers. Reg. § 1.162-3 applies different rules for amounts paid or incurred for non-incidental materials and supplies and for amounts paid or incurred for incidental materials and supplies. The taxpayer cannot use its provisions and also use Reg. § 1.263(a)-1(f), discussed above.

3. Trade or Business

A test for whether an activity constitutes a trade or business comes from *Commissioner v. Groetzinger*, 480 U.S. 23 (1987). The Court indicated that a taxpayer could be carrying on a trade or business, even if he did not deal with customers, if his activity was regular and continuous with the intent to make a profit.

The carrying on requirement was applied in *Frank v. Commissioner*, 20 T.C. 511, 513 (1953). The Franks deducted travel costs incurred while searching for a radio station or newspaper to operate. In disallowing those deductions, the court stated, "The petitioners were not engaged in any trade or business at the time the expenses were incurred. The trips ... were preparatory to locating a business venture of their own." The court noted another complication, addressed later in this chapter: the taxpayers had no home to be away from in pursuit of a trade or business. The § 195 deduction for start-up expenditures discussed in Section D partially overturns the result in *Frank*.

As the word "any" indicates, a taxpayer can have more than one trade or business. She can be self-employed in all of them, an employee in all of them, or self-employed in some and an employee in others. Although § 162 covers each business, there are important limitations. Section E considers situations in which status as an employee is less favorable than status as a self-employed individual. Chapter 15 considers a different situation—a taxpayer who deducts losses sustained in one business against profits earned in another business. The IRS may challenge the loss deductions by arguing that the endeavor is not really a trade or business. In that case, the § 183 "hobby loss" rules apply. It may also argue that the taxpayer does not "materially participate" in the unprofitable business. If so, the §469 passive activity rules might postpone his loss deduction.

4. Paid or Incurred

Although individuals are likely to use the cash receipts and disbursements method of accounting, many business entities choose—or are required to use—the accrual method. The language in §162(a) referring to expenses that are paid or incurred reflects these two accounting methods. I.R.C. §7701(a)(25). As a general rule, cash-method taxpayers report income and expenses when they receive or pay cash or its equivalent, and accrual-method taxpayers report income and expenses when they earn the income or are obligated to make outlays.

C. Section 162 Expenses

Section 162(a) lists three specific business deductions: reasonable salaries, travel expenses, and rental payments. These are not the only available deductions, as "ordinary and necessary" also encompasses advertising, insurance, professional dues, legal fees, repairs, utilities, and other items. The discussion in this section covers the specifically listed items, items that have mixed business and personal aspects, and public policy limitations.

1. Reasonable Salaries

Section 162(a)(1) lets an employer deduct a reasonable allowance for salaries or other compensation for personal services. The reasonableness requirement can be used to attack compensation as too high or too low. For example, a high-income employer may pay an unreasonably large salary to a relative who is in a lower tax rate bracket. Because it cannot deduct dividends, a closely held C corporation might call payments made to a shareholder-employee salary instead of dividends. But a pass-through entity, which is not subject to tax on its profits, has a different incentive. To reduce its exposure to employment taxes, it might call payments profit distributions rather than salary.

Not surprisingly, the IRS tends to scrutinize closely held corporations more than widely held companies because the parties are not acting at arm's-length in setting salaries. Reasonableness is judged as of the time the salary was negotiated if the contract was the result of a free bargain; that is more likely to be the case if the parties are unrelated. Reg. § 1.162-7(b)(3); *Harolds Club v. Commissioner*, 340 F.2d 861 (9th Cir. 1965).

> **Example 12-3.** Alvin is the sole shareholder and president of Closely Held C Corporation. Closely Held paid him its entire $100,000 pre-salary profit. If the payment is salary, Closely Held can deduct it. In that case, it has no taxable income and no tax liability. Alvin has $100,000 of gross income from salary. If the payment is a dividend, Closely Held cannot deduct it. In that case, it has taxable income of $100,000 and pays income tax on that amount. Alvin has $100,000 of gross income from dividends. Although Closely Held and Alvin both pay income tax on the $100,000, neither pays employment tax and Alvin's tax rate on a dividend is lower than his tax rate on salary. It is likely that part of the $100,000 should be treated as salary and part as a dividend.

Courts use different tests in determining if a salary is reasonable. Some courts use an independent investor test. A salary is presumed reasonable if the investors are obtaining a higher return than they had any reason to expect. It is merely a presumption, however, because the rate of return must be based on the performance of the person receiving the salary. For example, an increase in an executive's salary would not be justified if the higher return was attributable to the business unexpectedly finding minerals on its property. *Exacto Spring Corp. v. Commissioner*, 196 F.3d 833, 839 (7th Cir. 1999). On the other hand, a lower rate of return than expected suggests a lower salary is appropriate.

Some courts look to objective factors to determine the reasonableness of salary. *See Metro Leasing and Development Corp. v. Commissioner*, 376 F.3d 1015 (9th Cir. 2004) (five factors); *Eberl's Claim Service, Inc. v. Commissioner*, 249 F.3d 994 (10th Cir. 2001) (Tax Court used 12 factors). Other courts use a hybrid test, combining the independent investor test with the multi-factor approach. *See Haffner's Service Stations, Inc. v. Commissioner*, 326 F.3d 1 (1st Cir. 2003); *LabelGraphics, Inc. v. Commissioner*, 221 F.3d 1091 (9th Cir. 2000). Courts consider the type and extent of services rendered; the scarcity or availability of qualified employees; the employee's qualifications and prior earning capacity; the employee's contributions to the business; the employer's net earnings; the prevailing compensation paid employees with comparable positions; and any peculiar characteristics of the business.

Litigation regarding reasonable salaries also includes bonuses. In *Menard, Inc. v. Commissioner*, 560 F.3d 620, 624 (7th Cir. 2009), the Seventh Circuit held that a $17.5 million bonus (5% of earnings) was not a dividend even though Mr. Menard (who held all of the corporation's voting stock) received higher pay than his counterparts at Home Depot and Lowe's. Both of those larger companies had lower returns on shareholder equity. The Seventh Circuit noted its disagreement with the Tax Court:

> There is no suggestion that any of the shareholders were disappointed that the company obtained a rate of return of "only" 18.8 percent or that the company's success ... has been due to windfall factors, such as the discovery of oil under the company's headquarters. But besides thinking Menard's compensation excessive, the Tax Court thought it was *intended* as a dividend. It thought this because Menard's entitlement to his 5 percent bonus was conditioned on his agreeing to reimburse the corporation should the deduction of the bonus from the corporation's taxable income be disallowed by the Internal Revenue Service ... and because 5 percent of corporate earnings year in and year out "looked" more like a dividend than like salary.

Publicly traded corporations are limited to a deduction of $1 million for salary paid to an employee who was the chief executive officer or the principal financial officer at any time during the year or to an employee who was one of the three highest compensated officers other than the CEO or PFO. It also applies to compensation paid any employee who was so described in any preceding taxable year beginning after December 31, 2016. I.R.C. § 162(m). This limit does not apply to the company's other employees or to employees of most privately held companies. It also does not apply to payments from retirement plans or to payments that would be excluded from the employee's gross income. Prior to the Tax Cuts and Jobs Act of 2017, this section had exceptions for compensation paid as commissions or for meeting certain performance goals. The pre-2017 Act rules continue to apply to compensation paid pursuant to a written binding contract in effect on November 2, 2017, and not materially modified since then.

Section 280G limits the employer's deduction for excess parachute payments. A parachute payment is compensation that is contingent on a change in ownership or control of a corporation, or a change in ownership of a substantial portion of its assets. There is an excess parachute payment if the present value of the payments conditioned on the ownership change exceeds three times the individual's average compensation for the preceding five years (or shorter period in which he performed services). Section 280G covers payments to employees who are officers, shareholders, or highly compensated individuals. It does not disallow deductions for large severance payments to other individuals, nor does it disallow the *entire* payment made to a disqualified individual.

Issues related to "golden parachutes" are most likely to arise in larger corporations. Indeed, § 280G does not apply to corporations that could have qualified as S corporations. It also does not apply to corporations whose stock was not readily tradeable on an established securities market before the ownership change and that obtained shareholder approval for the payment.

2. Travel Away from Home

Section 162(a)(2) allows a deduction for traveling expenses incurred (including amounts expended for meals and lodging unless they are lavish or extravagant) while away from home in the pursuit of a trade or business. To determine whether a traveling expense is lavish, we consider the specific facts and circumstances. Outlays that are reasonable in New York City are likely to be considered lavish in a rural area.

Additional rules apply to meals. First, the taxpayer can deduct meals only if sleep or rest is required. *United States v. Correll*, 389 U.S. 299 (1967). Second, the deduction for a business meal is limited to 50% of its cost. I.R.C. §274(n)(1).

a. Away from Home

The taxpayer must have a home to be away from, and the reason for being away must be business rather than personal. *Commissioner v. Flowers*, 326 U.S. 465 (1946). Having a tax home is critical. Courts have, for example, disallowed deductions for costs incurred by a traveling salesman and by a stage hand employed by Disney traveling ice shows. *Rosenspan v. United States*, 438 F.2d 905 (2d Cir. 1971); *Henderson v. Commissioner*, 143 F.3d 497 (9th Cir. 1998). Although Henderson returned to his parents' home between shows, he established no business connection to the city in which they lived.

Establishing a tax home is only a first step. If the taxpayer's assignment at a new location exceeds a year, the IRS considers the assignment indefinite rather than temporary. Rev. Rul. 99-7, 1999-1 C.B. 361. It believes the taxpayer has made a personal choice not to move to the new location. Because her expenses reflect personal choice rather than business necessity, it disallows the deduction for travel away from home. This treatment can give seemingly harsh results in a depressed economy. A taxpayer who lost employment in one location may continue seeking employment in that location even if she accepts what she hopes is temporary employment elsewhere.

> **Example 12-4.** Arabella owns a business in Ohio. She plans to spend seven months in Maryland to open an office there. If she moves to Maryland for the seven months, she can deduct her travel expenses, including the cost of lodging and 50% of her meals.

> **Example 12-5.** After six months, Arabella realizes that it will take 14 months to set up the Maryland office. She can deduct her travel

expenses only for the first six months. Once the temporary work location is realistically expected to last more than one year, her travel expenses are no longer deductible.

If a taxpayer has homes in more than one location and conducts business in each location, only one can be his "tax home." Although many factors are relevant in determining which location is the tax home, the most important factor is usually the length of time spent at each home. The expenses for travel away from the tax home are deductible. *Andrews v. Commissioner*, 931 F.2d 132 (1st Cir. 1991).

b. Personal Aspects of Travel

There must be a direct relationship between the business and the travel expense. If there are no personal aspects to the trip, the full deduction is allowed. If there are both business and personal reasons for the trip, the principal purpose is critical. If the taxpayer's principal purpose is business, she can deduct all her expenses in traveling to and from the destination. If it is personal, she cannot deduct any of them. Reg. § 1.162-2(b). Different rules apply to outlays for lodging and meals. She can deduct 100% of lodging costs and 50% of meal costs for days spent on business. I.R.C. § 274(n)(1). She cannot deduct meals and lodging for days spent on personal matters.

A facts-and-circumstances test determines the principal purpose. The relative number of days spent on business and on personal activities is a strong indicator of the principal purpose. The taxpayer can count weekends as business days — even if she uses them for personal purposes — if business exigencies require a stay until the following week.

> Example 12-6. Bella, a self-employed architect, flew to New Orleans on Monday morning, met with clients on Monday and Tuesday, spent Wednesday visiting friends, and returned home Thursday morning. Because her trip had more business days than personal days, she can deduct all her airfare. She can also deduct lodging on Monday and Tuesday nights and 50% of her meals for every day except Wednesday.

> Example 12-7. Bella flew to Houston on Thursday evening to meet with clients all day Friday. She planned to return home Saturday morning. She met with one client Friday morning. Her Friday afternoon client had an unexpected conflict and was unavailable until Monday morning. She spent the weekend visiting museums, met with her other client Monday morning, and flew home Monday afternoon. Even though she spent more time on personal pursuits than business, the

imbalance was caused by her client's unexpected unavailability. All her days qualify as business travel days. She can deduct all her airfare, her lodging, and 50% of her meals for each day she was away.

c. Foreign Travel

The rules for foreign travel and domestic travel are identical with respect to meals and lodging. They differ with respect to transportation costs. For domestic travel, transportation costs are an all-or-nothing proposition. For travel outside the United States, the deduction is subject to a combination of that rule and a proportionality rule. I.R.C. § 274(c)(1); Reg. § 1.274-4.

Section 274(c)(1) disallows expenses that would otherwise be allowable; it does not affirmatively authorize deductions. If the trip is primarily personal, the rules applied to domestic travel apply; the transportation is not deductible. If the trip is primarily business, the cost of transportation is allocated between the business and personal days. Thus, if 60% of the days away from home are spent on business and 40% are spent on personal activities, the taxpayer can deduct only 60% of the cost of transportation. It is irrelevant that the trip was primarily for business reasons.

> **Example 12-8.** Adina traveled to Japan for four weeks. She spent three weeks in business meetings and one week on personal activities. She can deduct 75% of the cost of her plane ticket, lodging for three of the four weeks, and 50% of her meals for those three weeks.

There are two exceptions to the proportionality rule. If either applies, only the all-or-nothing rule applies to the transportation costs. First, the rule does not apply if the trip does not exceed one week. Second, it does not apply if the time in a foreign country that is spent on personal activities is less than 25% of the total time traveling abroad. I.R.C. § 274(c)(2).

> **Example 12-9.** Adina instead spent six days in Japan. She spent four days in business meetings and two days on personal activities. The proportionality rule for airfare does not apply because she did not spend more than a week on foreign travel. She can deduct the cost of her plane ticket, lodging for four of the six days, and 50% of her meals for those four days.

> **Example 12-10.** Adina instead spent six weeks in Japan. She spent five weeks in business meetings and one week on personal activities. The proportionality rule for airfare does not apply because she spent less than 25% of her time on personal activities. She can deduct the cost

of her plane ticket, lodging for five of the six weeks, and 50% of her meals for those five weeks. This is true even if she spent her weekends on personal activities; the weekends between business days would also be treated as business days.

d. Commuting Expenses

As a general rule, the taxpayer cannot deduct the cost of commuting between his residence and place of business or the cost of parking his car if he drives. Reg. §§ 1.162-2(e), 1.262-1(b)(5). He is treated as having made a personal decision to live further than walking distance from his place of work. Only the costs of transportation between his home and place of work are treated as nondeductible commuting. If he leaves the office to travel to another worksite, he can deduct those expenses.

> Example 12-11. Alan, an attorney in Washington, D.C., lives 20 miles away in Springfield, Virginia. He drives to the office each day. He cannot deduct his automobile expenses. If he drives from his office to a courthouse in D.C. for a hearing and then returns to his office, he can deduct the cost of driving between his office and the courthouse.

Local transportation expenses are deductible in limited circumstances. Rev. Rul. 99-7, *supra*. First, a taxpayer may deduct daily transportation expenses in going between his residence and a temporary work location *outside* the metropolitan area where he lives and normally works. Second, if he has at least one regular work location away from his residence, he may deduct daily transportation expenses in going between his residence and a temporary work location in that same business. This rule does not include a distance requirement. Third, if his residence is his principal place of business, he may deduct daily transportation expenses in going between it and a different work location in that same business. This rule does not include a distance requirement or a temporary location requirement.

> Example 12-12. Alan drove from his home in Springfield to a courthouse in Pittsburgh for a hearing and drove back to his home in Springfield. He can deduct the cost of driving from his home to Pittsburgh and back. If he had to remain in Pittsburgh for three days of depositions, he can also deduct the cost of lodging and 50% of his meals.

> Example 12-13. Alan closed his D.C. office and now operates his law firm from his home in Springfield. If he drives to the courthouse in

D.C. for a hearing, he can deduct the cost of driving from his home to the courthouse and back.

3. Rental Payments

Section 162(a)(3) lets a taxpayer deduct rental or other payments made as a condition to the continued use or possession of property. He cannot have taken title, be taking title, or have any equity in the property; in those cases, his outlay would be a capital expenditure. Calling such an outlay rent does not change its substance or make it currently deductible.

> Example 12-14. Abel rents office space for $25,000 per month, which is a reasonable rate in that location. He deducts his rental payments as a business expense. If he purchases the building, he cannot deduct its cost in the year of acquisition. Instead, he deducts the cost over the building's useful life through depreciation.

> Example 12-15. Bob plans to install a sprinkler system that costs $20,000 and has a useful life significantly greater than one year. The purchase would be a capital expenditure. He cannot change the outcome by "renting" the system for $10,000 per year for two years, with an option to continue renting it indefinitely for $10 per year thereafter. Although rental payments are currently deductible, the IRS would treat this as a disguised purchase. Bob would be paying the system's cost over a period that is substantially less than its useful life, and he could retain it thereafter for a nominal fee. The fact that he never takes title is irrelevant. *Estate of Starr v. Commissioner*, 274 F.2d 294 (9th Cir. 1959).

4. Educational Expenses, Seminars, and Meetings

A taxpayer can deduct educational expenses that maintain or improve her skills in her occupation or that are required as a condition of her employment or profession. She cannot deduct expenses incurred in entering a profession or meeting its minimum requirements. Reg. § 1.162-5.

> Example 12-16. Alice, a self-employed attorney, took a continuing legal education course. She can deduct its cost if it meets the state's requirements for retaining her license to practice law or maintains or improves her legal skills.

Much of the litigation involving educational expenses concerns advanced degrees (*e.g.*, M.B.A. or LL.M.). The decisions focus on whether the taxpayer is engaged in a trade or business at all or on whether the outlays qualify him for a new trade or business. For example, a taxpayer who obtains a law degree in May and begins an LL.M. program three months later, before even receiving bar examination results, is unlikely to be "carrying on a trade or business." An individual who interns with various businesses while obtaining an undergraduate degree faces the same hurdle in deducting an M.B.A. A tax accountant who attends law school may be improving his skills as an accountant, but he is also qualifying himself for a new trade or business.

The taxpayer faces other hurdles even if he satisfies the requirements of Reg. § 1.162-5. If he enters a full-time program that is expected to last more than a year, he risks the IRS arguing that he abandoned his trade or business to become a full-time student. *Sherman v. Commissioner*, T.C. Memo. 1977-301 (allowing a deduction for a two-year program). If he moves to a new city to take classes, it may disallow his living expenses in the new location on the ground that he is not temporarily away from home on business.

Section 274(h)(1) imposes significant limitations on expenses for a convention, seminar, or similar meeting held outside the North American area. The taxpayer must establish that the meeting is directly related to the active conduct of his business and that it is as reasonable to hold it outside the North American area as within it. The latter requirement considers the purpose of the meeting, the purposes of the sponsoring groups, the residences of the sponsoring organization's active members, and the locations of prior meetings. Section 274(h)(3) defines the North American area as the United States, its possessions, the Trust Territory of the Pacific Islands, Canada, and Mexico. The IRS can add Caribbean countries and Bermuda if they enter into exchange of information agreements with the United States. I.R.C. § 274(h)(6).

The rules are more limiting for events held on cruise ships. I.R.C. § 274(h)(2). The meeting must be directly related to the active conduct of the taxpayer's business, the cruise ship must be registered in the United States, and all ports of call must be in the United States or its possessions. The maximum deduction is $2,000 per year.

Finally, § 274(m)(2) provides that no deduction is permitted for travel as a form of education. This provision applies when the travel itself is the outlay that allegedly improves the taxpayer's skills. It does not apply to travel expenses incurred to enroll in an otherwise-deductible program.

5. Business Meals and Gifts

Although business meals and entertainment expenses can be ordinary and necessary, several limitations apply. Section 274(k)(1), which applies to business meals, disallows deductions for food or beverages unless the taxpayer (or one of his employees) is present and the outlay is not lavish or extravagant under the circumstances. Even if meals expenses satisfy these requirements, the taxpayer's deduction is generally limited to 50% of the amount spent. I.R.C. § 274(n)(1).

Before the Tax Cuts and Jobs Act of 2017, § 274 required a taxpayer to have more than a general expectation of deriving an income or business benefit to deduct outlays for entertainment. The expenses had to be directly related to the taxpayer's business or associated with his business. Repealed I.R.C. § 274(a)(1)(A). Because expenses for entertainment (including expenses for facilities used for entertainment) are no longer deductible, these distinctions are not currently relevant. Even before the 2017 legislation, § 274(a)(3) had eliminated deductions for amounts paid or incurred for membership in any club organized for business, pleasure, recreation, or other social purpose. This includes dues paid to country clubs and athletic clubs.

Although there is no longer a deduction for entertainment expenses, taxpayers must still determine if a meal is nondeductible entertainment or a 50%-deductible business meal. Proposed regulations issued in February 2020 address this question. The proposed regulations largely follow guidance in Notice 2018-76, 2018-42 I.R.B. 599, and treat food and beverages as deductible—even if they are provided as part of an entertainment event—if they are charged for separately or if the invoice or other record states these charges separately from the entertainment charges. Prop. Reg. § 1.274-11. Prop. Reg. § 1.274-12(a) discusses food and beverages provided to business associates. Outlays are deductible if the taxpayer (or an employee) is present, the outlay is not lavish or extravagant under the circumstances, and the food or beverage is provided to a business associate. A business associate is defined as a person with whom the taxpayer could reasonably expect to engage or deal in the active conduct of the taxpayer's business. It includes clients, customers, suppliers, and professional advisers. The person for whom food or beverages is provided can be an established or prospective business associate. Prop. Reg. § 1.274-12(b)(3). The 50% deduction limitation still applies in both proposed regulations. Prop. Reg. § 1.274-12 covers other aspects of § 274 in relation to meals; these include outlays for employees and outlays for meals provided to the general public.

Beginning in 2026, employers will no longer be able to deduct the costs of operating a § 132(e) eating facility for employees or the costs of food and beverages supplied at such a facility. They will also lose their deduction for meals provided to their employees that meet the § 119 convenience of the employer requirements. I.R.C. § 274(o).

Section 274(b)(1) limits the deduction for business gifts. If the donee can exclude the gift only under § 102, the donor's annual deduction cannot exceed $25 per donee (not $25 per gift). This provision does not apply to "gifts" to employees that are included in the employee's gross income because of § 102(c) or employee achievement awards excluded by § 74. It does apply to gifts to business associates and clients.

Section 274(d) imposes mandatory substantiation requirements for travel, gifts, and § 280F(d)(4) listed property. Expenses are substantiated by adequate records or by sufficient evidence corroborating the taxpayer's own statement. The records or evidence must demonstrate four items: (1) the amount of the expense; (2) the time and place of the expense and description of any gift; (3) the business purpose of the expense; and (4) the business relationship to the taxpayer of persons receiving the benefit. The taxpayer loses his entire deduction for any un-substantiated item; courts cannot estimate a reasonable deduction amount.

6. Job-Related Clothing

Several types of employment involve distinctive clothing. A public safety officer usually wears a uniform, a salesperson might wear clothing sold by her company, and a rock star might perform in a gemstone-encrusted jacket. The mere fact that the item is worn at work does not make its cost deductible. The IRS allows a deduction only if the item is specifically required as a condition of employment and is not of a type adaptable to general or continued use in place of ordinary clothing. Rev. Rul. 70-474, 1970-2 C.B. 34. Judicial decisions indicate that the test applied in determining whether clothing is adaptable to general use is an objective one. The taxpayer's subjective belief is not sufficient to justify the deduction. *Pevsner v. Commissioner*, 628 F.2d 467 (5th Cir. 1980). He may also have to demonstrate that he did not wear the clothing outside of the workplace.

7. Transportation Fringe Benefits

Before the Tax Cuts and Jobs Act of 2017, employers could deduct their outlays for providing qualified transportation fringe benefits: parking; transit passes; group transportation to work; and even costs of bicycle commuting. The employees who received those benefits excluded them, subject to dollar limits. As a result, neither the employer (who deducted them) nor the employee (who excluded them) was taxed on those benefits. Employees, as described in

Chapter 3, generally retain their tax exclusion. But employers can no longer deduct amounts paid to provide qualified transportation fringe benefits. I.R.C. §274(a)(4). Section 274(l)(1) disallows any deduction for any expense to provide transportation (or reimburse an employee's outlays) in connection with travel between the employee's residence and place of employment. This rule does not apply to outlays made to ensure the employee's safety. In addition, for 2018 through 2025, it does not apply to reimbursements of an employee's qualified bicycle commuting expenses. I.R.C. §274(l)(2). The different treatment reflects the difference in employee tax consequences. Unlike the benefits covered by §274(l)(1), the employee is taxed on reimbursements for qualified bicycle commuting expenses.

The employer's parking costs vary depending on whether it owns the parking facility its employees use (or leases the entire facility) or instead leases spaces in a facility owned by another person. Notice 2018-99, 2018-52 I.R.B. 1067, addresses guidance that will be superseded by a regulation. If the employer owns or leases the entire facility, it can use any reasonable method for determining the nondeductible amount. The notice indicates that the value of the parking is not a reasonable method. The notice provides a methodology that the IRS considers reasonable. First, the employer cannot deduct its cost for the percentage of total parking expenses that corresponds to the percentage of the facility's spaces that are reserved employee parking. Second, the employer is to determine the primary use of any remaining spaces. If the percentage of use by the public exceeds (or is expected to exceed) 50%, the remainder of the total parking expenses are deductible. If the percentage of use by the public does not exceed (or is not expected to exceed) 50%, the employer can deduct the percentage of total parking expenses allocable to spaces that are exclusively reserved for nonemployees. If any expenses remain unallocated, the employer is to make a reasonable determination of employee use of remaining spaces during normal business hours on a typical business day. Expenses allocated to employee use are not deductible.

If the employer instead pays another person for spaces in that person's parking facility, it cannot deduct the amounts it pays for those spaces. Because §274(e)(2)(A) does not disallow deductions for amounts included in an employee's taxable wages, an employer can deduct payments that exceed the amount the employee can exclude as a qualified transportation fringe benefit.

> **Example 12-17.** Ben paid ABC Parking $310 per employee per month in 2020 for reserved parking in the ABC lot. Because the inflation-adjusted exclusion limit for parking is $270 per month, Ben can deduct $40 per month for each employee who receives parking. Each employee

excludes $270 per month from gross income and is taxed on the additional $40 per month.

8. Public Policy Limitations

In considering the public policy limitations discussed below, keep three Supreme Court decisions in mind. In *Commissioner v. Sullivan*, 356 U.S. 27 (1958), the Court let a taxpayer deduct rents and salaries even though his gambling business was illegal under state law. But in *Tank Truck Rentals, Inc. v. Commissioner*, 356 U.S. 30, 36 (1958), the Court disallowed deductions for fines for overweight truck loads. *Sullivan* involved otherwise legal expenses of an illegal business, while *Tank Truck Rentals* involved a fine for an illegal act by a legal business. Most of the fines were for willful violations; a small number were for unintentional violations. The Court disallowed both. "But since the maximum weight statutes make no distinction between innocent and willful violators, state policy is as much thwarted in the one instance as in the other." Because a deduction reduces the cost of the fine by the tax savings, allowing it would frustrate a sharply defined state policy.

Finally, in *Commissioner v. Tellier*, 383 U.S. 687, 694 (1966), the Court let an individual convicted of securities fraud deduct his attorney fees: "No public policy is offended when a man faced with serious criminal charges employs a lawyer to help in his defense. That is not 'proscribed conduct.' It is his constitutional right."

a. Bribes and Kickbacks

Section 162(c) disallows deductions for certain bribes and kickbacks. It covers both direct and indirect payments (*e.g.*, payments to members of a government official's family). Section 162(c)(1) disallows deductions for payments to government officials or employees if those payments are illegal bribes or kickbacks. If a payment is to an official or employee of a foreign government, it disallows the deduction only if the payment violates the Foreign Corrupt Practices Act of 1977. This exception recognizes that "facilitation" payments are common in many foreign countries.

Section 162(c)(2) disallows deductions for bribes, kickbacks, or other payments that are illegal under any U.S. law or under any generally enforced state law. It covers payments to induce action, such as bribing a juror, and payments for the referral of clients, patients, or customers. It applies if the payment could result in criminal penalty or loss of a license or privilege to engage in a trade or business. If the payor could lose the right to practice law, style hair, or drive a taxicab, the payment is covered.

Section 162(c)(3) disallows deductions for kickbacks, rebates, or bribes made by a provider of services or items for which payment might be made under the Social Security Act. It also applies if payments might be made out of federal funds under a state plan approved under the Social Security Act. It disallows payments made in connection with furnishing items or services or the making or receipt of government-funded payments.

b. Lobbying Expenses

Section 162(e) disallows deductions for lobbying expenses. It does not apply to taxpayers for whom lobbying is a trade or business when they are lobbying on behalf of a client. It applies to the clients who pay their fees. I.R.C. § 162(e)(4)(A).

Disallowed payments fall into four major categories: (1) influencing legislation; (2) participation in, or intervention in, political campaigns on behalf of (or in opposition to) candidates for public office; (3) attempting to influence the general public (or segments thereof) with respect to elections, legislative matters, or referendums; and (4) direct communication with certain executive branch officials in an attempt to influence official acts or positions. Those officials are listed in § 162(e)(5). A $2,000 annual maximum deduction is allowed for in-house expenditures for items (1) and (4). I.R.C. § 162(e)(4)(B).

Section 162(e) is not limited to direct lobbying activity; § 162(e)(2) disallows the portion of dues paid to a tax-exempt organization that the organization allocates to lobbying.

c. Fines and Penalties

Section 162(f) disallows deductions for fines or similar penalties paid a government or governmental entity. Reg. § 1.162-21(b)(1) defines fines and similar penalties with reference to four alternative characteristics. The first covers any payment made pursuant to a guilty plea or a plea of no contest for a crime in a criminal proceeding. It does not matter if the crime is a felony or a misdemeanor. The second covers civil penalties (specifically including certain tax penalties) imposed by federal, state, or local law. The third covers amounts paid in settlement of actual or potential liability for a civil or criminal penalty. The fourth covers amounts forfeited as collateral posted in connection with a proceeding that could result in a fine or penalty. Section 162(f) applies to both intentional and unintentional violations. It also applies to the taxpayer's payments to a government or governmental entity in relation to the investigation into a potential violation. It does not apply to payments that are pursuant to a court order if no government or governmental entity was a party to the lawsuit. I.R.C. § 162(f)(3).

This section does not apply to restitution payments that are designed to make the victim whole as opposed to amounts imposed as punishment. The nature of a payment is determined based on the relevant facts and circumstances. If restitution is paid in lieu of forfeiture to the government, the taxpayer may lose the deduction on the ground that the payment is an indirect forfeiture. It also does not apply to amounts spent to come into compliance with the law. The taxpayer must establish that the payment was for restitution or to come into compliance, and the amount must be designated as such in a decree or settlement agreement. I.R.C. § 162(f)(2)(A).

Reg. § 1.162-21(b)(2) lists items that are not disallowed. Not surprisingly, in light of the Supreme Court's decision in *Tellier*, the wrongdoer can deduct legal fees and other costs of defending the action. The regulation also indicates that compensatory damages paid to a government are not treated as a fine or penalty. The regulations include several examples. Reg. § 1.162-21(c).

In *Wood v. United States*, 2002 WL 31973260 (S.D. Fla. 2002), the taxpayer attempted to deduct $5 million forfeited to the government after his conviction for illegally smuggling Freon. The court rejected his argument that the $5 million represented the deductible excise tax he would have paid. The funds went to the Customs Forfeiture Fund and were not available to the IRS as payment of the excise tax. The court also denied a deduction for a loss on a transaction entered into for profit even though § 165 does not include a provision mirroring § 162(f). It looked to decisions of other courts: "The rationale for such denial, in the absence of a specific Code provision, is that allowance of a deduction based on forfeiture would frustrate a sharply defined public policy against the related criminal activity." 2002 WL 31973260, at *4.

State law may determine whether a payment is criminal or restitutionary in nature. In PLR 200834016, the IRS determined that New Jersey treated restitution as non-penal even though it also had the penal aspects of rehabilitation and deterrence. The taxpayer pled guilty to insurance fraud, paid a criminal penalty, and was incarcerated. He also paid restitution to the defrauded insurance companies. The IRS let him deduct the restitution payments as a loss on a transaction entered into for profit, not as a loss incurred in a trade or business.

d. Clayton Act Treble Damages

Section 162(g) disallows a deduction for two-thirds of any damages a taxpayer pays after a conviction (or plea of guilty or nolo contendere) for violating the Clayton Act. It applies only to the extra amount imposed when damages are trebled.

e. Sexual Harassment/Discrimination NDAs

Section 162(q) disallows a deduction for settlements or payments related to sexual harassment or sexual abuse if the settlement or payment is subject to a nondisclosure agreement. This provision also disallows any deduction for attorney fees related to the settlement or payment.

f. Controlled Substances

The disallowance provisions discussed above apply because of the type of expense or loss, not the nature of the business. Section 280E, on the other hand, disallows deductions, even for such innocuous outlays as utilities, if the taxpayer's activity involves trafficking in controlled substances. No comparable Code section exists for other illegal businesses.

A federal definition applies in determining if drugs are controlled substances. The expense is disallowed if such trafficking is prohibited by either federal or state law. Although a majority of states allow sales of marijuana, § 280E still applies if the sale violates federal law.

Section 280E disallows any "deduction or credit," not any outlay. This distinction is important because the taxpayer's cost of the drugs he sells is not an expense deduction. It is an offset against the selling price to determine gross income from business. I.R.C. § 61(a)(2); Reg. § 1.61-3(a). It is analogous to the adjusted basis used in computing gain or loss realized on sales of non-inventory items. The Tax Court recognized this distinction in *Californians Helping to Alleviate Medical Problems, Inc. v. Commissioner*, 128 T.C. 173 (2007). It let the taxpayer offset the cost of goods sold (COGS) against sales revenue, but it did not let it deduct any other outlays for its marijuana business. In *Patients Mutual Assistance Collective Corp. v. Commissioner*, 151 T.C. 176 (2018), it limited the taxpayer's COGS to the price it paid for its inventory and the transportation and other costs incurred in acquiring the marijuana. It could not include indirect costs in its COGS because that would provide a way around the nondeductibility of those outlays.

D. Expenses with a Business Connection

1. Qualified Business Income Deduction

Section 199A, enacted in 2017, purports to reduce the disparity in rates between businesses that are incorporated (21% top rate) and those that are not (37% top rate). It lets unincorporated taxpayers deduct the smaller of two amounts. The first is the taxpayer's combined qualified business income; the second is 20% of the excess of his taxable income over his net capital gain. To reach combined qualified business income, the taxpayer considers each of his qualified businesses and also adds 20% of his aggregate qualified dividends from real estate investment trusts (REITs) and qualified publicly traded partnership (PTP) income. I.R.C. § 199A(b)(1). The discussion below ignores REIT and PTP income.

Qualified business income is the smaller of two amounts. The first is 20% of his qualified business income from a qualified trade or business. The second is the greater of 50% of the W-2 wages from that business or 25% of those wages plus 2.5% of the unadjusted basis immediately after his acquisition of all qualified property. I.R.C. § 199A(b)(2). Only tangible depreciable property is considered qualified property. I.R.C. § 199A(b)(6). Property ceases to be qualified when it has reached the end of its depreciable period (the later of the last day of the year when its § 168 recovery period ends or 10 years after it is placed in service), is no longer held by the qualified business at the end of the taxable year, or is not used during the taxable year in the production of qualified business income. I.R.C. § 199A(b)(6). Note the language describing qualified property. The taxpayer computes 2.5% of its unadjusted basis immediately after acquisition; the taxpayer does not annually reduce the amount he determined to reflect subsequent depreciation deductions.

So-called specified service businesses are ineligible for this deduction. That provision eliminates businesses involving the performance of services in the fields of health, law, accounting, actuarial science, performing arts, consulting, athletics, financial services, or brokerage services. It also eliminates any business whose principal asset is the reputation or skill of at least one of its employees, any business that involves investing or investment management, trading, or dealing in securities, partnerships, or commodities. I.R.C. § 199A(d)(2). A specified service business may nevertheless qualify for this deduction if the taxpayer's taxable income for the year is less than the sum of a threshold amount plus $50,000 ($100,000 on a joint return). But only a percentage of the taxpayer's qualified items can be considered in computing qualified business income, W-2 wages, and unadjusted basis. I.R.C. § 199A(d)(3). The § 199A(e)(2) threshold amount is indexed for inflation; for 2020, it is $163,300 ($326,600 on a joint return). The § 199A(d)(3)(B) applicable percentage begins at 100%. It is reduced (but not below zero) by the percentage that equals the ratio that the taxpayer's taxable income minus the threshold amount bears to $50,000 ($100,000 on a joint return).

2. Depreciation, Depletion, and Amortization

A taxpayer usually cannot deduct a capital expenditure in the year he acquires it. I.R.C. § 263(a)(1). If the property qualifies, he can depreciate its cost over its useful life. I.R.C. § 167. The depreciation deduction is available only for property that is used in a trade or business or that is held for the production of income. The property must be subject to exhaustion, wear and tear, or obsolescence. For example, land is not depreciable but improvements to land are depreciable. Because depreciation is computed using a formula, the deduction is for an "allowance" for depreciation rather than for the actual decline in value. Property that is subject to wear and tear when used may be depreciable even though it is also a collector's item and does not decline in value. *Simon v. Commissioner*, 68 F.3d 41 (2d Cir. 1995) (19th-century violin bows).

Although § 167 authorizes the depreciation deduction, the actual computations are governed by § 168. Its heading reads "Accelerated Cost Recovery System" (ACRS). IRS guidance usually refers to the Modified Accelerated Cost Recovery System (MACRS) to reflect amendments to § 168 that occurred after its enactment. MACRS has two components: the General Depreciation System (GDS) and the § 168(g) Alternative Depreciation System (ADS). The discussion below focuses on the GDS, which provides more rapid depreciation than the ADS. It ignores additional depreciation incentives that Congress enacts from time to time to spur economic growth or as relief measures. For example, § 168(k) (bonus depreciation) lets the taxpayer deduct 100% of the cost of qualifying property placed in service after September 27, 2017, and before January 1, 2023. Smaller percentages apply to later years: 80% for 2023; 60% for 2024; 40% for 2025; and 20% for 2026. This deduction is taken before any deduction for GDS depreciation. Unless Congress extends it, § 168(k) does not apply to most property acquired after 2026. As a general rule, property qualifies for this deduction if it has a 20-year or shorter recovery period. The Tax Cuts and Jobs Act of 2017 extended this benefit to used property. Previously, the original use had to begin with the taxpayer.

a. Applicable Method, Recovery Period, and Convention

Section 168(a) uses three terms of art. The applicable depreciation method reflects the formula used to allocate depreciation over the asset's life. The applicable recovery period is the asset's assigned life; it is not necessarily its actual useful life. The applicable convention is a statutory method for determining when the taxpayer acquired or disposed of the asset. The actual date of acquisition or disposition is not used in computing depreciation.

Applicable depreciation method. The applicable depreciation method depends on the type of property. Most tangible personal property uses the 200 percent declining balance method. Most real property uses the straight line method. Some property uses the 150 percent declining balance method, which has the same methodology as the 200 percent declining balance method but uses a slower rate. Because salvage value is ignored, we depreciate the asset's total cost or other basis. I.R.C. § 168(b).

If the asset's cost is spread equally over its recovery period, the taxpayer is using straight line as the applicable method. Although straight line depreciation is the easiest to calculate, it is probably not his preferred method. Because of time value of money principles, he usually benefits from taking higher deductions in the asset's earlier years even though he will have lower deductions in the future. The aggregate deduction is the same for all methods.

The 200 percent declining balance method is based on doubling the straight line rate. The doubled rate is applied each year to the asset's adjusted basis. Because it is impossible for this method to result in deducting his original basis within the assigned recovery period, a taxpayer using declining balance switches to the straight line method when it yields a larger deduction. I.R.C. § 168(b)(1)(B).

Applicable recovery period. The straight line rate (and, by derivation, the declining balance rate) depends on the asset's recovery period. Most tangible personal property is 3-year, 5-year, or 7-year property. Residential rental real estate has a recovery period of 27.5 years; nonresidential real property has a recovery period of 39 years. Other recovery periods range from 10 to 50 years. I.R.C. § 168(c).

If property is 5-year property, its straight line rate is 20% because each year is one-fifth (20%) of its life. If it is 7-year property, its straight line rate is approximately 14.3%. The 200 percent declining balance rates for those items would be 40% and 28.6%, respectively. Real property is depreciated using the straight line method; the relevant percentages for each year are approximately 3.6% (27.5-year life) or 2.6% (39-year life).

Applicable convention. Instead of counting the actual days he owned the property in the year he acquired it, the taxpayer applies a convention. I.R.C. § 168(d). If he acquires real property, he uses the mid-month convention. The property is treated as acquired (or disposed of) on the middle day of the relevant month. For tangible personal property, he usually uses the half-year convention. Property is treated as acquired (or disposed of) at the mid-point of the year. The otherwise allowable deduction is halved in the year of acquisition and the year of disposition.

A second applicable convention is applied to tangible personal property to prevent abuse. Because the half-year convention treats the taxpayer as owning the asset for half of the year, he might be tempted to place property in service at year-end but claim depreciation for a full six months. If he places in service during the last three months of the year more than 40% of the basis of the tangible personal property he placed in service that year, he uses the mid-quarter convention instead of the half-year convention. I.R.C. § 168(d)(3). Property acquired during the year is treated as acquired on the middle day of the relevant calendar quarter.

> **Example 12-18.** Amy acquired Machine #1 on April 10 (cost $100,000) and Machine #2 on December 1 (cost $300,000). Because she acquired more than 40% of her tangible personal property in the last three months of the year, she must use the mid-quarter convention. She is treated as acquiring Machine #1 on May 15 and Machine #2 on November 15.

b. Computing Declining Balance Depreciation

After determining the relevant depreciation method, recovery period, and convention, the taxpayer computes depreciation. He can mathematically compute the amount, or he can use the tables in Rev. Proc. 87-57, 1987-2 C.B. 687. These methods provide identical results. If you compute depreciation mathematically, apply the applicable percentage to the *adjusted* basis; you are applying a constant rate to a declining balance. If you use the IRS method, apply the table percentages to the *original* basis; you are applying a declining rate to a constant balance. Both methods switch to straight line to ensure deducting the full cost within the applicable recovery period.

The example below illustrates the declining balance method. It ignores §§ 168(k) and 179.

Example 12-19. In February of Year 1, Art paid $15,000 for a truck that is 5-year property. If this is the only property he acquired this year, he uses the half-year convention. Because the straight line rate is 20%, the 200 percent declining balance rate is 40%. He deducts the following amounts of depreciation in the first four years: Year 1, $3,000 ($15,000 cost multiplied by 40% and multiplied by .5 because of the half-year convention); Year 2, $4,800 (($15,000 cost minus $3,000 Year 1 depreciation) multiplied by 40%): Year 3, $2,880 (($15,000 cost minus $7,800 Year 1 and Year 2 depreciation) multiplied by 40%); Year 4, $1,728 (($15,000 cost minus $10,680 Year 1, Year 2, and Year 3 depreciation) multiplied by 40%).

At this point, Art has deducted depreciation for 3.5 years of the truck's life. If he continues using declining balance depreciation, he deducts $1,036.80 in Year 5 and $311.04 in Year 6. The amount in Year 6 is half the normal amount to reflect that he deducted half a year's depreciation in Year 1. The Year 5 and Year 6 amounts total $1,347.84, which is less than the $2,592 adjusted basis at the end of Year 4. To deduct the truck's full cost in the remaining 1.5 years, he switches to the straight line method in Years 5 and 6. He divides the truck's remaining $2,592 basis by the 1.5 years remaining; this gives straight line depreciation of $1,728. He deducts $1,728 in Year 5 and $864 in Year 6. That totals $2,592.

If Art uses Table 1 from Rev. Proc. 87-57, he multiplies his $15,000 basis by .20 in Year 1 ($3,000), by .32 in Year 2 ($4,800), by .192 in Year 3 ($2,880), by .1152 in Year 4 ($1,728) and in Year 5 ($1,728), and by .0576 ($864) in Year 6. Each computation method gives the same results.

c. First-Year Expensing

Section 179(a) lets taxpayers elect to expense the cost of certain property in the first year instead of depreciating that cost. This deduction is generally available only for § 1245 property that is acquired by purchase for use in the active conduct of a trade or business. Section 1245 generally applies to tangible personal property. The taxpayer can also use this section for certain computer software (an intangible) and for qualified real property. I.R.C. § 179(d)(1). Qualified real property is currently defined as qualified improvement property. Section 168(e) defines that term as improvements to a nonresidential real property's interior made after the property was placed in service; it does not include expenditures that are attributable to enlargements, elevators and escalators, or the building's internal structural framework. Qualified real property also includes roofs, HVAC property, fire protection and alarm systems, and security systems placed in nonresidential real property after that property had been placed in service. I.R.C. § 179(e).

Section 179(b) imposes three limits; the inflation-adjusted dollar limits are halved if a married couple files separate returns. First, the taxpayer cannot treat more than a specified amount as qualifying in any given year. That amount is $1,040,000 in 2020. Second, the maximum amount is reduced dollar-for-dollar by outlays exceeding a specified dollar limit. That limit is $2,590,000 in 2020. Finally, the deduction cannot exceed the taxpayer's taxable income from the active conduct of a trade or business. He uses his aggregate business income for this limitation; he is not limited to the income from the business for which he purchases the property. Section 179(b)(3)(B) allows a carryover of potential deductions that exceed his trade or business income.

A taxpayer who cannot fully expense property because of the dollar limits can depreciate the property's remaining cost using § 168 depreciation. If he stops using property predominately in a trade or business before the end of its recovery period, he recaptures the difference between the deduction he claimed and the deduction he would have claimed using only § 168 depreciation. Reg. § 1.179-1(e).

d. Listed Property

Section 280F includes additional depreciation limits for automobiles and for property of a type generally used for entertainment, recreation, or amusement. These items are called listed property. I.R.C. § 280F(d)(4). First, § 280F(a) applies maximum dollar limits to the annual depreciation deduction for passenger automobiles. These limits are often lower than the amount computed using § 168 or § 179. As a result, the taxpayer recovers her cost over a period that exceeds its recovery period. Second, § 280F(b)(1) limits a taxpayer's ability to use the normal § 168 computations if her business use of the property does not exceed 50%. Instead of depreciating the property over its § 168(c) recovery period and using the 200 percent declining balance method, she uses the ADS method prescribed in § 168(g). This involves longer depreciation periods and the straight line method. If an employee uses listed property, § 280F(d)(3) limits her deduction unless the use is for the convenience of the employer and is required as a condition of her employment.

A taxpayer whose business use drops to 50% or less in a subsequent year recaptures the unearned amount of any prior depreciation deduction. I.R.C. §280F(b)(2). For example, if a taxpayer's qualified business use of a car drops to 40% before the end of its five-year recovery period, recapture applies. If the use instead drops to 40% in a later year, recapture does not apply.

e. Depletion and Amortization

Unlike depreciable property, natural resources do not wear out; they are removed through mining or other extraction methods, thus depleting the available property. Section 611 authorizes recovering their cost through a depletion deduction. This deduction is available for mineral deposits, oil, gas, and timber. Depletion is measured by dividing the cost of the natural resource by the total number of available units. Section 613 provides for a depletion percentage that is used for most mines, wells, and other natural deposits; §613A provides for depletion in the case of oil and gas.

Amortization is the method of cost recovery applied to intangible assets (including patents, trademarks, leaseholds, customer lists, and goodwill). Section 197 provides for deducting the cost over 15 years, beginning in the month the property is acquired. Amortization is computed using the straight line method.

3. Start-Up Expenditures

A start-up expenditure is an amount paid or incurred in connection with (1) investigating the creation or acquisition of an active trade or business; (2) creating an active trade or business; or (3) any activity engaged in for profit and for the production of income before the day on which the active trade or business begins, in anticipation of such activity becoming an active trade or business. I.R.C. §195(c). The deduction allowed by this section covers only expenses that would be deductible if the taxpayer were already in that business. Outlays for training employees, property insurance, and salaries qualify. Outlays to acquire land and buildings, machinery and equipment, or intangibles do not qualify; they are capital expenditures.

Section 195 applies to taxpayers who actually create or acquire a trade or business. If a taxpayer takes sufficient steps to indicate a profit motive, but never begins operating the business, he deducts a loss incurred in an activity entered into for profit. I.R.C. §165(c)(2). If he does not take sufficient steps to reach that level, his loss is not deductible. If he enters the business but disposes of it before fully deducting his start-up expenditures, he deducts the remaining outlays as a loss. Section 195 is elective.

The taxpayer's deduction has two components: (1) up to $5,000 that can be deducted in the year the business begins and is not subject to amortization and (2) amounts that are amortized. The $5,000 deduction phases out on a dollar-for-dollar basis if start-up expenditures exceed $50,000. I.R.C. § 195(b)(1). If, for example, he incurs $52,000 in start-up expenditures, he can claim only $3,000 without amortizing. He amortizes any remaining start-up expenditures over 180 months (15 years), beginning with the month in which the trade or business begins. A taxpayer who spends more than $5,000 may have two deductions in the year in which he begins the active conduct of his business: $5,000 and an allocable portion of the additional outlay. A taxpayer who spends $55,000 or more amortizes his entire outlay.

> **Example 12-20.** Bert spent $20,000 on start-up expenditures this year. Because he began the active conduct of his business on April 1, his amortization deduction for the $15,000 excess outlays is multiplied by 9/180 this year (and by 12/180 in most future years). He deducts $5,750 this year ($5,000 plus 9/180 of $15,000). He deducts $1,000 (12/180 of $15,000) in each of the next 14 years and $250 in the final year.

4. Moving Expenses

Section 217 allows deductions for employment-related moving expenses, but the Tax Cuts and Jobs Act of 2017 limits eligibility to self-employed individuals and to members of the military whose move is occasioned by a military order and is incident to a permanent change of station. Members of the military are not subject to the distance and work requirements discussed in the next paragraph. I.R.C. § 217(g). Unreimbursed moving expenses are deducted in computing AGI. I.R.C. § 62(a)(15).

Section 217(c) imposes distance and work requirements. The distance between the new place of work and the former residence must be at least 50 miles farther than the distance between the former place of work and the former residence. Thus, a taxpayer who commuted 10 miles to work from his former residence cannot take a moving expense deduction if his new place of work is only 30 miles from that former residence. If he has no former place of work, the new place of work must be at least 50 miles from his former residence. Self-employed individuals must satisfy a 78-week work requirement during the first two years after the move; at least 39 weeks must be in the first 12 months. The work requirement is waived in cases of death or disability. I.R.C.

§217(d)(1).

The taxpayer can deduct the expenses using his normal method of accounting. He does not have to wait until he satisfies the work requirements. If he does not take the deduction in the year the moving expenses were paid or incurred and subsequently satisfies the work requirement, he amends the tax return for the earlier year. Reg. §1.217-2(d)(2)(ii). If he claims a deduction in the year that the moving expenses were paid or incurred and subsequently fails to satisfy the work requirement, he includes the previously deducted amount as gross income in the first taxable year in which the requirement cannot be met. I.R.C. §217(d)(3).

Section 217 covers costs to move household goods and personal effects of the taxpayer and members of his household as well as traveling and lodging expenses incurred in the process of moving. I.R.C. §217(b)(1); Reg. §1.217-2(b). Costs to pack, ship, transport, insure and store (up to 30 days) are deductible; costs to break leases and losses on property sold as a result of the move are not deductible. Employer reimbursements for losses sustained on the sale of a residence as part of a move are compensation for services. *Keener v. Commissioner*, 59 T.C. 302 (1972). The cost of meals is not deductible; Reg. §1.217-2(b) has not been amended to reflect that change in the Code.

> **Example 12-21.** Barry relocated his law office to a new city. He meets the distance requirement, and he assumes he will meet the work requirement. He spent $300 for packing belongings, $3,000 for moving household goods, $1,000 for travel en route (other than meals), and $200 for meals en route. Barry can deduct the expenses for packing and moving his household goods and for travel expenses other than meals. He cannot deduct any loss on selling his old home.

5. Interest and Taxes

Interest and taxes paid by a taxpayer engaged in a trade or business would normally be §162 deductions. Because the Code includes provisions that specifically address interest (§163) and taxes (§164), those sections govern instead. The discussion of interest and taxes in Chapter 13 focuses on rules applied to taxpayers who are not engaged in a trade or business or income-producing activity.

Interest paid or accrued on indebtedness properly allocable to a trade or business is not nondeductible personal interest. I.R.C. §163(h)(2)(A). The interest *is* nondeductible personal interest if the trade or business is performing services as an employee.

Section 163(j), as enacted in 2017, limits the deduction for interest paid or incurred in a trade or business. It cannot exceed the sum of the taxpayer's business interest income, 30% of his adjusted taxable income (ignoring negative adjusted taxable income), and his floor plan financing interest (interest paid or incurred on debt to finance motor vehicles held for sale or lease and secured by those vehicles). I.R.C. § 163(j)(1). He can carry excess interest expense forward; it will retain its character as business interest. I.R.C. § 163(j)(2).

Congress made two amendments to § 163(j) in response to the COVID-19 pandemic. First, the 30% limit is increased to 50% for 2019 and 2020. Second, taxpayers can elect to use 2019 income instead of 2020 income in computing their deduction limit. The latter provision responds to the likelihood that a taxpayer's business will be less successful in 2020 than it was in 2019. I.R.C. § 163(j)(10).

Section 163(j) does not apply to taxpayers that meet the § 448(c) gross receipts test (average annual gross receipts over the preceding three years of $25 million or less). The definitions of business interest income and interest expense refer to items properly allocable to a trade or business and do not include § 163(d) investment interest income or expense. I.R.C. § 163(j)(5)–(6). To reach adjusted taxable income, the taxpayer begins with taxable income and deletes income and deductions not properly allocable to a trade or business, business interest income and expense, any net operating loss deduction, any § 199A deduction, and (for years beginning before 2022) any depreciation, amortization, or depletion deduction. I.R.C. § 163(j)(8).

A taxpayer engaged in a trade or business is not limited to deducting the taxes specifically enumerated in § 164(a). If, however, the taxes are paid in connection with the acquisition or disposition of property, they are not deductible expenses. They are part of the cost of acquisition or disposition. I.R.C. § 164(a) (flush language).

E. Significance of Employee Status

Section 162 does not distinguish between an employer and an employee. Both are engaged in trade or business activities. Before 2018, both could deduct their ordinary and necessary expenses although an employee had a more difficult time in establishing that an outlay was ordinary and necessary unless it was required by her employer or by a licensing authority.

1. Expenses Deducted in Computing AGI

A self-employed taxpayer deducts business expenses in computing AGI. That general rule does not apply to an employee. Section 62(a)(2) and (13) lists employee business expenses that are deductible in computing AGI. If a deductible expense is not listed in §62, an employee cannot currently deduct it. Before 2018, she could deduct items not listed in §62 if she itemized.

Reimbursed expenses are listed in §62(a)(2)(A) as deductible in computing AGI. An employee cannot deduct an expense (for AGI or as an itemized deduction) if she voluntarily forgoes requesting an available reimbursement. In that situation, the expense is not ordinary and necessary. *Heidt v. Commissioner*, 274 F.2d 25 (7th Cir. 1959).

2. Phase-Outs and Deduction Limitations

Employee business expenses that are not allowed in computing AGI are miscellaneous itemized deductions. Until 2018, total miscellaneous itemized deductions were allowed only to the extent they exceeded 2% of AGI. I.R.C. §67(a). This limitation made it difficult for employees to benefit significantly from unreimbursed outlays. No deduction is available for miscellaneous itemized deductions paid or incurred in 2018 through 2025. I.R.C. §67(g).

Assuming these deductions become allowable again in 2026 (if not sooner), note that several deduction provisions impose stricter requirements on employees than they do on business owners. An employee can deduct expenses for a home office only if the use is for the convenience of the employer. This requirement is in addition to the other requirements for deducting home offices. As noted above, the listed property rules apply more stringently to employees than to self-employed taxpayers. In addition, indebtedness related to an employee's business outlays is personal indebtedness; interest paid on that debt is not deductible. I.R.C. §163(h)(2)(A). When a Code section allows a deduction for taxpayers engaged in a trade or business, read it carefully to see if it excludes rendering services as an employee.

F. Section 212 Expenses

Section 212 lets individuals deduct expenses in two settings: (1) for the production or collection of income; and (2) for the management, conservation, or maintenance of property held for the production of income. Prior to 2018, individuals could also deduct expenses in connection with the determination, collection, or refund of any tax. The first two items are discussed in this section. Section 212(3) is discussed in Chapter 13.

The discussion below is currently relevant for taxpayers whose expenses relate to property held for the production of rents and royalties. Expenses to produce other types of income, such as interest and dividends are miscellaneous itemized deductions and not allowed in 2018 through 2025.

Section 212 repeats much of the language from § 162(a)—the outlay must be an expense, it must be ordinary and necessary, and it must be paid or incurred during the taxable year. Congress enacted the predecessor of current §212(1)–(2) in 1942 in response to situations exemplified by *Higgins v. Commissioner*, 312 U.S. 212 (1941). Mr. Higgins deducted expenses associated with the oversight of his financial interests, including hiring assistants to manage his extensive holdings. The assistants maintained his records, received securities, interest, and dividend checks, made deposits, and reviewed investment decisions. Under the applicable statute, only trade or business expenses were deductible. The Court held that his activities did not constitute a trade or business and disallowed his deductions.

The outlays in *Higgins* were clearly for the production of income or for the management, conservation, or maintenance of property held for the production of income. They would be allowed by § 212 (but not in 2018 through 2025, when miscellaneous itemized deductions are disallowed). As the Fourth Circuit stated in 1944: "The purpose of this amendment was to permit deductions for certain non-trade and non-business expenses and thereby enlarge the allowable deduction for expenses which under previous revenue acts had been confined to expenses paid or incurred in carrying on any trade or business." *Bowers v. Lumpkin*, 140 F.2d 927, 928 (4th Cir. 1944).

Potential deductions include fees for investment counsel, custodial fees, clerical help, office rent, and similar expenses that are ordinary and necessary under the circumstances. Reg. § 1.212-1(g). Nondeductible items include outlays for special courses or training, improving the taxpayer's personal appearance, renting a safe-deposit box for storing jewelry, or seeking employment or securing the right to practice a profession. Reg. § 1.212-1(f). Depreciation is allowed for property that is subject to wear, tear, and obsolescence.

1. Interpretive Issues

Section 212 has not escaped litigation regarding its meaning. For example, what constitutes "for the production of income" or "management of property held for the production of income"? In *Surasky v. United States*, 325 F.2d 191 (5th Cir. 1963), the owner of a large amount of a corporation's stock deducted the cost of attempting to elect new board members in a proxy fight. He believed such action would eventually render the corporation more profitable. Reversing the trial court, which had focused on the speculative nature of the endeavor, the Fifth Circuit allowed the deduction. It held that Congress intended to allow deductions for expenses incurred in the exercise of reasonable business judgment in an attempt to produce income.

Deductibility is not contingent upon success. It is contingent upon exercising reasonable business judgment in an attempt to produce income. In Rev. Rul. 64-236, 1964-2 C.B. 64, the IRS conceded that expenditures related to proxy fights are deductible if the expenditures are proximately related to the production or collection of income, or are for the management, conservation, or maintenance of property held for the production of income. Because "income" includes profit, expenditures made with the anticipation of profit are likewise covered by § 212. Reg. § 1.212-1(b).

2. Litigation Expenses

Another common issue is the deductibility of expenses incurred during litigation. Many of these cases involve taxpayers who are divorcing. In *Fleischman v. Commissioner*, 45 T.C. 439 (1966), the taxpayer deducted legal expenses incurred in defending his wife's attempt to set aside their antenuptial agreement. The Tax Court rejected his arguments that the expenses were paid for the management, conservation, or maintenance of property held for the production of income. Citing to *United States v. Gilmore*, 372 U.S. 39 (1963), it held that legal expenses incurred in defending property rights in a divorce proceeding are personal expenses. The origin of the claim being litigated was the marital relationship and not an income-producing activity.

3. Reason for Holding Property

The issue of whether property is held for the production of income often arises in the context of vacation property, second homes, and property formerly used as a principal residence. *Lowry v. United States*, 384 F. Supp. 257 (D.N.H. 1974), involved when and how residential property is converted into income-producing property. The taxpayers abandoned their summer residence and immediately listed it for sale. During the next six years, they deducted maintenance expenses. They claimed the property was held for the production of income, namely a profit on its sale. The district court adopted the reasoning of the Tax Court in *Newcombe v. Commissioner*, 54 T.C. 1298 (1970). The critical question was whether they had a real expectation of profit. It identified several factors that are significant in that determination: (1) the length of time the taxpayer occupied the residence prior to abandonment; (2) its availability for his personal use while it was unoccupied; (3) its recreational character; (4) attempts to rent it; and (5) whether the offer to sell was an attempt to realize post-conversion appreciation.

Both cases involved taxpayers who offered their properties for sale but not for rent. Offering the property for rent strengthens the argument that the property is held for the production of income. Even if taxpayers can deduct maintenance expenses and depreciation, they may be unable to deduct a loss realized on selling the property. In *Cowles v. Commissioner*, T.C. Memo. 1970-198, the court held that "mere offers to sell or rent are insufficient to provide the necessary foundation for the deduction of a loss incurred in a 'transaction entered into for profit.'" Section 165(c)(2) uses that term rather than "held for the production of income."

4. Deduction Limitations

Although § 212 contains no formal limitation provisions, many such provisions apply. Congress enacted § 212 to authorize deductions for taxpayers who were not engaged in a business, not to place them in a better position than taxpayers who were. As a result, courts interpret § 212 to include limitations applied to § 162. For example, if a taxpayer hires an employee to manage his rental property, he cannot deduct any portion of the employee's salary that is unreasonable in amount. Likewise, if a business would treat an outlay as a capital expenditure instead of as an expense, an income-producing activity must also treat it as a capital expenditure.

Some Code sections treat income-producing activities less favorably than they treat business activities. For example, the § 179 expensing election is available only to taxpayers engaged in a trade or business. Section 163(d) limits a taxpayer's deductions for interest paid or accrued on indebtedness that is properly allocable to investment property. He deducts investment interest expense only to the extent his investment income exceeds his other investment expenses. Although capital gains and dividends are normally considered investment income, he cannot include them in computing investment income if he takes advantage of the lower tax rates for net capital gains and qualified dividends. Section 163(d)(2) lets taxpayers carry disallowed investment interest over for deduction in a future year. That interest is subject to the same limits in the later years.

Pay close attention to the language of Code provisions to determine which apply only to trade or business activities and which also apply to income-producing activities or to transactions entered into for profit.

G. Expenses to Produce Tax-Exempt Income

Section 265 disallows deductions associated with producing income that is exempt from tax. It prevents a taxpayer from receiving a double benefit—deducting the costs of producing income that is not taxed. Section 265(a)(1) applies to deductions allocable to income other than interest income. If the income is exempt from income tax, the deduction is not allowed. This limitation applies to all types of deduction—business, income-producing, and personal. For example, it disallows attorney fees to produce an award for personal physical injuries excluded by § 104(a)(2) or to obtain a property settlement that does not qualify as taxable alimony. Section 265(a)(6) provides an exception for taxpayers who receive tax-exempt military housing allowances and parsonage allowances. They can deduct home mortgage interest and real property taxes even if they use their tax-exempt allowances to pay these expenses. Section 265(a)(1) also applies to deductions that would be allowed by § 212 but that are allocable to interest that is exempt from income tax. Finally, § 265(a)(2) disallows deducting interest on debt incurred or continued so that the taxpayer can purchase or carry tax-exempt bonds. If any of these expenses is a miscellaneous itemized deduction, it would be disallowed in 2018 through 2025 even if there were no § 265.

H. Tax Credits

Because deductions reduce taxable income, their value depends on the taxpayer's marginal tax rate. A credit, on the other hand, reduces the tax that is due. A dollar of credit is worth a dollar. The Code includes several tax credits for outlays incurred in a business or income-producing activity. It also includes credits that are related to those activities. The first group includes credits for investing in particular types of property, hiring particular groups of individuals, or providing various benefits for employees during the COVID-19 pandemic. This chapter does not discuss those items. Four credits in the second group are briefly described below.

1. Household and Dependent Care Expenses

The credit for household and dependent care expenses, discussed in Chapter 3 in the context of an employer's dependent care assistance program, is allowed only if the taxpayer is engaged in a trade or business, including as an employee. Section 21 allows a credit for household service or care expenditures for a qualifying individual that are incurred to let the taxpayer continue working. A qualifying individual is a qualifying child who is under age 13 or a mentally or physically impaired dependent or spouse of the taxpayer.

To qualify, the taxpayer must pay at least half of the cost of maintaining a household in which the qualifying individual resides. The credit is between 20% and 35% of the expenses incurred in the qualifying individual's care. The credit percentage drops, but not below 20%, as the taxpayer's AGI increases. The maximum qualifying expenses are $3,000 for one qualifying individual and $6,000 for two or more qualifying individuals. Thus, the maximum credit ranges from $600 to $1,050 for one qualifying individual and from $1,200 to $2,100 for more than one qualifying individual.

2. Earned Income Tax Credit

The goal of the § 32 earned income tax credit is to encourage low-income taxpayers to work rather than depend on public assistance. The credit is equal to a percentage of the taxpayer's earned income and is affected by whether he has children. The credit is phased out as his income increases. The calculation of this credit is more complex than many tax calculations, which is unfortunate given its target beneficiaries.

To qualify for this credit, a taxpayer must have earned income and must not receive more than $3,650 (in 2020, as adjusted for inflation) in investment income. He must not be another taxpayer's dependent, must be a U.S. citizen or resident, and, if married, must file a joint return.

A taxpayer with no qualifying children must be at least 25 years old and less than 65 years old. His maximum credit is $538 for 2020, as adjusted for inflation. It is phased out over an AGI range that begins at $8,790 ($14,680 for taxpayers who file a joint return). The maximum 2020 credits for taxpayers with qualifying children range from $3,584 (one child) to $6,660 (three or more children). These amounts are also subject to phase-outs.

There is no minimum or maximum age for claiming the credit if the taxpayer has a qualifying child. A qualifying child can be either a son, daughter, stepchild, adopted child, foster child, or a descendant of the taxpayer or a brother, sister, stepbrother, stepsister, or a descendant of a brother, sister, stepbrother, or stepsister. The qualifying child must be 18 or younger as of the end of the year or be a full-time student who is younger than 24. A person who is permanently and totally disabled at any time during the year can be a qualifying child regardless of his age. The qualifying child must be a U.S. resident and live with the taxpayer for more than half of the year.

3. Credit for Retirement Savings

Section 25B allows a credit for contributions to a retirement account. The maximum annual credit is based on a percentage of $2,000 (or lesser amount the taxpayer contributes to the account). The credit percentage ranges from 0% to 50% to reflect a phase-out based on the taxpayer's AGI and filing status. The income levels used are inflation-adjusted. This credit is not available to taxpayers who are under age 18, dependents, or full-time students.

4. Foreign Tax Credit

The Code includes several relief provisions for taxpayers who earn income that might be subject to tax in both the United States and another country. Chapter 10 discusses the exclusions for foreign earned income and employer-provided housing allowances. Those exclusions have residence and source requirements. Chapter 13 covers the deduction available for foreign income taxes; those deductions are generally available only if the taxpayer itemizes deductions. Section 901 provides a third relief provision: the credit for foreign income taxes. Because taxpayers cannot use the exclusion, deduction, and credit with respect to the same income, they must compute the relative value of each benefit.

The foreign tax credit cannot exceed whichever of two amounts is smaller: the actual foreign tax or the U.S. tax attributable to the foreign income. The computation is made using a ratio comparing the foreign-source income to the taxpayer's entire taxable income. I.R.C. § 904(a). Unlike the deduction, which treats all foreign income taxes alike, the credit is separately computed on passive and active income. I.R.C. § 904(d). The taxpayer can carry over credits he is unable to use in a given year. I.R.C. § 904(c).

Checkpoints

- Taxpayers can deduct ordinary and necessary expenses paid or incurred in carrying on a trade or business.

- A taxpayer is in a trade or business if his activity is regular and continuous and he intends to make a profit.

- An expense qualifies if, under the facts and circumstances, it would be made by other taxpayers in that business.

- Capital expenditures are not expenses. This rule applies to the initial acquisition and to improvements made after that date.

- Outlays for an existing tangible asset are capital expenditures if they are betterments, restore the property, or adapt it to a different use.

- Taxpayers deduct most expenses using their accounting method.

- Reasonable salaries are deductible; dividends disguised as salaries are not.

- Publicly traded companies are subject to additional deduction limits for compensation.

- Business travel expenses are deductible only if they are not lavish. Only 50% of reasonable meal expenses are deductible.

- If the reason for travel is partly personal, deductions for meals and lodging are limited to the business days. The deductibility of transportation expenses depends on whether the trip was primarily for business or pleasure. Additional limitations apply to foreign travel expenses.

- Commuting expenses are generally not deductible.

- Rental payments are deductible unless the rental terms are designed to disguise a capital expenditure.

- Education expenses are deductible if they maintain or improve skills in an existing business or meet requirements for retaining a position or license. They are not deductible if they qualify the taxpayer for a new trade or business.

- Expenses for business gifts and travel are subject to substantiation rules and other conditions. Congress eliminated the entertainment deduction in 2017.

- Clothing is deductible only if it is required by the job, not suited for everyday wear, and not so worn.

- Outlays to provide qualified transportation fringe benefits are not deductible. The employee excludes these benefits from gross income.

- Numerous public policy limitations reduce or eliminate deductions for expenses that might otherwise be considered ordinary and necessary.

- Section 199A allows a limited deduction for qualified business income.

- Depreciation deductions allocate an asset's cost over its useful life using formulas prescribed in the Code. Some business property may qualify for bonus depreciation or first-year expensing. Listed property is subject to more stringent rules than other business property.

- Amortization is a method for recovering the cost of intangible assets on a straight line basis; depletion is a method for recovering the cost of natural resources.

- Up to $5,000 of business start-up expenditures can be deducted in the year the business begins; additional amounts are amortized over 180 months.

- Taxpayers who meet distance and work requirements can deduct moving expenses. This deduction is not available for most employees.

- Deduction limits apply to business interest; this rule has exceptions for taxpayers with average gross income below a threshold amount.

- Employee business expense deductions are usually itemized and may be subject to additional eligibility restrictions. Those that are treated as miscellaneous itemized deductions are not deductible in 2018 through 2025.

- Section 212 allows deductions for ordinary and necessary expenses that are paid or incurred for the production or collection of income, for managing property held for the production of income, or for determining tax obligations. It is currently unavailable for outlays that would be miscellaneous itemized deductions.

- Section 212 provides deductions similar to those allowed by § 162. Some deductions are limited by their terms to taxpayers engaged in a trade or business.

- In determining whether a residence is held for the production of income, courts consider the taxpayer's use of the property, attempts to rent the property after moving out, and attempts to realize post-conversion appreciation.

- Deductions to produce tax-exempt income are generally disallowed.

- Several tax credits are allowed only if connected to a taxpayer's trade or business (including performing services as an employee).

Chapter 13

Personal Expenses

A. Introduction

This chapter covers deductions and credits that do not require a trade or business or income-producing connection. Most are for actual expenses—such as interest expense, state, local, and foreign taxes, and medical expenses. One—the standard deduction—is a statutory surrogate for expenses; it does not require actual outlays. The deductions and credits discussed below are exceptions to the rule in §262, that personal, living, or family expenses are not deductible.

We begin with a group of provisions that are deducted in computing adjusted gross income (AGI). The remaining discussion focuses on itemized deductions, the standard deduction, the currently unavailable personal exemptions, and tax credits.

221

B. Deductions in Computing AGI

Adjusted gross income (AGI) is an intermediate step in getting from gross income to taxable income. Any deduction listed in § 62(a) is deductible whether or not the taxpayer itemizes deductions. In addition, AGI or modified AGI is used in computing her eligibility for other deductions or the amount of certain deductions. Even if they normally use the accrual method of accounting, taxpayers use the cash method to report the items discussed in this section.

1. Alimony and Alimony Recapture

Chapter 10 discusses the treatment of alimony by the recipient. The payor can deduct alimony payments only if § 71(a) includes them in the recipient's gross income. This deduction is available only for divorce or separation instruments finalized by the end of 2018.

2. Education Loan Interest

Although § 163(h) disallows any deduction for personal interest expense, § 163(h)(2)(F) excepts educational interest, and § 62(a)(17) makes it deductible in computing AGI. Interest described in § 221 does not require that the underlying loan have any relationship to a trade or business.

The taxpayer must pay the interest with respect to indebtedness incurred for his own, his spouse's, or any of his dependents' attendance at an eligible educational institution. He must pay the expenses within a reasonable period before or after incurring the debt. I.R.C. § 221(d)(1). The qualifying loan cannot exceed the institution's cost of attendance reduced by amounts covering those expenses that are excluded by provisions discussed in other chapters (*e.g.*, scholarships or qualified tuition programs). I.R.C. § 221(d)(2).

The maximum deduction is $2,500 per year; that amount does not get adjusted for inflation. The potential deduction is subject to phase-out based on modified AGI. I.R.C. § 221(b). The phase-out ratio uses modified AGI minus an inflation-adjusted amount as its numerator. Its denominator is $15,000. For 2020, the phase-out begins at modified AGI of $70,000 for unmarried individuals ($140,000 for married individuals filing a joint return). Married individuals cannot take any deduction if they file separate returns. I.R.C. § 221(e)(2).

> **Example 13-1.** Arnold pays education interest expense of $3,400 in 2020. He is single and has modified AGI of $73,000. Because his modified AGI exceeds $70,000 by $3,000, he loses 20% ($3,000/$15,000)

of his potential deduction. Although he paid interest of $3,400, he can count only $2,500 in computing his allowable deduction. Because he loses 20% of the maximum potential deduction, he can deduct only $2,000. If his modified AGI had been $70,000 or less, he could have deducted $2,500.

3. Qualified Tuition and Related Expenses

Section 222 allows a deduction for tuition and fees paid for qualified educational expenses of the taxpayer, his spouse, or his dependents. This deduction requires no relationship to a trade or business, and it is allowed in computing AGI. I.R.C. §62(a)(18). It has expired and been extended several times. Unless Congress extends it again, it is not available after 2020. I.R.C. §222(e).

The maximum deduction is $4,000 per year. I.R.C. §222(b)(2)(B). If AGI exceeds $65,000 but does not exceed $80,000, the maximum deduction drops to $2,000. No deduction is allowed if AGI exceeds $80,000. Each AGI limit is doubled if the taxpayer is married and filing a joint return, but the maximum deduction amounts are not doubled. This section does not provide for inflation adjustments.

Section 222(c) provides additional eligibility rules and computations. Taxpayers cannot deduct expenses that they deduct under any other Code section or for which they claim the §25A credit. Finally, they reduce their deduction by any exclusion they claim for these expenses using government bonds, a qualified tuition program, or a Coverdell education savings account.

Section 222 uses definitions found in §25A. The expenses that qualify are those for tuition and fees required for enrollment or attendance at an eligible educational institution. I.R.C. §25A(f)(1). The §25A(f)(2) definition of eligible educational institutions encompasses colleges, universities, and other postsecondary institutions. Expenses for courses involving sports, games, or hobbies are ineligible unless the course is part of the degree program. Student activity fees, athletic fees, insurance, and other expenses that are unrelated to the course of instruction also do not qualify. Fees for books, supplies, and equipment qualify only if they must be paid as a condition of enrollment or attendance. Fees for room, board, and transportation do not qualify. I.R.C. §25A(f)(1)(B)–(C); Reg. §1.25A-2(d).

4. Contributions to Health Savings Accounts

A taxpayer who contributes to a health savings account can deduct the amount allowed by §223 in computing AGI. I.R.C. §62(a)(19). This deduction is available only to taxpayers who are insured under high-deductible health plans. Taxpayers use these plans to cover current and future medical expenses. Withdrawals—including earnings on funds in the plan—are not gross income if they are used for medical care. I.R.C. §223(f).

Inflation adjustments apply to the maximum deduction and the dollar amount that makes a plan high-deductible. I.R.C. §223(g). This deduction does not phase out based on a taxpayer's income. Section 62(a)(16) allows a deduction in computing AGI for contributions to a §220 Archer medical savings account. These plans operate much like plans covered by §223.

These plans offer several potential tax benefits. Deductible contributions reduce the taxpayer's gross income and AGI. Earnings on plan funds are not taxed as they accumulate. Contributions and earnings are not taxed when withdrawn to pay medical expenses. Because §213 reduces any potential medical expense deduction as the taxpayer's AGI rises, and because that deduction requires the taxpayer to itemize, using HSA funds avoids those limitations. Unlike the use-it-or-lose-it flexible spending plans covered in Chapter 3, funds in HSA plans carry forward throughout the account holder's life. Note that numerous exceptions and special rules govern these plans.

5. Charitable Contributions

As discussed in Section E, charitable contributions are an allowable deduction for taxpayers who itemize their deductions. Legislation enacted in response to COVID-19 lets individuals deduct up to $300 of qualified charitable contributions made in 2020 in computing AGI. I.R.C. §62(a)(22). This deduction is available even for contributions made before this change was enacted. It is not available to individuals who itemize, and it is limited to cash contributions. I.R.C. §62(f).

C. Interest Expense

Section 163(a) allows a deduction for interest paid or accrued during the taxable year. In Rev. Rul. 69-188, 1969-1 C.B. 54, the IRS defined interest as "compensation for the use or forbearance of money per se and not a payment for specific services which the lender performs in connection with the borrower's account." Thus, a payment might not qualify even if the parties label it as interest and might qualify even if they call it something else. If a loan does not provide for adequate interest, §7872 imputes interest income to the lender and may provide a deduction for the borrower.

If the Code did not include § 163(a), taxpayers engaged in a trade or business or income-producing activity could still deduct interest expense. They would use §§ 162(a) and 212(1)–(2) as authority for their deductions. Although § 163(a) is broadly worded, it is limited by § 163(h), which prevents a noncorporate taxpayer from deducting personal interest. One exception to this categorization, the deduction for educational loan interest, is discussed in Section B. The discussion below focuses on the § 163(h)(2)(D) exception for qualified residence interest.

1. Qualified Residence

There are two types of qualified residence interest: interest paid or accrued on acquisition indebtedness and interest paid or accrued on home equity indebtedness. Each type of indebtedness must be with respect to a qualified residence. I.R.C. § 163(h)(3)(A). Only two residences can be qualified residences during any taxable year—the principal residence and one other residence that the taxpayer uses as a residence during the taxable year. I.R.C. § 163(h)(4)(A). Chapter 6 discusses principal residence; Chapter 15 discusses the concept of "used as a residence."

> Example 13-2. Alicia has three residences—her principal residence, a lakeside vacation home, and a condominium near a ski resort. Each is subject to a mortgage. Assuming all other requirements are met, she can deduct interest on the loans covering her principal residence and one of the other residences. She can select between the other residences each year.

2. Acquisition and Home Equity Indebtedness

Acquisition indebtedness must be secured by the residence *and* be incurred in acquiring, constructing, or substantially improving the qualified residence. I.R.C. § 163(h)(3)(B)(i). Although a taxpayer who constructs a residence lives elsewhere during the construction period, the indebtedness qualifies for up to 24 months if the residence becomes a qualified residence when it is ready to be occupied. Temp. Reg. § 1.163-10T(p)(5). If she later refinances acquisition indebtedness, the new debt also qualifies, but only up to the amount of debt it replaced.

> Example 13-3. Arabella purchased her only residence for $280,000 in 2015; it is now worth $425,000. She made a $50,000 down payment

and borrowed the remaining $230,000 with a loan that qualifies as acquisition indebtedness. She made monthly payments that reduced the loan balance to $204,000. If she refinances the loan and borrows $210,000, only $204,000 of the new loan is acquisition indebtedness. It is irrelevant that the new loan does not exceed the *original* loan amount.

No matter how much the taxpayer borrows, limits apply to the amount that can be treated as acquisition indebtedness. That amount varies based on when the taxpayer incurred the indebtedness. For indebtedness incurred before 2018 or after 2025, the maximum amount is $1 million. I.R.C. § 163(h)(3)(B)(ii). For indebtedness incurred in 2018 through 2025, the maximum amount is $750,000. I.R.C. § 163(h)(3)(F)(i)(II). The relevant limit applies in the aggregate, not per residence. If the taxpayer is married and files a separate return, the annual limit is halved even if the other spouse takes no deduction. *Bronstein v. Commissioner*, 138 T.C. 382 (2012). The limit is not halved if the two co-owners are not married to each other. *Voss v. Commissioner*, 796 F.3d 1051 (9th Cir. 2015); the IRS has acquiesced in that decision. AOD 2016-02.

Home equity indebtedness must be secured by a qualified residence, but the taxpayer can spend the borrowed funds for any purpose. I.R.C. § 163(h)(3)(C). If the indebtedness was incurred before 2018 or after 2025, the maximum qualifying amount is whichever amount is smaller: $100,000 or the excess of the property's value over any acquisition indebtedness secured by that property. That limit is halved if the taxpayer is married and filing a separate return. No deduction is allowed for interest paid on home equity indebtedness incurred between 2018 and 2025. I.R.C. § 163(h)(3)(F)(i)(I).

> **Example 13-4.** Bert borrowed $125,000 in 2016 to pay credit card debt. The loan is secured by his principal residence. The residence is worth $500,000 and is not subject to any acquisition indebtedness. Only $100,000 of Bert's loan qualifies as home equity indebtedness. He cannot deduct interest he pays on the $25,000 that does not qualify. If his principal residence had been subject to $410,000 of acquisition indebtedness when he borrowed the $125,000, only $90,000 of the new loan would qualify as home equity indebtedness. If Bert had instead borrowed the $125,000 in 2018, he could not deduct any of the interest on that debt.

If a taxpayer borrows more than the limit on qualified acquisition indebtedness, up to $100,000 of the excess debt may qualify as home equity indebtedness (assuming the indebtedness was incurred before 2018 or after

2025). Rev. Rul. 2010-25, 2010-44 I.R.B. 571. The IRS does not follow a Tax Court decision holding that such excess debt could not qualify because it was incurred to acquire, purchase, or substantially improve the residence and therefore was acquisition indebtedness even though it exceeded the $1 million limitation. *Pau v. Commissioner*, T.C. Memo. 1997-43.

> **Example 13-5.** Bess purchased her only residence for $1,450,000 in 2017. She made a $50,000 down payment and borrowed the remaining $1,400,000. The loan is secured by the residence. She can deduct interest with respect to $1,100,000 of this loan: $1 million is acquisition indebtedness and $100,000 is home equity indebtedness. Interest paid with respect to the remaining $300,000 debt is nondeductible personal interest. If Bess had purchased her home in 2020, she can deduct interest with respect to only $750,000 of her loan.

If a taxpayer refinances a qualifying loan, the new loan takes on the characteristics of the original loan. Two exceptions apply. First, the amount treated as a replacement for the original loan cannot exceed the amount refinanced. Second, the refinanced debt takes on the characteristics of the original loan only until the end of the original loan term. If the original loan was not being amortized over its term (perhaps it carried interest only, with a balloon payment of principal due at a set date), the new loan qualifies only until the earlier of two dates: the date on which the first refinancing expires or 30 years after the date of the first refinancing. I.R.C. § 163(h)(3)(F)(iii).

3. Mortgage Insurance

A lender may require that the borrower obtain mortgage insurance before making a loan. This insurance protects the lender if the borrower defaults when the home, which will be repossessed, is worth less than the loan balance. Although such insurance is not interest, § 163(h)(3)(E) treats insurance premiums paid with respect to acquisition indebtedness as qualified residence interest. The deduction phases out for taxpayers whose AGI exceeds $100,000 (halved for married taxpayers filing separate returns). Unless extended by Congress, this deduction is not available for premiums paid or accrued after 2020.

4. Points

Taxpayers may pay points to obtain a lower interest rate. Each point, which is 1% of the amount borrowed, is prepaid interest. Because the lower interest rate is a future benefit, the borrower cannot deduct the points in the year he pays them. Instead he allocates them over the loan term. I.R.C. §461(g)(1).

Section 461(g)(2) lets a cash-method taxpayer deduct points in the year she pays them. It applies to loans incurred in connection with the purchase or improvement of her principal residence. The loan must be secured by the residence, payment of points must be an established business practice in that locale, and the points must not exceed the amount generally charged. Section 461(g)(2) does not apply to accrual-method taxpayers or to loans to purchase or improve a secondary residence. It applies to home equity loans only if the proceeds are used to purchase or improve the principal residence. The taxpayer must actually pay the points when she borrows the funds. If the lender simply increases the loan amount, she has not actually paid them. In that case, she deducts them over the life of the loan as she repays her lender. *Cathcart v. Commissioner*, T.C. Memo. 1977-328.

> **Example 13-6.** Alina borrowed $150,000 to purchase her principal residence; the loan is secured by the residence. Taxpayers routinely pay points in her locale. Because she paid 2 points ($3,000), she could borrow at 5% instead of 5.25%. If she uses the cash method, she deducts the $3,000 in the year she pays the points. If she uses the accrual method, she deducts the $3,000 over the life of the loan.

One court allowed points paid on a refinanced loan to qualify for immediate deduction. *Huntsman v. Commissioner*, 905 F.2d 1182 (8th Cir. 1990). The taxpayers purchased the residence with a three-year loan and obtained permanent, longer-term financing before the three years elapsed. They paid points on the new loan. The court focused on the statutory language, which allowed the deduction for points on indebtedness incurred "in connection with" the purchase or improvement. If the statute had applied to indebtedness incurred "to" purchase or improve, it might have held differently. The IRS follows this opinion only in the Eighth Circuit. AOD 1991-02.

D. State, Local, and Foreign Taxes

Section 164(a) allows a deduction for certain state, local, and foreign taxes paid or accrued during the taxable year. If the Code did not include this section, taxpayers engaged in a trade or business or an income-producing activity would deduct taxes as an ordinary and necessary expense of those activities. The section's primary beneficiaries are taxpayers engaged in personal activities.

1. Real Property Taxes

Section 164(a)(1) lets a taxpayer deduct state, local, and foreign real property taxes paid or accrued during the taxable year. (Foreign real property taxes are not deductible in 2018 through 2025. I.RC. § 164(b)(6)(A).) The two-residence limit applied to qualified residence interest does not apply to real property taxes. Reg. § 1.164-3(b) defines real property taxes as "taxes imposed on interests in real property and levied for the general public welfare . . . ." An assessment for local benefits that increases the value of the taxpayer's property does not qualify. I.R.C. § 164(c)(1). These include street, sidewalk, and local improvements. Reg. § 1.164-4(a).

Cooperative apartment corporations are more common in some parts of the country than in others. Although they have many of the characteristics of condominiums, ownership of the underlying property is a major difference. Tenant-stockholders do not directly own their property. Instead they own shares of stock in the corporation that owns the apartments. They deduct their proportionate share of the corporation's real property taxes. I.R.C. § 216(a)(1).

If real property has multiple owners, each should pay his respective share of the property tax. But it is possible that one owner will pay more than her share. Reg. § 1.164-1(a) (flush language) provides that the taxes are deductible by the person on whom they are imposed. In one such situation, the Tax Court let the co-owner who paid the entire tax deduct it. *Powell v. Commissioner,* T.C. Memo. 1967-32.

> It seems to us that the proper test of whether or not a real property tax is deductible by the person who paid such tax is whether that person satisfied some personal liability or protected some personal right or beneficial interest in property. . . . This petitioner was not entitled merely to occupy one-sixth of the property held in common with her brothers and sisters, but she was entitled to occupy the whole in common with them.

The Tax Court requires the taxpayer to be either a legal or equitable owner as a condition of taking the deduction. *Daya v. Commissioner,* T.C. Memo. 2000-360.

Real property taxes are generally assessed on a particular date each year. If property is sold before that date, the buyer and seller do not know what the tax will be. They can allocate their respective liabilities based on the prior year's tax, but that is only an estimate. In addition to determining the appropriate amount to deduct, the timing of the deduction may be in doubt.

Section 164(d) allocates the actual tax, not the tax estimated by the parties. It treats the tax allocable to the period ending on the day before the sale as imposed on the seller. It treats the remainder of the tax as imposed on the buyer. If one party reports on the cash method, but the taxing authority makes the other party liable for actual payment, the first party is treated as paying her share of the tax on the day of the sale. I.R.C. § 164(d)(2)(A).

> **Example 13-7.** Amber sold real property to Bart on October 1 of Year 1. The local government assessed the tax against Bart on November 30. He paid the tax on February 4 of Year 2. If Amber uses the cash method, she is treated as paying (on October 1 of Year 1) the tax attributable to the period from January 1 through September 30 of Year 1. Bart deducts the rest of the tax.

Section 461(c) lets accrual-method taxpayers elect to accrue real property taxes ratably over the period covered by the taxes. If a taxpayer who sells property did not make that election, her share of the tax is treated as having accrued on the date of the sale. I.R.C. § 164(d)(2)(B). Reg. § 1.164-6(d) provides examples of when the purchaser and seller can take the deduction.

2. Personal Property Taxes

Some jurisdictions impose taxes on the ownership of personal property. These taxes primarily affect taxpayers engaged in a business or income-producing activity. A few jurisdictions impose these taxes on personal-use property, generally motor vehicles. Taxpayers who itemize can deduct state and local property taxes they pay or accrue with respect to personal-use personal property. I.R.C. § 164(a)(2).

Do not confuse a personal property tax with other charges a jurisdiction imposes. Only a tax imposed annually based on the property's value qualifies. I.R.C. § 164(b)(1). A tax imposed only when the property is transferred is not a property tax even if it is based on the property's value. A tax imposed on a car based on its weight is not a property tax even if it is imposed annually.

3. Income Taxes

Section 164(a)(3) provides a deduction for state, local, and foreign income taxes. You might assume that a tax imposed on income is a trade or business expense or an income-producing expense. If so, it would be deducted in computing

AGI by taxpayers who were self-employed or who received rental or royalty income. That view is contrary to the language in Temp. Reg. § 1.62-1T(d):

> To be deductible for the purposes of determining [AGI], expenses must be those directly, and not those merely remotely, connected with the conduct of a trade or business. For example, taxes are deductible in arriving at [AGI] only if they constitute expenditures directly attributable to a trade or business or to property from which rents or royalties are derived. Thus, property taxes paid or incurred on real property used in a trade or business are deductible, but state taxes on net income are not deductible [in computing AGI] even though the taxpayer's income is derived from the conduct of a trade or business.

The IRS also applies this rule to the § 212(3) deduction for expenses of determining a tax. The expense allocable to preparing the form covering income of a sole proprietorship is deducted in computing AGI; the expense of preparing the rest of the return is an itemized deduction. Rev. Rul. 92-29, 1992-1 C.B. 20. Because it is a miscellaneous itemized deduction, it is not allowed in 2018 through 2025.

4. Sales and Use Taxes

Congress repealed the deduction for state and local sales taxes in 1986. After that repeal, taxpayers who lived in states that did not impose an income tax but did impose a sales tax complained that the Code unfairly favored residents of states that imposed income taxes. They argued that a state's financing mechanism should not be "dictated" by federal tax distinctions. In 2004, Congress enacted § 164(b)(5)(A). That provision gives taxpayers a choice between deducting state and local general sales tax *or* state and local income tax.

The deduction covers both general sales tax and compensating use tax. A general sales tax is a tax imposed at a single rate on the retail sale of a broad range of categories. I.R.C. § 164(b)(5)(B). A tax can qualify even if food, clothing, medical supplies, and motor vehicles are not taxed or are taxed at a lower rate. With the exception of taxes imposed on the sale of motor vehicles, a sales tax imposed at a higher rate on any item is not deductible. The higher tax on motor vehicles is disallowed only to the extent it exceeds the general rate. I.R.C. § 164(b)(5)(C), (D), (F).

A compensating use tax is a tax imposed on the use, storage, or consumption of items that would be subject to the general sales tax. I.R.C. § 164(b)(5)(E). Use taxes are imposed when the taxpayer purchases property in a jurisdiction that imposes a lower sales tax than that imposed by her state of residence (or that imposes no sales tax). It is also imposed on property sold by out-of-state merchants that have no physical presence in her state of residence. Those merchants often collected no sales tax on such sales and states had to rely on their residents to file use tax returns and pay the tax. The decision in *South Dakota v. Wayfair, Inc.*, 138 S. Ct. 2080 (2018), now allows states to require such collection by the vendor.

Taxpayers can track their payment of sales and use tax, but they do not have to do so. Section 164(b)(5)(H) authorizes the IRS to publish tables based on income and sales tax rates. Taxpayers can deduct the sales tax on major purchases in addition to the table amount.

5. Limitation on Deduction for Taxes

The Tax Cuts and Jobs Act of 2017 imposed a $10,000 limit on the deduction for state, local, and foreign taxes that would otherwise be allowed as itemized deductions. This limit applies in 2018 through 2025. I.R.C. § 164(b)(6)(B). This limit is halved for married taxpayers who file separate returns. Because state and local tax burdens are not uniform throughout the United States, this limit affects residents of several states more severely than it affects residents of other states. In response, some states enacted statutes treating so-called contributions to state funds as charitable contributions rather than as taxes; taxpayers received a credit against their state taxes (or other state tax benefit) for these payments. Reg. § 1.170A-1(h)(3), issued in June 2019, limited taxpayers' ability to deduct these alternative payments as charitable contributions. The regulation differentiates between taxpayers who receive state tax credits, taxpayers who receive state tax deductions that do not exceed the amount they transfer to the state, and taxpayers who receive state tax deductions that exceed the amount they transfer to the state. Taxpayers in the first and third situation are to reduce their charitable contribution deduction by the state tax benefit they receive. The regulation includes a limited exception: the taxpayer does not have to reduce his charitable contribution if the state benefit is 15% or less of the amount he transferred to the state. He does have to reduce his contribution if his benefit exceeds 15%. In other words, the cut-off is a flat 15%, not the first 15% of his transfer.

E. Charitable Contributions

1. Definition

A charitable contribution is a contribution or gift to or for the use of an organization described in § 170(c):

(1) State, local, or federal governmental entities, if the contribution is made for exclusively public purposes;

(2) Organizations organized and operated exclusively for religious, charitable, scientific, literary, or educational purposes, for amateur sports purposes, or for the prevention of cruelty to children or animals and that meet conditions discussed below;

(3) Certain organizations of war veterans;

(4) Domestic fraternal societies if the gift will be used exclusively for religious, charitable, scientific, literary, or educational purposes, or for the prevention of cruelty to children or animals; and

(5) Nonprofit cemetery companies and corporations.

Because most charitable contributions are to organizations in the second category, this discussion focuses on § 170(c)(2). It includes corporations, trusts, community chests, funds, and foundations that are created or organized in the United States or one of its possessions. That requirement covers only creation or organization; the charity can benefit a foreign organization. The charity must be operated exclusively for one or more of the purposes described in the list above. None of its earnings can inure to the benefit of any private shareholder or individual. This requirement is designed to prevent it from benefiting those in control rather than using its funds for its charitable purpose. It cannot be disqualified for tax exemption because of attempting to influence legislation. It must limit its lobbying to limits provided in § 501(h). Organizations of war veterans, the third category of charity listed above, are not subject to this limitation. The Supreme Court upheld that disparate treatment in *Regan v. Taxation with Representation of Washington*, 461 U.S. 540 (1983). Finally, it cannot participate or intervene in any political campaign for or against a candidate for public office.

Section 170(c) treats a transfer as a contribution if it is to or for the use of a qualifying organization. In *Rockefeller v. Commissioner*, 676 F.2d 35 (2d Cir. 1982), the court held that out-of-pocket expenses paid in rendering services to a charity were gifts "to" rather than "for the use of" the charity. It agreed that the term "for the use of" referred to transfers in trust. The distinction is relevant in the discussion below of deduction limits. In *Davis v. United States*,

495 U.S. 472 (1990), the taxpayers argued that amounts they spent to support their sons on church missions were gifts for the use of the charity. The Court held that the payments did not qualify because the funds were not donated in trust for the church or in a similarly enforceable legal arrangement. It also disallowed the payments as out-of-pocket costs of rendering uncompensated services for the charity because the taxpayers did not perform the services.

Section 170(a)(1) allows a deduction only if the amount is paid. Mere commitments or promises to donate are not sufficient. Payment can be made through a credit card charge even if the taxpayer does not pay his credit card bill that same year. Rev. Rul. 78-38, 1978-1 C.B. 67.

The transfer must be a "voluntary transfer of money or property that is made with no expectation of procuring a financial benefit commensurate with the amount of the transfer." Rev. Rul. 83-104, 1983-2 C.B. 46. In other words, no deduction is allowed for quid pro quo transactions. Quid pro quo issues arise from contributions to schools because a taxpayer cannot deduct a contribution to a school his children attend if the payment is disguised tuition or enrollment is contingent upon making the payment. In *Sklar v. Commissioner*, 282 F.3d 610 (9th Cir. 2002), the taxpayer was unsuccessful in deducting the portion of his child's tuition that related to religious education. He argued that he received only intangible religious benefits in exchange. The court noted that the Supreme Court had rejected the intangible religious benefits claim in *Hernandez v. Commissioner*, 490 U.S. 680 (1989), involving payments to the Church of Scientology for auditing and training.

Another area of concern involves taxpayers who purchase items from a charity. For example, a taxpayer might buy tickets to a dinner, the proceeds of which go to charity. In Rev. Rul. 67-246, 1967-2 C.B. 104, the IRS ruled that the taxpayer must establish two elements: (1) the portion of the payment claimed as a gift must exceed the value of the benefit received; and (2) the excess payment must be made with the intention of making a gift. The IRS issues annual guidance on quid pro quo benefits that are inconsequential or insubstantial. A donor who receives items whose value is sufficiently small can deduct his entire donation. For 2020 a donation is fully deductible if the benefit does not exceed the lesser of 2% of the gift or $112.

2. Amount

a. Money, Other Property, and Forgone Income

If the contribution is in money, the gift is the amount contributed minus the value of any benefit the donor receives. If the contribution consists of unreimbursed expenses, the amount paid is generally treated as the amount of the gift. Section 170(i) provides a rate of 14 cents a mile for using a vehicle on behalf of a charity; this amount is not inflation-adjusted. Reasonable out-of-pocket costs for travel—including meals and lodging—on behalf of a charity are also deductible. There must be "no significant element of personal pleasure, recreation, or vacation" associated with the charitable travel. I.R.C. § 170(j).

If a taxpayer renders free services to a charity, he is forgoing the receipt of gross income. Not surprisingly, the regulations do not allow a deduction in this situation. Reg. § 1.170A-1(g). Similarly, § 170(f)(3)(A) treats the rent-free use of property as a transfer of less than the taxpayer's entire interest in the property. A deduction is allowed only to the extent it would have been allowed if the transfer had been in trust.

If the transfer is of the taxpayer's entire interest in property, the amount of the gift is generally governed by § 170(e). Reg. § 1.170A-1(c)(1) provides that the starting point is the property's fair market value, not its adjusted basis. The effect of this rule differs based on whether the property has unrealized gain or loss. Because a taxpayer does not have a realization event when she makes a gift, a taxpayer who donates property that has declined in value gives up any possibility of deducting her potential loss. If she can deduct the loss, she should sell the property and donate the cash to charity.

> Example 13-8. Amanda purchased 100 shares of XYZ stock for $1,000. Five years later, when the stock was worth $800, she donated it to a charity. She cannot deduct her $200 loss because the gift is not a re-alization event. The stock's $800 value is her charitable contribution. If she instead sold the stock and donated the money she received, she could deduct both her $200 loss and the $800 charitable contribution.

> Example 13-9. Arielle purchased a dining room table for $1,000. Five years later, when the table was worth $800, she donated it to a charity. Arielle could not have deducted the $200 loss even if she sold the table, because no Code section allows a deduction for selling personal-use property. The table's $800 value is her charitable contribution.

A taxpayer who donates appreciated property avoids reporting the gain as gross income. He receives a double benefit if he can also deduct the property's value as a contribution. Not surprisingly, § 170(e) limits this double benefit. Many of its rules are based on the property being a capital asset or a § 1231 asset. For purposes of this chapter, you can assume that personal-use property, investment property, and business real property all qualify.

The first limit applies if the potential gain would not have been long-term capital gain if the taxpayer had sold the property. This limit applies to capital assets that have not been held more than one year (short-term capital gain property) and to property that is not a capital asset (ordinary income property). In both cases, the taxpayer reduces the potential charitable gift by that gain. I.R.C. § 170(e)(1)(A).

> **Example 13-10.** Arthur purchased shares of DEF stock for $4,000. Four months later, when the shares were worth $6,000, he donated them to a charity. Because none of his gain would have been *long-term* capital gain if he had sold the stock, his charitable gift is not $6,000. He reduces the stock's value by the $2,000 potential gain. His charitable gift is his $4,000 basis.

Other limits apply even if the property would have produced long-term capital gain if sold. The first limit applies to tangible personal property if the use by the charity is unrelated to its exempt function. Because most tangible personal property does not produce income, a charity that has no use for it is likely to sell it; a sale is not a use in the charity's exempt function. If the charity's use is unrelated to its exempt function, the value of the gift is reduced by the amount of potential gain. I.R.C. § 170(e)(1)(B)(i)(I).

> **Example 13-11.** Bing purchased a stamp collection for $3,000. Ten years later, when his collection was worth $8,000, he donated it to a charity. The charity sold the collection to raise cash for its activities. Because the charity will not use the stamp collection in its exempt function, his charitable gift is only his $3,000 basis for the collection. If he instead donated the collection to the National Museum of Stamp Collecting, his charitable gift would be the collection's $8,000 value. The collection is related to the museum's exempt function.

The donor's gift is reduced, even if the tangible personal property is related to the charity's exempt function, if the charity disposes of it before the last day of the taxable year in which it receives it. This limitation applies to gifts valued at more than $5,000. She avoids this limitation if the charity certifies that its use of the property was substantial and related to its exempt function or explains why such planned use became impossible or infeasible to implement. I.R.C. §§ 170(e)(1)(B)(i)(II), (e)(7)(C)–(D), 6050L(a)(2)(A). Section 170(e)(7) adds another limitation. She recaptures the amount by which the value of the gift exceeds her basis if the charity disposes of the property after that taxable year but within three years after the date of the donation. Recapture does not apply if the charity makes the certification described earlier in this paragraph.

The donor also reduces her contribution by built-in long-term capital gain for donations to a private foundation (other than for gifts of publicly traded stock), donations of patents, certain copyrights, trademarks, and similar intellectual property, and donations of taxidermy property if she is the person who prepared, stuffed, or mounted the property (or who paid for the preparation, stuffing, or mounting). I.R.C. § 170(e)(1)(B)(ii)–(iv).

If none of the above limits apply, a taxpayer who donates long-term capital gain property or § 1231 property receives the double benefit described at the beginning of this discussion. Although she qualifies for this double benefit, the percentage limitations discussed below may reduce its availability.

> Example 13-12. Alyssa purchased land for $50,000 five years ago. It is currently worth $82,000. She received salary of $700,000 this year and had no other gross income. If she sells the land and contributes the $82,000 sale price to a charity, she increases her gross income by $32,000 of realized gain; her charitable contribution is the $82,000 she donated. The net result is a $50,000 decrease in her taxable income. If she instead donates the land to the charity, she has no additional gross income; her charitable contribution is the $82,000 value of the land. The net result is an $82,000 decrease in her taxable income.

b. Bargain Sales

In Chapter 4, we considered the part gift/part sale rules that apply when a transferor receives consideration for a primarily donative transfer. Different rules apply when he makes a bargain sale of appreciated property to charity. The bargain sale rules apply if he receives money (or other property) or the charity took the property subject to a mortgage or other encumbrance. The bargain sale is treated as two transactions: a sale and a donation. He reports gain if the consideration exceeds the basis allocated to the portion treated as sold. His adjusted basis for computing gain is based on the ratio of the amount realized to the property's value. I.R.C. § 1011(b). The amount of the gift, which represents the value for which he did not receive consideration, is subject to the rules in § 170(e) described above.

> Example 13-13. Armand purchased investment land 10 years ago for $100,000. It is currently worth $500,000 and is subject to a $25,000 mortgage. He donated the land, subject to the mortgage, to a charity. He is treated as selling 5% of the property ($25,000/$500,000) and donating the remaining 95%. He allocates 5% of his basis ($5,000) to the sale and includes long-term capital gain of $20,000 in gross income.

Because this is long-term capital gain property (and is not tangible personal property), his charitable gift is the $475,000 value of the portion he donated. He is not taxed on the $380,000 gain allocable to that part of the property.

Example 13-14. Assume instead that Armand purchased the investment land only 10 *months* ago. He includes short-term capital gain of $20,000 in gross income. Because this is not long-term capital gain property, the value of his gift ($475,000) is reduced by the $380,000 gain allocable to the gifted property. His charitable gift is his $95,000 basis for the portion of the property treated as a gift.

3. Percentage Limits and Carryovers

Section 170(b)(1) contains several percentage limits. These limits apply to the contribution base, *not* to the actual charitable gifts. The contribution base is AGI computed without regard to any net operating loss carryback to the taxable year. I.R.C. § 170(b)(1)(H). The discussion in this chapter refers to AGI because most taxpayers will not have net operating loss carrybacks.

In general. Section 170(b)(1)(A) contains an overall limit—50% of AGI. Contributions made *to* a qualifying organization qualify. Contributions *for the use of* the organization do not qualify. The list of organizations that qualify for the 50% limit is narrower than the list of organizations that can receive deductible contributions. It includes churches, educational organizations, organizations that provide medical care, medical education, or medical research, governments, and organizations that normally receive a substantial portion of their support from governments or the general public. Universities, charities such as the United Way, and nonprofit hospitals are examples of qualifying organizations.

Cash contributions to organizations described above qualify for a 60% of AGI limit. I.R.C. § 170(b)(1)(G)(i). The increased limit applies in 2018 through 2025.

Example 13-15. Algernon has AGI of $100,000. He donated $35,000 to a publicly supported charity in 2020 and made no other donations. His $35,000 gift is deductible because it does not exceed 60% of his AGI.

Example 13-16. Bea has AGI of $100,000. She donated $35,000 to each of two publicly supported charities in 2020. Although neither donation exceeded 60% of her AGI, the $70,000 total exceeds 60% of her AGI by $10,000. She can deduct only $60,000.

Gifts that do not qualify for the 50% or 60% limits cannot exceed 30% of AGI. The taxpayer deducts gifts qualifying for the higher limits first. As a result, the limitation is actually the lesser of (1) 30% of AGI or (2) 50% of AGI minus gifts qualifying for the 50% or 60% limit. I.R.C. § 170(b)(1)(G)(iii). Gifts to private foundations are likely to be subject to the 30% limit. These organizations are usually funded and controlled by smaller groups of private individuals or families.

> **Example 13-17.** Blaine has AGI of $100,000. He donated $22,000 to his private foundation in 2020. His $22,000 gift is deductible because it does not exceed 30% of his AGI.

> **Example 13-18.** Blaine made a last-minute cash gift of $40,000 to a publicly supported charity. That gift is deductible because it does not exceed 60% of his AGI. It is irrelevant that he made the gift to the private foundation first. Even though his gift to the private foundation is less than 30% of his AGI, it is not fully deductible. His normal $50,000 maximum deduction for the year is reduced by the $40,000 gift to the publicly supported charity. He can deduct only $10,000 of his gift to the foundation this year. If Blaine's last-minute gift had been $55,000, he would not be able to deduct any of his gift to the foundation this year.

Lower percentage limits also apply to donations of appreciated property. If the donee is a publicly supported charity, and the property's value is the amount of the gift, the limit is 30% of AGI. I.R.C. § 170(b)(1)(C). Because this deduction is considered after deductions for cash gifts to publicly supported charities and private foundations, the actual limit may be even lower.

> **Example 13-19.** Bethany has AGI of $100,000. She made one gift to a publicly supported charity: shares of ABC Corporation stock that she purchased for $10,000 several years ago. The shares were worth $32,000 when she donated them. That value qualifies as the amount of her gift. Because the limit for gifts of appreciated property is 30% of AGI under those circumstances, Bethany can deduct only $30,000 of her $32,000 gift this year. If she also made cash gifts to publicly supported charities or private foundations, those gifts would further reduce her ability to deduct her gift of ABC shares this year.

Similar rules apply to gifts of appreciated property to private foundations and to gifts of such property *for the use of* publicly supported charities. Those gifts are subject to a maximum limit equal to 20% of AGI instead of the 30%

that applies to cash gifts. I.R.C. § 170(b)(1)(D). Cash gifts and gifts of property to publicly supported charities are considered ahead of these gifts for purposes of the overall limit. Finally, contributions of qualified conservation easements qualify for the 50% limit and for a 15-year carryover of excess contributions, but they are considered after all other charitable gifts. I.R.C. § 170(b)(1)(E).

If a taxpayer's unrealized gain is relatively small, he might elect to treat his basis as the amount of the gift. In that case, the lower percentage limits for gifts of appreciated property do not apply. I.R.C. § 170(b)(1)(C)(iii). The carryover rules will affect his decision. Section 170(d)(1) lets individuals carry excess contributions eligible for the 50% of AGI limit forward up to five years. Gifts made in the subsequent years have priority in using up the taxpayer's overall limit. Comparable rules apply to gifts subject to the 60% limit (§ 170(b)(1)(G)(ii)) and to the lower percentage limits (§ 170(b)(1)(B) (flush language), (C)(ii), (D)(ii)). Because using basis as the amount of the gift results in a higher percentage limit, he is less likely to have a carryover.

> **Example 13-20.** Aaron has AGI of $100,000. He made one gift to a publicly supported charity: shares of ABC stock he purchased for $35,000 several years ago. The shares were worth $42,000 when he donated them. If he treats the amount of his gift as $42,000, he can deduct only $30,000 (30% of AGI) this year, and he can carry $12,000 over as a potential deduction in the next five years. If he instead treats the amount of his gift as his $35,000 basis, he can deduct the entire $35,000 because it does not exceed the 50% of AGI overall limit. Because the gift amount is fully deductible, he has no carryover. He must decide between a $35,000 deduction now and no carryover or a $30,000 deduction now and a $12,000 carryover to the next five years.

COVID-19 legislation. The percentage limits for cash contributions to most charities are suspended during 2020. The taxpayer's deduction cannot exceed her contribution base reduced by contributions, such as those made in property, that do not qualify for this treatment. This provision is elective. Pub. L. No. 116-136, § 2205.

4. Substantiation Rules

Section 170(a)(1) indicates that contributions are deductible only if verified under the regulations, and § 170(f) contains several substantiation rules. Section 170(f)(8) disallows any deduction for a contribution of $250 or more unless the donor receives a contemporaneous written acknowledgement from the donee. The acknowledgement must indicate the amount of cash or describe the property. It must also provide a description and estimate of the value of any goods and services provided to the donor. An exception applies if the donor received only intangible religious benefits. Additional substantiation rules apply to property donations exceeding $500 (§ 170(f)(11)) (with further requirements if the donation exceeds $5,000 or $500,000) and donations of vehicles (§ 170(f)(12)). Deductions of cash or checks are disallowed unless the donor maintains a bank record or confirmation from the donee. I.R.C. § 170(f)(17).

5. Miscellaneous Rules

The discussion in this section covers a few of the additional rules governing the charitable contribution deduction. It ignores provisions covering, among other topics, donations of inventory, property used in scientific research, or buildings in registered historic districts, contributions to donor-advised funds, and expenses paid by whaling captains.

The taxpayer might transfer a future interest, retaining the right to enjoy the property for a fixed period or for his life. He might transfer a term interest and retain a reversion. The value of the gift is clearly less than the full value of the property in these situations.

Section 170 imposes limits on deductions for partial gifts. If the donor transfers a future interest in tangible personal property, his deduction is delayed even if the charity's gift is vested. He cannot deduct his gift until all intervening interests (held by him or by a related person) expire. I.R.C. § 170(a)(3). If he donates a remainder interest in trust, he cannot deduct the present value of the remainder unless the trust qualifies as a § 664 charitable remainder annuity trust or charitable remainder unitrust or a § 642 pooled income fund. I.R.C. § 170(f)(2)(A). If he donates any other interest in trust, the gift is deductible only if the charity will receive a guaranteed annuity or percentage of the trust value and the trust is treated as a grantor trust. I.R.C. § 170(f)(2)(B). Finally, if the partial interest is not donated in trust, he receives a deduction only if (1) the interest would be deductible if it had been transferred in trust; (2) he transferred a remainder interest in a personal residence or farm; (3) he transferred an undivided portion of his entire interest in property; or (4) the contribution was of a qualified conservation easement. I.R.C. § 170(f)(3).

Section 170(e)(1)(B)(iii) limits the deduction for gifts of patents, certain copyrights, and other types of intellectual property to the donor's basis if it is less than the property's fair market value. She can take an additional deduction based on a specified percentage of income that the charity receives from the donated property. I.R.C. § 170(m). The additional deduction is 100% of income for the first two years. It decreases by 10 percentage points per year, reaching 10% for the 11th and 12th years and then dropping to zero.

Although conservation easements are not subject to the partial interest limits of § 170(f)(3), deductions for contributions of easements are frequently litigated. The IRS may challenge whether the easement actually reduced the value of the taxpayer's property (particularly in the case of façade easements in registered historic districts), or it may challenge the property's appraisal or the documentation supplied with the tax return. Section 170(h) covers these contributions. A donor can deduct contributions of clothing and household goods only if those items are in good used condition or better. I.R.C. § 170(f)(16).

F. Expenses to Determine a Tax

Section 212(3) allows a deduction for amounts paid or incurred in connection with the determination, collection, or refund of any tax. Outlays can be for tax planning (including the tax consequences of a divorce), tax return preparation, and tax litigation. This deduction applies to determining both federal and other taxes. It applies even if the underlying tax (*e.g.*, the federal income tax) is not itself deductible. Deductions related to tax planning or determination in a personal context are miscellaneous itemized deductions; they cannot be deducted in 2018 through 2025.

G. Medical Care Expenses

1. General Rules

Section 213(a) allows an itemized deduction for uncompensated medical expenses. Although insurance is the most common means of covering medical expenses, it is not the only option. The taxpayer may have entered into a salary reduction agreement that results in untaxed income being placed in a flexible spending account. If he receives reimbursement for his medical expenses from that account, those expenses are compensated. Likewise, if he was injured and receives an award for future medical expenses, outlays he makes in the future — up to the amount previously allocated to medical care — are considered compensated.

Section 213(a) lets the taxpayer deduct medical expenses he pays for himself, his spouse, and his dependents. A dependent generally means an individual for whom the taxpayer deducts a dependency exemption (which is not available in 2018 through 2025). One exception applies to children whose parents are divorced (or who never married each other). If § 152(e) applies to determine which parent can treat the child as a dependent, each parent can use the amount he or she pays for the child's medical care in computing any deduction for that year. I.R.C. § 213(d)(5).

Taxpayers can take this deduction only for outlays that exceed 10% of AGI. I.R.C. § 213(a). Outlays need only exceed 7.5% of AGI in 2020. I.R.C. § 213(f). Taxpayers report this deduction on the cash method. Neither the taxpayer's normal accounting method nor the timing of the injury or sickness matters. Reg. § 1.213-1(a)(1). Payment made by credit card is treated as actual payment for this purpose even if the taxpayer does not pay the credit card company until a later year. Rev. Rul. 78-39, 1978-1 C.B. 73.

2. Qualifying Outlays

Section 213(d)(1)(A) defines medical care as "amounts paid for the diagnosis, cure, mitigation, treatment, or prevention of disease, or for the purpose of affecting any structure or function of the body." The expense must be primarily incurred in connection with a specific medical problem. Expenses that are merely beneficial to the individual's general health do not qualify. Reg. § 1.213-1(e)(1)(ii). In addition to expenses for doctor and dentist visits, medical care includes "quit smoking" programs, service animals for medical reasons, laser eye surgery, organ transplants, prescribed birth control pills, alcohol rehabilitation treatment, crutches, and obesity weight loss programs.

a. Drugs

Section 213(b) provides that medicines or drugs are considered medical expenses only if they are prescribed drugs or insulin. A prescribed drug is a drug or biological that requires a prescription from a health care provider. I.R.C. § 213(d)(3)–(4). A drug is not a prescribed drug if the taxpayer can acquire it without a prescription. A physician's recommendation alone is not sufficient to transform medication available over the counter into a prescribed drug. For this reason, although the IRS generally treats the costs of "quit smoking" programs as medical care, nicotine patches available without a prescription do not qualify. Rev. Rul. 99-28, 1999-1 C.B. 1269. The prescription requirement applies only to drugs. For example, bandages qualify as medical care because they help prevent infection. The fact that they are available without a prescription is irrelevant; they are not drugs.

Drugs must be legally obtained, and illegal treatments are not deductible. Reg. § 1.213-1(e)(1)(ii). If the treatment is illegal at the federal level, the IRS

considers its legality under state law irrelevant. It applied this limitation to
medical marijuana in Rev. Rul. 97-9, 1997-1 C.B. 77. We cannot predict whether
increased state-level legalization will affect the tax treatment of marijuana.

b. Capital Expenditures

Some medical outlays involve capital expenditures. They may be for discrete
assets, such as motorized wheelchairs, or for additions to a home, such as a
pool. A business could not immediately deduct comparable outlays, but it
could depreciate their cost over multiple years. Because § 167 does not allow
a depreciation deduction for personal-use items, a taxpayer who makes a capital
expenditure for medical purposes can deduct only those amounts authorized
by the regulations.

The regulations divide capital expenditures into two categories. Items that
relate only to the person needing care qualify in full as medical care expenses
if they are not permanent improvements to property. These include outlays
for eyeglasses, crutches, hand controls for a car, and room air conditioners.
Deductions for permanent improvements that primarily benefit the sick person
are subject to a limitation. They qualify as medical care only to the extent they
exceed the increase in the value of the underlying property. Outlays to maintain
the improvement also qualify as medical care. Reg. § 1.213-1(e)(1)(iii).

> Example 13-21. Adelle suffers from acute coronary insufficiency, and
> her doctor recommended that she install an elevator in her home. It
> cost $20,000 and it increased the value of her home by $3,000; none
> of its cost was covered by insurance. Adelle treats $17,000 of the
> elevator's cost as medical care for the year. She increases her adjusted
> basis for her home by any nondeductible amount.

c. Travel, Transportation, Meals, and Lodging

Transportation costs to receive medical care qualify as medical care. I.R.C.
§ 213(d)(1)(B). The IRS issues a revenue procedure each year indicating the
cost per mile when a taxpayer uses her car for this purpose; she can instead
compute her actual transportation costs. Taxpayers who travel to other areas
to receive medical care can treat the costs of reaching the location where care
occurs as medical care. There must be a specific medical problem being
targeted. Travel expenses are not medical care if incurred to improve her
general health.

The treatment accorded meals and lodging depends on the setting in which
they are incurred. If the taxpayer is institutionalized for a medical condition,
the entire cost of her care qualifies even though a portion could be allocated

to meals and lodging. In addition to hospitalization, this provision may cover attendance at a school that has facilities to treat a learning disability or other medical condition. On the other hand, if she is institutionalized but medical care is not the primary reason, only the cost allocable to medical care qualifies. The portion allocable to meals and lodging does not. Reg. § 1.213-1(e)(1)(v).

A taxpayer who is receiving out-patient medical care at a licensed hospital (or similar medical facility) can deduct up to $50 per night for lodging near the facility. The lodging must not be lavish under the circumstances and there must be no significant element of personal pleasure, recreation, or vacation in the travel away from home. I.R.C. § 213(d)(2).

Meals and lodging while traveling to obtain medical care, and meals while at the location where care is given are an area of confusion. Although § 213(d)(2) allows a limited deduction for outpatient lodging, it does not mention meal costs. The Tax Court and Sixth Circuit allowed a deduction for meals and lodging en route in *Montgomery v. Commissioner*, 428 F.2d 243 (6th Cir. 1970). They distinguished the disallowance in *Commissioner v. Bilder*, 369 U.S. 499 (1962), because *Bilder* related to expenses after the taxpayer arrived, while *Montgomery* involved expenses in getting to the treatment. The IRS disagrees with the *Montgomery* decision, which predates the enactment of § 213(d)(2).

Another issue involves individuals whose medical conditions require them to avoid certain foods. The cost of substitute items may exceed the cost of the prohibited items. Does that make any of the increased cost an outlay for medical care? An IRS ruling limits the deduction to outlays that supplement the taxpayer's diet but are not substitutes for it. Rev. Rul. 55-261, 1955-1 C.B. 307. The Tax Court was somewhat more generous in *Randolph v. Commissioner*, 67 T.C. 481 (1976). It let a taxpayer who was allergic to the chemicals in pesticides treat the extra amount paid for substitute food as medical care. In AOD 1979-66, the IRS indicated its disagreement with *Randolph*. In its view, allocating part of an item's cost to medical care violates the "primarily" for medical care requirement of Reg. § 1.213-1(e)(1)(ii).

d. Care Provided by Nonprofessionals

With the exception of the rules governing medicines and drugs, § 213 does not focus on the decisions of medical professionals. Treatment by unlicensed practitioners is allowed if the nature of the services meets the definition of medical care. Rev. Rul. 63-91, 1963-1 C.B. 54. But payments for qualified long-term care made to a care provider who is the taxpayer's spouse or is related to the taxpayer do not qualify unless the service is provided by a licensed professional. I.R.C. § 213(d)(11). The definition of related person includes both individuals and entities in which the taxpayer has an interest covered by § 267(b) or § 707(b).

e. Outlays for Changes in Taxpayer's Appearance

Section 213(d)(9)(A) provides that cosmetic surgery does not qualify as medical care unless "necessary to ameliorate a deformity arising from, or directly related to, a congenital abnormality, a personal injury resulting from an accident or trauma, or disfiguring disease." An outlay is cosmetic surgery if it is directed at improving the patient's appearance and does not meaningfully promote the proper function of the body or prevent or treat illness or disease. I.R.C. § 213(d)(9)(B).

The fact that an outlay improves the patient's appearance does not necessarily disqualify it as medical care. Laser eye surgery is one such example. Although the patient may prefer his appearance without glasses, the surgery does correct vision problems. Because teeth are likely to yellow with age, teeth whitening treatments do not usually qualify. But procedures to lighten teeth darkened by antibiotics may qualify. Routine teeth cleaning procedures to help prevent gum disease qualify.

The decision in *O'Donnabhain v. Commissioner*, 134 T.C. 34 (2010), illustrates these distinctions. The taxpayer underwent hormone treatment, male-to-female gender reassignment surgery, and breast augmentation surgery. Because the court determined that gender identity disorder was a disease, it treated the hormone treatment and gender reassignment surgery as medical care. It treated the breast augmentation surgery as nondeductible cosmetic surgery. There was no documentation that the hormone treatment failed to enlarge her breasts sufficiently to give her comfort in her social gender role.

f. Insurance

Medical care includes premiums paid for insurance policies covering medical care. I.R.C. § 213(d)(1)(D). Premiums paid through a salary reduction agreement do not qualify. Otherwise the taxpayer would be excluding and deducting the same amount. He is also prevented from deducting premiums for policies that pay a flat amount based on an event — for example, being hospitalized or losing an arm — rather than reimbursing for actual medical care costs.

In addition to insurance for current medical care, § 213(d)(1)(D) covers premiums for qualified long-term care contracts. The maximum premium that qualifies for this purpose is based on the taxpayer's age. I.R.C. § 213(d)(10). The inflation-adjusted amounts for 2020, for example, range from $430 for a taxpayer who is age 40 or less to $5,430 for a taxpayer who is older than age 70. Self-employed individuals may deduct the premiums for medical insurance covering themselves, their spouses, and their dependents as business expenses instead of as medical care expenses. I.R.C. § 162(l).

3. Coordination with Other Code Sections

Some outlays might qualify as medical expenses or as ordinary and necessary business expenses. Under Rev. Rul. 75-316, 1975-2 C.B. 54, a taxpayer can use § 162 instead of § 213 if he meets three conditions: (1) his work necessitates that such expenses be incurred; (2) the expenses incurred are clearly not required or used in his personal life; and (3) the Code and regulations do not otherwise address the treatment of the item. The ruling involved a blind individual who employed a reader solely for his business duties. The IRS distinguished other rulings in which it had limited taxpayers to medical expense deductions because they involved outlays covering both business and personal activities. Section 162 might provide a larger deduction for a self-employed taxpayer because it escapes the AGI limitations applied to medical expenses. An employee might treat these as medical expenses if his other medical expenses exceed the applicable floor. Otherwise, he could deduct them as business expenses. Deductions for impairment-related work expenses are not miscellaneous itemized deductions and therefore not disallowed in 2018 through 2025. I.R.C. § 67(b)(6), (d).

A taxpayer may have a child or other dependent for whom care is necessary while the taxpayer works. If the individual has a physical or mental condition that renders her incapable of self-care, outlays for a caregiver might qualify for the medical expense deduction. They might also qualify for the § 21 household and dependent care credit discussed in the previous chapter. Section 213(e) provides that any amount allowed as a § 21 credit cannot be deducted as a medical expense.

H. Standard Deduction

After determining AGI, most taxpayers have a choice. They may itemize (§ 63(e)) or take the standard deduction (§ 63(b)). The standard deduction does not require them to incur any deductible expenses or to have substantiating records. Section 63(c)(6) prevents three groups of individuals from taking the standard deduction: (1) a married individual who files a separate return and whose spouse itemizes; (2) a nonresident alien; and (3) a taxpayer whose return involves a change in accounting period.

Taxpayers are entitled to a basic standard deduction, which reflects their filing status. I.R.C. §63(c)(2), (7). An additional amount is added for taxpayers who are elderly or blind. I.R.C. §63(c), (f). Both standard deduction amounts are adjusted annually for inflation. The basic amounts for 2020 are $12,400 for unmarried individuals and married individuals filing separate returns, $18,650 for heads of households, and $24,800 for married individuals filing jointly and surviving spouses.

When the taxpayer compares the standard deduction to her available itemized deductions, she considers both the basic amount and any increases or decreases caused by age, blindness, or status as a dependent. A taxpayer who is not married increases her 2020 standard deduction by $1,650 if she is blind or has reached age 65. She increases it by $3,300 if she satisfies both conditions. A taxpayer who is either married or a surviving spouse increases her 2020 standard deduction by $1,300 if she is blind or has reached age 65. She increases it by $2,600 if she satisfies both conditions. Because the additional amounts are available per taxpayer, married taxpayers who both are blind and at least age 65 qualify for a total additional standard deduction of $5,200 in 2020.

Some individuals who file their own tax returns are dependents of other taxpayers. The 2020 standard deduction available to a dependent is the greater of (1) $1,100 or (2) $350 plus her earned income. I.R.C. §63(c)(5). If she is at least age 65 or blind, she qualifies for the additional standard deduction even though she is a dependent.

> **Example 13-22.** Astrid is age 19, a full-time student, and her parents' dependent. In 2020, she earned $2,200 from a part-time job and realized a $500 gain from selling stock. She reports gross income of $2,700 and takes a standard deduction of $2,550 ($350 plus her earned income). If she earned only $700 from her part-time job, she reports gross income of $1,200 and takes a standard deduction of $1,100.

I. Personal Exemptions

1. Overview

The deduction for personal exemptions before 2018 was based on the number of individuals in the taxpayer's "family." He subtracted this deduction from AGI, along with either the standard deduction or itemized deductions. When

Congress increased the standard deduction for 2018 through 2025, it eliminated the separate deduction for personal exemptions.

Although this deduction is not currently available, the related rules defining qualified dependents retain their relevance in other areas. I.R.C. § 151(d)(5)(B). For that reason, we retain them in this chapter.

2. Qualifying Dependents

The discussion below focuses on the differences between a qualifying child and a qualifying relative. Do not be misled by this terminology. An individual who is not the taxpayer's child can be a qualifying child; an individual who is not the taxpayer's relative can be a qualifying relative.

a. Qualifying Child

As a general rule, an individual must meet five tests to be a qualifying child. I.R.C. § 152(c)(1). These tests cover relationship, place of abode, age, self-support, and filing status. The relationship test is satisfied if the potential dependent is the taxpayer's child, a descendant of his child, or his brother, sister, stepbrother, or stepsister (or one of their descendants). I.R.C. § 152(c)(1)(A), (c)(2). The definition of child includes the taxpayer's stepchild, adopted child, and eligible foster child. I.R.C. § 152(f)(1). Half-brothers and half-sisters are included in the definition of brothers and sisters. I.R.C. § 152(f)(4).

The place of abode test requires that the potential dependent share the same principal place of residence as the taxpayer for more than half of the year. I.R.C. § 152(c)(1)(B). There are exceptions for temporary absences. Reg. § 1.152-1(b). Although these regulations relate to prior law, many of the circumstances, including illness, education, or death during the year, are relevant.

A child who has reached age 19 by year-end cannot qualify unless she is a full-time student for at least five months and has not reached age 24 by year-end. I.R.C. § 152(c)(1)(C), (c)(3)(A), (f)(2). The age limit is waived if she is permanently and totally disabled. I.R.C. § 152(c)(3)(B). Unless she is permanently and totally disabled, she must be younger than the taxpayer who is claiming her as a dependent. I.R.C. § 152(c)(3)(A).

A dependent can be a qualifying child even if the taxpayer provides none of her support. The support test is satisfied if the qualifying child does not provide more than half of her own support. I.R.C. § 152(c)(1)(D). Although Reg. § 1.152-1(a)(2) has not been amended to reflect current § 152, its guidelines as to what qualifies as support, including "food, shelter, clothing, medical and dental care, education, and the like" are relevant. We ignore scholarships for purposes of this requirement if the dependent is the taxpayer's child and a student. I.R.C. § 152(f)(5). Student loans are considered support on the child's part if she is responsible for their repayment.

If the potential qualifying child is married, the joint return test is satisfied if she does not file a joint return. It is also satisfied if the only reason for filing the joint return is to claim a refund, not to reduce her spouse's tax liability. For example, the couple may be entitled to a refund of withheld taxes. I.R.C. § 152(c)(1)(E).

By eliminating the support test for qualifying child status, Congress made it possible for more than one taxpayer to treat an individual as a qualifying child. For example, the child might live with both parents, but they are not married (and thus cannot file a joint return). Or she might live with both parents and a grandparent or with one parent and a grandparent.

Section 152(c)(4) contains tie-breaker rules for determining whose dependent the child is. If only one potential claimant is the child's parent, she is the qualifying child of the parent. If no potential claimant is the child's parent, she is the qualifying child of the potential claimant with the highest AGI. If both parents are potential claimants, she is the qualifying child of the parent with whom she resided for the longer time that year. If the times are equal, the parent with the higher AGI can claim the exemption. Finally, if the parents are entitled to claim the child but do not do so, she can be claimed by another taxpayer who meets the tests, but only if the other taxpayer's AGI exceeds that of either parent.

> **Example 13-23.** Delia lives the entire year with her mother Alaina, her father Boris, and her grandmother Chloe. Alaina and Boris are not married to each other. Alaina has an AGI of $25,000; Boris has an AGI of $30,000. As between Alaina and Boris, Boris is entitled to claim Delia as a qualifying child. Chloe can claim Delia only if neither parent claims her *and* Chloe's AGI exceeds $30,000. If Boris did not join the household until April, the tie-breaker rules favor Alaina over Boris because Delia resided with her for a longer period that year.

Section 152(e) contains four requirements for shifting qualifying child status to the "noncustodial" parent. First, the parents must provide more than half of the child's support. Second, they must be divorced or legally separated under a decree, separated under a written separation agreement, or living apart throughout the last six months of the year. Third, the child must be in the custody of one or both parents for more than half of the year. Fourth, the custodial parent must sign a written declaration releasing the exemption. Reg. § 1.152-4 includes numerous examples for determining which parent is the custodial parent. Section 152(e) does not apply if the child is covered by a multiple support agreement, discussed later in this section.

The requirements for the release are strictly enforced. A state court decree alone is not sufficient. The noncustodial parent must attach to his return a Form 8332 (or a document that conforms to its substance) signed by the custodial parent. *Swint v. Commissioner*, 142 T.C. 131 (2014). Slightly different rules apply to decrees issued before the current regulations were adopted.

b. Qualifying Relative

As a general rule, the individual must meet four tests to be a qualifying relative. I.R.C. § 152(d)(1). These tests cover relationship, gross income, support, and status. Section 152(d)(2) lists eight categories of individuals who satisfy the § 152(d)(1)(A) relationship test: (1) the taxpayer's child or a descendant of his child; (2) his brother, sister, stepbrother, or stepsister; (3) his father or mother, or an ancestor of either; (4) his stepfather or stepmother; (5) a son or daughter of his brother or sister; (6) a brother or sister of his father or mother; (7) his son-in-law, daughter-in-law, father-in-law, mother-in-law, brother-in-law, or sister-in-law; and (8) an individual who has the same principal place of abode as the taxpayer and is a member of his household.

Only individuals in the last category must live with the taxpayer. This group includes relatives who are not covered by the first seven categories (*e.g.*, his brother's grandchild). It also includes individuals who are not related to him at all. It does not include an individual who was his spouse at any time during the year. I.R.C. § 152(d)(2)(H). Nor does it include an individual whose relationship with him violates local law. I.R.C. § 152(f)(3). Adopted children, foster children, and half-siblings can meet the relationship test. I.R.C. § 152(f)(1), (4).

The gross income test is satisfied if the individual's gross income is less than the exemption amount. I.R.C. § 152(d)(1)(B). The support test is met if the taxpayer provides more than half of the individual's support. I.R.C. § 152(d)(1)(C). The final requirement is that the individual not be a qualifying child of any taxpayer that year. I.R.C. § 152(d)(1)(D). If an individual could be both a qualifying child and a qualifying relative, the qualifying child rules govern.

If more than one taxpayer contributes to supporting an individual, it is possible that none of them provides more than half of her support. Section 152(d)(3) loosens the support test if they qualify for a multiple support agreement. These agreements have four requirements. First, no one person provides more than half of the individual's support. Second, at least two taxpayers who could have treated her as a dependent, but for the support requirement, provide more than half of her support. Third, at least one taxpayer provides more than 10% of her support. Fourth, each taxpayer (other than the one who will claim the dependent) who provides more than 10% of the support files a written declaration that he will not claim the person that year.

J. Tax Credits

The tax otherwise due can be reduced by personal credits. A taxpayer may qualify for a $2,000 child tax credit for each qualifying child who is less than 17 years old at year-end. I.R.C. §24(c)(1), (h)(2) ($1,000 after 2025). A portion of this credit may be refundable. I.R.C. §24(d)(1), (h)(5). This credit is subject to a phase-out based on AGI and filing status. It is reduced by $50 for every $1,000 (or fraction of $1,000) by which modified AGI exceeds the threshold. I.R.C. §24(b)(1). The Tax Cuts and Jobs Act of 2017 set the threshold amount for 2018 through 2025 at $400,000 for joint returns ($200,000 for all other taxpayers). I.R.C. §24(h)(3). It also added a $500 credit for each of the taxpayer's dependents who was not a qualifying child. I.R.C. §24(h)(4).

Taxpayers may also take a nonrefundable credit for the expenses of adopting a child. I.R.C. §23. We discuss this credit in Chapter 3 because taxpayers may have to coordinate taking this credit with excluding outlays provided by an employer-provided adoption assistance plan.

Two other credits associated with children are discussed in the previous chapter because they are available only if the taxpayer has earned income. These are the §21 credit for household and dependent care expenses and the §32 earned income tax credit. The §32 credit is refundable.

Taxpayers may take a credit authorized by §25A for a portion of qualified tuition and related expenses. The credit can be as high as $2,500 per year in a student's first four years of education, when the American Opportunity Tax Credit applies. The Lifetime Learning Credit is equal to 20% of the first $10,000 of qualified educational expenses the taxpayer pays for all eligible students that year. These credits are subject to phase-outs based on income.

Checkpoints

- Personal outlays are deductible only if a specific Code section authorizes the deduction.

- Taxpayers can deduct qualified education interest, qualified tuition, and contributions to health savings accounts in computing AGI. Nonitemizers can also deduct up to $300 of qualified charitable contributions in 2020.

- Most personal deductions are allowed only if the taxpayer itemizes.

- Taxpayers can deduct interest on loans incurred to purchase, construct, or substantially improve up to two qualified residences.

- There are limits on the amount of debt that qualifies as acquisition indebtedness or home equity indebtedness.

- Taxpayers can deduct state and local real property taxes, state and local personal property taxes, and state, local, and foreign income taxes.

- Taxpayers can elect to deduct state and local sales and use taxes instead of income taxes.

- The deduction for state, local, and foreign taxes is limited to $10,000 for taxable years between 2018 and 2025. No deduction is allowed for foreign real property taxes during those years.

- Taxpayers can deduct contributions made to qualifying charities. The overall maximum deduction is usually 50% of AGI, with a five-year carryover allowed for excess contributions. The limit is increased to 60% of AGI for cash gifts to qualifying charities (and is further increased during 2020 for most cash gifts).

- The deduction computation varies depending on whether the gift was outright or in trust, whether the gift was cash or other property, and whether the charity was publicly supported or not.

- Expenses for determining or disputing the amount of any tax are miscellaneous itemized deductions and cannot be taken in 2018 through 2025.

- Taxpayers may deduct unreimbursed expenses for medical care for themselves, their spouses, and their dependents. For most taxpayers, the deduction is available only for expenses exceeding 10% of AGI (7.5% in 2020).

- Most taxpayers can take the standard deduction instead of deducting itemized deductions. The standard deduction is adjusted for inflation each year and varies based on filing status.

- Taxpayers could deduct personal exemptions for themselves, their spouses, and their qualifying dependents but not in 2018 through 2025. Different tests apply in determining whether a potential dependent is a qualifying child or a qualifying relative.

- Many personal deductions are subject to phase-outs based on the taxpayer's AGI.

Chapter 14

Losses from
Discrete Events

Roadmap

- Introduction
- Overall losses, activity losses, and losses from discrete events
- Basis for loss
- Loss deductions allowed by Section 165
- Bad debt losses
- Disallowed losses

A. Introduction

This chapter discusses voluntary and involuntary losses from discrete events. Before doing so, we distinguish those losses from a taxpayer's overall losses and activity losses. We discuss overall losses and activity losses in other chapters.

Four topics are relevant when dealing with losses from discrete events: qualifying for a loss deduction; computing the deductible amount; determining the appropriate taxable year; and determining the character of the loss.

B. Overall Losses, Activity Losses, and Losses from Discrete Events

A taxpayer has an *overall loss* if his allowable deductions exceed his gross income. Because we use an annual accounting period, a taxpayer who sustains an overall loss benefits from his excess deductions only if the Code provides for carrying that loss to another year.

A taxpayer suffers an *activity loss* if his deductions for an activity exceed his gross income from that activity. The net loss provides a tax benefit only if he can deduct it against net income from other activities or carry the net loss to another year.

Finally, a taxpayer suffers a *discrete loss* if he sustains a loss with respect to one or more assets. He may sell shares of stock at a loss, or his uninsured car may be stolen. Although this chapter focuses on individual events, some of the computations require aggregating similar events occurring during the year.

C. Basis for Loss

We use the computation introduced in Chapter 5 to determine loss from a discrete event. It is the excess of adjusted basis for loss over the amount realized. I.R.C. § 1001(a). A mere decline in value, without a sale or other disposition, does not result in a realized loss.

The term "adjusted basis for computing loss" is critical. Although taxpayers usually have a single adjusted basis, they occasionally have one adjusted basis for computing gain and a lower adjusted basis for computing loss. Chapter 4 covered one such situation: the taxpayer received property as a gift, and its value on the date of gift was lower than the donor's adjusted basis. I.R.C. § 1015(a). This chapter covers another: the taxpayer converted personal-use property into business-use property (or to property held for profit), and it was worth less than his basis when the conversion occurred.

> Example 14-1. Alvin purchased a personal-use car for $24,000. Two years later, when the car was worth $15,000, he began using it exclusively in his chauffeur business. Immediately after the conversion, his basis for gain was $24,000 and his basis for loss was $15,000.

D. Loss Deductions Allowed by Section 165

Section 165(a) authorizes deducting "any loss sustained during the taxable year and not compensated for by insurance or otherwise." Section 165(b) provides that the taxpayer uses her adjusted basis for loss in computing any loss deduction.

Despite the "any loss" language, § 165(c) lets individuals deduct only three types of losses: (1) losses incurred in a trade or business; (2) losses incurred in a transaction entered into for profit even though not related to a trade or business; and (3) losses to personal-use property that arise from fire, storm, shipwreck, other casualty, or theft. Section 165(c)(3) is often called the casualty loss deduction, personal casualty loss deduction, or the personal casualty or theft loss deduction. Using the term casualty without "personal" is risky, as the limits imposed on casualty and theft losses of personal-use property do not apply to similar losses sustained for other types of property.

1. Losses Incurred in a Trade or Business or a Transaction Entered into for Profit

a. Sales and Exchanges

Section 165(c)(1) applies to a taxpayer who realizes a loss on selling or exchanging property used in a trade or business. Section 165(c)(2) applies if she realizes a loss on property acquired in a transaction entered into for profit. If the taxpayer sold property, we compare her adjusted basis for loss to her amount realized. The loss realized is the difference in those two amounts. Assuming she did not sell the property to a related person, as discussed later in this section, she deducts the loss. She prefers an ordinary loss because capital losses have deduction limits, and they reduce her ability to benefit from the lower tax rates applied to net capital gains. Chapter 19 addresses capital losses.

If the taxpayer exchanged her property for other property, her amount realized reflects the fair market value of any property she received in addition to money. After computing the loss, she determines whether a nonrecognition provision applies. If, for example, the exchange is a § 1031 like-kind exchange, she does not recognize her loss. Instead, she adjusts the basis of her new property to reflect her unrecognized loss. That gives her the opportunity to deduct it in a future year.

> Example 14-2. Beth purchased investment land several years ago for $100,000. It declined in value to $98,000. She transferred the land to an unrelated person in exchange for an airplane worth $98,000. Beth realized a loss of $2,000. Because this was not a like-kind exchange, she has a potential $2,000 loss deduction this year. Her basis for the airplane is its $98,000 value.

> Example 14-3. Beth instead received other investment land worth $98,000. Because this was a like-kind exchange, she cannot recognize her potential $2,000 loss deduction this year. Instead, her new land has an initial basis of $100,000, which is $2,000 higher than its actual

value. If she sells it for $98,000, she recognizes her previously unrecognized loss.

b. Casualties and Thefts

Although § 165(c)(3) authorizes a deduction for casualty or theft losses, it does not apply to losses incurred in a trade or business or in a transaction entered into for profit. Those losses are instead covered by § 165(c)(1) for a trade or business and § 165(c)(2) for a transaction entered into for profit.

Three factors are relevant: (1) whether the taxpayer received insurance proceeds or other compensation for the loss; (2) whether her loss was total or partial; and (3) whether she ever held the property for personal use.

The computation is simple if her property is stolen or destroyed, she receives no compensation, and she never used the property for personal purposes. Her loss equals her adjusted basis. If the only difference is that she received some compensation, her loss is the excess of her adjusted basis over the amount she received. She always uses her adjusted basis when computing a total loss of business property or property held for profit. She would have used that basis if she had sold the property immediately before the event.

> Example 14-4. Arlene's office was burglarized. She had insured the building but not its contents. Two items were taken: (1) a desk worth $10,000 before the theft (adjusted basis of $14,000) and (2) a desk chair worth $500 before the theft (adjusted basis of $300). She realized a loss of $14,000 for the desk and $300 for the chair. If she had carried insurance, she would compare the insurance proceeds to her adjusted basis to determine the amount of any gain or loss.

If her property is only damaged, she receives no compensation, and she never used the property for personal purposes, the computation is slightly different. Her loss is the lesser of her adjusted basis or the decline in value caused by the casualty. Reg. § 1.165-7(b)(1). Because she still owns the property, she cannot deduct the full adjusted basis if it exceeds the decline in value. And, if the decline in value is greater than her adjusted basis, she is still limited to adjusted basis as a maximum deduction.

> Example 14-5. Belle's delivery truck was damaged in a hailstorm. Her adjusted basis was $15,000. Its value before the storm was $18,000; its value after the storm was $14,000. Belle was not insured for hailstorm damage. Her potential loss deduction is $4,000, the decline in value caused by the casualty. If her truck instead had an adjusted basis of $2,500, her potential loss deduction would be only $2,500.

If she had carried insurance, she would compare the proceeds to her adjusted basis (or the decline in value caused by the storm) to determine her loss.

The regulations let the taxpayer use the cost of repairs to establish the decline in value. Reg. § 1.165-7(a)(2)(ii). The repairs she takes into account cannot exceed the amount necessary to restore the property. She cannot count amounts paid to improve its pre-casualty condition.

If she initially used the property for personal purposes and then converted it to business use or began holding it to realize a profit, the computation depends on the property's adjusted basis and its value when the conversion occurred. If the property was appreciated, the computations are the same as for property that was always used for business or held with a profit motive. If the property was worth less than its adjusted basis when she converted it, her initial basis for loss is that lower value. Her basis for gain is still the original adjusted basis. The computations for total or partial loss reflect these basis rules.

> **Example 14-6.** Alisa purchased a dining room table for $5,000 and used it for personal purposes. When it was worth $2,400, she converted it to business use in her newly opened restaurant. Unfortunately, the restaurant caught fire two weeks later. Her basis for loss is the table's $2,400 value at the time she converted it to business use. If the table was worth $6,300 when Alisa converted it to business use, her basis for loss is its $5,000 basis at the time of the conversion.

> **Example 14-7.** Barb purchased a minivan for personal use for $23,000. When it was worth $18,000, she converted it to business use. When the van was worth $16,200, it was damaged by an uninsured motorist and is now worth $12,000. Her loss (before considering any insurance) is the lesser of her basis for loss (the $18,000 value when she converted the property minus any depreciation she deducted after converting it) or the $4,200 decline in value caused by the casualty.

The taxpayer incurs a casualty loss in the year in which the loss is sustained. Reg. § 1.165-7(a)(1). If he has a claim for compensation, that part of the loss is not sustained until the compensation claim is resolved. This may result in his loss deduction being split between years.

> **Example 14-8.** Abe's business truck was destroyed in a collision when its adjusted basis was $42,000. He filed a claim with his insurer for the value of the truck minus the policy's $7,000 deductible. The insurer and Abe had not agreed by year-end on the truck's value before the

collision. Abe can deduct $7,000 in the year the collision occurred, because that amount is not covered by insurance. When his claim is resolved, he will compare the insurance proceeds to his remaining $35,000 adjusted basis ($42,000 minus the $7,000 loss he deducted) to determine any additional loss.

The taxpayer incurs a theft loss in the year he discovers the theft. I.R.C. § 165(e). There must be an actual event that constitutes a theft under state law—a taking that was illegal and done with criminal intent. The term theft includes larceny, embezzlement, and robbery. Reg. § 1.165-8(d). The facts are critical in establishing theft. For example, the IRS disallows theft loss deductions for declines in stock value based on corporate wrongdoing when the stock was purchased on the open market. In that situation, there is no theft under state law because the corporate employees involved in the wrongdoing did not intend to defraud the person who bought the stock. Notice 2004-27, 2004-1 C.B. 782. The investor can still deduct his loss if he sells the stock for less than his basis or if the stock becomes completely worthless.

Rev. Rul. 2009-9, 2009-14 I.R.B. 735, provides relief for victims of fraudulent investment schemes, which often occur over a multi-year period. Many investors lose their original investment, plus the income taxes paid on phantom income reported to them by the investment firm. The ruling allows them a theft loss deduction for their initial investment, plus any additional investments, plus any amounts reported as income, minus any amounts withdrawn before the scheme collapsed. This deduction is not subject to the limits for personal theft losses, discussed below, because the investors had a profit motive.

c. Other Compulsory or Involuntary Conversions

The taxpayer can deduct his loss from the condemnation or seizure of property used in a trade or business or acquired in a transaction entered into for profit. I.R.C. § 165(c)(1), (2). The computations are the same as those for casualties and thefts, which are themselves a class of involuntary conversion. We separate them here for two reasons. First, there are differences between casualties and thefts of business or for-profit property and personal-use property. Second, casualties and thefts are treated differently from other compulsory or involuntary conversions when we consider the capital gain and loss provisions in Chapter 19.

Example 14-9. Arnie paid $100,000 for land he used as a business parking lot. The county took his land by eminent domain and paid him its value, which was then $92,000. Arnie realized a loss of $8,000. Section 165(c)(1) makes that loss deductible. If he held the land for investment, § 165(c)(2) allows the deduction.

d. Abandonment

A taxpayer might abandon property, perhaps because it is no longer useful. If it is not depreciable, Reg. § 1.165-2(a) lets him deduct the loss in the year the "business or transaction is discontinued or where such property is permanently discarded from use therein …." The year in which the loss is sustained is not necessarily the year in which an overt act of abandonment occurs. We do not address the rules governing depreciable property, which are more complex.

Losses related to worthless securities are discussed later in this section. Although worthlessness has much in common with abandonment, the worthless security rules overlap with the bad debt rules discussed later in this chapter. In addition, losses from worthless securities have their own timing rules.

e. Placement on the Tax Return

Losses from the sale or exchange of property are deductible in computing AGI. Losses from casualties or thefts are not losses from sales or exchanges. If the taxpayer sustains these losses, his tax treatment is affected by the existence of casualty or theft gains, his holding period for the property involved, and the results of other transactions described in § 1231. The summary in the next paragraph assumes he had only one transaction, and it resulted in a casualty or theft loss.

A casualty or theft loss is deductible in computing AGI if it is incurred in a trade or business that he owns or is incurred in connection with property held for the production of rents and royalties. I.R.C. § 62(a)(1), (4). If he holds his business property as an employee or has an investment loss that is not attributable to property held for the production of rents and royalties, his loss may be an itemized deduction unless he has offsetting gains.

2. Casualty or Theft Losses of Personal-Use Property

No Code section allows a deduction for a loss from the sale, exchange, seizure, requisition, or abandonment of property held for personal use. The only deductible loss authorized for personal-use property is for losses caused by casualty or theft. I.R.C. § 165(c)(3). This deduction shares some features of the casualty or theft loss deduction for business or for-profit property, but additional limits apply to personal-use property.

a. Requirements

A casualty loss results from an identifiable event that causes physical damage to the taxpayer's property. Value reductions attributable to physical damage to *neighboring* property are not sufficient. *Pulvers v. Commissioner*, 407 F.2d 838 (9th Cir. 1969). The same is true for value reductions caused by nonphysical attributes, such as adverse publicity. For example, the Tax Court disallowed a casualty loss deduction based on buyer resistance in *Chamales v. Commissioner*, T.C. Memo. 2000-33. The taxpayers lived next door to O.J. Simpson. They claimed that their property was devalued after his arrest, which led to reporters and sightseers inundating the neighborhood.

Section 165(c)(3) provides that deductions for losses to personal-use property are permitted if "such losses arise from fire, storm, shipwreck, or other casualty." To be an "other casualty," the event must be similar to the listed events. In other words, it must be sudden, unexpected, or unusual in nature. An earthquake is one such event. Gradual losses, such as structural damage caused by termites occurring over a span of years, do not meet the suddenness standard. Rev. Rul. 63-232, 1963-2 C.B. 97. The Tax Court disallowed a deduction for trees destroyed by Dutch elm disease because disease is not a sudden event. *Coleman v. Commissioner*, 76 T.C. 580 (1981). More recently, the Tax Court denied the taxpayer's deduction for gambling losses caused by a reaction to medicine he was taking to treat Parkinson's Disease. *Mancini v. Commissioner*, T.C. Memo. 2019-16. The losses occurred over a multi-year period, and thus were not sudden, and the depletion of his assets did not constitute damage to his property.

Judicial decisions involving rings illustrate the fact-intensive nature of the suddenness requirement. The court allowed a deduction in *White v. Commissioner*, 48 T.C. 430 (1967). Mr. White inadvertently slammed a car door on his wife's hand; this apparently broke the prongs on her ring. When she shook her hand in pain, the diamond flew out and was never recovered. It previously allowed a deduction in *Carpenter v. Commissioner*, T.C. Memo. 1966-228. Mrs. Carpenter placed her ring in a glass of ammonia to clean it and left the glass by the sink. Mr. Carpenter did not notice the ring when he emptied the glass into the disposal. Several years earlier, a district court disallowed the deduction when a husband flushed tissues down the toilet. He did not realize that his wife's rings were in one of the tissues. *Keenan v. Bowers*, 91 F. Supp. 771 (E.D.S.C. 1950). The opinion in *Carpenter* does not mention *Keenan v. Bowers*.

These cases illustrate more than the need for suddenness. They also illustrate that the taxpayer's own negligence does not bar the deduction. Reg. § 1.165-7(a)(3) mentions only willful act or willful negligence as a bar in its discussion of damage to automobiles. In denying a deduction for a loss sustained when the taxpayer, who set fire to his estranged wife's clothing, ended up burning down the house, the Tax Court cited both the taxpayer's willful behavior and the state's public policy against arson. *Blackman v. Commissioner*, 88 T.C. 677 (1987).

A taxpayer who claims a theft loss deduction has the burden of proving that the property was stolen. *Allen v. Commissioner*, 16 T.C. 163 (1951). No presumption of theft arises simply because the property is missing. *Popa v. Commissioner*, 73 T.C. 130, 133 (1979), is based on unusual facts. Mr. Popa was away from Vietnam when Saigon fell and was unable to return for his belongings. The Tax Court majority allowed a deduction even though he could not prove whether his loss occurred from sudden destruction, theft, or government seizure. "We can hardly fault petitioner for not remaining to determine whether his property was destroyed by gun fire, by looting, by fire, or some form of seizure by the remaining Saigon residents, the Vietcong, or the North Vietnamese." Although he could deduct the loss if his property was destroyed or stolen, he could not deduct it if his property was seized by the government. *Powers v. Commissioner*, 36 T.C. 1191 (1961). The dissenters believed that he had not met his burden of proof as to what happened to his property.

b. Year of Deduction

Generally, a casualty loss is deductible in the year it is sustained. Reg. § 1.165-7(a)(1). In certain circumstances, such as a casualty loss that occurs during a federally declared disaster, the taxpayer can elect to deduct the loss in the year before the casualty occurred by filing an amended return for the prior year. I.R.C. § 165(i)(1). For losses resulting from theft, the deduction is taken in the year the theft is discovered. I.R.C. § 165(e). If there is a reasonable prospect of recovering compensation, the deduction is postponed until the situation is resolved. If the taxpayer takes a deduction, and then later receives compensation, he includes the amount received in gross income in the year it is received, subject to any exclusion based on the § 111 tax benefit rule. Reg. § 1.165-1(d)(2)(iii).

c. Amount of Deduction

The amount the taxpayer can deduct depends on the amount of the loss, the amount of her AGI, and whether she also realizes personal casualty or theft gains that year. If the casualty or theft loss occurred in 2018 through 2025, it may also depend on whether it arises from a federally declared disaster.

Event is a federally declared disaster. A federally declared disaster is a disaster that the President determines warrants assistance under the Robert T. Stafford Disaster Relief and Emergency Assistance Act. An area that is determined to warrant that assistance is a "disaster area." I.R.C. § 165(i)(5).

If the taxpayer's property is destroyed, her loss is computed using the lesser of its value immediately before the event or her adjusted basis for computing loss. Reg. § 1.165-7(b)(1). This differs from the rule applied to casualty and theft losses incurred in a business or for-profit setting. In those settings, the taxpayer whose property is stolen or destroyed uses her adjusted basis for loss. She ignores the property's value before the event.

If her property is only damaged, her loss is the lesser of the decline in value caused by the casualty or her adjusted basis for computing loss. In both this situation and the situation described in the preceding paragraph, she reduces the loss by any insurance or other compensation received.

The taxpayer reduces every personal casualty or theft loss by $100. I.R.C. § 165(h)(1). The reduction is $100 per event, not per item of property stolen or destroyed. If she has no personal casualty gains that year, she also reduces her potential deduction for personal casualties and thefts by 10% of her AGI. I.R.C. § 165(h)(2)(A). The 10% reduction is per year, not per event. Examples 14-10 through 14-12 assume that the tornado and hurricane resulted in April's county being declared a disaster area.

> **Example 14-10.** April had salary income of $200,000. Her home was destroyed by a major tornado when it was worth $350,000. Her adjusted basis was $480,000, she had no insurance, and she suffered no other personal casualties that year. Her potential casualty loss is $350,000 because that amount is less than her adjusted basis. She subtracts $100 and also subtracts $20,000 (10% of her AGI). Her casualty loss deduction is $329,900.

> **Example 14-11.** Assume instead that April's adjusted basis for her home was $265,000. Her potential casualty loss is now $265,000 because that is less than the value of her home before the casualty. She again subtracts $20,100. Her casualty loss deduction is $244,900.

> **Example 14-12.** Assume instead that April's home was damaged but not destroyed in Example 14-10. It was worth $350,000 before the tornado hit and $242,000 after. The $108,000 decline in value is less than her $480,000 adjusted basis, so it is the amount of her loss. After subtracting $20,100, she has a casualty loss deduction of $87,900. If her uninsured car was destroyed in a major hurricane two weeks later,

she computes an additional loss (the lesser of its value before the storm or its basis). That loss is also reduced by $100 because it was a separate event from the tornado.

The casualty loss deductions in Examples 14-10 and 14-11 exceeded April's AGI. Even though her loss was personal, the excess loss qualifies as a business loss for purposes of the § 172 net operating loss deduction. She can carry an NOL over and deduct it from income in the carryover years.

The computation is more complex if personal casualty or theft gains and personal casualty or theft losses occur in the same year. First, any gain is from a compulsory or involuntary conversion. Section 1033 lets the taxpayer postpone being taxed on the gain if she reinvests any insurance or other proceeds in qualifying replacement property. Thus, she has three general choices: (1) don't reinvest the proceeds and report her gain as gross income; (2) reinvest the proceeds but report her gain as gross income anyway; (3) reinvest the proceeds and elect to defer reporting her gain. She has personal casualty or theft gains for purposes of computing the casualty or theft loss deduction only for gains she includes in gross income.

The discussion below assumes that she reports her gain as gross income rather than replacing the property and electing nonrecognition. It covers taxpayers who have a net casualty or theft loss and taxpayers who have a net casualty or theft gain separately. This discussion covers only personal casualties or thefts because § 165(c)(3) does not apply to casualties or thefts of business or for-profit property.

The 10% of AGI deduction limit is affected by the existence of personal casualty or theft gains. The $100 per event limit is not affected by those gains. If personal casualty or theft losses exceed personal casualty or theft gains, the taxpayer's loss deduction has two components. She deducts the losses in computing AGI to the extent that they do not exceed the gains. She deducts the remaining loss amount only to the extent it exceeds 10% of AGI. I.R.C. § 165(h)(2)(A). If personal casualty or theft gains exceed personal casualty or theft losses, the only limit that applies to her loss deduction is the $100 per event reduction. As was true for the preceding examples, we assume the fire and earthquake occurred in federally declared disaster areas.

> Example 14-13. Bunny had salary income of $300,000. Her principal residence was destroyed by an uncontrollable forest fire when it was worth $200,000. Her adjusted basis was $225,000, and she had no insurance. Her vacation home was destroyed by an earthquake when it was worth $124,000. Her adjusted basis was $82,000, and it was insured for its full value. Bunny sustained a $200,000 personal casualty loss

on her principal residence, which she reduces by $100. She realized a $42,000 personal casualty gain on her vacation home. Of her $199,900 personal casualty loss, Bunny can deduct $42,000 in computing AGI because she included a $42,000 personal casualty gain in gross income. She reduces her remaining $157,900 personal casualty loss by 10% of her $300,000 AGI. That gives her a $127,900 itemized deduction. Bunny's total personal casualty loss deduction is thus $169,900, part of which is deducted in computing AGI and part of which is an itemized deduction.

Example 14-14. Assume instead that Bunny's vacation home was worth $500,000. Because it was insured for its value, she realized a personal casualty gain of $418,000. She can deduct her full $199,900 personal casualty loss because her personal casualty gain exceeds her personal casualty loss. Her $418,000 gain increases her AGI; her $199,900 loss deduction decreases it.

Event is not a federally declared disaster. Until the Tax Cuts and Jobs Act of 2017, the taxpayer's deduction did not depend on there being a federally declared disaster. That act added § 165(h)(5), which applies in 2018 through 2025. A taxpayer who suffers a personal casualty or theft that does not occur in a disaster area (or is not attributable to the federally declared disaster even if it occurs in the disaster area) cannot deduct his loss except to the extent he has personal casualty or theft gains that he has not used to offset federally declared disaster losses.

Example 14-15. Arthur had salary income of $300,000. His principal residence was destroyed by lightning in 2019 when it was worth $200,000. His adjusted basis was $225,000, and he had no insurance. His vacation home was destroyed when his child accidentally started a fire. His adjusted basis was $82,000, and it was insured for its $124,000 value. He sustained a $200,000 personal casualty loss on his home, which he reduces by $100. He realized a $42,000 personal casualty gain on his vacation home. Of his $199,900 personal casualty loss, Arthur can deduct $42,000 in computing AGI because he included a $42,000 personal casualty gain in gross income. Because the lightning strike did not occur in a federally declared disaster area, he cannot deduct his remaining $157,900 personal casualty loss.

Insurance claim requirement. A taxpayer who suffers a personal casualty or theft might fear a rate increase or a policy cancellation; he would rather claim a larger casualty loss deduction and not ask his insurer for compensation. That tactic will not succeed. Section 165(h)(4)(E) disallows any portion of the deduction that would be covered by insurance unless he timely files an insurance claim. This rule does not apply to losses of business property or property acquired in a transaction entered into for profit.

d. Placement on the Tax Return

If a taxpayer has deductible personal casualty or theft losses and no personal casualty or theft gains, he has an ordinary loss deduction; it is an itemized deduction. If he has both deductible personal casualty or theft losses and personal casualty or theft gains, the losses are deducted in computing AGI but only up to the amount of personal casualty gains. I.R.C. § 165(h)(4)(A). The remaining deductible personal casualty loss is an itemized deduction. If his personal casualty or theft gains exceed his deductible personal casualty or theft losses, all the gains and losses are treated as capital gains and losses. I.R.C. § 165(h)(2)(B). The losses are deducted in computing AGI.

3. Worthless Securities

The tax consequences of worthless securities are governed by § 165(g) even if the security is a debt instrument. Section 166, which applies to bad debt losses, does not apply to debt evidenced by a security. If the security is a capital asset, § 165(g)(1) treats the loss as a loss from a sale or exchange that occurs on the last day of the taxable year. The loss is deducted in computing AGI. I.R.C. § 62(a)(3).

Classification as a capital loss occurring on the last day of the year has two consequences. First, the loss is subject to the § 1211 capital loss deduction limits if total capital losses exceed total capital gains. Second, the taxpayer's holding period may be lengthened enough to make the loss long-term rather than short-term. This might reduce his ability to benefit from the lower tax rates available for net capital gains.

Section 165(g)(2) defines securities as shares of stock, rights to subscribe for or receive shares of stock, and bonds, debentures, notes, certificates, or other evidences of indebtedness. The instrument must have been issued by a corporation or a government with interest coupons or in registered form. An account payable due from a corporation is not a security. A note issued by an individual is not a security.

E. Bad Debt Losses

Section 166 allows a deduction for debts that become uncollectible in a taxable year. Unlike § 165(c), which divides losses into business, transaction entered into for profit, and personal, § 166 divides bad debts into two categories: business and nonbusiness.

1. Requirements

The taxpayer can deduct a loss only for bona fide debt. The regulations define a bona fide debt as "a debt which arises from a debtor-creditor relationship based upon a valid and enforceable obligation to pay a fixed or determinable sum of money." Reg. § 1.166-1(c). He should have little difficulty establishing a debt is bona fide if it arose in an arm's-length transaction. The IRS will argue that transfers to a close friend or family member were meant as a gift rather than as a bona fide loan. It can also argue that the taxpayer-lender canceled the loan for donative reasons even if it was originally a bona fide loan. He loses his deduction if the IRS prevails on either argument.

The gift presumption can be rebutted if the transaction has the characteristics we expect to see in an arm's-length transaction. These include a formal promissory note, a fixed payment schedule, and interest. The analysis involves looking at all the facts and circumstances, including enforcement of the loan terms.

In *Bugbee v. Commissioner*, T.C. Memo. 1975-45, the taxpayer made loans to a close friend. He charged interest, but the friend never paid interest or any part of the principal. The Tax Court allowed the deduction. It stated that determining "[w]hether a transfer of money creates a bona fide debt depends upon the existence of an intent by both parties, substantially contemporaneous to the time of such transfer, to establish an enforceable obligation of repayment." This is largely a facts-and-circumstances analysis, and the relevant question is whether the parties intended that the lender be repaid. The court held that the friend's poor financial condition did not preclude the deduction — a bad debt may still be deductible even if the loan involved a substantial amount of risk.

As was true for determining whether the debt is a bona fide debt, determining whether it is worthless is based on the relevant facts and circumstances. Reg. § 1.166-2(a). The lender does not have to file a lawsuit to determine collectability if the surrounding circumstances indicate that the debt is worthless. Reg. § 1.166-2(b). For example, if the debtor has filed for bankruptcy, the lender has persuasive evidence that the debt is worthless. Reg. § 1.166-2(c).

2. Basis for Loss

We compute the deduction using the taxpayer's basis for loss. I.R.C. § 166(b). If he has no basis, there can be no deduction. This rule is most likely to affect a cash-method taxpayer. Because he does not report gross income until he receives payment, he has no basis for an account receivable and therefore has no bad debt deduction. An accrual-method taxpayer has a tax-cost basis equal to the amount he previously included in income.

> **Example 14-16.** Last year, Avery drafted articles of incorporation and billed the client $1,500. The client declared bankruptcy this year, and Avery will not be paid. If he uses the cash method, he never reported the $1,500 as gross income. As a result, he has no basis for the account receivable and no bad debt deduction. If he uses the accrual method, he reported $1,500 gross income last year. That gave him a basis of $1,500 for the account receivable. He can deduct a $1,500 bad debt this year. Avery's two-year tax consequences are the same for each method, but the year of reporting differs. Both methods net out to zero.

The distinction between cash and accrual methods is less important if the debt represents money lent to the debtor. Taxpayers using either method have a basis equal to the amount lent. An accrual-method taxpayer also has a basis for unpaid interest he reported as gross income.

3. Type of Loss

For individuals, § 166(d) treats a nonbusiness bad debt as a loss from the sale or exchange of a capital asset held not more than one year. In other words, it is treated as a short-term capital loss and is subject to the deduction limits applied to capital losses. The deduction is allowed only for a total loss; the taxpayer cannot estimate and deduct a partial loss. Section 166(d) defines nonbusiness debt in the negative by indicating what it is not. It is not a debt that was created or acquired in connection with the trade or business. Nor is it a debt the loss from whose worthlessness was incurred in the trade or business.

If the debt is a business bad debt, the taxpayer can deduct the loss as an ordinary loss. In addition, he may be able to estimate and deduct a partial loss rather than waiting for the debt to become totally worthless. I.R.C. § 166(a)(2). Determining whether a debt is a business debt is illustrated in Reg. § 1.166-5 and case law. To be a debt created or acquired in connection with a trade or business, the obligation must bear a direct relationship to the taxpayer's trade or business.

If there is more than one motive for making the loan, the business motive must be the dominant motive. *United States v. Generes*, 405 U.S. 93 (1972). For example, if a shareholder makes a loan to a corporation, the loan is a nonbusiness loan because investing is not considered a trade or business. *Whipple v. Commissioner*, 373 U.S. 193 (1963). But if he is also an employee, and his dominant motive for making the loan is to stay employed, the loan may be a business loan. *Haslam v. Commissioner*, T.C. Memo. 1974-97. Unlike Mr. Generes, who failed the dominant motive test, Mr. Haslam was a full-time employee of the debtor and had no other employment.

4. Recovery of Previously Deducted Loss

A taxpayer who properly deducted a debt based on evidence that it was un-collectible may later receive full or partial repayment. In that case, he has gross income equal to the amount recovered, or the amount deducted, whichever is less. He reports that income in the year of recovery, subject to any exclusion based on the § 111 tax benefit rule. Reg. § 1.166-1(f).

F. Disallowed Losses

1. Taxpayer Wrongdoing

Section 165 does not include public policy limitations. Nevertheless, courts have disallowed loss deductions based on public policy when they felt the taxpayer's conduct deserved this treatment. In *Wood v. United States*, 2002 WL 31973260 (S.D. Fla. 2002), a district court disallowed a deduction for amounts forfeited to the government by a smuggler. The Tax Court disallowed a deduction for funds lost by a taxpayer who thought he was participating in a counterfeiting scheme but was actually being robbed by the other "participants." *Mazzei v. Commissioner*, 61 T.C. 497 (1974).

2. Transactions with Related Persons

A taxpayer cannot deduct a loss unless it is sustained in an actual transaction or event. Problems arise when she wants to deduct a decline in value *and* keep the property. She might sell the property to a family member but plan to reacquire it later. Alternatively, she might sell it to an entity over which she has control. If § 267(a)(1) applies, she cannot deduct the loss.

Section 267(a)(1) applies bright-line tests to sales between related persons. This lets courts avoid fact-intensive litigation over whether the seller sufficiently cut her ties to the property. The deduction is disallowed even if the buyer and seller are hostile to each other. For example, the deduction was disallowed for sales by one brother to another that were "ordered by binding arbitration to separate the interests of the hostile brothers...." *Miller v. Commissioner*, 75 T.C. 182 (1980).

a. Transactions Covered

Section 267(a)(1) provides that "No deduction shall be allowed in respect of any loss from the sale or exchange of property, directly or indirectly, between" taxpayers falling into certain listed categories. Taxpayers falling into those categories are "related." Thus, this section applies if there is a direct or indirect sale or exchange between related taxpayers. When a corporation is involved, both actual and constructive ownership count in determining if parties are related.

If § 267(a)(1) covered only direct sales, taxpayers could avoid it by transferring property to individuals or entities that were not included in the list of related persons but were nevertheless closely associated with the transferor. Because it also applies to indirect sales and exchanges, the IRS can claim that a direct sale to an unrelated taxpayer is really an indirect sale to a related taxpayer. For example, if an individual sold investment property to her son-in-law, the IRS might claim this was really an indirect sale to her daughter.

Another indirect sale device involves third-party intermediaries. For example, in *McWilliams v. Commissioner*, 331 U.S. 694, 700–01 (1947), the Supreme Court disallowed losses when one spouse sold stock through a broker and the other spouse bought the same number of shares in the same company, also through a broker. "Congress ... could not have intended to include within the scope of [§ 267(a)(1)] only simple transfers made directly or through a dummy, or to exclude transfers of securities effected through the medium of the Stock Exchange, unless it wanted to leave a loophole almost as large as the one it had set out to close." Since the enactment of § 1041 in 1984, § 267(a)(1) no longer applies to sales involving spouses. *McWilliams* remains relevant to indirect sales involving other related persons.

b. Categories of Related Persons

Section 267(b) lists 13 categories of relationships that result in loss disallowance. In addition to family members, these categories include certain corporations, partnerships, trusts, and estates. Those entities are included based on relationships reflecting ownership or status.

Section 267(b)(1) lists "members of a family," and § 267(c)(4) defines that term as brothers and sisters, including half-brothers and half-sisters, spouse, ancestors, and lineal descendants. Full effect is given to legal adoptions. Reg. § 1.267(c)-1(a)(4). Section 267(c)(4) does not include aunts, uncles, nieces, nephews, or cousins in its definition of relatives. A taxpayer who sold loss property to his mother's sister (his aunt) could deduct that loss unless the government established that it was an indirect sale to his mother. This definition of family differs from the definition used in some other Code sections. For example, for purposes of treating a taxpayer as a dependent, stepsiblings are treated as family members. I.R.C. § 152(c)(2), (d)(2).

> **Example 14-17.** Anthony owns investment property, which is worth $5,000 less than his basis. He cannot deduct his loss on selling that property to Bert if they are brothers or half-brothers. He can deduct his loss if they are stepbrothers.

Section 267(b) lists several relationships involving corporations. If any of these relationships exists, losses are disallowed on sales between the parties. It does not matter whether the corporation or the other party makes the sale or exchange. Most of these relationships involve actual or constructive ownership of more than 50% of the value of the corporation's stock. If a corporation issues more than one class of stock, the rights of each class (*e.g.*, to vote or receive dividends) are relevant to its value.

Section 267(b) also lists several relationships involving trusts. These include the trust's grantor and its fiduciary and the trust's beneficiary and its fiduciary. Disallowance provisions also cover a tax-exempt entity and any person who controls it or whose family controls it. This provision is most likely to apply to foundations that are funded by a small donor group, often a single family. Section 267(b)(13) disallows losses on sales or exchanges between the executor of an estate and a beneficiary of the estate. This rule does not apply if the transaction satisfies the beneficiary's right to a pecuniary bequest.

> **Example 14-18.** In her will, Anita bequeathed $10,000 to Ben. After the executor finished paying debts, there was no cash left to pay that bequest. The estate owned shares of stock worth $10,000, for which it had a basis of $10,300. Because this was a pecuniary bequest, the executor could deduct the $300 loss if it transferred the stock directly to Ben.

Section 267(b) does not cover the treatment of sales or exchanges between partners and their partnerships. Instead § 707(b)(1) disallows losses on sales or exchanges between a partnership and a person that owns more than 50% of either the capital interest or profits interest in that partnership. It also disallows losses between two partnerships if the same persons own more than 50% of the capital interests or profits interests.

c. Constructive Ownership

A shareholder could try to prevent §267(a)(1) from applying to sales between himself and a corporation by transferring stock to family members. If he reduced the value of his shares to 50% or less, it would apply only if the IRS could establish that he owned the stock indirectly—perhaps because he controlled how family members voted or limited their ability to sell the shares to a third party.

The constructive ownership rules reduce the need for litigation regarding indirect ownership. When they apply, a taxpayer is treated as owning the shares that he actually owns *and* the shares that he constructively owns through attribution from another person. Although attribution may appear to result in total ownership that exceeds 100%, that is only a fiction used for applying §267(a)(1). It is not actual ownership.

Section 267(c) covers attribution from entities, from family members, and from partners. It also covers reattribution following attribution from one of the first three groups. These rules are used in determining if parties to a transaction are related. Examples of constructive ownership appear in Reg. §1.267(c)-1(b).

If an entity (corporation, partnership, trust, or estate) owns shares in a corporation, those shares are constructively owned by its shareholders, partners, or beneficiaries. The attribution is proportionate to their interest in the entity. I.R.C. §267(c)(1).

> **Example 14-19.** Alana is a 30% partner in ABCD Partnership. She is not related to the other partners. ABCD owns 80% of the shares of LMN Corporation. Because of §267(c)(1), Alana constructively owns 24% of the LMN shares. Because she does not own more than 50% of the value of its shares, she and LMN are not related persons.

> **Example 14-20.** Buzz is a 75% partner in BCDE Partnership. He is not related to the other partners. BCDE owns 80% of the shares of OPQ Corporation. Because of §267(c)(1), Buzz constructively owns 60% of the OPQ shares, and he and OPQ are related persons. He cannot deduct a loss on selling property to OPQ; it cannot deduct a loss on selling property to him.

An individual constructively owns stock owned by other family members. I.R.C. §267(c)(2). She constructively owns stock owned by her partner only if she actually owns stock or if she constructively owns stock because of attribution from an entity. I.R.C. §267(c)(3).

> **Example 14-21.** Alec and Brandon are brothers. Alec owns 60% of the shares of XYZ Corporation. Unrelated persons own the remaining

40%. All XYZ shares are equal in value. Alec has actual ownership of 60% of the XYZ shares. Brandon has constructive ownership of the same shares. Alec is actually related, and Brandon is constructively related, to XYZ for purposes of loss disallowance.

Example 14-22. Amara and Brenda, two unrelated individuals, are equal partners in the AB Partnership. In addition, each of them owns 30% of the shares of ZZ Corporation. Because each partner actually owns shares in ZZ, each also constructively owns shares owned by her partner. Each is treated as owning 60% of the ZZ shares (30% actual ownership and 30% constructive ownership). Amara and Brenda are each related to ZZ for purposes of the loss disallowance rules. If Amara owned no ZZ shares and Brenda owned 60% of the ZZ shares, Amara would not constructively own the ZZ shares owned by Brenda. She and ZZ would not be related parties.

If a person constructively owns stock, can that stock be reattributed to yet another person? Section 267(c)(5) provides that reattribution is allowed only for stock owned constructively through attribution from an entity. Individuals who constructively own stock owned by a family member or a partner are not treated as actually owning that stock for the purpose of making yet another person a constructive owner.

Example 14-23. Adler and Betty are equal shareholders (50%) in Aster Corporation and are married to each other. Aster owns 60% of the Jasmine Corporation shares. Unrelated persons own the remaining Jasmine shares. Because of attribution from Aster, Adler and Betty each constructively owns 30% of the Jasmine shares (50% of the 60% owned by Aster). In addition, the shares Adler constructively owns are reattributed to Betty, and vice versa. Each of them thus constructively owns 60% of the Jasmine shares. Adler and Betty are both treated as related to Jasmine. The result would be the same if Adler and Betty were brother and sister or parent and child instead of spouses.

d. Treatment of Related Purchaser

The tax attributes of the person who acquires the property depend on the method of acquisition. If he purchases the property, he takes a cost basis. I.R.C. § 1012. If he acquires it in a nonrecognition transaction, such as a § 1031 like-kind exchange, his basis is computed with reference to the property he relinquished. His basis does not include the transferor's disallowed loss. Reg.

§ 1.267(d)-1(c)(1). That disallowed loss has no effect on whether the property is a capital asset in his hands, and his holding period does not include the transferor's holding period. Reg. § 1.267(d)-1(c)(3).

> **Example 14-24.** Amy purchased investment land for $18,000. She later sold it to her son Basil for $14,000, which was its value at the time of the sale. Basil will use this land in his parking lot business. His basis is his $14,000 cost. Although the land was a capital asset in Amy's hands, it will be § 1231 property for Basil if he holds it for more than one year before disposing of it. He does not include Amy's holding period in determining his holding period.

If § 267(a)(1) disallows the transferor's loss deduction, the transferee may benefit when he disposes of that property. Section 267(d)(1) lets him offset any gain realized on a later disposition by the transferor's disallowed loss. If he disposes of the property in a like-kind exchange, his replacement property qualifies for the relief. Reg. § 1.267(d)-1(a)(2).

> **Example 14-25.** Aden sold investment land to his brother Baden and realized a $32,000 loss. Because he and Baden are related, Aden could not deduct his loss. Five years later, Baden sold the land for a gain of $60,000. Baden's gross income includes only $28,000 of his gain. His $60,000 gain realized is reduced by Aden's $32,000 disallowed loss.

> **Example 14-26.** Instead of selling the land he acquired from Aden, Baden exchanged it with Caden (an unrelated person) for like-kind investment land. Baden's basis for the original land became his basis for the new land. Baden later sold the new land for a gain of $33,000. His gross income includes only $1,000 of that gain. Because he acquired the new land in a like-kind exchange, Baden still qualifies for § 267(d)(1) relief and can reduce his taxable gain by Aden's $32,000 disallowed loss.

Section 267(d)(1) reduces taxable gain on the subsequent disposition. It does not produce or increase a loss. It benefits only the original related transferee. Reg. § 1.267(d)-1(a)(3). If she transfers the property by gift instead of by selling it, no one benefits from the previously disallowed loss. In addition, it applies only if the transferor's loss would have been taken into account in computing taxable income if it had been allowable. I.R.C. § 267(d)(3).

> **Example 14-27.** Amanda sold investment land to her sister Betsy and realized a $15,000 loss. Because she and Betsy are related, Amanda could not deduct her loss. Five years later, Betsy sold the land for a gain of $4,000. Because Amanda's disallowed loss exceeds Betsy's gain,

Betsy reports none of her gain as gross income. She cannot deduct the additional $11,000 of Amanda's disallowed loss. If Betsy instead gave the land to her son Al and he sold it, he cannot offset his gain by any of Amanda's disallowed loss. He was not the original transferee.

e. Coordination with Nonrecognition Provisions

If § 267(a)(1) applies to a sale or exchange, the transferor can never deduct his loss. If a nonrecognition provision applies, he postpones deducting his loss; it is not permanently disallowed. If a transaction could be covered by both § 267(a)(1) and a nonrecognition provision, we must determine which Code section applies.

A taxpayer generally does not recognize gain or loss if he exchanges real property held for productive use in a trade or business or for investment for like-kind property that will be held for either purpose. I.R.C. § 1031. To preserve the deferred gain or loss, he computes his basis for the new property using the basis for his old property as a starting point. I.R.C. § 1031(d). If the two parties to the exchange are related, either § 267(a)(1) or § 1031 could theoretically apply. These sections give very different results.

> **Example 14-28.** Anton owns investment land worth $200,000. His basis is $240,000. He exchanges the land with his sister Batya and receives investment land worth $200,000. Anton has a realized loss of $40,000. If § 267(a)(1) applies, he can never deduct that loss. His initial basis for the new property is $200,000. Batya can offset the $40,000 disallowed loss against her gain if she later sells the property at a gain. If § 1031 instead applies, Anton can deduct his $40,000 loss when *he* sells the new property; his basis for it will be $240,000. Batya will get no benefit from Anton's loss.

In this situation, § 1031 appears to govern the transaction. Rev. Rul. 72-151, 1972-1 C.B. 225. Section 1031(f) contains anti-abuse rules that apply to related-party like-kind exchanges; we discuss those in Chapter 17.

Section 267(g) provides that losses realized on sales between spouses are not covered by § 267(a)(1). Instead, those losses are subject to the nonrecognition rules of § 1041. The recipient spouse takes the transferor's basis, holding period, and potential for depreciation recapture. Although § 267(a)(1) does not apply to sales between spouses, Example 14-23 illustrates how a spouse's status as a related person is relevant in computing constructive ownership.

A taxpayer cannot currently deduct a loss on selling stock or securities if he acquires substantially identical stock or securities within a period beginning 30 days before the sale and ending 30 days after it. I.R.C. § 1091(a). He benefits from the disallowed loss at a later date because it increases his basis for the stock or securities acquired within the specified time period. If his original sale was to a related person, § 267(d)(1) does not apply. I.R.C. § 267(d)(2). As a result, the transferee cannot reduce her later gain by the transferor's disallowed loss. The taxpayer who sustained the disallowed loss is the one who ultimately benefits from it.

Checkpoints

- Individuals can deduct losses incurred in a trade or business, incurred in a transaction entered into for profit, or that are personal casualty or theft losses.

- Taxpayers engaged in a trade or business or who hold property acquired in a transaction entered into for profit can deduct losses from both voluntary and involuntary dispositions.

- If the taxpayer sustains a total loss with respect to business or for-profit property, his loss computation uses his adjusted basis for loss even if that exceeds the property's value before the loss.

- If the taxpayer converted personal-use property to business or for-profit use, his basis for loss cannot exceed the value of the property when he converted it. His basis for gain is not subject to that limit.

- The deduction for casualty and theft losses of personal-use property is based on the lesser of the taxpayer's basis or the decline in value caused by the casualty or theft. The amount computed by this formula is reduced by $100 per event in addition to being reduced by any insurance or other compensation received.

- To be a casualty loss, the loss must be sudden, unexpected, and unusual in nature.

- Personal casualty and theft losses are itemized deductions to the extent that they exceed personal casualty and theft gains. Only the amount of the net loss that exceeds 10% of AGI is deductible.

- In 2018 through 2025, personal casualty and theft losses that are not incurred in a federally declared disaster area are not deductible except to the extent the taxpayer has personal casualty gains that are not used to offset personal casualty and theft losses incurred in a disaster area.

- Losses from worthless securities that are capital assets are treated as capital losses occurring on the last day of the taxable year.

- Taxpayers can deduct bad debt losses if the debt is bona fide and uncollectible.

- Business bad debts are deductible as ordinary losses. Nonbusiness bad debts are treated as short-term capital losses.

- Although § 165 does not contain public policy limitations, courts may disallow a loss based on public policy grounds.

- A taxpayer cannot deduct a loss if he sells the property to certain family members or related entities.

- Section 267(a)(1) applies a bright-line test. The taxpayer's motive does not matter.

- Section 267(a)(1) applies even if the taxpayer uses a third-party and sells indirectly to a related person.
- Constructive ownership rules apply in determining if a corporation and another party are related.
- The related buyer can reduce any gain he realizes on a subsequent sale by the seller's previously disallowed loss.

Chapter 15

Losses from Activities

Roadmap

- Introduction
- Mixed use of a dwelling unit
- Activities not engaged in for profit
- Activities for which the taxpayer is not at risk
- Passive activities
- Excess business losses
- Wagering losses

A. Introduction

This chapter covers provisions that prevent a taxpayer from offsetting a loss from one activity against profits from another activity. Some limitations are permanent in nature. Others merely defer the deduction until a later year.

Most of these limitations apply in a business or income-producing setting. Limitations apply to certain activities that produce income but also have significant personal elements. Still others apply because the taxpayer does not have a sufficient investment in the activity or is not sufficiently engaged in the activity

B. Mixed Use of a Dwelling Unit

1. Definitions

Taxpayers who use a home for personal and for business or income-producing activities may claim tax deductions to reduce their cost of ownership. Not surprisingly, the Code limits their ability to do so. Those limits are found in § 280A, which applies to deductions allocable to the use of a dwelling unit that the taxpayer also uses as a residence during the same taxable year.

A dwelling unit includes a house, apartment, condominium, mobile home, boat, or similar property. It also includes all structures or other property appurtenant to the dwelling unit; these include garages, sheds, and similar property. It does not include any portion of a unit that is used exclusively as a hotel, motel, inn, or similar establishment. I.R.C. § 280A(f)(1).

A dwelling unit is used as a residence if the taxpayer makes "excessive" personal use of it. Days devoted to each use are important when taxpayers split their use of the residence between personal days and rental days. Taxpayers who conduct a business using a portion of their residence make continuous personal use of the residence. These definitions are expanded upon later in this section.

The terms dwelling unit and structure are not co-extensive. A single building may include multiple dwelling units, as is the case with an apartment building. Section 280A applies only to a dwelling unit that is used for multiple purposes, one of which is personal. On the other hand, a dwelling unit can include appurtenant structures that are not themselves used as dwelling units. Prop. Reg. § 1.280A-1(c)(1).

2. Rental Use

A taxpayer who rents a dwelling unit to others is treated as using it as a residence if her personal use exceeds the greater of 14 days or 10% of the days on which it is rented at a fair rental. I.R.C. § 280A(d)(1). A taxpayer who uses a dwelling unit no more than 14 days for personal purposes is not subject to § 280A(a) even if her days of personal use exceed the rental days.

> **Example 15-1.** Alyssa owns a vacation cottage, which she rents at a fair rental 20 days each year. Section 280A(a) applies if her personal use exceeds 14 days. If she instead rents the cottage at a fair rental for 180 days, it applies only if her personal use exceeds 18 days.

Section 280A(d)(2) provides that use is personal if the dwelling unit is used for personal purposes by the taxpayer, by any other person who has an interest in the unit, or by any family member of the taxpayer or the other person. Family is defined as brothers, sisters, spouse, ancestors, and lineal descendants. Her use is also personal if the dwelling unit is used by an individual who uses it under an arrangement that lets her use a different dwelling unit. It does not matter if she pays rent for using the other unit. Use is also personal if it is used by any individual and she does not charge him a fair rental.

Several exceptions apply. Use is not personal if the user qualifies for the § 119 exclusion for lodging furnished on the employer's business premises as a condition of employment. Use to make repairs and annual maintenance is not personal use. In addition, § 280A(d)(3) provides exceptions if she charges a fair rental to a tenant who makes the residence his principal residence even if that tenant is a member of her family. Section 280A(d)(4) ignores personal use that precedes or follows a qualified rental of her principal residence; that rental usually must cover a 12-month term.

Section 280A does not apply if the taxpayer does not use a dwelling unit as a residence. If she makes no personal use, or she limits her personal use to the greater of 14 days or 10% of the rental days, she avoids the § 280A allocations. Unless rental use is de minimis, she reports the rents received as gross income and deducts rental expenses allocable to the rental days. If the expenses exceed her income, § 280A does not prevent her from deducting the loss against other income.

> Example 15-2: Alma rents a dwelling unit to others and also uses it for personal purposes. This year, she rented it for 180 days and used it for personal purposes for 10 days. She is not treated as using the dwelling unit as a residence. If the expenses allocable to the rental days exceed her rental income, § 280A does not prevent her from deducting her loss. She does not have to itemize her deductions to deduct rental expenses. If she itemizes her deductions, she can also deduct mortgage interest or property taxes allocable to the personal use.

The number of personal days is irrelevant if the taxpayer rents the dwelling unit for 14 or fewer days during the year. In that case, § 280A(g) excludes the rents from gross income, and she cannot deduct any expenses related to the rental activity. This exclusion could benefit taxpayers who rent their homes to movie studios for location shots or to individuals attending local sporting events.

If a taxpayer rents a dwelling unit and also uses it as a residence, no deductions are allowed other than those authorized by § 280A. Section 280A(a) does not apply to deductions she could take even if she made no trade or business or income-producing use of the dwelling unit. I.R.C. § 280A(b). The deductions covered by this category are those for home mortgage interest and real property taxes. The limited deduction for casualty losses to personal-use property might also be available. Because the standard deduction was increased markedly in 2017, while the casualty loss deduction was significantly curtailed, many taxpayers will take the standard deduction instead of itemizing otherwise-deductible expenses allocable to personal use of the residence.

Although § 280A(b) does not disallow deductions granted by those other sections, the taxpayer must allocate them between her rental use and her personal use. The allocations are important because deductions allocable to the production of rent are allowed in computing adjusted gross income (AGI). They are deductible even if she does not itemize deductions. I.R.C. §62(a)(4).

Section 280A(e)(1) provides a ratio for allocating expenses to the rental days. The numerator is the number of days that the unit is rented at a fair rental; the denominator is the total number of days the unit is used. The taxpayer ignores days on which the unit is not used. Two appellate courts use a different allocation for mortgage interest and property taxes. *Bolton v. Commissioner*, 694 F.2d 556 (9th Cir. 1982); *McKinney v. Commissioner*, 732 F.2d 414, 416 (10th Cir. 1983). Because they treat those items as accruing throughout the entire year, they use the total number of days in the year as the denominator. The *McKinney* opinion included this language: "Maintenance expenses have a direct relationship to the extent the unit is used while interest and taxes accrue on a regular annual basis regardless of use. This difference should require a different treatment." The IRS disagrees with that treatment. Its Publication 527, Residential Rental Property, uses the total days of use as the denominator for *all* expenses.

> **Example 15-3.** Agnes rents her vacation cottage for 100 days each year. She uses it for personal purposes for 50 days each year. It is vacant the rest of the year. The ratio for allocating repairs to the rental days is 100/150. If *Bolton* and *McKinney* are correct; the ratio for allocating mortgage interest is 100/365. If the IRS is correct, it is 100/150.

The *Bolton-McKinney* formula for allocating interest and property taxes may be more favorable to the taxpayer than the government's formula. Because it allocates a smaller percentage of these expenses to the rental use, her rental income is more likely to exceed those expenses. This is important because she can deduct rental-related expenses (such as repairs) only if there is excess rental income. In addition, if she itemizes, she can still deduct the remaining mortgage interest and property taxes. She may prefer allocating more interest and taxes to the rental days, particularly if she does not itemize or she does itemize but pays state and local taxes that exceed the current $10,000 deduction cap.

Section 280A(c)(5) limits some of the taxpayer's deductions attributable to a dwelling unit that is used as both a rental property and a residence. Deductions it covers cannot exceed the amount by which the gross income derived from the rental use exceeds the sum of two amounts: (1) the amount of deductions that would be allowed whether or not the unit was rented and that are allocable to the rental activity; and (2) deductions allocable to the rental *activity* that are not allocable to the rental *use*.

Section 280A(c)(5) divides deductions into categories, only one of which is limited by its formula. The first category—deductions allowable even if there were no rental activity—is not limited. The taxpayer can deduct mortgage interest and property taxes allocable to the rental activity even if they exceed its gross income. The second category—deductions that are allocable to the rental activity but not to the actual rental use—includes such outlays as advertising. They are not limited by the gross income from the activity. The third category—other expenses allocable to the rental use—is limited. This category includes repairs and maintenance, utilities, and depreciation. Those outlays are allocated to the rental use based on the ratio provided in § 280A(e)(1). They are deductible only to the extent the gross income from the rental activity exceeds expenses in the first two categories. The taxpayer carries any excess expenses to future years and deducts them if he has sufficient rental income in those later years. I.R.C. § 280A(c)(5) (flush language).

> Example 15-4. Amos made both personal and rental use of his vacation cottage. He received rent of $10,000. The mortgage interest and property taxes allocable to rental use totaled $5,500. He paid $400 for items that were not allocable to the rental use but were allocable to the rental activity. His expenses for repairs, utilities, property insurance, and depreciation allocable to the rental period were $6,000. He could deduct only $4,100 of the expenses in the third category. If he received only $4,000 of rent, he could deduct the expenses in the first two categories, even though they exceeded the rent. He could not deduct any of the expenses in the third category.

The third category of expenses has two subcategories: expenses that affect basis (e.g., depreciation) and expenses that do not. The taxpayer deducts expenses that do not affect basis before deducting those that do. He does not reduce his basis for the property by any nondeductible depreciation. Prop. Reg. § 1.280A-3(d)(3). Note that Example 15-4 did not indicate which formula (IRS or *Bolton-McKinney*) Amos used in allocating mortgage interest and property taxes to the rental activity. The allocation used for those items affects his ability to deduct expenses in the third category.

3. Business Use

Section 280A(c)(1) applies if a taxpayer uses part of a dwelling unit for personal purposes and another part for business. If she satisfies its requirements, she can deduct at least some of the expenses allocable to the business portion. Otherwise, her deductions related to the home are limited to amounts she could deduct even if she made no business use of the home. I.R.C. § 280A(b).

To satisfy § 280A(c)(1), she must use the portion of the dwelling unit exclusively and on a regular basis as either: (1) the principal place of business for any trade or business she conducts; (2) a place of business used by clients, patients, or customers for meeting with her in the ordinary course of her trade or business; or (3) a separate structure used in connection with her trade or business. Section 280A(a) does not limit deductions for any item allocable to her regular use of space as a storage unit for product samples or inventory. I.R.C. § 280A(c)(2). This exception applies only if her trade or business is selling products at retail or wholesale and she has no other fixed location for it.

An employee must satisfy an additional requirement—the use must also be for the convenience of her employer. If the employer provides no space and requires her to telecommute, she should satisfy this requirement. If she is furnished office space but also works at home after normal business hours, she is unlikely to qualify. She cannot avoid § 280A by renting the portion of the dwelling unit to her employer. I.R.C. § 280A(c)(6). Even if she meets the convenience of the employer test, an employee cannot deduct expenses related to a home office for which she is not reimbursed unless she itemizes instead of taking the standard deduction. And, because these deductions would be miscellaneous itemized deductions, she cannot take them at all in 2018 through 2025.

a. Exclusive Use on a Regular Basis

The regular and exclusive use tests are separate requirements. A taxpayer who uses part of the dwelling unit exclusively for meeting with customers for two weeks of the year fails the regular use test. A taxpayer who regularly uses space that is also used by family members fails the exclusive use test. The exclusive use test applies to the portion of the dwelling unit used for business purposes. That portion can be one or more rooms; it can even be a dedicated area within a single room. Section 280A(c)(4) is an exception to the exclusive use test enacted for taxpayers who provide day care services. It includes an allocation formula based on the amount of time the home is used for that purpose.

Courts may apply the exclusive use test strictly. For example, in *Bulas v. Commissioner*, T.C. Memo. 2011-201, the taxpayer converted a bedroom into a home office and built a half bathroom across the hall for use by his clients. Family members and personal guests occasionally used the bathroom. The court allowed deductions only for the office. The bathroom failed the exclusive use test.

The taxpayer's regular and exclusive use must be for one of the three purposes listed in § 280A(c)(1). The first purpose is as his principal place of business. He does not have to use the dwelling unit in his *main* trade or business. It can be the principal place of business for *any* of his trades or businesses. Space can also qualify even though the primary earning activity for a business occurs elsewhere if the taxpayer uses the space for administrative or management duties (such as billing clients). There must be no other fixed location where he conducts substantial administrative or management duties. This provision effectively overrules the result in *Commissioner v. Soliman*, 506 U.S. 168 (1993). Dr. Soliman spent 30 to 35 hours per week rendering services to patients at three hospitals. None of them provided administrative space for his use. He spent two to three hours daily in a room in his condominium that he used exclusively for contacting patients, surgeons, and hospitals by telephone, maintaining billing records and patient logs, and doing other professional tasks. In holding that he did not satisfy the principal place of business test, the Court focused primarily on the relative importance of the duties performed at each location and the relative amount of time spent at each location.

The second purpose is as a regular place for meeting with patients, clients, or customers in the normal course of the trade or business. This test can be satisfied even if the location is not the taxpayer's principal place of business. Although the meetings must be regular, he does not have to meet regularly with any one patient, client, or customer. Meetings must be in person rather than over the telephone. *Green v. Commissioner*, 707 F.2d 404 (9th Cir. 1983); *Frankel v. Commissioner*, 82 T.C. 318 (1984).

The third purpose applies only if the taxpayer uses a separate structure. In that case, the taxpayer only needs to show that the area is used in connection with his trade or business. A detached garage qualifies as a separate structure; an attached garage does not.

b. Computing Allowable Deductions

The taxpayer computes his allowable deductions using the formula in §280A(c)(5). The starting point is the gross income derived from using the dwelling unit. A taxpayer who regularly meets patients, clients, or customers there, but also has other business locations, must allocate gross income among the locations. He then deducts the allocable portion of expenses that are allowable even if the space is not used for business—generally, mortgage interest and property taxes. He also deducts expenses that are allocable to the business but not to the residence. If he has no other business location, this category includes all his professional dues and subscriptions, required licenses, the business telephone line, salaries for employees, and supplies. If his gross income exceeds the expenses in the first two categories, he deducts business expenses that are allocable to the home. The third category includes property insurance, depreciation, utilities, and repairs of the space used for business (or repairs that benefit the entire property and must be allocated). His deductions for those expenses cannot exceed the activity's gross income reduced by expenses in the first two categories. Expenses in the third category that do not affect basis are deducted before those that do. Prop. Reg. § 1.280A-2(i)(5). Excess deductions are carried over for deduction in future years. I.R.C. § 280A(c)(5) (flush language).

Taxpayers can allocate expenses between business and personal use based on a reasonable allocation. Allocating based on the percentage of total space is reasonable. Allocating based on the number of rooms is reasonable if the rooms are of approximately equal size. Prop. Reg. § 1.280A-2(i)(3).

> **Example 15-5.** Allan regularly meets with clients in a home office, which is approximately 20% of the home's square footage. He received fees of $7,000 from those clients. His mortgage interest and property taxes allocated to the home office totaled $3,000. He paid license fees and professional dues of $1,300. The electric bills and property insurance premium allocable to the home office totaled $1,800. He computed $2,000 of depreciation with respect to the home office. His total expenses covered by § 280A are $8,100. He deducts the interest, property taxes, license fees, and professional dues; those total $4,300. He can also deduct $2,700 of his remaining expenses: $1,800 for electricity and property insurance and $900 of depreciation. He reduces his basis for the home by the $900 of depreciation he can deduct.

In 2013, the IRS announced an optional safe harbor deduction. Rev. Proc. 2013-13, 2013-6 I.R.B. 478. Instead of deducting actual expenses, the taxpayer can deduct $5 per square foot, with a maximum deduction of $1,500 (300 square feet). The deduction based on square footage cannot exceed the excess of his gross income derived from the home office over any business deductions that are not allocated to the home. Mortgage interest and property taxes are ignored in this computation; they are instead deducted as itemized deductions. Depreciation is not deducted at all. The election can be changed from year to year, so that a taxpayer can deduct the safe harbor amount in one year and actual expenses in another. Taxpayers can use the safe harbor if they meet any of the exclusive use on a regular basis tests, the storage test, or the qualified day care services test. Employees who receive reimbursements or advances from an employer with respect to a home office cannot use it.

4. Coordination with Other Code Sections

Section 280A may interact with three provisions discussed below. If a dwelling unit used as a residence is involved in an activity not engaged in for profit, § 280A(f)(3) provides that § 280A rather than § 183 applies. If the taxpayer is not at risk with respect to the activity, perhaps because nonrecourse financing is involved, § 465 might disallow loss deductions. And because rental activities are usually classified as passive activities, the § 469 limitations on deducting passive activity losses could have applied if § 469(j)(10) did not provide otherwise.

C. Activities Not Engaged in for Profit

Although § 183 is often called the hobby loss section, "hobby" does not appear in its text. Instead, it disallows deductions if an activity "is not engaged in for profit." Section 183(c) defines that term as an activity that does not qualify for deductions allowable by either § 162 or § 212(1)–(2). In other words, it applies to an activity that is not a trade or business or an income-producing activity. Unfortunately, § 183 provides no guidance as to whether an activity qualifies under either category. It is likely to apply to "activities which are carried on primarily as a sport, hobby, or for recreation." Reg. § 1.183-2(a). The determination is made using objective standards. If the taxpayer can establish that his primary motive for entering into or continuing the activity was profit, the fact that his expectation was unreasonable is not fatal. A small chance of a large profit may suffice for speculative ventures such as investing in wildcat oil wells. When the activity has recreational aspects, courts give less weight to the small chance of a large profit.

1. Determining the Status of the Activity

Reg. § 1.183-2(b) lists nine factors used in evaluating an activity.

(1) *Manner in which activity is conducted.* Does the taxpayer carry on the activity in a businesslike manner and maintain accurate records?

(2) *Expertise of taxpayer or advisors.* Did he prepare for the activity by studying its business, economic, and other practices or consult with others who had such expertise?

(3) *Time and effort spent.* Did he devote significant personal time to the activity or withdraw from another occupation to spend time on the activity?

(4) *Potential asset appreciation.* Does he expect to realize profit based on appreciation in the assets used in the activity?

(5) *Success in other ventures.* Has he converted other unprofitable activities into profitable activities?

(6) *History of income or losses.* If he has incurred losses, have they continued beyond a normal start-up period? If so, are they caused by factors beyond his control?

(7) *Amount of profits.* How does the amount of profits relate to losses incurred, his investment, and the value of the activity's assets?

(8) *Taxpayer's financial status.* Does he have substantial other sources of income or capital, or is the activity likely to be an important source of his income?

(9) *Elements of personal pleasure or recreation.* Does the activity have any personal or recreational appeal, or is profit the main appeal?

Courts regularly cite to and evaluate activities based on these factors. Loss-producing activities that result in litigation tend to involve taxpayers with substantial income or assets. Many of them are highly paid professionals who deduct losses from breeding or showing animals, farming, or their children's recreational activities.

Although litigation usually involves activities with personal or recreational aspects, the IRS occasionally argues that a profession is not engaged in for profit. It successfully disallowed an attorney's deductions in *Cohen v. Commissioner*, T.C. Memo. 1984-237. It was unsuccessful in making the same challenge in *Westphal v. Commissioner*, T.C. Memo. 1994-537. Mrs. Westphal devoted significantly more effort to her law practice than did Mr. Cohen.

Multiple undertakings can be treated as one activity if they are sufficiently interrelated. Reg. § 1.183-1(d)(1). A taxpayer can offset the loss from one interrelated undertaking against the income from the other undertaking and potentially avoid § 183. The taxpayer was successful in doing so in *Topping v. Commissioner*, T.C. Memo. 2007-92. The court held that her success (other than financial) as an equestrian competitor was responsible for more than 90% of the client base for her horse barn-interior design activities and that the two were a single integrated business even though her CPA reported them on separate tax return schedules.

Section 183(d) provides a presumption regarding the status of an activity, and § 183(e) allows the taxpayer time before it applies. If he fails to satisfy the presumption, he can still argue that his activity is engaged in for profit. An activity is presumed to be engaged in for profit if his gross income from the activity exceeds his deductions. For this purpose, he includes all deductions that would be allowed if the activity were engaged in for profit. The presumption, which the government can attempt to rebut, has a time limit. His gross income must exceed his deductions in at least three taxable years in the five-year period ending with the year in which the presumption is to be applied. If the activity consists in major part of breeding, racing, showing, or training horses, the period is two years out of seven.

The taxpayer can elect to delay the determination of whether the presumption applies to a taxable year. The determination is not made before the close of the fourth taxable year following the year in which he first engages in the activity. I.R.C. § 183(e). The time is extended two years for activities involving horses. If he makes the election, and satisfies the requirements of § 183(d), the presumption applies to every year in the five- or seven-year period. A taxpayer who makes this election extends the statute of limitations with respect to any tax deficiency relating to the activity. Without this extension, the government could be precluded from litigating the early years of the activity with respect to taxpayers who fail to satisfy the presumption.

2. Limitations on Deductions

If the taxpayer establishes that the activity is engaged in for profit, the normal § 162 or § 212 deduction rules apply. If not, deduction limits provided in § 183(b) apply. He cannot deduct even those limited amounts unless he itemizes his deductions. Section 183 does not provide a carryover to future years; deductions it disallows are permanently disallowed.

Section 183(b)(1) allows any deductions that would be allowed without regard to whether the activity was engaged in for profit. This includes state and local property taxes, but it does not include repairs, dues and subscriptions, or depreciation. Interest is allowed only to the extent connected with property used as a residence. Section 280A, discussed in Section B, provides that § 183 does not apply to the dwelling unit in any year in which § 280A(a) applies. That year is still counted for purposes of the § 183(d) presumption discussed above. I.R.C. § 280A(f)(3).

The taxpayer then determines if his gross income, if any, from the activity exceeds the deductions allowed without regard to whether the activity was engaged in for profit. If those deductions exceed his gross income, he cannot take any additional deductions. If the gross income exceeds the deductions, he may also deduct expenses that would be allowed if the activity was engaged in for profit. I.R.C. § 183(b)(2). Those deductions cannot exceed the amount by which his gross income from the activity exceeds the first group of expenses. Expenses that affect the basis of his property are deducted last. Reg. § 1.183-1(b). He reduces his basis for depreciable assets only to the extent he could deduct depreciation.

> **Example 15-6.** Alonzo received $1,000 in prize money for racing go-karts. He paid $225 in property tax on his go-karts. He also paid $3,000 for gasoline and $600 for insurance. If he cannot establish that his

racing was an activity engaged in for profit, he reports $1,000 of gross income. If he itemizes his deductions, he can deduct the $225 property tax and $775 of the $3,600 he spent on gasoline and insurance. (He gets no deduction in 2018 through 2025 for any expense that is a miscellaneous itemized deduction.) He cannot deduct the remaining $2,825 he spent, nor can he deduct depreciation of his go-karts. If he establishes go-kart racing as a trade or business, he can deduct all his expenses— even if he shows a loss—and he does not have to itemize.

D. Activities for Which the Taxpayer Is Not at Risk

1. Overview

When a taxpayer purchases property, her basis includes her down payment and any amount she promises to pay in the future even if the debt is nonrecourse. *Crane v. Commissioner*, 331 U.S. 1 (1947); *Commissioner v. Tufts*, 461 U.S. 300 (1983). If she fails to pay a nonrecourse debt, the creditor can foreclose on the encumbered property, but he cannot make her liquidate other assets. Although she is not at risk (other than for losing any money she actually paid) with respect to this debt, her basis for depreciation includes the nonrecourse debt. The debt is disregarded only if the government establishes that it is significantly greater than the value of the property. *See Estate of Franklin v. Commissioner*, 544 F.2d 1045, 1048 (9th Cir. 1976) ("No such meshing occurs when the purchase price exceeds a demonstrably reasonable estimate of the fair market value."); Rev. Rul. 77-110, 1977-1 C.B. 58.

Section 465 disallows loss deductions when the taxpayer is not at risk in a business or income-producing activity. This section governs her loss if her deductions allocable to the activity exceed the income received or accrued. Income includes only amounts actually received or accrued; we ignore amounts included in income because of the rule discussed in Subsection 3. I.R.C. §465(d). Section 465(a)(2) lets taxpayers carry disallowed deductions forward.

2. Computing the Amount at Risk

The taxpayer is considered at risk for any money and for the adjusted basis of any other property she contributes to the activity. She is also considered at risk for certain amounts borrowed with respect to the activity. She must be personally liable for the borrowed amounts or must have pledged assets not used in the activity as security for those amounts. When pledged assets are used instead of personal liability, she cannot count more than the value of her interest in the pledged property. Section 465(b) includes several other limitations on the computation of amounts at risk.

She reduces her amount at risk by any loss she deducts with respect to the activity. I.R.C. § 465(b)(5). This reduction is made for the year following the deduction year. She also reduces her amount at risk if she takes funds out of the activity. She increases her amount at risk by any net profit and by any additional money she invests in the activity. Prop. Reg. § 1.465-22.

> **Example 15-7.** Arabella invested $100,000 in an income-producing activity for which she has limited liability. Her share of the deductions was $15,000 greater than her share of the income in Year 1. Because she was at risk for $100,000 in Year 1, she could deduct the entire $15,000 loss. Her amount at risk would be $85,000 at the beginning of Year 2. If she had invested property worth $100,000, for which she had a $60,000 basis, instead of investing cash, her initial amount at risk would have been only $60,000. She could still deduct her $15,000 Year 1 loss. Her amount at risk at the beginning of Year 2 would be $45,000.

> **Example 15-8.** Arabella's share of the activity's net loss was $92,000 in Year 2. She cannot deduct the full loss because her amount at risk is less than $92,000. Her amount at risk is reduced to zero by the amount she can deduct. Her remaining loss is carried to future years and deducted when she has sufficient amounts at risk.

3. Amount at Risk Reduced Below Zero

Although the taxpayer cannot reduce her amount at risk below zero through loss deductions, she can do so by taking distributions. If she does, § 465(e) recaptures previously deducted losses. She reports gross income equal to the lesser of (1) the negative balance of her amount at risk or (2) her aggregate loss deductions in prior years reduced by amounts she previously included in income with respect to the activity. This provision prevents her from withdrawing funds on a tax-free basis after deducting losses that reduced her amount at risk to zero.

E. Passive Activities

1. Avoiding Section 469

Section 469 disallows losses from activities in which the taxpayer does not materially participate, so-called passive activities. Section 469(c)(2) provides that rental activities are considered passive unless excluded by §469(c)(7), which is discussed below. Section 469 may apply to activities the taxpayer engages in himself or as a partner, S corporation shareholder, or LLC member.

The taxpayer can avoid §469 by establishing that he materially participates in the activity. He can limit its effect, with respect to certain rental real estate activities, by establishing that he actively participates in the activity or that he is in a real property trade or business.

a. Material Participation

Section 469 does not apply if the taxpayer materially participates in the activity. As a general rule, he must be involved on a regular, continuous, and substantial basis. I.R.C. §469(h)(1). Section 469(h)(5) includes participation by his spouse in determining if he materially participates.

The temporary regulations provide seven ways for the taxpayer to establish material participation in the activity. Temp. Reg. §1.469-5T(a). These include participation for more than 500 hours during the year, participation that constitutes substantially all the participation of all individuals for the year, and participation for more than 100 hours during the year if that participation is at least equal to the participation of any other individual. If the activity is a significant participation activity, he can qualify if he has aggregate participation for more than 500 hours during the year in all significant participation activities. If the activity is a personal service activity, he can qualify if he had material participation for any three preceding taxable years. He can also qualify by establishing material participation for any five taxable years in the ten preceding taxable years. Finally, he can qualify if he can establish participation that is regular, continuous, and substantial during the year.

Many of the tests include a numerical count of hours and make record-keeping important; some introduce additional terminology. One such test involves significant participation activities, which can be aggregated in determining if the taxpayer participates for more than 500 hours. A significant participation activity is a trade or business in which the taxpayer participates for more than 100 hours during the year and for which he does not satisfy any of the other material participation tests. Temp. Reg. §1.469-5T(c). A personal service activity involves performance of personal services in health, law, engineering, architecture, accounting, actuarial science, performing arts, or consulting. It also includes performance of personal services in any other field in which capital is not a material income-producing factor. Temp. Reg. § 1.469-5T(d).

The term participation is defined in both a final regulation and a temporary regulation. Reg. § 1.469-5(f)(1) provides that it means any work the individual performs in connection with an activity in which he has an ownership interest. It defers to exceptions, which currently appear in the temporary regulations. Temp. Reg. § 1.469-5T(f)(2) provides that participation does not include performing work not customarily performed by an owner if one of the principal purposes for performing the work is avoiding the § 469 limitations. It also provides that participation in the individual's capacity as an investor does not qualify unless he is involved in day-to-day management.

The form in which the activity operates is relevant. Unless an exception in Temp. Reg. § 1.469-5T(e)(2) applies, a limited partner is not considered to materially participate in the activity with respect to his limited partnership interest. In *Thompson v. United States*, 87 Fed. Cl. 728 (2009), the court held that an LLC member could be treated as a material participant even though he had limited liability. It stated that the provisions applicable to limited partners, who generally do not participate in management, did not apply to LLC members. It noted that shareholders in S corporations had limited liability but could participate in management and satisfy the material participation tests in Temp. Reg. § 1.469-5T(a). The Tax Court had previously held that interests in LLCs are not limited partnership interests. *Garnett v. Commissioner*, 132 T.C. 368 (2009). The IRS acquiesced in the result in *Thompson* in AOD 2010-02.

b. Real Estate

Section § 469(c)(2) provides that rental activities are passive activities, and § 469(c)(4) provides that material participation does not change this classification. Nevertheless, taxpayers who actively participate in rental real estate activities can deduct up to $25,000 in losses each year. I.R.C. § 469(i)(1)– (2). The activity remains passive even if the loss deduction is allowed.

Eligibility is determined in part through an ownership test. I.R.C. § 469(i)(6). If the taxpayer's interest in the activity is less than 10% of all interests in the activity, she is not an active participant. This determination is made based on value, not on management or other rights in the activity. She can include her spouse's interest in determining the value of her interest. An interest as a limited partner is generally not treated as an interest with respect to which she actively participates.

Even if she actively participates, the maximum deduction phases out as her modified AGI increases. The $25,000 limitation is reduced by 50 cents for each dollar of AGI greater than $100,000. I.R.C. § 469(i)(3). Because the maximum deduction is $25,000, the phase-out completely eliminates the deduction when her modified AGI reaches $150,000. Both the $25,000 deduction limit and the $100,000 phase-out threshold are halved if she is married and files a separate return. I.R.C. § 469(i)(5).

> **Example 15-9.** Althea is actively engaged in a rental real estate activity. She received $30,000 of rental income and had $38,000 of rental expenses this year. If her AGI is $100,000 or less, she can deduct all her rental expenses. Her $8,000 loss will offset her gross income from other sources. If her AGI is instead $146,000, her maximum loss deduction is only $2,000. The $25,000 maximum allowable loss is reduced by $23,000 (50% of her $46,000 excess AGI).

Section 469(c)(7) provides more favorable treatment for rental real estate if the taxpayer qualifies by virtue of his participation in a real property trade or business. A real property trade or business is "any real property development, redevelopment, construction, reconstruction, acquisition, conversion, rental, operation, management, leasing, or brokerage trade or business." I.R.C. § 469(c)(7)(C). He must render more than half of the personal services he renders in all businesses in real property trades or businesses in which he materially participates. In addition, he must perform more than 750 hours of services during the year in real property trades or businesses in which he materially participates. I.R.C. § 469(c)(7)(B). Services he performs as an employee do not count unless he qualifies as a 5% business owner, a term defined in § 416(i)(1)(B). I.R.C. § 469(c)(7)(D)(ii). If he satisfies those requirements, rental real estate activities are not treated as passive.

> **Example 15-10.** Alfred works 1,200 hours per year as a veterinarian. He also is engaged in renting apartment buildings. He spends 800 hours per year reviewing tenant applications, arranging for repairs, and performing general management functions. Although he materially participates in the rental real estate activity, he does not render more than half of the services he renders in all businesses in a real property trade or business. As a result, the rental activity is considered passive. Unless his AGI for the year is sufficiently low, he cannot offset any

rental losses against the net income produced by his veterinary practice or other income-producing source.

Example 15-11. Alfred plans to reduce the hours he devotes to his veterinary practice and will work only 700 hours per year as a veterinarian. If he continues spending 800 hours per year in his real estate activity, that activity will not be considered a passive activity. He can offset losses from the rental activity against the net income produced by his veterinary practice or other income-producing source.

2. Applying Section 469

Unless one of the exceptions applies, a taxpayer cannot deduct a passive activity loss from non-passive income. The same disallowance applies to any credits related to passive activities. I.R.C. §469(a). A taxpayer has a passive activity loss if his aggregate losses from all passive activities exceeds his aggregate income from all such activities. I.R.C. §469(d)(1). Determining which activities are passive is only the first step. Even if an activity is passive, some income or deduction items associated with it may be treated as non-passive. Those items are eliminated from the computation.

Section 469(e)(1) lists items that are not treated as passive. Interest, dividends, annuities, and royalties are excluded if they are not derived in the ordinary course of a trade or business. These items are often called portfolio income. Expenses, other than interest expense, are excluded if they are clearly and directly allocable to those gross income items. Interest expense properly allocable to those items is also excluded. Gains and losses are excluded if they are not derived in the ordinary course of a trade or business and are derived from disposing of property producing the excluded types of income or held for investment. Income, gain, or loss attributable to the investment of working capital is not considered to be derived in the ordinary course of a trade or business.

Example 15-12. Art had two passive activities. Activity #1 had gross income of $100,000, which included $2,000 of dividend income that was not derived in the ordinary course of a trade or business. None of the activity's $101,000 of expenses was attributable to the dividend income. Activity #2 had income of $50,000 and expenses of $43,000. Art had a passive activity loss of $3,000 from Activity #1 and passive activity income of $7,000 from Activity #2. Because the aggregate income from passive activities exceeded the aggregate losses, he deducts his $3,000 loss from Activity #1.

Example 15-13. If the gross income from Activity #1 instead included $15,000 of dividend income (and no related expenses), Art would have a $16,000 passive activity loss from Activity #1. That exceeds the passive activity income attributable to Activity 2 by $9,000. He cannot deduct his $9,000 net passive activity loss.

Although passive activity losses can generally be deducted only against passive activity income, the opposite is not true. Losses from activities that are not passive can be deducted against net income from passive activities.

The taxpayer carries his disallowed passive activity losses to future years and deducts them against passive activity income generated in those years. I.R.C. §469(b). If a passive activity changes its status because he meets one of the participation tests, it becomes a former passive activity. I.R.C. §469(f)(3). He can deduct the losses carried over from passive activity years against the income of the activity in any year in which it is a former passive activity. If the loss exceeds the income, he continues to carry it forward as a passive activity loss. I.R.C. §469(f)(1).

If a taxpayer disposes of a passive activity in a taxable transaction, he can deduct any unused loss in the year in which the disposition occurs. I.R.C. §469(g)(1). If the disposition results in recognition of all realized gain or loss, he treats the unused loss as non-passive. I.R.C. §469(g)(1)(A). If the disposition is made to a related person, the loss is not treated as non-passive until the activity is disposed of in a taxable transaction to a non-related person. I.R.C. §469(g)(1)(B). If he disposes of his entire interest in a transaction taxed using the installment method, he deducts a portion of the loss as he receives each payment. I.R.C. §469(g)(3).

If an interest in the activity is transferred because of his death, §469(g)(2) provides for treating the losses as non-passive, but this treatment is subject to limits. It applies only to losses that are greater than the excess of the transferee's basis for the property over the decedent's basis immediately before his death. Any remaining losses will never be deducted. If he instead transfers the activity by inter vivos gift, his basis immediately before the gift is increased by the suspended losses allocable to the interest transferred. The losses are not allowed as a deduction in any future year. I.R.C. §469(j)(6). Because they increase basis, they may result in a smaller gain or a larger loss realized when the interest is ultimately sold.

3. Coordination with Other Code Sections

A taxpayer's passive activity may involve a dwelling unit covered by §280A(c)(5). In that situation, any income, deduction, gain, or loss allocable to that activity is ignored for purposes of the passive activity loss provisions. This determination is made on a year-by-year basis. I.R.C. §469(j)(10). A taxpayer may not be at risk with respect to an activity that is also regarded as passive. In that situation, §465 applies before any §469 limitations are applied. Any deduction disallowed by §465 is not a passive activity deduction for that year. Temp. Reg. §1.469-2T(d)(6). Finally, the excess business loss deduction limitation discussed in the next section is applied after we apply the passive activity loss limitation. I.R.C. §461(l)(6).

F. Excess Business Losses

The Tax Cuts and Jobs Act of 2017 added §461(l), effective for 2018 through 2025. This provision was amended in response to the COVID-19 pandemic and is now effective for 2021 through 2025. This section applies even if the taxpayer is at risk with respect to the activity and actively participates in it. Section 461(l)(1) disallows deductions for excess business losses. The disallowed losses can be carried forward for deduction in a future year. I.R.C. §461(l)(2). It is treated as a §172 net operating loss carryover.

A taxpayer has an excess business loss if her deductions attributable to her trades or businesses exceed the sum of her gross income attributable to those trades or businesses plus a safe harbor amount. The safe harbor amount, initially set at $250,000 (doubled on a joint return), is indexed for inflation.

> **Example 15-14.** Alicia operated a consulting firm as a sole proprietor. In 2021, one of her major clients declared bankruptcy and did not pay the $600,000 fee it owed her. That year, Alicia's firm had gross income of $2,000,000 and expenses of $2,400,000. Alicia also had $800,000 of gross income from various investments. If Congress had not enacted §461(l), Alicia would have deducted her $400,000 of excess expenses against her nonbusiness income. Instead, she could deduct only the applicable safe harbor amount in 2021; she would carry the remaining loss to 2022 (and beyond if necessary).

G. Wagering Losses

A taxpayer may place a bet or buy a lottery ticket sporadically, or he may wager on a regular basis. If he loses money, §165(d) limits his deduction for wagering losses to the amount of his wagering gains. Because wagering often results in a loss, and has recreational aspects, the IRS is likely to argue that he is not engaged in the activity for profit, using the tests found in Reg. § 1.183-2(b). *See Chow v. Commissioner*, T.C. Memo. 2010-48.

Because § 165(d) applies even to professional gamblers, the distinction between wagering losses and expenses of a wagering activity was important before 2017. That was because the Tax Court held that a gambler's business expenses (*e.g.*, newsletters and travel) were not subject to § 165(d). *Mayo v. Commissioner*, 136 T.C. 81 (2011). Although the IRS acquiesced in *Mayo* in AOD 2011-06, Congress amended § 165(d) in 2017 to treat expenses as part of the loss rather than as a separate deduction. This change currently applies only to 2018 through 2025.

> **Example 15-15.** Adam is in the business of wagering. In 2019, he made winning wagers of $100,000, losing wagers of $98,000, and incurred $5,000 of expenses related to his wagering activity. He had gross income of $100,000 and could deduct $100,000 (his $98,000 of wagering losses plus $2,000 of his expenses).

If the taxpayer's wagering activity qualifies as a business, his deductions are allowable in computing AGI. If his wagering activity qualifies only as an activity engaged in for the production of income, or an activity not engaged in for profit, his deductions are allowed only if he itemizes. The deductions are not miscellaneous itemized deductions and are therefore not disallowed in 2018 through 2025. I.R.C. § 67(b)(3).

Checkpoints

- Section 280A limits the deductions a taxpayer may take if he makes both business or income-producing use and personal use of a residence.

- Section 183 disallows deductions that would normally be taken by a business or income-producing activity if the taxpayer does not engage in the activity for profit.

- Section 465 disallows deductions when a taxpayer is not at risk with respect to an activity. This may occur if the loss reported by the venture exceeds his contributions and he is not at risk because of nonrecourse financing.

- Section 469 disallows deductions for losses from activities in which the taxpayer's participation is too passive. The definition of a passive activity varies based on the type of activity.

- Section 461(l) disallows business losses that exceed the sum of business income plus an inflation-adjusted safe harbor amount.

- Wagering losses are not deductible to the extent they exceed wagering gains. This rule also applies to wagering expenses in 2018 through 2025.

- Several disallowance provisions provide for carrying disallowed items to future years.

Chapter 16

Taxable Year and Accounting Methods

Roadmap

- Introduction
- Appropriate taxable year
- Cash and accrual accounting methods
- Accounting for inventory
- Accounting for installment sales
- Accounting for long-term contracts
- Accounting for interest income

A. Introduction

Previous chapters focused on *whether* certain items are included in gross income or are deductible. This chapter focuses on timing. *When* should an item be reported? Reporting income or deductions in Year 1 as opposed to Year 2 can alter the tax that is due. Substantive laws may change, different tax rates may apply, or filing status may change.

Taxpayers compute taxable income on an annual basis even though some events affect more than one year. A transaction completed in one year may be reversed in another year when different tax rates apply. Likewise, a taxpayer's outlays for the year may exceed his income. Strict adherence to the annual accounting principle would prevent him from ever deducting the excess outlays. This chapter discusses the tax benefit rule, claim of right computations, and net operating loss deduction; the first two deal with earlier events that are reversed in a later year, while the third covers a loss carryover. All three reduce what might otherwise be unfortunate results caused by ignoring prior year events.

303

Because the appropriate reporting year is usually governed by the taxpayer's accounting method, we also discuss several accounting methods. We cover the cash receipts and disbursements method, the accrual method, and methods used to account for inventory, installment sales, long-term contracts, and certain types of interest income.

B. Appropriate Taxable Year

1. General Rules

Taxable income is computed for a taxable year. Section 441 defines the available taxable years and prescribes eligibility rules for electing them.

Most taxpayers use either a calendar year or their "annual accounting period." A taxpayer has an annual accounting period if there is a period he regularly uses in computing his income in keeping his books. Although most individuals use a calendar year, many entities use a fiscal year that ends on the last day of a month other than December.

A taxpayer must use the calendar year if he keeps no books, if he does not have an annual accounting period, or if his annual accounting period does not qualify as a fiscal year. I.R.C. §441(g). Most trusts must use the calendar year. I.R.C. §644. A personal service corporation must use the calendar year unless it satisfies the IRS that there is a business reason for not using its shareholders' taxable year. A corporation is a personal service corporation if its principal activity is the performance of personal services that are substantially performed by employee-owners. I.R.C. §441(i). Having a year-end that corresponds to the entity's normal business cycle can be a business purpose. Deferral of income is not a business purpose.

A partnership's taxable year is based on the taxable year of partners having a majority interest in partnership capital or profits or the taxable year of all its principal partners. The calendar year is the default taxable year. The partnership can use a different taxable year if it establishes a business purpose. I.R.C. §706(b). An S corporation can select a fiscal year only if it establishes a business purpose. I.R.C. §1378(b). Partnerships, personal service corporations, and S corporations can adopt a fiscal year without showing a business purpose—but only if the deferral period is three months or less. I.R.C. §444(b).

Each taxable year generally stands alone, thus "preserving the integrity of separate taxable years." *Fox v. Commissioner*, 82 T.C. 1001, 1027 (1984). *See Burnet v. Sanford & Brooks Co.*, 282 U.S. 359 (1931). If a transaction is reversed in a later year, the taxpayer reports the reversal in that later year unless an exception applies.

> **Example 16-1.** Antonia rendered services and billed Client in Year 1. She included her fee in gross income that year, even though she hadn't yet been paid, because she used the accrual method. In Year 3, Client's obligation was discharged in bankruptcy. Instead of amending her Year 1 tax return, Antonia deducted a loss on her Year 3 return.

2. Tax Benefit Rule

The recovery of a previously deducted amount is not gross income if the deduction provided no tax benefit. Section 111(a) excludes any amount recovered "to the extent such amount did not reduce the amount of tax imposed...." This rule makes sense from the perspective of fairness. If the outlay provided no tax benefit, the taxpayer should not have gross income when he recovers it. To determine if a deduction reduced his taxes, he computes what the tax would have been without it. If the recomputed tax does not exceed the originally computed tax, the deduction provided no tax benefit.

> **Example 16-2.** Arthur's 2017 gross income was $3,000. He had itemized deductions of $5,200 attributable to county property taxes and home mortgage interest. His 2017 taxable income and federal income tax were both zero. In 2019, he received a refund of $1,000 of the property taxes he paid in 2017. The tax assessor had incorrectly valued every home on his block. If he had paid the correct property tax in 2017, his itemized deductions would have been only $4,200. Because even $4,200 exceeded his 2017 gross income, his taxable income would still have been zero. The $1,000 is excluded from his 2019 gross income because it provided no tax benefit in 2017.

In appropriate cases, the recomputation might involve switching from itemized deductions to the standard deduction. Rev. Rul. 2019-11, 2019-17 I.R.B. 1041, provides examples of taxpayers who received refunds of state and local taxes; the ruling includes the effect of taking the standard versus itemized deductions and addresses the post-2017 cap on deducting state and local taxes.

> **Example 16-3.** If Arthur's refund was instead $2,000, he still reports none of it as gross income in 2019. If he had been assessed and paid the correct property tax, his 2017 itemized deductions would have

been $3,200. Because even $3,200 exceeded his 2017 gross income, his taxable income would still have been zero. The $2,000 is excluded from his 2019 gross income because it provided no tax benefit in 2017.

You might wonder why Arthur itemized his deductions in the examples above, given that the $6,350 standard deduction exceeded his gross income. If he filed a separate return, and his spouse itemized deductions, he would also have to itemize. I.R.C. § 63(c)(6)(A). In any event, his 2017 personal exemption ($4,050) exceeded his taxable income.

A more likely scenario involves an outlay that provided some tax benefit, perhaps because it was deducted in computing AGI or was affected by a phase-out in the earlier year. A detailed computation involving phase-outs appears in Rev. Rul. 93-75, 1993-2 C.B. 63.

The increased standard deduction (and elimination of the personal exemption deduction) for 2018 through 2025 should reduce the significance of the tax benefit rule, at least with respect to itemized deductions. It will continue to be relevant for a self-employed taxpayer's business deductions.

> **Example 16-4.** Anson's 2018 gross income from operating a business was $29,000. His business deductions were $18,000. Because those deductions plus his $12,000 standard deduction exceeded his gross income by $1,000, he had no 2018 taxable income or income tax liability. In 2020, he received a refund of a $1,200 business expense he deducted in 2018. If he had not deducted this amount, his 2018 taxable income would have been $200; he would have paid a tax of $20. Of the $1,200 he received in 2020, only $200 provided a tax benefit in 2018. He includes $200 in his 2020 gross income.

The amount of tax in the year of recovery is based on taxable income, filing status, and tax rates in that year. *Alice Phelan Sullivan Corp. v. United States*, 381 F.2d 399 (Ct. Cl. 1967). The rates might be higher (or lower) than those applied in the earlier year. The use of the later year's rates reflects the annual accounting principle. If Anson's business was more profitable in 2020 than in 2018, it is likely that the tax rate on that $200 will be greater than 10%.

The discussion above considered only two years—the year of the deduction and the year of the recovery. A deductible outlay might also produce a tax benefit if it increased a carryover to a different tax year even if it saved no tax in the original year. I.R.C. § 111(c). Determining eligibility for § 111(a) may thus require examining several taxable years. The need to consider carryovers makes the computations more complex, but the governing principle still applies:

the taxpayer excludes a recovery to the extent the original item did not provide a tax benefit.

Section 111(a) does not specifically indicate whether it applies only to the taxpayer who took the original the deduction. It thus differs from the depreciation recapture provisions, which apply to gain attributable to depreciation "allowed or allowable to the taxpayer or to any other person...." *See* I.R.C. § 1245(a)(2)(A). Should § 111(a) be limited to the original taxpayer, or should it also apply to a taxpayer whose basis for a previously deducted item reflects the original taxpayer's basis? What about a taxpayer who inherits a previously deducted item and whose basis is therefore equal to the value of the property when the decedent died? The Tax Court uses a four-part test to determine if the tax benefit rule applies: (1) there must have been a deduction in an earlier year; (2) that deduction must have resulted in a tax benefit; (3) an event that occurred in a later year must be fundamentally inconsistent with the premises on which the original deduction was based; and (4) no nonrecognition provision applies to prevent including the item in the later year. *Frederick v. Commissioner*, 101 T.C. 35 (1993) (interpreting the tax benefit rule in light of *United States v. Bliss Dairy, Inc.*, 460 U.S. 370 (1983)). In *Estate of Backemeyer v. Commissioner*, 147 T.C. 526 (2016), Mr. Backemeyer properly deducted various farming supplies in late 2010 but died in early 2011 before using them. Mrs. Backemeyer inherited these supplies, for which she received a § 1014 fair market value basis. She deducted them as her own expenses of farming. The court held that the tax benefit rule did not apply to Mr. Backemeyer; a transfer at death was not fundamentally inconsistent with the premises on which the original deduction was based.

3. Restoring Amounts Received Under Claim of Right

Section 1341 applies when a taxpayer reported income in one year and repaid it in a later year. He reported gross income in the earlier year because he received the amount under a claim of right. He would normally deduct the repayment in the later year when it was determined that he did not have a right to the income. *North American Oil Consolidated v. Burnet*, 286 U.S. 417 (1932); *United States v. Lewis*, 340 U.S. 590 (1951). The *Lewis* decision rejected the taxpayer's argument that he should be allowed to recompute the earlier year's tax. As a result, the tax paid in the later year reflected that year's rates. Section 1341 changes that outcome for taxpayers who meet its requirements. If it applies, the tax savings in the later year equals or exceeds the extra tax paid in the earlier year. Not surprisingly, given this potential benefit, this section does not apply every time someone receives income in one year and repays it in another.

a. Applying Section 1341

Section 1341 applies if the taxpayer meets three requirements. First, it must have appeared that she had an unrestricted right to the income in the earlier year. Second, she must be entitled to deduct the repayment because it is established in a later year that she did not have an unrestricted right to the income. Third, the deduction in the later year must exceed $3,000. I.R.C. §1341(a)(1)–(3).

The unrestricted right requirement is critical. The item must have been "included in gross income because it appeared from all the facts available in the year of inclusion that the taxpayer had an unrestricted right to such item...." Reg. §1.1341-1(a)(2). A taxpayer who knew funds were received wrongfully cannot meet this requirement. This rule was applied to an embezzler in *McKinney v. United States*, 574 F.2d 1240 (5th Cir. 1978). It was applied to a taxpayer who paid an arsonist and collected insurance proceeds in Rev. Rul. 82-74, 1982-1 C.B. 110.

A taxpayer also fails this test if he had an actual right, rather than an apparent right, to the funds. This determination is made using the facts available at the end of the year in which the funds were received. The IRS has often interpreted "apparent right" fairly narrowly. Initially, it argued that a repayment condition was a subsequent event, and that a taxpayer who received income in that situation had an actual right to it in the earlier year. This position was rejected in *Van Cleave v. United States*, 718 F.2d 193 (6th Cir. 1983). In that case, the taxpayer received salary subject to an agreement to repay any portion the IRS determined was unreasonable. The court held that the taxpayer's right appeared unrestricted at the time of the payment and let him use §1341.

If a taxpayer voluntarily returns funds, it is never established that he did not have an unrestricted right to them. He may be able to deduct the repayment as an ordinary and necessary business expense, but §1341 does not apply. This was the outcome in *Pike v. Commissioner*, 44 T.C. 787 (1965), in which an attorney voluntarily repaid certain amounts because he did not want the dispute to endanger his professional career.

In Rev. Rul. 67-48, 1967-1 C.B. 50, the IRS ruled that the taxpayer who breached his employment contract could deduct repaying compensation but could not use §1341. If he had rendered the required future services, no repayment would have been required. This situation differs from the audit that the government unsuccessfully treated as a subsequent event in *Van Cleave*. Mr. Van Cleave was required to repay the compensation if a third party determined it was unreasonable; the taxpayer in the ruling had to repay the compensation because of his own subsequent actions.

A taxpayer who satisfies the § 1341(a)(1)–(3) requirements performs two tax computations for each year. She compares the tax she would have paid in the earlier year if she had not received the item to the tax she actually paid. She compares the tax that would be due in the later year if she deducted the repayment to the tax she would pay if she did not deduct it. I.R.C. § 1341(a)(4)–(5); Reg. § 1.1341-1(b)(1)(i)–(ii). If deducting the amount in the later year reduces her tax more than reducing the earlier year's gross income does, she takes the deduction in the later year. If reducing the earlier year's gross income results in a greater tax saving, she does not take the deduction in the later year. She instead treats the reduction in the earlier year's tax as a payment of tax for the later year. I.R.C. § 1341(b)(1). It has the effect of a tax credit in the later year.

To determine the reduction in the earlier year's tax, the taxpayer does not merely subtract the item she repaid in the later year. Because the Code includes floors and phase-outs of tax benefits based on income, she may have to recompute her previous deductions for charitable contributions or other items affected by her income. Reg. § 1.1341-1(d)(4)(ii).

b. Failure to Satisfy Requirements

A taxpayer who cannot satisfy the § 1341(a)(1)–(3) requirements may be able to deduct the amount she repays in the later year. Her tax savings in the year she repays the original amount are based only on her taxable income and tax rates in that later year.

The reason for failing to satisfy the requirements is important. A taxpayer whose repayment does not exceed $3,000 simply fails a mathematical test. She deducts the repayment as a business expense, an expense related to an income-producing activity, or a loss from a transaction entered into for profit. A taxpayer who fails the unrestricted claim of right requirement may confront public policy arguments against her deduction. An embezzler is a typical example. She cannot satisfy § 1341 because she had no unrestricted claim of right to the funds even if she reported them as gross income. But she certainly had a profit motive that would justify a § 165(c)(2) deduction; the repayment is a loss on a transaction entered into for profit. But no deduction is allowed for repayments that are treated as fines or penalties.

4. Net Operating Loss Deduction

In general. Taxpayers who engage in a trade or business are favored when their activity results in a loss. If a business taxpayer's deductions exceed her gross income, she can use the excess loss to reduce future taxable income. She takes a net operating loss (NOL) deduction in those future years, which are referred to as carryover years. I.R.C. § 172.

The NOL computation begins with taxable income. I.R.C. § 172(c). A taxpayer who has even a minimal amount of taxable income does not have an NOL. For example, a taxpayer who sustains a business loss does not have an NOL if her gross income from other sources covers that loss and her other deductions.

Even if she has negative taxable income, modifications required by § 172(d) may reduce or eliminate her NOL. She must eliminate capital losses in excess of capital gains, and she cannot use the § 1202 exclusion (discussed in Chapter 6). She must also eliminate nonbusiness deductions in excess of nonbusiness gross income and the § 199A qualified business income deduction. She treats deductible casualty and theft losses of both personal-use property and property acquired in a transaction entered into for profit as business losses. She treats net nonbusiness capital gains as nonbusiness income. She treats salary as business income. Reg. § 1.172-3(a)(3).

Before 2018, a taxpayer generally carried an NOL back to the two taxable years preceding the loss year and forward to the 20 taxable years following it. The loss could offset 100% of any income available in the carryover year. Most NOLs sustained after 2017 are ineligible for a carryback, but there is no longer a 20-year limit on deducting them in future years. I.R.C. § 172(b)(1). There is, however, a deduction limit. The NOL deduction allowed in any year is the lesser of the carryover amount or 80% of that year's taxable income (before considering the carryover). I.R.C. § 172(a).

COVID-19. Congress amended § 172(a) for NOLs sustained in 2018 through 2020 by suspending the 80% limit. It also allowed such losses to be carried back up to five years. I.R.C. § 172(b)(1)(D).

> **Example 16-5.** In 2021, Arlene had $28,000 of gross income and $58,950 of potential deductions. Her negative taxable income is $30,950, but her NOL is smaller. Arlene reported $20,000 of business income and $8,000 of dividends. She also reported $43,000 of business deductions, and $15,000 of nonbusiness mortgage interest and property taxes. In computing her NOL, she offsets $8,000 of mortgage interest and property taxes against her $8,000 of dividend income; she cannot deduct the other $7,000. Her NOL was only $23,000.

> **Example 16-6.** In 2022, Arlene had taxable income of $25,000 before considering her $23,000 NOL carryover from 2021. Because $20,000 (80% of $25,000) is less than $23,000, Arlene could deduct only $20,000 of her NOL in 2022; she carries the remaining $3,000 forward to 2023.

Arlene could have deducted the entire $23,000 in 2022 if her taxable income for that year had been at least $28,750.

Arlene's business loss did not exceed the §461(l) safe harbor discussed in Chapter 15. If it had, she would have had an excess business loss. She could not have deducted the excess loss against nonbusiness income. Instead, she would have carried it forward as an NOL.

5. Other Events Affecting Multiple Years

Several deductions disallowed in one year might ultimately be allowed in a future year because of carryovers. Some carryovers are limited in duration; others can be taken whenever the taxpayer ultimately qualifies. Carryovers discussed elsewhere in this book include those for investment interest expense (§163); charitable contributions (§170); use of a dwelling unit as a residence (§280A); excess business losses (§461); losses from an activity for which the taxpayer is not at risk (§465); passive activity losses (§469); and net capital losses (§1211).

Recapture provisions are designed to prevent taxpayers from bunching deductions or from trying to convert ordinary deductions into capital gain income. Examples include recapture of first-year expensing if property is no longer used predominantly in a business (§179); recapture of ordinary losses on §1231 property; and depreciation recapture or rate adjustments (§§1245 and 1250). The interplay between damages excluded by §104 and the medical expense deduction in §213 is another example of how events in one year affect the tax treatment of events in another year.

6. Forced Matching of Reporting Periods

If the parties to a transaction don't use the same accounting methods, distortions may result. For example, the payor might take a deduction before the payee reports gross income. Code provisions that prevent this result are exceptions to the general accounting rules. The forced matching provisions differ from rules discussed in Chapter 13 that require the cash method for charitable contributions, medical expenses, interest on education loans, qualified tuition, and health savings accounts. The rules discussed in those chapters apply whether or not the parties are related and whether or not a taxpayer uses the accrual method for other items.

Section 267(a)(2) applies when an accrual-method payor is related to a cash-method recipient. In that situation, the payor cannot take a deduction until the taxable year in which the recipient reports gross income. The definition of related person discussed in Chapter 14 applies.

> **Example 16-7.** Algernon receives a salary of $5,000 per month, payable a week after the month ends. He uses the cash method. His employer, Beryl, uses the accrual method. Algernon received his salary for December 2019 on January 7, 2020. If Beryl is not related to Algernon, she deducts his December 2019 salary on her 2019 tax return. If she is his mother, she deducts his salary on her 2020 return.

Before the enactment of § 467, parties involved in a multi-year rental agreement could designate payment terms that did not reflect economic reality but that did affect the year in which they reported rental income and expense. Section 467 requires a present value computation that results in a constant rental accrual. It applies to rental agreements covering tangible property if the total consideration exceeds $250,000, at least one payment will be made in a year later than the year in which the property is used, and the agreement calls for increasing amounts of rent. I.R.C. § 467(d). Both the lessor and lessee report rent and interest based on a "section 467 rental agreement." Interest is computed annually based on rents for prior years that remain unpaid at year-end. I.R.C. § 467(a).

In Chapter 3, we discuss property transferred in connection with the performance of services but subject to a substantial risk of forfeiture. The transferor's deduction is deferred until the service provider reports the item as gross income. I.R.C. § 83(h).

C. Cash and Accrual Accounting Methods

The two basic accounting methods are cash receipts and disbursements (cash method) and accrual. I.R.C. § 446(c). A taxpayer can use different accounting methods for different activities (*e.g.*, business and personal or two separate businesses). I.R.C. § 446(d). Once he selects an accounting method, he uses it until he receives IRS permission to change or a court determines the method does not clearly reflect income. I.R.C. § 446(e).

Sections 451 and 461 provide general rules for reporting gross income and deductions. Most Code sections involving deductions use one of two terms: "paid or accrued" or "paid or incurred." Accrued refers to expenses that are determined based on the passage of time. Interest, property taxes, and rent are examples of such expenses. Incurred refers to expenses that are identified with an event. These include supplies, professional fees, and hourly wages. Despite the alternative language, taxpayers cannot deduct expenses when they are paid *or* when they are accrued or incurred. We construe these terms using the taxpayer's method of accounting. I.R.C. §7701(a)(25). Unless an exception applies, a cash-method taxpayer deducts expenses when paid and an accrual-method taxpayer deducts them when accrued or incurred.

1. Cash Receipts and Disbursements Method

Individuals normally use the cash method, in large part because it is easier to understand and use than the accrual method. The cash method operates like a checkbook. A cash-method taxpayer reports gross income in the year he receives cash or its equivalent. He reports expenses in the year he makes payment.

Section 448 prevents certain taxpayers from using the cash method. Section 448(a) does this for tax shelters. Although it purports to prevent all C corporations (and partnerships with a C corporation partner) from using the cash method, §448(b) lets farming businesses, corporations with 3-year average annual gross receipts of $25 million or less, partnerships whose C corporation partners meet that gross receipts test, and qualified personal services corporations use the cash method. The gross receipts limitation is indexed for inflation. §448(c). The §448(c) test has relevance beyond cash versus accrual accounting. We refer to provisions applicable to taxpayers meeting this test at other points in this book.

A corporation is a qualified personal services corporation if substantially all of its activities are in the fields of health, law, engineering, architecture, accounting, actuarial science, performing arts, or consulting, and substantially all of its stock value is directly or indirectly held by the employees or retired employees who perform services for it in connection with these activities. Stock held by an employee's or retired employee's estate also qualifies as does stock received by any other person on account of an employee's or retired employee's death, but only for a two-year period. I.R.C. §448(d)(2).

a. Gross Income

If a cash-method taxpayer receives payment in the year in which she performs services, she reports the amount received that year. There are other possibilities. She might receive a check at year-end, receive only a promise that the other party will pay, or receive payment in property other than cash. She might be offered payment and refuse to accept it.

In *Kahler v. Commissioner*, 18 T.C. 31 (1952), the Tax Court held that a cash-method taxpayer who received a check after banking hours on the last day of the year had gross income. Inability to access cash after banking hours is rarely a problem now; taxpayers can use direct deposit and 24-hour ATMs.

The taxpayer has no gross income if he receives only a promise that the other party will pay. The promise could be represented by an account receivable or by a more formal note receivable. Because the receipt of a note is not treated as payment, he does not report gross income. In *Williams v. Commissioner*, 28 T.C. 1000, 1002 (1957), the taxpayer received a note that bore no interest and was unsecured. He was unable to sell it to a bank or finance company. The note had no fair market value and was thus not a cash equivalent in the year of receipt. "A note received only as security, or as an evidence of indebtedness, and not as payment, may not be regarded as income at the time of receipt.... A simple change in the form of indebtedness from an account payable to a note payable is insufficient to cause the realization of income by the creditor."

If the taxpayer receives payment in property other than cash, she reports gross income equal to the value of the property received. Her basis for that property is the amount she reported as gross income. In effect, she is treated as if she received cash and used it to purchase the property.

A taxpayer who receives a prepayment cannot avoid reporting gross income merely because he has not earned the money. This is true even if he might have to return the funds because he does not render the services. The cash method requires him to report income when he actually or constructively receives it. Reg. § 1.446-1(c)(1)(i). Income is constructively received when an amount is credited to his account or is made available to him or his designee without restriction. Income is not constructively received if his ability to control receipt is subject to substantial limitations or restrictions. Reg. § 1.451-2(a). For example, if a client requires her attorney to place a fee in his trust account until all appeals are heard, he has not constructively received the fee. But if she offers him a check, which does not have to be placed in the trust account, he cannot avoid gross income by refusing to take the funds until the next year or by voluntarily placing them in his trust account.

b. Expenses

If the taxpayer pays cash for an item that benefits her that year, she deducts it that year. Payments by check or by cash are essentially equal for tax purposes. *Estate of Witt v. Fahs*, 160 F. Supp. 521 (S.D. Fla. 1956). Likewise, payment through an agent occurs when the agent mails checks to creditors, transfers funds to their accounts, or makes actual delivery of the checks. Rev. Rul. 80-335, 1980-2 C.B. 170. Payment by credit card is generally treated as payment in cash. The credit card statement is proof of payment if it shows the amount of the charge, the transaction date, and the name of the payee. Rev. Proc. 92-71, 1992-2 C.B. 437. A mere promise to pay is not treated as payment.

Example 16-8. Alton purchased a radio station advertisement in November 2019. He charged the station's bill to his credit card in December 2019 and paid the credit card company in January 2020. He deducts the expense in 2019. If he had instead paid the invoice by credit card in January 2020, he would deduct the expense in 2020.

Chapter 12 discussed the difference between expenses and capital expenditures. Even a cash-method taxpayer cannot deduct capital expenditures in the year of payment. I.R.C. § 263. Unless he qualifies for a first-year deduction, he recovers a depreciable asset's cost over its useful life.

A cash-method taxpayer might prepay expenses that benefit multiple years. Because a full deduction would not clearly reflect income, he should not be allowed a current deduction. *See Commissioner v. Boylston Market Association,* 131 F.2d 966 (1st Cir. 1942); Reg. § 1.263(a)-4(d)(3). Instead, he should allocate the outlay to the years covered by the prepayment. Although allocation makes sense in theory, many prepayments cover only a short period. Accounting for them over multiple years increases his compliance costs without appreciably affecting the government's tax collections. This is particularly true for recurring outlays. Several judicial decisions took this view in cases involving rent, insurance premiums, permits, and license fees. *See Zaninovich v. Commissioner,* 616 F.2d 429 (9th Cir. 1980). In *U.S. Freightways Corp. v. Commissioner,* 270 F.3d 1137 (7th Cir. 2001), the court indicated that accrual-method taxpayers might also deduct such items. The payments involved did not benefit the taxpayer for more than a year following the year of payment.

The regulations include a 12-month rule for intangibles. Reg. § 1.263(a)-4(f)(1). A taxpayer may take a current deduction if the payment will not benefit her after the earlier of two dates: (1) 12 months after the first date on which she realizes the benefit; or (2) the end of the taxable year following the year in which she makes the payment. She allocates the deduction over the years benefited if she fails this test.

Example 16-9. Adela paid $12,000 in 2019 for business insurance covering 60 months, beginning on September 1, 2019. Because this payment benefits her for more than 12 months after she first benefits from it, she allocates it to the periods it covers and deducts $200 in each of the 60 months. If she had instead paid for a policy covering 12 months, she could deduct her entire premium in 2019. The payment would not cover a period beyond 12 months after she first benefited from it, and the benefit would not extend past December 31, 2020.

Because the taxpayer pays points to obtain a lower interest rate on his loan, points represent prepaid interest. Points differ from most prepayments in one important respect. A taxpayer who prepays an expense such as insurance premiums receives a partial refund if he cancels the policy early. A taxpayer who repays a loan early does not receive a refund of the points he paid. The accounting rules governing points are discussed in Chapter 13.

2. Accrual Method

Accrual-method taxpayers report gross income when all events that fix their right to receive the income have occurred. That is usually the year in which they render services or accrue interest owed them. They deduct expenses in the year in which their obligation to pay is fixed. It is usually irrelevant whether an amount is actually received or paid.

Unlike the cash method, for which eligibility rules apply, any taxpayer can use the accrual method. Exceptions, many of which are covered in Chapter 13, place the taxpayer on the cash method for some expense deductions.

a. Gross Income

Under the accrual method, it is the *right* to receive and not the *actual* receipt that determines the inclusion of an item in gross income. But a taxpayer who receives a prepayment enjoys an accession to wealth. Can he postpone being taxed until he earns the income?

We first determine whether the amount received was prepaid income or a security deposit. That topic is discussed in Chapter 8. If it is prepaid income, the IRS argues for immediate taxation because the taxpayer has the ability to pay in the year of receipt. The Supreme Court upheld the IRS position in several decisions rendered shortly after the 1954 Code was enacted. *Schlude v. Commissioner*, 372 U.S. 128 (1963); *American Automobile Association v. United States*, 367 U.S. 687 (1961); *Automobile Club of Michigan v. Commissioner*, 353 U.S. 180 (1957). *Schlude* involved prepayments for dance lessons. The dance studio promised a specific number of lessons but did not prescribe fixed dates for those lessons. That made it more difficult to allocate income among accounting periods. The other two organizations provided various automobile- and travel-related services to members.

Congress later enacted Code sections allowing certain accrual-method taxpayers to report prepayments when they earned the income rather than in the earlier year of receipt. Section 455 applies to prepaid subscription income, and § 456 applies to prepaid dues of membership organizations.

In the Tax Cuts and Jobs Act of 2017, Congress amended § 451 to provide rules for advance payments. Accrual method taxpayers with applicable financial statements are deemed to satisfy the all events test, and must report gross income, no later than the year in which they report the income on the applicable financial statement. Qualifying statements are prepared in accordance with generally accepted accounting principles and submitted to government agencies or creditors for a substantial nontax purpose. I.R.C. § 451(b). Section 451(c) applies to taxpayers who receive certain advance payments. Payments covered by this section must meet three tests: (1) the payments would be fully included in gross income in the year of receipt under a permissible method of accounting; (2) a portion of the payment would be included in a later year on a financial statement; and (3) the payment is for goods, services, or any other item identified by the Treasury Department. I.R.C. § 451(c)(4)(A). The taxpayer receives the item if he actually receives it, constructively receives it, or it is due and payable. I.R.C. § 451(c)(4)(C). He can include the item in gross income in the year he receives it. Alternatively, he can elect to report the amount required to be reported in the year of receipt in that year and report the remaining amount in the next year. I.R.C. § 451(c)(1).

The IRS had previously issued Rev. Proc. 2004-34, 2004-1 C.B. 991, which let an accrual-method taxpayer defer reporting a prepayment allocable to income it would earn before the end of the next taxable year. It applied to several types of income from performing services and selling goods. The IRS clarified and modified these rules in several subsequent revenue procedures. In Notice 2018-35, 2018-18 I.R.B. 520, the IRS indicated that taxpayers could continue to rely on the revenue procedure until it issued further guidance implementing the amendments to § 451.

b. Expenses

An accrual-method taxpayer deducts expenses in the year that the liability arises. Two tests are relevant in determining the appropriate year for deducting the outlay. These are the all events test and the economic performance test.

The all events test has two components. All events necessary to fix the taxpayer's liability must have occurred and he must be able to determine the amount with reasonable accuracy. I.R.C. § 461(h)(4). The all events test could justify a current deduction for services he will receive many years in the future but that he could estimate now. The economic performance test, the other requirement for deductibility, prevents such distortions. Section 461(h)(1) provides that the all events test is not treated as met any earlier than when economic performance occurs.

Section 461(h)(2) governs when the economic performance test is satisfied. For example, it is satisfied when the taxpayer has received the property or services that the other party will provide. It is satisfied with respect to workers compensation liability or tort liability when the taxpayer makes payments to the other person. The Federal Circuit has held that the economic performance requirement applies to the computation of basis as well as to the deductibility of expenses. *AmerGen Energy Co., LLC v. United States*, 113 Fed. Cl. 52 (2013). The taxpayer wanted the basis for its nuclear power plants to include the liability it assumed for future decommissioning costs.

> **Example 16-10.** Arvin ordered a month's worth of office supplies in November 2019. The supplies arrived in December 2019, along with a bill from the supplier. Arvin paid the supplier in January 2020. He deducts the expense on his 2019 tax return because he became liable for the expense in 2019. All events had occurred to fix the liability, the amount of the liability could be determined, and economic performance occurred.

Section 461(h)(3) lets the taxpayer take the deduction if he meets only the all events test. Items covered by this exception must be recurring in nature, and he must regularly treat items of that kind as occurring when they meet the all events test. If the item is material in amount, he must establish that accruing it in the earlier year results in a more proper match against income than accruing it when economic performance occurs. Finally, economic performance must occur within a reasonable period of time after the close of the taxable year and no later than 8.5 months after the close of that year. This exception is not available for workers compensation and tort liabilities.

D. Accounting for Inventory

A business usually uses the accrual method to account for purchases and sales of inventory. The discussion below focuses on a taxpayer who purchases goods at wholesale and sells them to the public rather than manufacturing them herself. She is likely to have two types of inventory: items she has purchased for resale and supplies used in the course of her business but not held for resale. Accounting for a manufacturer's inventory is more complicated because it has at least three components: (1) raw materials, on which she has not yet begun work; (2) work-in-process, which she has not yet completed; and (3) completed goods, which are available for sale. She may also have inventories of supplies.

Because inventory accounting is rarely covered in depth in the basic income tax course, this chapter also ignores exceptions to the general rules.

Items held for sale. Inventory accounting affects one component of gross income from business: cost of goods sold (COGS). The taxpayer reduces sales revenue by COGS in computing gross income from business. I.R.C. § 61(a)(2); Reg. § 1.61-3(a). Unless he specifically tracks each item and its cost (specific identification method), he uses an *accounting convention* to determine the order in which he sells his inventory. The specific identification method is appropriate for unique goods, such as real property and fine jewelry. An accounting convention is easier to administer for other items.

The first-in, first-out (FIFO) method assumes that the business sells goods in the order in which it purchased them. In determining the COGS, it begins with the oldest unit in inventory, then the second oldest, and so on. In an inflationary market, this method inflates reported earnings because sales revenue is matched with inventory purchased when costs were lower.

The last-in, first-out (LIFO) method assumes that the business sells goods in the reverse order of their purchase. In determining the COGS, it begins with the newest unit in inventory, then the second newest, and so on. In an inflationary market, the balance sheet understates the inventory's replacement cost because it reports the cost of the oldest inventory. Taxpayers cannot use LIFO in computing taxable income unless they also use it on their financial statements or other reports prepared for owners or creditors. I.R.C. § 472(c). Congress has considered repealing the use of LIFO on several occasions.

The average-cost method averages the cost of all the units in inventory. In an inflationary economy, it would produce earnings that are lower than those produced by FIFO (because the COGS would be higher) and higher than those produced by LIFO (because the COGS would be lower). The Code does not specifically authorize the average cost method, but § 471(c) lets small businesses use the method they use on an applicable financial statement. Taxpayers who lack an applicable financial statement may use the method they use in preparing their books and records. The taxpayer's status as a small business is based on § 448(c). The taxpayer has an applicable financial statement if he meets the requirements of § 451(b), discussed earlier in this chapter.

> **Example 16-11.** Angela sells books. She began the year with no inventory and acquired 100 books for sale: (1) 10 in January for $30 each ($300); (2) 30 in March for $40 each ($1,200); (3) 25 in July for $50 each ($1,250); and (4) 35 in October for $60 each ($2,100). Her total cost was $4,850. Her average cost was $48.50. She sold 62 books

for $100 each ($6,200). To compute her gross income from sales, Angela subtracts her COGS from her $6,200 sales revenue. Her FIFO COGS would be $2,600 (all books purchased in January and March and 22 books purchased in July). Her LIFO COGS would be $3,430 (all books purchased in October and July and two books purchased in March). The COGS using average cost is $3,007.

E. Accounting for Installment Sales

Section 453(a) provides that income from an installment sale is reported using the installment method. The use of "income" means that this section applies only to dispositions resulting in gain. The discussion and examples in this section ignore interest. You should assume that each sale provided for interest in addition to payments of the sale price.

1. Definitions

An installment sale is a disposition in which the taxpayer will receive at least one payment after the close of the taxable year in which the disposition occurs. I.R.C. §453(b)(1). This definition does not require any payment in the year of disposition, more than one payment, or a payment more than a full year after the sale. A taxpayer who sold gain property in December 2019 and received full payment in March 2020 made an installment sale.

We allocate the seller's gain by multiplying each payment received by the ratio of gross profit to total contract price. I.R.C. §453(c). These terms and the term selling price are defined in the regulations. The regulations refer to the ratio itself as the "gross profit ratio." Reg. §15a.453-1(b)(2)(i).

Gross profit is the selling price minus the adjusted basis. If the taxpayer is a non-dealer and sells real property or makes a casual sale of personal property, she adds selling expenses to adjusted basis for this computation. Reg. §15a.453-1(b)(2)(v).

The contract price is the selling price reduced by qualifying indebtedness the buyer assumes or takes the property subject to. The reduction by qualifying indebtedness cannot exceed the seller's basis. Reg. §15a.453-1(b)(2)(iii). Because we subtract qualifying indebtedness that the purchaser assumes, we allocate gain only over the payments the seller will *actually* receive. This methodology does not reduce the gain reported; it simply allocates it somewhat differently than we would do if we had to report gain each time the purchaser made a payment on the assumed debt.

2. Computations

a. Basic Computations

If there are no selling expenses or debt encumbering the property, the computations are relatively simple. They are more complicated if the seller incurs selling expenses or the buyer assumes qualifying indebtedness because those items affect the gross profit ratio. If the mortgage exceeds the seller's basis, the excess is reported as gain in the year of the disposition.

> **Example 16-12.** Amanda sold Blackacre to Ben for $100,000. He will pay $20,000 a year for five years. Her adjusted basis was $75,000, Blackacre was not subject to a mortgage, and she had no selling expenses. The selling price and total contract price are both $100,000. The gross profit is $25,000 (selling price minus adjusted basis). Because the gross profit is 25% of the total contract price, each payment is $5,000 gain and $15,000 basis recovery.

> **Example 16-13.** Bill sold Purpleacre to April for $100,000. She will pay $15,600 a year for five years and will also assume a $22,000 mortgage encumbering Purpleacre. His adjusted basis was $75,000, and he paid selling expenses of $1,000, which increased his adjusted basis to $76,000. The selling price is $100,000, but the total contract price is $78,000 (selling price minus qualifying indebtedness). The gross profit is $24,000 (selling price minus adjusted basis). Because the gross profit is 30.769% of the total contract price, each payment is $4,800 gain and $10,800 basis recovery.

If the buyer gives the seller a note receivable or other evidence of indebtedness rather than merely promising to make the installment payments, the transaction is somewhat more formal but the computations remain the same. The note is not treated as a payment even if a third party guarantees it. I.R.C. § 453(f)(3). It is treated as a payment only if it is payable on demand or is readily tradable in an established securities market. I.R.C. § 453(f)(4)–(5).

b. Contingent Payments and Open Transactions

The computations are adjusted if the contract includes contingencies that affect the selling price. In rare circumstances, the transaction is treated as an open transaction. In that case, the seller recovers her basis tax-free before reporting any gain.

The starting point is § 453(j)(2), which authorizes regulations providing for ratable basis recovery if the gross profit or total contract price cannot be readily ascertained. This grant of authority is designed to limit the situations in which basis is recovered using an open transaction approach. In determining the effect of contingencies, we ignore any contingency that is resolved by the end of the year in which the sale occurs. Reg. § 15a.453-1(c)(1).

The regulations cover three categories involving contingencies. The first category covers sales for which the seller can ascertain the maximum selling price assuming all contingencies relating to selling price are met. For example, the contract might call for a selling price equal to 5% of sales but not more than $150,000. The computation of selling price, contract price, and gross profit are based on $150,000. If he later determines that he will receive a smaller amount, he applies an adjusted ratio to later payments. Reg. § 15a.453-1(c)(2).

The second category covers sales for which the seller cannot ascertain the maximum selling price but there is a fixed payment period. In that case, he allocates his basis in equal amounts over the fixed period. If the payment for any period is less than the basis allocated to it, he reports no gain that period. He carries any unrecovered basis forward to the next period. In the last year, he can deduct any unrecovered basis as a loss. Reg. § 15a.453-1(c)(3).

The third category covers sales for which the seller cannot ascertain either the maximum selling price or the payment period. We scrutinize these transactions to be sure they are sales and not transactions producing rent or royalty income. If sale treatment is appropriate, he generally allocates his basis over the 15-year period beginning with the date of sale. If he receives less than the allocated basis in any given year, he allocates the unrecovered basis for that year equally to any remaining years. If he does not recover his basis by the end of the 15 years, he carries it forward until he recovers his basis or payments cease. Reg. § 15a.453-1(c)(4).

Special rules apply if computations based on one of the three categories will result in a substantial and inappropriate acceleration of income. Reg. § 15a.453-1(c)(7). The regulations include an income forecast method for allocating basis in appropriate situations. Reg. § 15a.453-1(c)(6).

The open transaction doctrine applies when it is impossible to ascertain a reasonable estimate of the selling price or gross profit. The regulations are designed to prevent this doctrine from applying in most situations. When it does apply, the transaction is not treated as closed; gain or loss is not computed. Instead, the seller applies payments to recovery of basis. After he recovers his basis, he reports all subsequent payments as gain. If payments end before he recovers his basis, he reports a loss equal to the unrecovered basis.

The case most frequently cited for the open transaction doctrine is *Burnet v. Logan*, 283 U.S. 404 (1931). It involved a sale of stock in a corporation that had a right to a percentage of the ore extracted from a leased mine. The purchaser agreed to pay the shareholders a fixed amount and an additional amount per ton of ore allocated to it. Neither buyer nor seller could estimate the amount of ore that would be extracted. The lease contract did not include minimum or maximum tonnage requirements or any definite payments. The Court held that the amount the taxpayer would receive was not ascertainable. Even if it believed that the fair market value of what she received was equal to the value of the stock she relinquished, the latter value was subject to the same contingency—the amount of ore extracted from the mine. If *Burnet v. Logan* were decided today, it would likely be covered by the regulation discussed above.

3. Special Rules

a. Depreciation Recapture

Section 453(i)(1) taxes gain attributable to depreciation recapture in the year of sale. Only the remaining gain qualifies for installment method reporting. Recapture income is that part of the gain that would be taxed as ordinary income under § 1245 or § 1250 if all payments were received in the year of disposition. I.R.C. § 453(i)(2). Because real property acquired since December 31, 1986, is depreciated using the straight line method, gain from its sale is not taxed as ordinary income if the property was held more than one year. Although the entire gain on its sale can be reported on the installment method, payments are not allocated pro rata between unrecaptured § 1250 gain and other gain. Instead, unrecaptured § 1250 gain is taxed before gain taxed at lower capital gains rates. Reg. § 1.453-12(a), (d). *See* PLR 200937007.

> **Example 16-14.** Arnold purchased a building several years ago for $300,000. He deducted straight line depreciation of $45,000, leaving him with a $255,000 adjusted basis. He sold it for its current $500,000 value and will receive $50,000 a year for 10 years. He had no selling expenses, and the building was not subject to any encumbrances. His $245,000 gain has two components: $45,000 of unrecaptured § 1250 gain and $200,000 of other gain. He reports all his gain on the installment method; because he used straight line depreciation, none of his gain is taxed as ordinary income. Each $50,000 payment is $25,500 basis recovery and $24,500 gain. In Year 1, the $24,500 gain is unrecaptured § 1250 gain.

In Year 2, $20,500 of the gain is unrecaptured § 1250 gain and $4,000 is § 1231 gain. All $24,500 gain in each of Years 3 through 10 is § 1231 gain.

b. Sale of Depreciable Property to Related Entity

Chapter 18 discusses § 1239, which requires a taxpayer to report gain as ordinary if he sells depreciable property to a related party. The critical factor is the related transferee's ability to depreciate the property. I.R.C. § 453(f)(7). Section 453(g) generally prevents a taxpayer from using the installment method for reporting gain from such a sale. If the seller can establish that tax avoidance is not one of the principal purposes for the sale, he can use the installment method. I.R.C. § 453(g)(2).

If § 453(g) applies, the seller treats all payments as received in the year of sale. He can recover basis ratably only with respect to payments that are contingent in amount and for which he cannot reasonably ascertain a fair market value. The purchaser cannot increase its basis for the property by any amount before that amount is includible in the seller's gross income. I.R.C. § 453(g)(1).

> **Example 16-15.** This year Blake sold his vacation home for its value to his wholly owned corporation. It will pay the sale price in five annual installments and will use the property as a conference center. If he can establish that tax avoidance was not a principal purpose for the sale, he reports his gain on the installment method. If he cannot establish that, he reports his entire gain on the building this year. Because land is not depreciable, he can use the installment method to report any gain on the land.

c. Like-Kind Exchanges

A taxpayer who receives both like-kind property and other property or money recognizes at least part of any gain realized. I.R.C. § 1031(b). If the money is received in installments, § 453(f)(6) governs how gain is reported. In that case, the contract price is smaller than in the computations described at the beginning of this section. The selling price is reduced by qualifying obligations assumed by the buyer *and* by the value of like-kind property the seller receives. The gross profit is reduced by any gain that is not recognized because of the receipt of like-kind property. The seller does not treat the value of that property as a payment.

Example 16-16. Angie and Bud exchanged like-kind properties. She transferred investment land with a basis of $100,000 and a fair market value of $150,000. He transferred investment land worth $120,000 and will pay her $6,000 a year for the next five years. Angie had no selling expenses, and her property was not encumbered. She has a realized gain of $50,000. If she received all $30,000 cash in the year of sale, she would recognize $30,000 of gain. Because she can report her gain on the installment method, she allocates the $30,000 recognized gain to each year using the installment method. Her total contract price is $150,000 minus the $120,000 value of the qualifying property she received from Bud, or $30,000. Her gross profit is also $30,000 ($50,000 gain realized minus the $20,000 gain she will not recognize). Because her gross profit ratio is 100%, each $6,000 payment is gross income.

d. Disposition by Related Purchaser

With the exception of the rules governing depreciable property described above, §453 does not prevent a taxpayer from using the installment method for sales to a related person. Instead, §453(e) applies if the related person disposes of the property within two years and has not yet made all the payments called for in the sales contract. Section 453(e) does not apply if the taxpayer can establish that neither the original disposition to the related person, nor the subsequent disposition by the related person, had tax avoidance as one of its principal purposes. I.R.C. §453(e)(7). In addition, the gain is not accelerated if the disposition by the related person was caused by a compulsory or involuntary conversion (e.g., casualty, theft, or government taking) or occurred after the death of one of the related persons. I.R.C. §453(e)(6).

The definition of related person for this purpose draws on the rules in §§318(a)(1)–(3) (attribution rules applied in certain corporate transactions) and 267(b) (attribution rules used for disallowing losses on transactions between related persons). I.R.C. §453(f)(1). These rules include sales to family members, to entities controlled directly or indirectly by the seller, and between certain other related persons (such as a fiduciary and a beneficiary of a trust).

The original installment sale is the first disposition; the disposition by the related person is the second disposition. When §453(e) applies, the amount realized from the second disposition is treated as received at that time by the original seller. Section 453(e)(3) provides adjustments to prevent him from being taxed both at the time of the second disposition and again when the related buyer pays him. If the second disposition is not a sale or exchange, the amount realized on that disposition is the property's fair market value. I.R.C. § 453(f)(4).

> **Example 16-17.** Aaron purchased investment land several years ago for $120,000. He sold it in 2018 to his daughter Bree for its $160,000 value, payable in five annual installments of $32,000. She made her 2018 and 2019 payments, and he reported $8,000 gain each year. Later in 2019, Bree sold the land for $175,000. Unless Aaron can establish that tax avoidance was not a principal purpose for either disposition, he reports his remaining $24,000 gain in 2019. He does not report additional gain when he receives the remaining payments from Bree.

> **Example 16-18.** Bree instead received $175,000 from an insurer because the land was destroyed by a meteor in 2019. In that case, Aaron does not report his remaining gain until he actually receives payments from Bree. The second disposition was an involuntary conversion.

e. Reacquiring the Property Sold

If the buyer doesn't pay the amount due in full, the seller may reacquire the property through foreclosure or agreement. Section 1038 (Chapter 17) governs the relevant tax consequences.

4. Exceptions

A taxpayer may elect to forgo using the installment method and report her gain in the year of disposition. She may need income to offset an expiring carryover or may expect tax rates to rise in the future. The election can be revoked only with the permission of the IRS. I.R.C. § 453(d). A taxpayer who reports the entire selling price as an amount realized on the tax return for the year of sale is deemed to have made an election even if she does not formally elect out of the installment method. Reg. § 15a.453-1(d)(3)(i). The regulations provide for late elections if the IRS concludes there was good cause for the late election. They do not allow conditional elections. Reg. § 15a.453-1(d)(3)(ii).

5. Interest on Deferred Tax

If the taxpayer uses the installment method, § 453A may require her to pay interest on her deferred tax liability. This provision does not apply unless the sales price exceeds $150,000. It applies to an obligation arising during a taxable year only if the face amount of all installment obligations arising during the year and outstanding at year-end exceeds $5 million. Sales of personal-use property, farm property, time shares, and residential lots are exempt. I.R.C. § 453A(b)(1)–(4). If the obligations arising during the year do not meet the $5 million threshold, they are never subject to § 453A.

The interest rate charged is the rate applied to underpayments of income tax by § 6621(a)(2). That amount is the Federal short-term rate plus three percentage points. Because the gain that is deferred retains its character as ordinary income or capital gain, the deferred tax computation uses the appropriate § 1 ordinary income and net capital gain rates. The computation uses tax rates in effect each year the obligation remains unpaid, not the rates in effect when the taxpayer made the sale. I.R.C. § 453A(c)(3).

6. Dispositions of Installment Obligations

If the taxpayer disposes of an installment obligation, § 453B applies. If she sells or exchanges the obligation, she reports gain or loss equal to the difference between the selling price and her basis for it. The same rule applies if the obligation is satisfied at less than face value. If she disposes of it in some other manner, she uses its value instead of the selling price in determining gain. I.R.C. § 453B(a). Her basis for the obligation is its face value reduced by any income she would report if it were satisfied in full. I.R.C. § 453B(b). The character of the gain or loss reflects the character of the original property sold. I.R.C. § 453B(a) (flush language).

> **Example 16-19.** Anna sold investment land to Bruce. The selling price was $500,000, and her basis was $300,000. He agreed to make four payments of $125,000 each. She reported long-term capital gain of $50,000 (25% of her $200,000 gain) when she received each payment. After Bruce made three payments, Anna sold the installment obligation to Buyer for $118,000. Her basis for the unpaid obligation is $75,000 (its $125,000 face value reduced by the $50,000 gain she would report if Bruce paid her in full). Because the land was a capital asset, she reports $43,000 long-term capital gain on selling the obligation (amount realized minus her basis for the obligation).

Unless the income in respect of a decedent rules apply, § 453B does not apply if the obligation is transmitted at the taxpayer's death. I.R.C. § 453B(c). If it is transferred to a spouse or to a former spouse incident to a divorce, the recipient spouse reports income on the installment method in the same manner as the transferor spouse. I.R.C. § 453B(g). Additional rules apply to certain corporate distributions of installment obligations. I.R.C. § 453B(d), (h).

F. Accounting for Long-Term Contracts

A taxpayer who constructs property may take more than one taxable year to complete the project. It is likely that he will receive progress payments during the construction period rather than waiting to receive payment when he completes the project. Should he report income based on those progress payments, based on the percentage of the project he has completed, or when he finally completes the project? Although § 460(a) provides for using the percentage of completion method for long-term contracts, exceptions apply. The discussion in this section ignores many of the complexities involved in long-term contracts.

A long-term contract is a contract to manufacture, build, install, or construct property that is not completed in the taxable year in which the taxpayer enters into the contract. I.R.C. § 460(f)(1). Manufacturing is included only if the item manufactured is a unique type of item that the taxpayer does not normally include in its finished goods inventory or is an item that normally requires more than 12 calendar months to complete; the contract period is irrelevant in this situation. I.R.C. § 460(f)(2).

As a general rule, the taxpayer reports profit each year based on the percentage that his costs incurred that year are of his estimated total costs. I.R.C. § 460(b)(1)(A).

> **Example 16-20.** Armando agreed to build an office complex for Bart. Armando will receive $50 million from Bart and expects to spend $45 million in completing the contract; as a result, he expects a profit equal to 10% of the contract price. Armando and Bart anticipate the complex will be complete in Year 3. In Year 1, Armando received $32 million from Bart and spent $15 million. The project was 25% complete by the end of Year 1. Because Armando expended $15 million of his $45 million expected cost, he reports one-third of his expected profit in Year 1.

Section 460(b) includes special computation rules, including a so-called look-back method of computing interest to compensate the taxpayer (or the government) if the profit reported based on the percentage of completion method differs from that based on the difference between actual and estimated costs.

Section 460(e)(1) exempts home construction contracts from the percentage of completion method. It also exempts contracts entered into by a taxpayer who meets the § 448(c) gross receipts test (maximum average of $25 million gross receipts for the prior three years) with respect to contracts estimated to be completed within two years of their commencement date.

G. Accounting for Interest Income

1. U.S. Savings Bonds

Cash-method taxpayers who purchase U.S. savings bonds issued at a discount can elect to report the interest as it accrues. I.R.C. § 454. Alternatively, they can report it in the year they collect the bond purchase price and accrued interest. In other words, they can report small amounts each year over a multi-year period or they can defer reporting until they receive all of the interest on surrendering the bond. If a government bond issued at a discount has a fixed maturity date of one year or less, § 454(b) provides that interest is not considered to accrue until the maturity date (or earlier date of disposition).

As discussed in Chapter 10, some taxpayers qualify to exclude the bond interest if they use the bond proceeds for qualified higher education expenses. I.R.C. § 135.

2. Original Issue Discount

The original issue discount (OID) rules provide a framework for computing interest and allocating it to the appropriate taxable year. If there is OID, the bond owner reports it as interest, not as capital gain. The discussion below provides an overview of these complex provisions, which govern a debt instrument's issue price, amount of OID, treatment of OID while the taxpayer owns the instrument, and treatment of OID when the taxpayer disposes of the instrument.

a. Issue Price

The OID rules apply to bonds, debentures, notes, or certificates or other evidences of indebtedness. I.R.C. § 1275(a)(1)(A). A debt instrument has OID if its stated redemption price at maturity exceeds its issue price. I.R.C. § 1273(a). OID is computed based on the original issue price, not on the amount a later purchaser pays to acquire the instrument from a prior owner. We ignore de minimis OID. I.R.C. § 1273(a)(3).

To compute any OID, we must determine the issue price. That price varies based on the consideration received when the instrument is issued. If it is publicly traded, the issue price is the initial offering price at which a substantial amount of the debt instruments was sold. This rule does not apply to instruments issued for property other than money. I.R.C. § 1273(b)(1). Section 1273(b)(5) defines property to include services and the right to use property. If a debt instrument is not publicly offered and is not issued for property, the issue price is the price paid by its first buyer. I.R.C. § 1273(b)(2).

> **Example 16-21.** Argo Corporation issued bonds that it will redeem in
> 10 years. The bonds were publicly offered and sold for $800 each.
> Each bond has a redemption price of $1,000. The issue price of each
> bond is $800, and each bond has OID of $200.

The issue price of an instrument issued for property is the fair market value
of that property if one of two conditions is satisfied. First, the instrument was
part of an issue of which a portion is traded on an established securities market.
Second, the instrument was issued in exchange for stock or securities that are
traded on an established securities market or for other property of a kind
regularly traded on an established market. I.R.C. § 1273(b)(3). Property satisfying
either condition is easy to value because it trades on an established market.

Unless the instrument falls into one of the categories described above, or is
governed by § 1274, the issue price is the stated price at maturity. I.R.C.
§ 1273(b)(4). Section 1274 determines the issue price of certain debt instruments
issued for property and not governed by § 1273(b)(3). If the instrument provides
for adequate stated interest, the issue price is the stated principal amount. Otherwise, it is the imputed amount computed using a present value computation
for the payments due under the instrument. I.R.C. § 1274(a). In either situation,
§ 1274 applies if the redemption price exceeds the relevant issue price and at
least one payment is due more than six months after the issue date. I.R.C.
§ 1274(c)(1). As is true for the other OID provisions, several exceptions apply.

Section 1274A(a) imposes a maximum discount rate of 9% for qualified
debt instruments for purposes of § 1274. If the stated principal amount exceeds
a maximum amount, the instrument is not qualified. I.R.C. § 1274A(b). The
maximum amount is adjusted for inflation. I.R.C. § 1274A(d)(2). For 2020,
it is $6,039,100.

b. Accruing OID

A taxpayer who owns a debt instrument issued with OID accrues the discount
using a constant interest rate (the yield to maturity). I.R.C. § 1272(a)(1). Each
accrual period is generally six months in length. I.R.C. § 1272(a)(5). This corresponds to the interval between interest payments generally associated with
corporate bonds. Each accrual period ends on the date of the year that
corresponds to the bond's maturity date (or a date six months earlier). For example, a bond that matures on July 31 has accrual periods that end on January
31 and July 31 of each year it is outstanding.

Within each accrual period, the taxpayer allocates OID on a daily basis to
the debt instrument's adjusted issue price. The adjusted issue price increases
each period by the amount treated as that period's OID. I.R.C. § 1272(a)(3)–

(4). Because the adjusted issue price increases, the OID allocated to each successive accrual period is larger than the amount allocated to the preceding period. This method reflects compound rather than simple interest. The amount allocated to each period is computed by multiplying the yield to maturity by the adjusted issue price at the beginning of that period. I.R.C. § 1272(a)(3). Interest provided for by the instrument is deducted from the OID amount so that the holder is not taxed twice on the same amount.

> **Example 16-22.** Alfred paid $800 for one of the Argo Corporation bonds described in Example 16-21. Every six months he computes OID and includes it in gross income. For the first six-month period, he computes the allocable OID by multiplying the yield to maturity by the $800 issue price. He adjusts the issue price upward by that amount. For the next six-month period, he multiplies the yield to maturity by the increased adjusted issue price. He continues this process until the bond matures and is redeemed or he disposes of it before its maturity.

Section 1272 generally does not apply to tax-exempt obligations, U.S. savings bonds, debt instruments with a maturity date not more than one year from their issue date, and loans that do not exceed $10,000 made between natural persons that are not made in the ordinary course of the lender's trade or business. I.R.C. § 1272(a)(2).

c. Sale, Exchange, or Retirement

Section 1271 applies when the holder sells or exchanges a debt instrument or the issuer retires it. If the issuer intended to call the obligation before its maturity, the holder's gain has two components: the OID that he had not previously included in gross income and any remaining gain. I.R.C. § 1271(a)(2)(A).

> **Example 16-23.** ABC Corporation issued publicly traded debt instruments at a discount of 10% from the redemption price. It intended to call the instruments as soon as it could borrow at a lower interest rate. Adam purchased one of these bonds for $900. Because the redemption price was $1,000, the bond was issued with $100 of OID. He reports the OID as interest income over the period he holds the bond. He increases his basis as he reports OID. If ABC retires the bond before maturity, and Adam realizes a gain, he first allocates his gain to the OID he has not already reported as gross income. Any remaining gain may qualify as capital gain. The same rules apply if he sells the bond to Bertha before its maturity date.

d. Related Provisions

Sections 1276 through 1278 apply to market discount bonds whose stated redemption price at maturity exceeds the taxpayer's basis for the bond immediately after she acquires it. As was the case for bonds issued with OID, market discount bonds require recalculations to allocate an appropriate amount to ordinary income. Because the market discount provisions generally apply to taxpayers who acquired the bonds after their original issue, the OID rules are unlikely to apply. If both sets of rules do apply, § 1278(a)(2)(B) provides a method for coordinating them. Exclusions apply for short-term bonds, U.S. government bonds, and bonds with de minimis market discount.

Sections 1281 through 1283 apply to obligations that have a fixed maturity that is no more than one year from their issue date. If the amount due at maturity exceeds the taxpayer's basis for the obligation, the obligation has acquisition discount. When these provisions apply, the taxpayer accrues the acquisition discount and reports it as interest over the life of the bond (which might straddle two taxable years) in addition to reporting any interest actually received.

At one time bonds were issued with interest coupons attached. The bondholder detached the coupon and submitted it for payment. When coupons are separated from the bond, so that one person owns the bond and another person owns the coupons that are not yet payable, the bond is a stripped bond and those coupons are stripped coupons. Section 1286 treats the stripped bonds and coupons as having OID. The OID for the bond is equal to the excess of the stated redemption price at maturity over its ratable share of the combined purchase price. The OID for each stripped coupon is the excess of the amount payable on its due date over its ratable share of the combined purchase price. A taxpayer who strips the bond and disposes of either the bond or coupons includes the accrued coupon interest and the accrued OID in his gross income. He adjusts his basis upward to reflect the amount included in gross income.

Bonds are now generally issued in registered form, and the issuer sends a check (or makes an electronic transfer) to the bondholder. If a registration-required bond is not registered, § 1287 requires the bondholder to report gain on sale or other disposition as ordinary income. A bond is registration-required unless it is issued by a natural person, is not of a type offered to the public, or has a maturity date at issue of one year or less. I.R.C. § 163(f).

Section 1288 provides rules for computing OID on tax-exempt obligations. The bondholder accrues OID and increases her basis to reflect the accrual even though the bonds produce tax-exempt interest. If she did not increase basis, she would be taxed on an artificial gain when she disposed of the bond.

3. Imputed Interest

a. Section 483

Section 483 applies when property is sold or exchanged, payments are due more than a year after the sale occurs, and the contract does not provide for adequate interest. It does not apply if: (1) the OID rules apply; (2) the total sales price is $3,000 or less; (3) payments are treated as interest using the carrying charge rules of § 163(b); or (4) amounts paid with respect to the transfer of a patent are contingent on productivity. I.R.C. § 483(d).

If part of the sales price is treated as unstated interest, the seller's gain is reduced (or his loss is increased) by the amount that is treated as interest. The interest is taxed at the rates applied to ordinary income. The gain or loss may, depending on the nature of the property sold, qualify for capital gain or loss treatment.

Although § 483 does not apply unless at least one payment is due more than a year after the date of sale, when it does apply its reach extends to any payment due more than six months after the date of sale. I.R.C. § 483(c)(1).

> **Example 16-24.** Art owned investment land worth $800,000, for which he had a basis of $600,000. He agreed to sell it to Barb for 10 annual payments of $82,000 each; the contract did not provide for interest. If § 483 did not apply, Art would report his gain using the installment method. Each payment would be $22,000 of capital gain and $60,000 tax-free return of his basis. Because the contract did not provide for adequate interest, Art must treat part of each payment as interest instead of capital gain.

As a general rule, the taxpayer determines an adequate rate of interest using the applicable Federal rate determined under § 1274(d). I.R.C. § 483(b). The applicable rate varies based on the term; anything over nine years is based on the Federal long-term rate. He reduces each payment to its present value. The total unstated interest is the difference between the payments called for and the present value of those payments.

Section 1274A(a) imposes a maximum discount rate of 9% for qualified debt instruments covered by § 483. Section 483(e) limits the maximum discount rate to 6%, compounded semiannually, if the taxpayer sells land to a family member. The definition of family member is taken from § 267(c)(4): brothers, sisters, spouse, ancestors, and lineal descendants. The maximum 6% rate applies to no more than $500,000 of land sales between the taxpayer and each related party in any year. It does not apply if either party is a nonresident alien.

b. Section 7872

In 1961 the Tax Court held that a borrower had no gross income when he was not charged interest. *Dean v. Commissioner,* 35 T.C. 1083 (1961). In 1984, the Supreme Court held that a taxpayer who made an interest-free loan as a gift made a taxable gift of the forgone interest. *Dickman v. Commissioner,* 465 U.S. 330 (1984). That year, Congress enacted § 7872, which applies for both income tax and gift tax purposes.

Section 7872 applies to below-market loans. When it applies, the loan transaction is recharacterized to provide for adequate interest. The lender is taxed as if he received that interest. He may also be subject to gift tax on the forgone interest or be able to deduct it as compensation expense. The borrower's tax consequences depend on whether the interest was forgone for donative or compensatory purposes and whether § 163 would have allowed a deduction if she had paid interest. The type of loan determines the years in which these events are deemed to occur.

> **Example 16-25.** Adler loaned $500,000 to his sister Beth and did not charge interest. If § 7872 applies, Adler is treated as making a gift of the forgone interest to Beth and then receiving that amount back from her as interest income. Beth is treated as paying interest to Adler.

Below-market loans are categorized in two overlapping ways. One is based on motive: gift or compensation. The other is based on length: term or demand. A gift loan is a loan for which the lender forgoes interest as a gift and not as compensation or other taxable payment. I.R.C. § 7872(f)(3). A demand loan is a loan that is payable in full at any time on demand of the lender. I.R.C. § 7872(f)(5). Term loans are loans that do not meet the definition of a demand loan. I.R.C. § 7872(f)(6).

A demand loan is a below-market loan if interest is payable at a rate that is less than the applicable Federal rate. A term loan is a below-market loan if the amount loaned is greater than the present value of the called-for loan payments. I.R.C. § 7872(e)(1). Present value is computed using the applicable Federal rate as a discount rate. The difference between the amount of interest that would have been paid and the actual amount due represents forgone interest. I.R.C. § 7872(e)(2). Applicable Federal rates are published every month in the Internal Revenue Bulletin. We use the short-term rate if the term does not exceed three years; the mid-term rate if the term is more than three years but not more than nine years; and the long-term rate if the term is more than nine years. I.R.C. § 1274(d).

Gift Loans. Section 7872 does not apply to gift loans between individuals for any day on which the total loans between them does not exceed $10,000. The borrower must not use the loan proceeds to acquire or carry income-producing assets. I.R.C. § 7872(c)(2). This exception does not apply for gift tax purposes if the loan was a term loan at any time. It does apply for income tax purposes. I.R.C. § 7872(f)(10).

If total gift loans between individuals do not exceed $100,000, the forgone interest will not exceed the borrower's net investment income. He computes his net investment income using the computations provided in § 163(d). That provision governs the deduction of investment interest expense. The borrower's net investment income is treated as zero in any year in which it does not exceed $1,000. I.R.C. § 7872(d)(1). This provision applies to both term and demand loans.

> **Example 16-26.** Arthur made interest-free demand loans to his children. He loaned $6,000 to Amelia, $12,000 to Angelique, and $15,000 to Astrid. Amelia had no investment income or income-producing assets. Angelique had $800 of investment income and no investment expenses. Astrid had $1,500 of investment income and $300 of investment expenses. None of the loans had a tax-avoidance motive.
>
> Arthur has no imputed interest income from the loans to Amelia or Angelique. The loan to Amelia did not exceed $10,000, and she had no income-producing assets. The loan to Angelique did not exceed $100,000, and her net investment income is treated as zero because it did not exceed $1,000. He has imputed interest income from the loan to Astrid. His gross income is the lesser of her $1,200 net investment income or the amount computed by applying the short-term Federal rate to the $15,000 demand loan.

If § 7872 applies to a gift loan, the applicable Federal rate depends on whether the loan is a demand loan or a term loan. The applicable Federal rate for a demand loan is the Federal short-term rate in effect under § 1274(d), compounded semiannually; that rate fluctuates as the Federal rate fluctuates. The applicable Federal rate for a term loan is based on the length of the loan; the rate is determined when the loan is made and does not fluctuate. I.R.C. § 7872(f)(2).

Any forgone interest is treated as having been transferred from the lender to the borrower and then retransferred by the borrower to the lender. These transfers are deemed to occur on the last day of the relevant calendar year. I.R.C. § 7872(a). Because the forgone interest is transferred from the lender as a gift, the borrower has no gross income. I.R.C. § 102(a). The lender reports interest income each year the loan is outstanding unless one of the exceptions for gift loans applies. The borrower can deduct the interest only if § 163 provides a deduction.

Compensation-Related Loans. Compensation-related loans may be made between an employer and a service provider (an employee or an independent contractor). I.R.C. § 7872(c)(1)(B). The employer is deemed to have received interest from the service provider and to have paid him compensation. The service provider reports compensation income and is treated as paying interest.

If the loan is a demand loan, the forgone interest is computed at the end of each year. The parties report compensation income one year at a time. The interest computation follows that for gift loans. I.R.C. § 7872(a). The applicable Federal rate is the short-term rate in effect under § 1274(d), compounded semi-annually. Section 7872 does not apply on any day that the total loans between the borrower and lender do not exceed $10,000. I.R.C. § 7872(c)(3). This exception does not apply if the loan was a term loan at any time. I.R.C. § 7872(f)(10).

If the loan is a term loan, the applicable Federal rate is determined when the loan is made. The payments due are discounted to present value on that day. The entire discount is treated as compensation that year. The forgone interest income or deduction is spread over the life of the loan using the OID rules. I.R.C. § 7872(b).

> **Example 16-27.** Alan loaned his employee Baxter $15,000 and charged no interest. Because Baxter must repay the loan in four years, it is a term loan; the forgone interest is computed using the Federal mid-term rate in effect when the loan is made. If the present value of the loan is $12,000, Alan is treated as paying Baxter $3,000 of compensation when the loan is made. Alan deducts the $3,000, and Baxter includes it in gross income that year. In addition, in each year the loan is outstanding, Alan reports an allocable amount of the $3,000 as interest income. Baxter deducts that amount only if his interest expense is covered by § 163.

Other Loans. Section 7872 also applies to loans between a corporation and a shareholder. I.R.C. § 7872(c)(1)(C). If the shareholder is the lender, the forgone interest is treated as a contribution to the corporation's capital. If the corporation is the lender, it is treated as a distribution to the shareholder. The distribution is probably a dividend if the corporation is a C corporation. If it is an S corporation, the rules governing distributions from S corporations apply. Prop. Reg. § 1.7872-4(d)(1). Loans to continuing care facilities are treated more favorably than most below-market loans. I.R.C. § 7872(g)–(h).

Checkpoints

- Individuals usually use a calendar year. Entities often use a fiscal year.

- Taxable income is generally computed with respect to a single year's income and outlays.

- The use of the annual accounting period may not accurately reflect the economic consequences of transactions that affect multiple years.

- Several Code sections provide relief by limiting the tax in a later year or allowing a carryover to another year. These include sections covering deductions that provided no tax benefit, income received under a claim of right and then repaid, and net operating losses.

- The cash method allocates revenues and expenses to the year in which amounts are received or paid. Income is constructively received when it is made available to the taxpayer without restriction.

- The accrual method allocates revenues and expenses to the year in which amounts are earned or incurred. The taxpayer deducts expenses when all events fixing the liability have occurred and the amount of the liability can be ascertained with reasonable accuracy. Economic performance may also be required.

- Some Code sections force both parties to a transaction to report the item in the same taxable year to prevent potential abuse.

- Some Code sections force (or allow) taxpayers to use a particular accounting method for certain items even if they report other items using a different method.

- Businesses that have inventory usually use the accrual method for their inventory. If the business does not track the specific items it sells, it uses an assumption about the order in which it sells its inventory.

- The FIFO method assumes that the inventory was sold in the order in which it was purchased. The LIFO method assumes a reverse order of sale. The average cost method assumes that the cost of each unit is equal to the average cost of all units on hand.

- If a seller will receive a payment after the year of sale, the gain is reported on the installment method unless she is ineligible or elects out of that method.

- The installment method generally allocates the seller's gain to each installment she receives. If she sold depreciable property, gain allocable to depreciation recapture is taxed immediately.

- The installment method is available even if the sales price is subject to contingencies.

- Anti-abuse rules apply if the installment sale is made to a related person who resells the property within two years.

- Taxpayers who perform long-term contracts generally report their profits using the percentage of completion method instead of reporting their profit when they complete the contract.

- Cash method taxpayers who acquire U.S. savings bonds at a discount may choose between reporting the interest as it accrues or reporting it when the bond is redeemed.

- If a borrower issues a debt instrument that does not provide for adequate interest, the OID rules treat part of the redemption price as interest. The interest is included in gross income over the life of the instrument.

- The OID rules use a present value computation to compute the interest. The discount rate for determining present value is the applicable Federal rate.

- Section 483 applies to sales that are not covered by the OID rules but that also fail to provide for adequate interest.

- Section 7872 applies to loans that do not provide for adequate interest. Imputed interest is computed based on the applicable Federal rate and reflects whether the loan is payable on demand or for a fixed period.

- If the loan is compensation-related, the borrower has gross income from compensation, and the lender has a business expense deduction. If the loan is a gift loan, the lender may have made a gift that is subject to gift tax.

Chapter 17

Gain and Loss: Nonrecognition Provisions

Roadmap

- Introduction
- Like-kind exchanges
- Compulsory or involuntary conversions
- Wash sales
- Transfers to a spouse or a former spouse
- Reacquisition of real property
- Other nonrecognition transactions

A. Introduction

If a nonrecognition provision applies, we report realized gain or loss in a later year instead of in the year we realize the gain or loss. These provisions also affect the basis and holding period of property involved in the transaction. In dealing with nonrecognition transactions, keep these statements in mind:

- Most gains and losses are recognized in the year in which they are realized. Nonrecognition applies only to situations covered by a specific Code section.
- Some nonrecognition provisions are mandatory. Others are elective.
- Some nonrecognition provisions apply to both gains and losses. Others apply only to gains or only to losses.
- Some nonrecognition provisions apply to a wide array of dispositions. Others apply only to particular disposition methods (*e.g.*, exchanges), particular types of property (*e.g.*, shares of stock or securities), or particular taxpayers engaged in the disposition (*e.g.*, spouses).

- If a transaction involves both property eligible for nonrecognition treatment and other property, nonrecognition treatment applies only to the eligible property.
- Nonrecognition differs from exclusion and nondeductibility. Nonrecognition merely postpones the tax consequences of a taxable gain or a deductible loss.
- Tax attributes other than unrecognized gains or losses also carry over to the new property or new owner. These include adjusted basis, holding period, and depreciation recapture potential.
- Most nonrecognition provisions provide a general rule and exceptions added to prevent hardship or abuse.
- Some transactions might qualify for nonrecognition in form but not in substance or vice versa.

B. Like-Kind Exchanges

1. Overview

Section 1031 applies to exchanges. Although the parties may use boot to equalize values, the transaction primarily involves the exchange of one property for another. When it applies, the taxpayer does not recognize any realized gain or realized loss. Her new property is in most ways the alter ego of her old property.

Section 1031(a)(1) provides that "no gain or loss shall be recognized on the exchange of real property held for productive use in a trade or business or for investment if such property is exchanged solely for real property of like kind which is to be held either for productive use in a trade or business or for investment." That sentence covers many of the principles introduced in Section A. This section is mandatory, it applies only to exchanges, only two property uses are covered, and the properties exchanged must be both real property and of "like kind" to each other.

As the word "either" indicates, a taxpayer does not have to exchange business property for business property or investment property for investment property. He can also exchange business property for investment property or vice versa. He can even exchange a single piece of business property or a single piece of investment property and receive multiple pieces of like-kind business or investment property (or both). But both properties must be held for one of the two named uses.

Example 17-1. Axel exchanged real property held for investment and realized a $100,000 gain. He received only real property of like kind that he plans to hold for productive use in a trade or business. He does not recognize his gain.

The example ignored the other party's tax consequences because § 1031 applies separately to each taxpayer. When two taxpayers exchange property, there are three potential outcomes: neither qualifies for nonrecognition; both qualify; or only one qualifies. We do not have enough information about the other party to know if she also qualifies.

2. Qualifying Property

a. Type of Property

Section 1031 and its regulations do not define "property held for productive use in a trade or business" or "property held for investment." Those definitions are determined through other administrative pronouncements and judicial decisions.

Section 1031(a)(2) currently includes only one limitation: real property held primarily for sale cannot qualify. Because the pre-2018 version of § 1031(a) also covered exchanges of personal property used in a trade or business or held for investment, the pre-2018 version of § 1031(a)(2) also included an extensive list of nonqualifying items of intangible personal property. That list does not help us determine what property qualifies.

A second limitation appears in § 1031(h). Real property located in the United States is not of like kind to real property located outside the United States.

b. Reason for Holding Property

Section 1031 applies only if the property exchanged was held for productive use in a trade or business or for investment and the property received will be held for one of those purposes. Establishing that property was held for investment can be difficult if the taxpayer made personal use of the property. For example, the taxpayer may have a vacation home that she uses for part of the year but rents to tenants at other times. Section 280A, discussed in Chapter 15, limits her expense deductions because of the personal use, but that section uses bright-line tests that are not found in § 1031. A taxpayer who makes no personal use is more likely to succeed in claiming her property was held for investment than a taxpayer who uses it for personal purposes while also hoping it will appreciate. The situation is analogous to that faced by taxpayers who claim a loss on selling property that has both personal and investment characteristics. Section 165(c)(2) lets them deduct losses realized on transactions entered into for profit but not losses on selling personal-use property.

Rev. Proc. 2008-16, 2008-1 C.B. 547, provides objective standards for exchanges of dwelling units held for personal and rental purposes. The taxpayer must have owned the relinquished property at least 24 months. She must have rented it at a fair rental for at least 14 days in each of the two 12-month periods ending on the day before the exchange. Her personal use of the property during each of the two periods cannot exceed the greater of 14 days or 10% of the days at which it was rented at a fair rental. Similar rules apply if she wants § 1031 to apply to a dwelling unit she received in an exchange. Beginning the day after the exchange, she must rent the new property at a fair rental value for at least 14 days in each of the next two 12-month periods. Her personal use in each period must not exceed the greater of 14 days or 10% of the rental days.

Multiple uses are not limited to personal versus business. Property held only for lease to customers can qualify for like-kind exchange treatment. Property held only for sale to customers cannot qualify. But what if the taxpayer held the property for both purposes? The IRS has treated such dual-use property as inventory, making it ineligible for like-kind exchange treatment, depreciation deductions, and § 1231 status, but Notice 2013-13, 2013-12 I.R.B. 659, may indicate a reconsideration of that position. It requested input on factors the IRS should consider in determining if construction and agricultural dual-use property is inventoriable or depreciable and whether it is eligible for § 1031 treatment. The notice also asked for input on other industries that could use guidance with respect to this issue.

Another problem area involves taxpayers who dispose of the property received, or convert it to personal use, too soon after the exchange. The situation is complicated if the taxpayer retains an indirect interest in the property after the exchange. For example, in *Magneson v. Commissioner*, 753 F.2d 1490, 1495 (9th Cir. 1985), the taxpayers exchanged a fee simple interest in property held for investment and received an undivided fee simple interest in like-kind property. They and their co-tenant transferred that second property to a limited partnership in exchange for general partnership interests. Both transactions occurred the same day. The court ruled that the original exchange qualified under § 1031. It noted that "They exchanged their investment property for like-kind investment property which they continue to hold for investment, albeit in a different form of ownership."

The *Magneson* opinion distinguished a transfer to a corporation in exchange for its stock from a transfer to a partnership in exchange for a partnership interest. The court noted that corporate stock could not qualify for § 1031 treatment but that a partnership interest could. Section 1031 was subsequently amended to preclude partnership interests from qualifying for § 1031. The real issue in both situations should be how soon a taxpayer can change his relationship to like-kind property by holding it through a corporation or partnership and whether it matters if the transfer was prearranged.

If the taxpayer instead transfers the new property to a family member or to a charity, he retains no interest unless the transfer was a sham. Judicial decisions and administrative rulings have considered these situations and the underlying facts and circumstances. As a general rule, if the transfer was prearranged, he cannot establish that he held the new property for use in a trade or business or for investment.

c. Attempting to Avoid Section 1031

If the taxpayer's business or investment property is worth less than its adjusted basis, he probably prefers to sell it and deduct his loss. In appropriate circumstances, the IRS will assert a substance over form argument when it believes a sale should be treated as an exchange. For example, in Rev. Rul. 61-119, 1961-1 C.B. 395, the taxpayer sold loss property. He purchased like-kind property from the same dealer in what purported to be a separate transaction. The IRS applied § 1031 because the two steps were reciprocal and mutually dependent transactions. The Fifth Circuit applied this rule to a corporation that sold its old trucks and had its subsidiary purchase new trucks. Both corporations dealt with the same manufacturer, and most of the trucks were actually delivered to the parent. The manufacturer considered the transactions integrated. *Redwing Carriers, Inc. v. Tomlinson*, 399 F.2d 652 (5th Cir. 1968). The Fourth Circuit held that § 1031 did not apply to a taxpayer that was misled into believing it dealt with separate parties in unrelated transactions. *Bell Lines, Inc. v. United States*, 480 F.2d 710 (4th Cir. 1973). Although § 1031 now applies only to exchanges of real property, those decisions remain relevant for taxpayers who want to recognize a loss but continue an investment in real property.

The discussion above focused on a taxpayer's relinquishing one item of property and receiving a different item in exchange. But what if the taxpayer purports to sell her property to another person and then leases it back? Did the sale-leaseback involve two independent transactions, or did the taxpayer make a like-kind exchange? If she would realize a deductible loss on selling her property, treating the transactions as independent has potential tax benefits. First, she could deduct the loss. Second, she could deduct paying rent to the transferee. If she owned the property, she could not depreciate the basis represented by land, and it is possible that straight-line depreciation on her building would be less than the deductible rent. This is an area where the IRS might claim the form of the transaction does not accord with its substance.

In *Leslie Co. v. Commissioner*, 539 F.2d 943 (3d Cir. 1976), the taxpayer was able to treat the transactions as independent. The court found several factors significant, most importantly that the leasehold had no separate value because it involved a market rate of rent. If the leasehold had no separate value, the taxpayer received only money and therefore had not made an exchange. Also relevant were the fairness of the sale price and the fact that the transferee would receive the eminent domain proceeds if the property were ever condemned.

Note that like-kind exchange versus sale may not be the only possibility a court could consider. In appropriate circumstances, the transaction might be treated as a financing arrangement. In that situation, we would ignore the sale and the purported seller would deduct part of her payments as interest instead of deducting all of them as rent. *See Frank Lyon Co. v. United States*, 435 U.S. 561, 584 (1978) ("[S]o long as the lessor retains significant and genuine attributes of the traditional lessor status, the form of the transaction adopted by the parties governs for tax purposes.").

3. Like-Kind Property

The regulations provide a somewhat limited definition of like kind, which is expanded upon in other administrative pronouncements. Reg. § 1.1031(a)-1(b) states that the term refers to the property's nature or character and not to its grade or quality. It then states that property of one kind or class cannot be exchanged for property of another kind or class. It does not directly define any of these terms. It continues by saying that whether real estate is improved or unimproved does not matter, as that relates to its grade or quality and not its kind or class.

Reg. § 1.1031(a)-1(c) provides limited examples that specifically involve real property: city real estate for a ranch or farm; a leasehold of a fee with 30 or more years to run for real estate; and improved real estate for unimproved real estate.

Two factors are important in determining whether an exchange of something other than outright ownership qualifies for nonrecognition. Each property must qualify as an interest in real property, and each interest must be extensive enough. As noted above, the regulations allow an exchange of improved for unimproved real property to qualify and allow an exchange of a leasehold with at least 30 years to run for actual ownership to qualify. The IRS has supplemented those limited examples with other guidance. For example, in PLR 200805012, it held that an exchange of real property for development rights could qualify as like kind. The development rights were treated as an interest in real property for some purposes under state law and they appeared to be perpetual in nature.

In CCA 201238027, it held that all the facts and circumstances were relevant, and that state law property classification was not necessarily determinative of whether the properties were of the same nature or character. The two properties were of the same type but were located in different states. One state classified the property as real and the other as personal.

4. Receipt of Boot

If the properties being exchanged are not of equal value, one party will transfer non-like-kind property or money to equalize values. The Code refers to the like-kind property as property permitted to be received for purposes of the relevant nonrecognition provision. It differentiates that property from the other property or money, which practitioners call "boot." A taxpayer who receives both like-kind property and boot fails the "solely" test of § 1031(a)(1).

If a taxpayer realizes a loss on an exchange of like-kind properties, she does not recognize that loss even if she also receives boot. I.R.C. § 1031(c). If she has a gain, § 1031(b) limits her recognized gain to the amount of boot received ("the sum of such money and the fair market value of such other property"). Section 1031(b) never increases the gain recognized above the amount of realized gain.

> Example 17-2. Becky exchanged investment real estate worth $100,000 (for which she had a basis of $80,000). She received investment real estate worth $92,000 and $8,000 cash. Although she realized a gain of $20,000, she recognizes only $8,000. The amount of money she received is less than her realized gain. The results would be the same if she received a tractor worth $8,000 instead of cash.

Transfers involving real estate often involve mortgaged property. There are three possible scenarios: (1) the transferor's property is encumbered; (2) the other party's property is encumbered; or (3) both properties are encumbered. Only the first and third involve debt assumed by the other party. In the second situation, the transferor is not receiving debt relief. She is promising to pay the other party's debt. Unless she receives money or other property, she is governed by the general rule of § 1031(a)(1) and recognizes no gain or loss.

If the transferor is the only party with encumbered property, and the other party assumes the debt (or takes the property subject to the debt), the transferor is treated as receiving money. This rule appears in the last sentence of § 1031(d). *See* Reg. § 1.1031(d)-2, Example 1. Because she received money, she recognizes some of her gain.

Example 17-3. Anya owned investment real estate worth $500,000 that was subject to a $150,000 mortgage. Her adjusted basis was $320,000. Beau, who owned real estate worth $350,000, exchanged his real estate for Anya's and took her real estate subject to the $150,000 mortgage. Anya will hold the new real estate for investment. Because the debt assumption was treated as money received, she recognized $150,000 of her $180,000 realized gain.

If both parties' properties are encumbered, the regulations net the obligations. Only the taxpayer who enjoys a net debt reduction is treated as receiving money. Reg. §§ 1.1031(b)-1(c), 1.1031(d)-2, Example 2.

Example 17-4. Anya instead exchanged her real estate for real estate owned by Brandon. Brandon's real estate had a fair market value of $900,000 and was subject to a $550,000 mortgage. Each took the other party's property subject to the debt. Although the values of the two properties differed significantly before the mortgages were considered, their net values were identical. Anya had equity equal to $350,000 ($500,000 value minus $150,000 mortgage). Brandon had equity equal to $350,000 ($900,000 value minus $550,000 mortgage). Because Anya was not relieved of debt, she was not treated as receiving money. She recognized none of her $180,000 gain.

Example 17-5. Anya instead exchanged her real estate for real estate owned by Belinda. Belinda's real estate had a fair market value of $400,000 and was subject to a $50,000 mortgage. Each took the other's property subject to the debt. Anya was relieved of debt in this transaction. Because the net $100,000 debt reduction was treated as money, she recognized $100,000 of her $180,000 gain.

The exchange may involve both debt assumption and receipt of boot in addition to the exchange of like-kind properties. Reg. § 1.1031(d)-2, Example 2, illustrates this situation. Each taxpayer transferred property subject to debt, and one of them also received money to equalize the net values. A party who receives money recognizes gain even if he does not have a net debt reduction.

5. Transfer of Other Property or Money

If a taxpayer's like-kind property is worth less than the property he is receiving, the other party will want to receive money or other property to equalize the values. The main exchange still qualifies under § 1031(a)(1). The taxpayer is receiving only like-kind property in the exchange. His tax consequences from transferring the money or other property are considered separately.

If he transfers money to equalize the values, that does not affect his gain or loss recognition. It does increase his basis for the property received. If he transfers other property, however, he recognizes gain or loss on the property that is not of like kind to the property he is receiving. That is why the § 1031(d) basis computation mentions recognized loss. Although he cannot recognize loss with respect to any like-kind property he transfers, he can recognize loss on any other property he transfers. Reg. § 1.1031(d)-1(e).

> **Example 17-6.** Armando exchanged investment real estate with Bradley and received investment real estate. Armando's real estate was worth $250,000 (basis of $220,000). Bradley's real estate was worth $275,000. To equalize the values, Armando also transferred shares of stock in XYZ Corporation worth $10,000 (basis of $12,000) and a delivery truck he used in his business worth $15,000 (basis of zero). Armando recognizes none of his $30,000 gain on the real estate. He recognizes his $2,000 loss on the XYZ stock and his $15,000 gain on the truck.

Nonrecognition transactions do not provide an independent basis for deducting a nondeductible loss. If Armando had transferred his personal-use automobile worth $10,000 (basis $12,000) instead of the XYZ stock, his $2,000 recognized loss would not be deductible. No Code section makes a loss on selling or exchanging personal-use property deductible.

6. Tax Consequences of Recognized Gain or Loss

As noted above, the taxpayer will recognize gain, but not loss, if she receives boot in addition to qualifying like-kind property. That recognized gain is likely to be long-term capital gain or § 1231 gain and qualify for the lower tax rates applied to net capital gain.

A taxpayer who transfers non-like-kind property to equalize values will recognize gain and loss (assuming the loss is deductible) with respect to that non-like-kind property. That recognized gain or loss is also likely to be long-term capital gain or loss or § 1231 gain or loss.

An important limitation involves recognized gain attributable to prior depreciation. A taxpayer who transfers depreciable real property and receives boot may still have net capital gain, but any of her gain that is unrecaptured § 1250 gain will be taxed at a different rate from other capital gains. A taxpayer who transfers depreciable personal property to equalize values will be subject to § 1245 depreciation recapture for any gain on that property. Depreciation recapture is discussed in Chapter 18.

7. Tax Attributes of Property Received

Section 1031(d) provides a formula for computing the basis of property received in a like-kind exchange. The formula builds any unrecognized gain or loss into the basis of the like-kind property that the taxpayer received. That increases the likelihood that she will be taxed on the gain, or will get to deduct the loss, if she ever sells the new property.

Her basis computation starts with the basis of the property she exchanged. If she *paid* money in addition to transferring property, she includes that money in this step. She subtracts any money she received, including debt relief treated as money. She adds any gain she recognized on the like-kind and non-like-kind property she transferred. Finally, she subtracts any loss she recognized on the non-like-kind property she transferred. If she receives more than one item of property, she allocates the basis among the properties received. The number of steps in her basis computation depends on what she exchanges and what she receives.

Because her basis for the like-kind property she received reflects her basis for the property she relinquished, the taxpayer's holding period for the property she received includes her holding period for the property she relinquished. I.R.C. § 1223(1). If she received boot in the exchange, her holding period for the boot begins the day after she acquired it.

a. Exchange Involves Solely Like-Kind Property

The basis computation is uncomplicated if the taxpayer's exchange involved only like-kind properties. It does not matter how many properties she transferred or how many she received. If she receives more than one item of like-kind property, she allocates her new basis among those properties according to their relative values.

> **Example 17-7.** Ariadne exchanged investment land for which she had a basis of $100,000 and received only investment land in exchange. Both properties were worth $120,000. She recognized none of her $20,000 realized gain. Her basis for her new land is the $100,000 basis she had in her old land. Because her new land is worth $120,000, the $100,000 basis preserves the $20,000 unrecognized gain from her old land.

Example 17-8. Britney exchanged investment land worth $125,000 for which she had a basis of $100,000 and received two tracts of investment land in exchange. Tract A was worth $75,000; Tract B was worth $50,000. She recognized none of her $25,000 gain. Her basis for her new land is the $100,000 basis she had in her old land. Because her new land is worth $125,000, the $100,000 basis preserves the $25,000 unrecognized gain from her old land. She allocates the $100,000 basis between Tracts A and B. Tract A takes 60% ($75,000/ $125,000) of the total basis, $60,000. Tract B takes 40% of the total basis, $40,000.

If Britney instead received improved property—*e.g.*, land and a building— the allocation has immediate tax consequences. She can depreciate the basis assigned to the building.

b. Exchange Involves Receipt of Boot

If the taxpayer received boot, the basis computation takes that receipt into account. The starting point is his basis for the property (or properties) exchanged. As illustrated below, his final basis equals his original basis if he realizes a gain (unless the boot exceeds his realized gain). It is less than his original basis if he realizes a loss because he reduces his original basis by the amount of boot received.

Example 17-9. Brett exchanged investment land for which he had a basis of $100,000 and which was worth $120,000. He received investment land worth $115,000 and $5,000 cash in exchange. He recognized only $5,000 of his $20,000 gain. His basis for his new land is the $100,000 basis he had in his old land, minus the $5,000 cash he received, plus the $5,000 gain he recognized. That computation results in a $100,000 basis. Because his new land is worth $115,000, the $100,000 basis preserves the unrecognized $15,000 gain from his old land.

Example 17-10. Alberta exchanged investment land for which she had a basis of $100,000 and which was worth $86,000. She received investment land worth $80,000 and $6,000 cash in exchange. She recognized none of her $14,000 loss. Her basis for her new land is the $100,000 basis she had in her old land, minus the $6,000 cash she received. The computation results in a $94,000 basis. Because her new land is worth $80,000, the $94,000 basis preserves the unrecognized $14,000 loss from her old land.

The examples above involved the receipt of money. If the taxpayer instead receives other property, a basis allocation is necessary. He allocates basis to the boot property first; it takes a basis equal to its value. I.R.C. § 1031(d) (second sentence). Any remaining basis is allocated to the like-kind property received.

> **Example 17-11.** Bertram exchanged investment land for which he had a basis of $100,000 and which was worth $86,000. He received investment land worth $80,000 and a motorcycle worth $6,000 in exchange. He recognized none of his $14,000 loss. His combined basis is the $100,000 basis he had in his old land. He allocates that basis between the two properties by assigning a $6,000 basis to the motorcycle. The new investment land receives the remaining $94,000 basis. Because that land is worth $80,000, the $94,000 basis preserves the unrecognized $14,000 loss from his old land.

c. Exchange Involves Transfer of Other Property or Money

If the taxpayer transferred other property or money, the basis computation reflects those items. The starting point is his basis for both the like-kind and non-like-kind property and the amount of any money he paid the other party. The computation also reflects any gain or loss recognized on the non-like-kind property he transferred.

> **Example 17-12.** Bob exchanged investment land for which he had a basis of $200,000 and which was worth $225,000. Because the investment land he received was worth $240,000, he also transferred $15,000 of cash. He recognized none of his $25,000 gain. His basis for the new land is the sum of the $15,000 he paid and his $200,000 basis for the land he exchanged. The computation results in a basis for the new land of $215,000. Because his new land is worth $240,000, that basis preserves the unrecognized $25,000 gain from his old land and gives him credit for the $15,000 cash he paid.

> **Example 17-13.** Instead of money, Bob transferred shares of stock in XYZ Corporation that were worth $15,000. His basis for the stock was $9,000. In addition to the $25,000 gain he realized on his land, Bob realized a $6,000 gain on the stock. He recognizes that $6,000 gain because the stock is not like-kind property. His basis for the new land is the sum of his $9,000 basis for the stock and the $200,000 basis for

the land, increased by the $6,000 gain he recognized on the exchange of his stock. That results in a $215,000 basis for his new land. Because his new land is worth $240,000, that basis preserves the unrecognized $25,000 gain from his old land.

8. Multi-Party Transactions

Potential parties to a transaction may have disparate goals. One may want to avoid gain recognition; the other may want to deduct a loss or to cash out. Although they cannot accommodate their disparate goals by dealing directly with each other, they can use a third-party intermediary to carry out the transaction. They can do so even if the first taxpayer transfers funds that the intermediary uses to purchase the second taxpayer's property.

> **Example 17-14.** Allison owns investment land worth $100,000; her basis is $80,000. Blair owns investment land worth $100,000; his basis is $110,000. Accommodator purchases Blair's land for $100,000 and transfers it to Allison in exchange for her land. Accommodator then sells the land it received from Allison. Allison has exchanged her land and avoids recognizing her gain; Blair has sold his and can recognize his loss. Accommodator receives a fee for rendering this service.

Exchanges using intermediaries can involve more than two transferors. For example, although Allison wanted Blair's property, Blair may have wanted Celia's property. Celia may want Allison's property, a different piece of property, or cash. If the parties who desire a like-kind exchange avoid receiving boot, they can all achieve their goals. The regulations include a detailed set of rules regarding who can serve as a qualified intermediary. Reg. § 1.1031(k)-1(g)(4).

9. Deferred Exchanges

A taxpayer who receives an offer to purchase his property may prefer a like-kind exchange. If the other party does not own like-kind property, she may be willing to acquire it. If the exchange must be simultaneous, it cannot occur until she acquires the like-kind property. If the exchange does not have to be simultaneous, the first taxpayer can transfer his property before the other party acquires and transfers the like-kind property.

In *Starker v. United States*, 602 F.2d 1341 (9th Cir. 1979), the court approved a non-simultaneous exchange. The *Starker* contract allowed up to five years for identifying the new like-kind property. The new property was not fully acquired until almost two years after the initial transfer.

Section 1031(a)(3) now governs deferred exchanges. It provides time limits for identifying the replacement property and for completing the exchange. If the parties do not meet both time limits, the taxpayer who transferred his property recognizes gain or loss even if he eventually receives like-kind property. The Code refers to the taxpayer's property as the property relinquished in the exchange or as the relinquished property. The other property is the property to be received in the exchange.

The taxpayer must identify the property to be received no later than 45 days after he transfers the relinquished property. I.R.C. § 1031(a)(3)(A). He must receive the new property on the earlier of two dates: the day which is 180 days after the date on which he transferred the relinquished property or the due date (including any extension) of the tax return for the year in which he transferred the relinquished property. I.R.C. 1031(a)(3)(B). Note that the 180-day period ends 135 days (*not* 180 days) after the end of the 45-day period.

> **Example 17-15.** On March 1, 2020, Arlo transferred appreciated investment land to Blythe. She did not own like-kind property but agreed to acquire such property for him or pay him the value of his property in cash. To avoid recognizing his gain, Arlo had to identify replacement property by April 15, 2020, and receive it by August 28, 2020.

The regulations refer to the 45-day period as the "identification period" and the second period as the "exchange period." If the taxpayer relinquishes more than one piece of property in the exchange, she begins each period on the date she relinquished the first property. Reg. § 1.1031(k)-1(b)(1)–(2).

The time limits could present problems if the taxpayer is limited to selecting one piece of property. What if she selected a piece of property but the other party could not acquire it before the exchange period ended because of problems with getting clear title? Fortunately, the regulations include methods for selecting more than one property that can be used to complete the exchange. Reg. § 1.1031(k)-1(c)(4).

Parties involved in deferred exchanges often use intermediaries to hold property or funds for the purchase of property. It is important that the intermediary not be viewed as the taxpayer's agent, which might result in her constructively receiving any money it holds. Reg. § 1.1031(k)-1(g) provides safe harbors, including use of a qualified intermediary, that let the taxpayer avoid constructive receipt.

Rev. Proc. 2000-37, 2000-2 C.B. 308, provides safe harbor guidance for a taxpayer who identifies property she wants to acquire before she identifies the property she will exchange. It provides for § 1031 treatment of property that is held in a qualified exchange accommodation arrangement (QEAA). It includes the 45-day and 180-day time periods used in § 1031(a)(3) deferred exchanges. It limits the combined period the acquired and relinquished properties are held in the QEAA to 180 days.

10. Related Party Exchanges

Related parties do not qualify for nonrecognition if either of them disposes of the property received within two years of the exchange. I.R.C. § 1031(f). This provision is designed to limit a taxpayer's ability to shift basis and then sell property. If a taxpayer who had a relatively high basis for her property exchanged it with a related party who had a much lower basis for property with the same value, and § 1031 applied, the first taxpayer could then sell the new property and report much less gain than the related party would have reported on the sale.

The Tax Court has applied § 1031(f) to situations involving qualified intermediaries. In *Ocmulgee Fields, Inc. v. Commissioner*, 132 T.C. 105 (2009), the taxpayer transferred appreciated property to a qualified intermediary (QI); an unrelated third party purchased that property from the QI. A related party sold property to the QI, and the QI transferred that property to the taxpayer. The court treated the transaction as a sale by the related party to the taxpayer. The Tax Court reached the same result in *Teruya Brothers, Ltd. v. Commissioner*, 124 T.C. 45 (2005). The court cited to § 1031(f)(4), which applies to transactions that are structured to avoid the purposes of § 1031(f).

Section 1031(f) does not apply if the taxpayers establish that neither the exchange nor the disposition had avoidance of federal income tax as one of its principal purposes. It also does not apply to a disposition after either party dies or to a disposition in a compulsory or involuntary conversion that was not imminent before the exchange. I.R.C. § 1031(f)(2).

11. Exchanges Involving a Principal Residence

Section 121(d)(10) limits a taxpayer's ability to benefit from both § 1031 nonrecognition and the § 121 exclusion. A taxpayer who receives property in a like-kind exchange and later makes it her principal residence cannot take advantage of the exclusion until five years after the exchange. This rule also applies to anyone who takes the taxpayer's basis, as would be the case if she transferred the property by gift. This rule is discussed in Chapter 6.

Another interaction between §§ 121 and 1031 involves an exchange of property the taxpayer used as a principal residence and also used for business or rented to tenants. For example, she may have an office in her home that she uses exclusively and on a regular basis for one of the purposes listed in § 280A(c), which is discussed in Chapter 15. In this situation, gain on the exchange might qualify in part for exclusion and in part for nonrecognition. Reg. § 1.121-1(e) provides that the portion of the property used for business can satisfy the § 121 two-year use-as-a-principal-residence requirement, and qualify for the exclusion, if it is in the same dwelling unit as the principal residence.

Rev. Proc. 2005-14, 2005-1 C.B. 528, applies § 121 before applying § 1031 when property that is exchanged is covered by both sections. It indicates that § 1031 can prevent recognition of the depreciation that could not be excluded under § 121. It treats the taxpayer as receiving boot for purposes of § 1031 only to the extent the boot he received exceeds the gain excluded by § 121 attributable to the business property. His basis for the new home includes any amount he could exclude under § 121. Rev. Proc. 2005-14 includes six examples.

> **Example 17-16.** Aubrey purchased a house for $210,000. After using it as his principal residence for two years, he converted it to rental property. He claimed depreciation deductions of $20,000 before exchanging it two years later for a house worth $460,000 and $10,000 cash. He will rent the new home to tenants. Aubrey realized a gain of $280,000 (amount realized of $470,000 minus adjusted basis of $190,000). Because he used the home as his principal residence for periods aggregating at least two years during the five-year period ending on the exchange, he qualified for § 121. He excluded $250,000 of his gain. The remaining $30,000 of gain qualified for § 1031 nonrecognition. The cash he received was not taxed because it was less than his $250,000 exclusion. The depreciation did not give rise to taxable gain because it was allocable to the gain covered by § 1031. His initial basis for the new house was $430,000 ($190,000 basis for the old house, plus the $250,000 excluded gain, minus the $10,000 cash received).

C. Compulsory or Involuntary Conversions

Section 1033 applies when property that is compulsorily or involuntarily converted is replaced with qualifying property. It applies only to gain; it does not affect a taxpayer's otherwise deductible losses. Section 1033 applies to personal use as well as to business and investment property. Unless § 1033(a)(1) applies, it is elective.

1. Section 1033(a)

a. General Rule

Section 1033(a) applies if property is compulsorily or involuntarily converted as a result of destruction in whole or in part, theft, seizure, or requisition or condemnation. It also applies to conversions as a result of threat or imminence of requisition or condemnation. No gain is recognized if the property is converted into property that is similar or related in service or use to the converted property. I.R.C. § 1033(a)(1). This is a mandatory provision.

If, as is more likely, the taxpayer receives money, § 1033(a)(2) applies. It provides that gain is recognized only to the extent she does not purchase qualifying replacement property within the required period. And, because it is elective, she can include the gain in gross income even if she does purchase qualifying replacement property.

> Example 17-17. Andrea had a basis of $85,000 for an item of property that was stolen. The property was insured for its $100,000 value. If she makes a timely purchase of qualifying replacement property costing $98,000, she can elect to recognize only $2,000 of her $15,000 realized gain. If she does not make the election, she recognizes the entire $15,000 gain in the year she receives the insurance proceeds even if she purchases replacement property.

The depreciation recapture rules discussed in Chapter 18 apply if the taxpayer recognizes gain or acquires qualifying replacement property that is not covered by § 1245 or § 1250. I.R.C. §§ 1245(b)(4), 1250(d)(4). Other limits apply to taxpayers who purchase replacement property from a related party. I.R.C. § 1033(i).

> Example 17-18. Barney's delivery truck was destroyed in a collision. It was insured for its $50,000 value. He had purchased the truck for $65,000 and taken depreciation deductions of $55,000, giving him a $10,000 adjusted basis. He spent the $50,000 insurance proceeds on a new delivery truck. He does not recognize any of his $40,000 gain even though it is all attributable to prior depreciation.

> Example 17-19. Barney instead used the $50,000 and additional funds he had saved and acquired a controlling interest in the GH Corporation. GH owns a fleet of delivery trucks. Barney would not normally

recognize any gain because he purchased a controlling interest in a corporation that owned qualifying replacement property. Because stock is not § 1245 property, he recognizes $40,000 of ordinary gain. Reg. § 1.1245-4(d)(2), Example 2.

b. Compulsory or Involuntary Conversion

Section 1033 applies to compulsory or involuntary conversions. The meaning of those terms may seem self-evident, but there are important differences between those terms and similar terms used in § 165(c)(3) (Chapter 14). You should not assume § 1033 covers only gains from events for which § 165(c)(3) covers losses.

Section 165(c)(3) lets taxpayers deduct losses with respect to personal-use property that are caused by fire, storm, shipwreck, other casualty, or theft. Although fire, storm, shipwreck, or other casualty lead to destruction in whole or part, and theft is listed in both sections, § 1033 applies more broadly. First, it does not use the term casualty. It applies even to destructions that are not as sudden as fire, storm, or shipwreck. For example, Rev. Rul. 66-334, 1966-2 C.B. 302, held that gradual salt water contamination of a fresh water supply constituted a destruction for purposes of § 1033. Because of its gradual nature, that type of event would not have been a § 165(c)(3) casualty loss even before the federally declared disaster requirement was added in 2017. Second, § 165(c)(3) applies only to personal-use property. Section 1033 applies to business, investment, *and* personal-use property.

There is also overlap between the treatment of compulsory or involuntary conversions in §§ 1033 and 1231. Both use almost identical language: destruction, theft or seizure, or requisition or condemnation. But there are several differences. Section 1231 (Chapter 19) applies only to property with a long-term holding period used in a trade or business and to long-term capital assets held in connection with a trade or business or a transaction entered into for profit; § 1033 also applies to personal-use property and to short-term capital assets. Section § 1231 applies to both gains and losses; § 1033 applies only to gains.

Because § 1033 is a nonrecognition provision, a taxpayer's decision to recognize (or not recognize) gain affects the computations he makes for purposes of §§ 165(c)(3) and 1231 in addition to affecting the ultimate computation of capital gain or loss. The deduction for personal casualty losses allowed by § 165(c)(3) is subject to the limits found in § 165(h). For example, the taxpayer must reduce his otherwise allowable deduction by 10% of his adjusted gross income. That limit does not apply if his personal casualty gains exceed his personal casualty losses. But we consider only *recognized* gains for this purpose. If he elects § 1033 nonrecognition for his personal casualty gains, he cannot take advantage of this rule. The § 1231 and capital gain and loss computations also consider only recognized gains and losses.

> **Example 17-20.** Arvin realized a gain of $15,000 when his fully insured 3-year-old vacation home was destroyed by fire. He realized a loss of $6,000 when his uninsured personal car was destroyed in a tornado that resulted in a federal disaster declaration. Arvin's other gross income (and AGI) was $100,000. If he replaces his vacation home and elects to use § 1033, he recognizes none of his gain. Because his personal casualty loss must be reduced by $100 and 10% of his adjusted gross income, he could not deduct any of the loss on his car. If he does not elect § 1033 treatment for his gain, he recognizes personal casualty gain of $15,000 and can deduct $5,900 of his personal casualty loss. The gain and loss are treated as capital gain and capital loss. His $9,100 net gain would be taxed at the lower capital gains rates.

c. Qualifying Replacement Property

Replacement property usually must be similar or related in service or use to the property converted. Alternatively, the taxpayer can purchase control of a corporation that owns qualifying property. The taxpayer must own stock possessing at least 80% of the corporation's total combined voting power and at least 80% of the total number of shares of all other classes of stock. Reg. § 1.1033(a)-2(c)(1).

The Code does not define "similar or related in service or use," and the regulations provide only three examples, all of property that does not qualify: (1) conversion of unimproved real estate and acquisition of improved real estate; (2) conversion of real property and use of funds to reduce indebtedness previously incurred to purchase a leasehold; and (3) conversion of a tug and acquisition of barges. Reg. § 1.1033(a)-2(c)(9).

The taxpayer's use of both properties is an important factor in determining if replacement property qualifies. If he used the converted property, his use of the replacement property must be similar. If he rented both properties to others, his risks and rewards in being a landlord must be similar. The tenants' uses do not matter. This rule was established in *Liant Record, Inc. v. Commissioner*, 303 F.2d 326, 329 (2d Cir. 1962). The court noted that decisions involving taxpayers who used their properties invoked a functional test. Their actual physical use of both properties had to be similar or related. When rental property was involved, the relevant test considered such factors as "the extent and type of the lessor's management activity, the amount and kind of services rendered by him to the tenants, and the nature of his business risks connected with the properties."

In Rev. Rul. 64-237, 1964-2 C.B. 319, the IRS announced it would adopt the test described in *Liant Record*. It would continue to look at the taxpayer's end use, and whether it changed his relationship to the property, when he used the property. In Rev. Rul. 79-261, 1979-2 C.B. 295, it indicated that a taxpayer that leased the converted property to tenants could qualify for §1033 in part when it leased part of the replacement property to tenants but used another part of the replacement property itself.

In most cases involving an owner-user, the functional use test makes sense. We assume he would have continued using his property in the same manner if the conversion had not occurred. Subsections 2 and 3 discuss situations in which the test is relaxed because of potential difficulty in acquiring qualified replacement property. Neither provision requires a showing of actual difficulty.

d. Time Period for Purchasing Replacement Property

The type of conversion affects the replacement period. That period usually begins with the date of disposition. If the disposition is by requisition or condemnation, it can begin at the earliest date of threat or imminence of requisition or condemnation. Because finding replacement real property may be difficult, the taxpayer benefits from a longer period in which to look for suitable replacement property. The period ends at the end of the second taxable year after the year in which she first realizes a gain from the conversion. The IRS can extend that date if she can show reasonable cause for not replacing the property by the normal ending date. I.R.C. §1033(a)(2)(B); Reg. §1.1033(a)-2(c)(3).

Note that the events setting the relevant dates differ. The period begins with the disposition (or threat or imminence of requisition or condemnation if earlier). That date might precede the date on which the taxpayer realizes a gain. The period ends with reference to the year in which she realizes gain. It ends on the last day of the second taxable year after gain is realized. Unless gain is actually realized on the last day of the year, the period ends more than two years after the date on which gain is realized.

> **Example 17-21.** Anna's office building was destroyed by fire on December 1 of Year 1. She realized a gain when she received the insurance proceeds on March 15 of Year 2. Her replacement period began on December 1 of Year 1. It ended on December 31 of Year 4, the last day of the year which is two years after the year in which she realized gain.

> **Example 17-22.** Alice's vacation home and the land on which it sat were taken by eminent domain on May 1 of Year 2. She realized a gain

when she received an eminent domain award for the property's value on August 3 of Year 3. The city had notified her on November 8 of Year 1 that it planned to take her property. Her replacement period began on November 8 of Year 1 even though the actual disposition did not occur until May 1 of Year 2. It ended on December 31 of Year 5, the last day of the year which is two years after the year in which she realized gain.

2. Condemnation of Real Property

Section 1033(g) applies to conversions of real property held for productive use in a trade or business or for investment if the conversion resulted from seizure, requisition, or condemnation (or threat or imminence thereof). It does not apply to conversions of personal property held for any purpose, to conversions of real property held for personal use, or to conversions of property by destruction or theft.

Section 1033(g)(1) lets a taxpayer avoid gain recognition by acquiring property that meets the § 1031 like-kind test discussed in Section B. He can acquire real property held for either productive use in a trade or business or for investment. He is not bound by the similar or related in service or use requirement. Section 1033(g) does not prevent him from acquiring replacement property that satisfies that requirement; it merely provides an additional qualifying option. Section 1033(g)(2) includes one limitation: a taxpayer cannot purchase stock of a corporation holding like-kind property and qualify for nonrecognition.

This section also gives the taxpayer an additional year to acquire replacement property. The replacement period ends three years after the close of the taxable year in which gain is realized. I.R.C. § 1033(g)(4).

The IRS bifurcates its analysis when property is converted as a result of both destruction and condemnation. For example, in Rev. Rul. 89-2, 1989-1 C.B. 259, the taxpayer's property was rendered unsafe because of chemical contamination. The city offered to purchase it for public health reasons and threatened to acquire it by eminent domain proceedings if the taxpayer did not sell. The city paid the value of the property, determined *before* the chemical contamination. The chemical contamination was a § 1033(a) destruction. The sale was a sale of real property used in a trade or business as a result of seizure, requisition, or condemnation (or threat or imminence thereof). The ruling divided the amount realized from the sale into two parts: the part that related to the destruction and the part that related to the sale of the destroyed property. Section 1033 could apply to both parts, but only the second part could qualify for § 1033(g).

3. Federally Declared Disasters

Section 1033(h) applies to conversions of property located in a disaster area if the property is converted as a result of a federally declared disaster. It applies to the taxpayer's principal residence and its contents and to property held for productive use in a trade or business or for investment. It does not apply to other personal-use property, such as a taxpayer's second residence. It does apply to the contents of the taxpayer's principal residence even if he is a tenant instead of an owner. I.R.C. § 1033(h)(4).

The insurance policy covering the taxpayer's residence also covers its contents. Coverage for most contents is simply an amount based on the value of his home; he does not submit a list of contents when he purchases the policy. Because the basic policy may limit the value of his personal property, he might separately list and insure particularly valuable items, such as silverware, jewelry, or electronics. The separately listed items are "scheduled property."

He recognizes no gain with respect to amounts received for personal property that was part of the home's contents and was not scheduled property. I.R.C. § 1033(h)(1)(A)(i). He does not have to replace the property. Given that his records for unscheduled property may have been destroyed in the disaster, automatic nonrecognition is a relief provision. The government probably loses relatively little revenue from this provision because he is more likely to have realized a loss than a gain on unscheduled property.

He treats proceeds received for the principal residence or for scheduled property as received for the conversion of a single item of property. He can treat any replacement property as similar or related in service or use to that single item so long as the replacement property is similar or related in service or use to the residence or its contents. In other words, the proceeds are treated as a common fund and can be reinvested as a common fund. I.R.C. § 1033(h)(1)(A)(ii). His replacement period for property described in § 1033(h)(1) ends four years after the close of the taxable year in which he realizes any gain from the conversion. I.R.C. § 1033(h)(1)(B).

The legislative history of § 1033(h)(2) indicates that a business may be closed for an extensive period after a federally declared disaster. During that time, it might lose its customer base, and the taxpayer might decide that insurance or other funds would be better used in a different business. This provision lets him treat tangible property of a type held for productive use in a trade or business as being similar or related in service or use to the property converted in the disaster. This rule even applies if the property converted was held for investment. When § 1033(h)(2) applies, his use of the replacement property does not have to satisfy an actual "similar or related in service or use" test.

Example 17-23. Ari owned the building in which he practiced law. The building was insured for its value, which exceeded his adjusted basis. If it is destroyed by lightning, he can avoid recognizing his gain by purchasing a new building for his law practice (or rebuilding his existing building). If it is taken by eminent domain, he can avoid recognizing his gain by acquiring any real property held for productive use in a trade or business or for investment. If it is destroyed in a federally declared disaster, he can avoid recognizing his gain by acquiring tangible property held for productive use in a trade or business.

4. Conversion of the Principal Residence

If a principal residence is compulsorily or involuntarily converted, the taxpayer's gain is potentially subject to § 1033 nonrecognition if she replaces the property. It is also potentially eligible for the § 121 exclusion. If her realized gain is less than the allowable § 121 exclusion, she will usually exclude her gain and will not have to reduce the basis of her replacement residence. If her gain exceeds the § 121 limitation, she can use both provisions. Reg. § 1.121-4(d). Chapter 6 discusses using both Code sections.

5. Tax Attributes of Replacement Property

The taxpayer's basis for replacement property reflects any gain he did not recognize on the original conversion. If the original property was directly converted into qualifying property, the new property takes the basis of the old property. I.R.C. § 1033(b)(1).

If the taxpayer received money or other property and purchased replacement property, his basis computation begins with the purchase price of the new property. He reduces that amount by the gain he did not recognize on the conversion. I.R.C. § 1033(b)(2). When he sells the replacement property, he will report a larger gain (or a smaller loss) because of that reduction.

Example 17-24. Benny realized a gain of $8,000 on an involuntary conversion for which he received proceeds of $150,000. He purchased qualifying replacement property for $150,000 and elected not to recognize his gain. Benny's initial basis for the replacement property is $142,000. This represents his $150,000 cost reduced by the $8,000 of unrecognized gain. Assuming its value does not change, he will recognize a gain of $8,000 if he later sells the replacement property.

Example 17-25. If Benny spent only $149,000 on replacement property, he recognizes $1,000 of his $8,000 gain. His basis for the replacement property is $142,000. This represents his $149,000 cost reduced by the $7,000 of unrecognized gain.

If the taxpayer uses the conversion proceeds to acquire multiple items of property, the basis reduction applied to these items reflects their relative cost. If, for example, one replacement property cost three times as much as the other replacement property, the basis of the first property is reduced by 75% of the unrecognized gain; the basis of the other property is reduced by 25% of the unrecognized gain. Each asset's share of the combined basis reflects the ratio of its cost to the combined cost. Reg. § 1.1033(b)-1(b).

Section 1223(1) treats a compulsory or involuntary conversion as a transaction in which the taxpayer's basis for the replacement property is computed with reference to his basis for the converted property. If the converted property was a capital asset or § 1231 property, he includes its holding period in his holding period for the replacement property. He does not include any time gap between the conversion and the purchase of replacement property. If he does not elect to apply § 1033 to his gain, his holding period for the replacement property begins the day after he acquires it.

If the taxpayer took depreciation deductions with respect to the converted property, the replacement property is subject to depreciation recapture when it is later sold. Sections 1245(a)(2)(A) and 1250(b)(3) apply to depreciation that is reflected in the property's basis even if that depreciation was deducted for a different property.

D. Wash Sales

1. Transactions Covered

Section 1091(a) is a mandatory nonrecognition provision. It applies to sales or other dispositions of stock or securities on which the taxpayer realizes a loss that would otherwise be deductible under § 165. It applies if he acquired substantially identical stock or securities within a 61-day period that begins 30 days before the disposition date and ends 30 days after it. It also applies if he entered into a contract or option to acquire the substantially identical stock or securities. The contract date, not the acquisition date of the shares subject to the contract, is subject to the 61-day period.

Unlike the other nonrecognition provisions discussed in this chapter, § 1091(a) uses loss disallowance language. Instead of saying "no loss shall be recognized if," it says "no deduction shall be allowed under section 165." Despite the different language, § 1091 transactions have the two significant features that distinguish nonrecognition provisions from disallowance provisions: (1) the basis of the new property reflects the disallowed loss; and (2) the holding period of the new property reflects the holding period of the old property.

Section 1091(a) does not apply to dealers in stock or securities who sustain the loss in the ordinary course of their business. Other taxpayers are excluded from coverage if the acquisition was by gratuitous transfer, such as by inheritance, or in a nonrecognition transaction.

> **Example 17-26.** Arnie sold 10,000 shares of XYZ Corporation stock at a loss. Ten days later, he purchased 10,000 identical shares of XYZ. He cannot deduct the loss on the XYZ shares he sold 10 days before. That loss will be reflected in his basis for the new shares.

> **Example 17-27.** Borden sold 10,000 shares of XYZ Corporation stock at a loss. Ten days later, his grandmother died, and he inherited 10,000 shares of XYZ. He can deduct the loss on the XYZ shares he sold 10 days before.

Section 1091 applies to both direct and indirect transactions. For example, Rev. Rul. 2008-5, 2008-1 C.B. 271, applied it to a sale of corporate stock. The seller had his Individual Retirement Account buy identical shares the next day.

Section 1091 does not require that the taxpayer purposefully acquire the substantially identical stock or securities. A taxpayer who participates in a corporation's dividend reinvestment plan acquires shares or fractional shares on every dividend payment date, often every three months. The funds used to purchase those shares are in lieu of cash dividends and are taxed in the same manner as cash dividends. I.R.C. § 305(b)(1). If he sold 100 shares at a loss and acquired four reinvested dividend shares within the 61-day period, § 1091 applies to four of the 100 shares he sold.

2. Substantially Identical Stock or Securities

Section 1091 requires that the stock or securities acquired be *substantially* identical to the stock or securities relinquished. Possible differences include shares of the same type (*e.g.*, both are common) but issued by different corporations, shares of different type (*e.g.*, common versus preferred) but issued by the same corporation, and shares of common stock and shares of preferred stock convertible into that corporation's common shares.

Shares issued by different corporations are not substantially identical. Common stock and preferred stock, even if issued by the same corporation, are generally not substantially identical. But if voting preferred stock is convertible into common stock of the same corporation and both classes have the same dividend restrictions, the IRS considers the two classes to be substantially identical. Rev. Rul. 77-201, 1977-1 C.B. 250. When debt instruments are involved, courts look to maturity dates, interest rates, and underlying security of any assets secured by the debt in determining whether the instruments are substantially identical.

3. Tax Attributes of Stock or Securities Acquired

Section 1091(d) provides the formula for computing the basis of the stock or securities whose acquisition prevented the taxpayer from deducting his loss. Because the computation is designed to preserve his loss potential, his basis for the new shares should be their cost increased by the disallowed loss.

The formula starts with the basis of the stock or securities disposed of at a loss. If the new stock or securities cost more than the sale price of the old, the basis is increased by that difference. If the new stock or securities cost less than the sale price of the old, the basis is decreased by that difference. This result follows from the somewhat fuzzy language of § 1091(d): "increased or decreased, as the case may be, by the difference, if any, between the price at which the property was acquired and the price at which such substantially identical stock or securities were sold or otherwise disposed of." The examples in Reg. § 1.1091-2(a) illustrate these results.

> **Example 17-28.** Ashton purchased 100 shares of XYZ stock for $1,000 on March 1 of Year 1. He purchased another 100 shares for $1,400 on June 1 of Year 1. On July 1 of Year 1, he sold the original 100 shares for $940. He realized a $60 loss on that sale but cannot deduct it because he sold those shares within 30 days after purchasing the June 1 shares. His basis for the shares acquired on June 1 is $1,000 (the basis of the shares acquired on March 1), increased by the $460 difference between the $1,400 purchase price of the June 1 shares and the $940 sale price of the March 1 shares. That amount is $1,460. In other words, his original cost for the June 1 shares is increased by the $60 loss Ashton realized on selling the March 1 shares.

Section 1223(3) provides that the holding period of the stock or securities whose acquisition resulted in the loss disallowance includes the holding period of the stock or securities on which the loss was disallowed.

Section 1091(b) provides that the regulations will determine which losses are not deductible if the amount of stock or securities acquired during the 61-day period is less than the amount of stock or securities sold. Section 1091(c) provides that the regulations will determine which stock or securities caused the loss disallowance (and which therefore have their basis adjusted) if the amount of stock or securities acquired is not less than the amount sold. Note the difference between those provisions. Section 1091(b) applies to determine which loss is disallowed. Section 1091(c) applies to determine which purchase resulted in a disallowed loss. Examples of the relevant computations appear in Reg. § 1.1091-1(h).

E. Transfers to a Spouse or a Former Spouse

1. General Rule

Section 1041(a) provides for nonrecognition of both gains and losses when property is transferred to a spouse or to a former spouse incident to a divorce. If the property is transferred to a spouse, this section applies even if the spouses are not dissolving their marriage and even if the recipient spouse provided consideration for the transfer. If property is transferred to a former spouse, it applies only if the transfer is incident to a divorce. Examples 4-15 and 4-16 in Chapter 4 illustrate the tax consequences.

2. Exceptions

Section 1041(a) does not apply to property transfers made before marriage, even if made pursuant to a prenuptial agreement. It is also inapplicable if the transferee spouse is a nonresident alien. I.R.C. § 1041(d).

A limited exception applies if the property transferred is subject to debt and is transferred to a trust. If the liabilities assumed and the liabilities to which the property is subject exceed the transferor's adjusted basis, he recognizes that excess as gain. This exception applies only to transfers in trust. If he transfers encumbered property directly to his spouse or former spouse, he recognizes no gain even if the liabilities exceed his basis. Temp. Reg. § 1.1041-1T(d), Q&A-12.

If the transfer does not satisfy the criteria in § 1041 and its regulations, its tax consequences are governed by the Code sections that would otherwise apply. These are the § 1001(c) general gain or loss recognition rules, the § 1015 basis for gift rules, and the part gift/part sale rules in Reg. §§ 1.1001-1(e) and 1.1015-4(a). These rules are discussed in Chapters 4 and 5.

3. Incident to a Divorce

Because these transfers are most likely to occur as part of a marital dissolution, it is important to determine if the transfer was incident to a divorce. Section 1041(c) indicates that a transfer is incident to the divorce if it occurs within one year after the date on which the marriage ceases or if it is related to the cessation of the marriage. In these situations, the transferor spouse recognizes no gain or loss, and the transferee spouse takes a transferred basis in the property transferred. The one-year test is a bright-line test. If the transfer occurs within that period, then the second option (related to the cessation of marriage) is irrelevant.

If the transfer does not occur within one year after the marriage ceases, we consider the regulations in determining if it is related to the cessation of marriage. Temp. Reg. § 1.1041-1T(b). Transfers are related to the cessation of marriage if they occur within six years after the date on which the marriage ceases and are made pursuant to a written divorce or separation instrument. Transfers that are not pursuant to a divorce or separation instrument, or that occur more than six years after the cessation of the marriage, are presumed not to be related to the cessation of the marriage. This presumption may be rebutted only by showing that the transfer could not be made within the one-year period or six-year period because of factors that hampered an earlier transfer. These include legal or business reasons and valuation disputes. Once any legal or business impediment or valuation dispute is resolved, the former spouses must promptly effectuate the transfer.

Section 1041 is not limited to transfers of property acquired before or during the marriage. It also applies to property acquired after the marriage ceased and transferred within the time limits discussed above. Temp. Reg. § 1.1041-1T(a), Q&A-5. Transfers to a third party on behalf of the spouse also qualify. Temp. Reg. § 1.1041-1T(c), Q&A-9.

4. Redeeming Stock in a Closely Held Corporation

Special rules apply when a stock redemption is used to eliminate one spouse's interest in a closely held corporation. The spouse whose stock is not redeemed benefits when the corporation uses its funds to buy out the other spouse; he increases his ownership percentage at no cost. If the spouse whose stock is redeemed treats the transaction as a taxable redemption, the other spouse does not report a constructive dividend. If the spouse whose stock is redeemed treats the redemption as an indirect transfer from the other spouse, she reports no gross income; the other spouse reports a constructive dividend from the corporation. Reg. § 1.1041-2.

F. Reacquisition of Real Property

Section 1038(a) provides for nonrecognition of gain or loss when a taxpayer who sold real property reacquires it in full or partial satisfaction of indebtedness secured by the property. The debt must have arisen in the taxpayer's sale of the real property.

If the seller received partial payment from the buyer, § 1038(b) provides for limited gain recognition. The gain from the reacquisition equals any money or other property she received from the buyer in excess of the gain she reported as gross income before reacquiring the property. I.R.C. § 1038(b)(1). The gain so computed will not exceed the excess of the sales price over the adjusted basis, reduced by the sum of gain reported before the reacquisition and any money or other property the seller paid or transferred in connection with the reacquisition. I.R.C. § 1038(b)(2). The selling price used for purposes of § 1038(b)(2) is the gross sales price reduced by commissions, fees, and other expenses of the sale. Reg. § 1.1038-1 provides examples of these computations.

The seller's basis for the reacquired property is her basis for the indebtedness on the date of reacquisition increased by the gain she recognizes on the reacquisition and by any amounts she pays in connection with the reacquisition. She treats the basis of any debt that was not discharged as zero. I.R.C. § 1038(c). Her basis for the debt for this purpose is generally her basis for the property sold reduced by the basis she recovered as the buyer made payments. Examples in Reg. § 1.1038-1(h) illustrate these computations.

If the seller treated any of the debt as worthless before reacquiring the property, she reports income equal to the amount she previously deducted. She increases her basis for that indebtedness by the amount she is treated as receiving. I.R.C. § 1038(d). This provision in effect reverses her prior deduction.

If the reacquired property was the seller's principal residence, she may have excluded gain because of § 121. If she resells the residence within one year after reacquiring it, the rules for gain recognition, basis, and treatment of the debt do not apply. Instead, she treats the resale as if it was part of the original sale of the property. I.R.C. § 1038(e); Reg. § 1.1038-2. Note that a significant portion of this regulation no longer applies. It was last amended in 1967; since then, Congress repealed § 1034 and significantly increased the § 121 exclusion.

G. Other Nonrecognition Transactions

As noted in Chapter 7, gain or loss is not recognized on certain exchanges of life insurance, annuity, endowment, and long-term care contracts. The § 1031(d) basis computation rules apply to these exchanges. If the exchange also involves other consideration (*e.g.*, money), the § 1031 gain and loss recognition rules apply. I.R.C. § 1035(d).

Section 1040 includes nonrecognition rules that apply to certain transfers of real property by an estate or trust to a decedent's qualified heir. The property must have been used as farmland or in another trade or business, and a § 2032A election to reduce its estate tax value must have been made. Section 2032A is covered in courses focused on estate tax or estate planning.

Section 1043 provides for nonrecognition of gain from sales of property to comply with conflict-of-interest provisions. It applies to certain federal executive branch employees and judges, their spouses, and minor or dependent children. A taxpayer who must divest property can elect nonrecognition if he reinvests the sales proceeds by acquiring permitted property within 60 days of the sale. If he reinvests less than the entire proceeds, he recognizes the lesser of the gain realized or the proceeds that he does not reinvest. U.S. government obligations and diversified investment funds are permitted property. The taxpayer reduces his basis for the new property by his unrecognized gain.

Sections 1400Z-1 and 1400Z-2 were added to the Code by the Tax Cuts and Jobs Act of 2017. They let taxpayers elect to postpone recognizing any realized capital gains that they reinvest in qualified opportunity zone funds. Section 1231 gains qualify only if the taxpayer has a net § 1231 gain that year. Reg. § 1.1400Z2(a)-1(b)(11)(iii)(A). These funds invest in low-income population census tracts or tracts contiguous to them. I.R.C. § 1400Z-1. The gain realized must be from a transaction with an unrelated party. The taxpayer has up to 180 days from realizing his gain to invest in one of these funds. I.R.C. § 1400Z-2(a)(1). These provisions apply only to sales or exchanges made before December 31, 2026. I.R.C. § 1400Z-2(a)(2)(B).

These provisions differ from the other nonrecognition sections discussed in this chapter. First, to qualify for nonrecognition, the taxpayer needs only to reinvest some of his realized *gain*. Compare that to § 1033, which requires the taxpayer to reinvest the *entire proceeds* of a compulsory or involuntary conversion to avoid recognizing any of his gain. Second, the taxpayer must recognize the deferred gain by December 31, 2026, even if he has not sold his interest in the qualified opportunity zone fund (or disposed of it in a Reg. § 1.1400Z2(b)-1(c) inclusion event). I.R.C. § 1400Z-2(b)(1). The final regulations issued in January 2020 treat a transfer by gift, a transfer to a spouse, and a transfer to a former spouse incident to a divorce as inclusion events; a transfer by reason of death is not an inclusion event. Reg. § 1.1400Z2(b)-1(c)(3)–(4). If the value of the investment is less than the deferred gain, he recognizes that lower amount. I.R.C. § 1400Z-2(b)(2)(A). He increases his basis for his investment, which is initially zero, by that recognized gain. I.R.C. § 1400Z-2(b)(2)(B)(i)–(ii). The other nonrecognition provisions in this chapter provide for gain recognition only when the taxpayer disposes of the property. Third, the taxpayer can increase his basis by part of the deferred gain if he holds the property long enough. He increases his basis by 10% of his deferred gain if he holds his interest for at least five years. If he holds his interest for at least seven years, he can increase his basis by an additional 5% of his deferred gain. I.R.C. § 1400Z-2(b)(2)(B)(iii)–(iv). If he holds his fund interest for at least 10 years, he can elect to treat the value of his interest as its basis. I.R.C. § 1400Z-2(c). If his interest has increased in value since December 31, 2026, that election would be beneficial, as it would exclude that later increase if he sold his interest at a gain. Fourth, § 1400Z-2 does not provide for including his holding period for the original property in his holding period for the qualified investment fund. If he transferred property to the fund instead of transferring cash, his holding period for the fund does not include his holding period for the property he transferred. Reg. § 1.1400Z2(b)-1(d)(i). The regulations issued for § 1400Z-2 include numerous definitions, examples, and special rules.

Courses focusing on taxation of business entities cover the nonrecognition rules that apply to the formation and reorganization of corporations and partnerships. Other nonrecognition provisions apply to transfers of property from a partnership to a partner or from a corporate subsidiary to its parent when the subsidiary is liquidated.

Checkpoints

- When a nonrecognition provision applies to a sale or other disposition, the taxpayer postpones including gains in gross income or deducting losses.

- The postponed gain or loss is usually reflected in the taxpayer's basis for his replacement property. When the transfer is between spouses, or is between former spouses incident to a divorce, the transferee's basis for the property received reflects the transferor's postponed gain or loss.

- If a taxpayer receives property that qualifies for nonrecognition but also receives nonqualifying property or otherwise disinvests, she recognizes gain equal to the value of the boot she receives.

- A taxpayer's holding period for replacement property generally includes the period she held the original property.

- Section 1031 is a mandatory provision governing exchanges of like-kind real property held for productive use in a trade or business or for investment. It applies to gains and losses.

- Section 1033 covers gains from compulsory or involuntary conversions of any type of property. The replacement property must usually be similar or related in service or use to the property converted, but exceptions apply. Section 1033 is primarily elective.

- Section 1091 is a mandatory provision covering losses from taxable dispositions of stock or securities. It applies when the taxpayer acquires substantially identical stock or securities within 30 days before or after the loss disposition.

- Section 1041 is a mandatory provision covering gain or loss when a taxpayer transfers property to a spouse or to a former spouse. The section applies to transfers to a former spouse only if they are incident to their divorce.

- Section 1038 is a mandatory provision covering gain or loss when a taxpayer who sold real property reacquires it in full or partial satisfaction of debt secured by the property.

- Section 1400Z-2 is an elective provision covering gain when a taxpayer sells appreciated property and invests at least some of his gain in a qualified opportunity fund. The taxpayer does not have to use his entire sales proceeds to obtain nonrecognition.

Chapter 18

Character of Gain and Loss; Depreciation Recapture; Section 1239

Roadmap

- Introduction
- Depreciation recapture
- Section 1239

A. Introduction

Several chapters indicate that a particular gain or loss might be a capital or § 1231 gain or loss, as opposed to ordinary gain or loss. In this chapter, we discuss the significance of treating an item as capital or § 1231 as opposed to ordinary. Although we focus on gains and losses and their effect on tax rates, we begin with a general discussion of tax rates. We then introduce gains and losses that may (or may not) be taxed as capital gains and losses. In the next chapter, we expand our discussion of characterizing gains and losses while focusing on the treatment of capital and § 1231 gains and losses.

Section 1(j) imposes a tax on taxable income at rates ranging from 10% to 37%, while § 1(h) provides for lower rates if the taxpayer has a net capital gain. But neither subsection defines net capital gain. Section 63 defines taxable income but also fails to define net capital gain or indicate how we might refer to taxable income that is not net capital gain.

Sections 64 (defining ordinary income) and 65 (defining ordinary loss) are marginally helpful. Both were enacted in 1976 and never amended. Ordinary income is defined as gain from the sale or exchange of property that is neither a capital asset nor an asset described in § 1231. Ordinary income also includes any gain from the sale or exchange of an asset if another Code section provides that the gain is treated as ordinary income. Ordinary loss is defined as loss from the sale or exchange of property that is not a capital asset and any loss from a sale or exchange that another Code section treats as ordinary. Neither section has an associated regulation. Neither section indicates how to treat income and deductions that are not sales or exchanges.

Because § 1(h) prescribes a different rate structure for net capital gains, it is appropriate to divide taxable income into two components: net capital gain and other taxable income. Fortunately, § 1222(11) defines net capital gain. A net capital gain is the excess of the taxpayer's net long-term capital gains over his net short-term capital losses. Section 1222 also defines the terms we use to get to that definition. Section 1222 starts from the presumption that we have a capital gain or loss from a sale or exchange; it divides gains and losses by the taxpayer's holding period. The definition of capital asset appears in § 1221; most holding period rules appear in § 1223. As we discuss in the next chapter, we cannot determine our § 1222 gains and losses until we work through § 1231 and other Code sections that might result in capital gain or loss treatment.

At this point, we can generalize. All income and deductions are ordinary unless they are capital gains or losses or treated as capital gains and losses. Gains and losses fall into one of the following categories: (1) gains that are always ordinary; (2) gains that are sometimes ordinary and sometimes capital; (3) gains that are always capital; (4) losses that are always ordinary; (5) losses that are sometimes ordinary and sometimes capital; (6) losses that are always capital. Some results may be bifurcated into capital and ordinary segments. Finally, some gains that are capital or treated as capital are subject to different rates than other capital gains and losses. This chapter discusses ordinary income attributable to depreciation recapture and § 1239. The next chapter covers other transactions giving rise in whole or part to capital gain or loss.

B. Depreciation Recapture

Sections 1245 and 1250 apply to a transferor's depreciable property. The list of covered property in § 1245(a)(3) makes it clear that § 1245 is the dominant section. Real property is subject to § 1250 only if it is not described in § 1245. I.R.C. § 1250(c). The discussion below assumes that depreciable real property is governed by § 1250 and that depreciable personal property is governed by § 1245. Remember that the term personal property means property that is not real property. Although it does not mean personal-use property, personal-use property can be subject to depreciation recapture if its basis reflects prior depreciation.

Recognized gain subject to § 1245 is always ordinary. Recognized gain subject to § 1250 is ordinary only if it reflects "additional depreciation." If the depreciation taken was not additional depreciation, the recognized gain is referred to as "unrecaptured § 1250 gain"; it is usually either capital gain or § 1231 gain. If § 1231 applies, the taxpayer's gains and losses are treated as capital unless those gains do not exceed those losses that year or the taxpayer has to recapture previously deducted net § 1231 losses. Unrecaptured § 1250 gain that becomes a component of net capital gain is subject to a maximum tax rate of 25%.

1. Rationale for Depreciation Recapture

Depreciation deductions and first-year expensing reduce the property's adjusted basis. I.R.C. § 1016(a)(2). Because depreciation is based on formulas and incentive provisions, the deductions may exceed the actual decline in the property's value. In that case, gain realized on a sale may reflect depreciation deductions in addition to (or instead of) actual appreciation.

> Example 18-1. Several years ago, Arlene purchased a building for $100,000. She deducted depreciation expense of $10,000, and properly reduced her adjusted basis to $90,000. She sold the building this year for $92,000. Although her building declined in value while she owned it, Arlene realized a gain for tax purposes. That gain is attributable to the depreciation deduction, which reduced her basis below the property's value.

Section 1231 may allow long-term capital gain treatment for sales of property held for business use. If no recapture provision applied, Arlene would enjoy two benefits. First, she would have deducted more depreciation than actually occurred; this deduction reduced her taxes at the higher tax rates applied to ordinary income. Second, when she sold the property, her gain—including gain attributable to the prior deductions—would be taxed at the lower capital gain rates. The recapture provisions eliminate the second benefit for § 1245 property and reduce it for § 1250 property.

2. Factors Affecting Recapture

Five factors are relevant to depreciation recapture: (1) whether there was a gain or a loss; (2) the type of property; (3) the taxpayer's holding period; (4) when the depreciation was deducted; and (5) the type of disposition. If the property is subject to recapture, we compute the tax results in the manner described later in this chapter.

Gain or loss. Recapture applies only to gains. Reg. §§ 1.1245-1(d), 1.1250-1(a)(5)(i). This distinction reflects its purpose. Taxpayers who take depreciation deductions against ordinary income should not automatically qualify for capital gain rates when they dispose of the property. Gain deemed attributable to prior depreciation, rather than to appreciation, should be taxed as ordinary gain. A taxpayer who suffered a loss did not deduct excessive depreciation, making depreciation recapture unnecessary.

Type of property. If § 1245 applies, we consider all prior depreciation in computing recapture. If § 1250 applies, we consider only "additional" depreciation. I.R.C. §§ 1245(a)(2)(A), 1250(a)(1). Section 1250(a)(1)(B) treats certain types of property, such as low-income housing, more favorably than other types. This chapter covers only the general rule of § 1250(a)(1)(B)(v). It subjects 100% of additional depreciation taken after December 31, 1975, to recapture computations.

Holding period. Section 1245 applies to all depreciation irrespective of holding period. If the taxpayer's holding period exceeds one year, only gain that exceeds prior depreciation can qualify for capital gain rates. If § 1250 property is held one year or less, all depreciation is additional depreciation. I.R.C. § 1250(b)(1). If the holding period exceeds one year, gain that exceeds "additional" depreciation can qualify for lower capital gain rates than gain attributable to additional depreciation. The discussion in this chapter assumes a holding period greater than one year.

When deduction occurred. Congress enacted the recapture provisions in the 1960s. Although § 1245 treats all depreciation as subject to recapture, the § 1250 computation depends on when the depreciation deduction occurred and whether the depreciation is "additional." For this purpose, we divide additional depreciation into three time periods: (1) after December 31, 1975; (2) between January 1, 1970, and December 31, 1975; and (3) before January 1, 1970. I.R.C. § 1250(a)(1)–(3). The examples we use focus on additional depreciation taken after December 31, 1975. They reflect a 1986 statutory change to § 168, which mandated the straight line method for newly acquired § 1250 property.

Type of disposition. Both sections provide that they trump other Code provisions. For example, §§ 1245(a)(1) and 1250(a)(1)(A) include the following language: "Such gain shall be recognized notwithstanding any other provision of this subtitle." In addition, §§ 1245(d) and 1250(h) state: "This section shall apply notwithstanding any other provision of this subtitle." That language appears to require immediate recapture even if a nonrecognition provision applies or the taxpayer disposed of the property by gift.

Neither section applies as strictly as the quoted language implies. Both exempt transfers by inter vivos gift and transfers at death. Both limit the amount of gain recognized on like-kind exchanges, involuntary conversions, and certain transactions involving entities and their owners. I.R.C. §§ 1245(b), 1250(d). The IRS has ruled that recapture does not occur in a transfer incident to a divorce that is covered by § 1041. PLR 8719007. These sections *do* affect the treatment of gains reported on the installment method, as discussed in Chapter 16.

3. Section 1245

a. Computations

If a taxpayer disposes of § 1245 property at a gain, he must determine the portion taxed as ordinary income. I.R.C. § 1245(a)(1). To do so, he subtracts his adjusted basis from the lower of (1) the property's "recomputed basis" or (2) the amount realized from the sale or exchange. If the disposition is not a sale or exchange, the second amount is the property's fair market value.

To determine recomputed basis, he increases his adjusted basis by prior depreciation deductions. I.R.C. § 1245(a)(2). If his actual deductions were less than the allowable deductions, he uses those lower amounts. I.R.C. § 1245(a)(2)(B); Reg. § 1.1245-2(a)(7).

> **Example 18-2.** Ajay purchased depreciable § 1245 property for $50,000. He properly deducted $20,000 in depreciation and has an adjusted basis of $30,000. He realized a gain of $8,000 when he sold the property this year for $38,000. His recomputed basis is $50,000—his $30,000 adjusted basis increased by the $20,000 depreciation deduction. Because his $38,000 amount realized is lower than his $50,000 recomputed basis, his depreciation recapture is computed by comparing $38,000 to his $30,000 adjusted basis. His $8,000 gain is § 1245 ordinary income.

> **Example 18-3.** If Ajay instead sold the property for $71,000, his gain realized is $41,000. His recomputed basis is $50,000—his $30,000 adjusted basis increased by the $20,000 depreciation deduction. Because his $50,000 recomputed basis is lower than his $71,000 amount realized, his depreciation recapture is computed by comparing $50,000 to his $30,000 adjusted basis. Only $20,000 of his $41,000 gain is § 1245 ordinary income.

The examples above illustrate a useful rule: § 1245 applies to the lesser of actual gain or prior depreciation deductions. If prior depreciation deductions are less than actual gain, the remaining gain may qualify for long-term capital gain treatment.

Section 1245 also applies to real property with a basis that reflects amortization deductions. Items treated as amortization include elective first-year expensing (§ 179) and certain other first-year deductions, such as outlays to remove architectural and transportation barriers affecting individuals who are elderly or who have disabilities. Those additional deduction sections are listed in § 1245(a)(2)(C).

b. Other Section 1245 Issues

Change in property's use. A taxpayer who converts § 1245 property to personal use does not realize gain because there is no disposition. Rev. Rul. 69-487, 1969-2 C.B. 165. Although § 1245 does not apply, § 179 recapture may apply if he converts business property to personal use or income-producing use. I.R.C. § 179(d)(10). Section 179 recapture applies if business use declines to 50% or less before the end of the property's normal depreciation period. Reg. § 1.179-1(e).

> **Example 18-4.** In Year 1, Aubrey purchased an office desk for $1,000. He elected to use § 179 and deducted the entire $1,000 in the year he acquired it; he then had a zero basis. In Year 10, the desk was worth $50. If he converted it to personal use, § 1245 would not apply. If he sold it for $50, § 1245 would apply to his $50 gain. There would be no § 179 recapture because he did not stop using the desk in his business before the end of its 7-year recovery period. If he had instead converted it to personal use in Year 4, he would have recaptured some of his § 179 deduction as ordinary income that year.

The recapture rules are more stringent for § 280F listed property. Section 280F requires partial recapture of § 168 depreciation if the business use of listed property (*e.g.*, certain motor vehicles) drops to 50% or less even if the taxpayer did not use § 179. I.R.C. § 280F(b)(2). That is because depreciation of listed property that is not used more than 50% in a trade or business is computed using straight line instead of accelerated depreciation.

Transfer of recapture potential. Section 1245(a)(2)(A) requires adding back depreciation: "(whether in respect of the same or other property) allowed or allowable to the taxpayer or to any other person." Thus, § 1245 taint follows property to an inter vivos donee. It also follows property transferred to a spouse or to a former spouse incident to a divorce. If a taxpayer disposes of her § 1245 property in an involuntary conversion, the recapture potential is transferred to her new property.

> **Example 18-5.** Anita purchased office equipment for $50,000. She properly deducted $20,000 of depreciation and has an adjusted basis

of $30,000. After fire destroyed her equipment, she received $38,000 in insurance proceeds and used that amount to buy replacement office equipment. This was a § 1033 involuntary conversion, and she elected not to recognize her $8,000 realized gain. When she sells the replacement equipment, her depreciation recapture computation includes the depreciation she deducted on the original equipment.

4. Section 1250

a. Computations

Section 1250 mandates ordinary income treatment only for additional depreciation. All depreciation is additional if the property is held for one year or less. If it is held for more than one year, only depreciation taken in excess of straight line depreciation is additional. I.R.C. § 1250(b)(1). Because property acquired after 1986 is depreciated using the straight line method, it will not have additional depreciation if held more than one year. However, it may have unrecaptured § 1250 gain.

Unrecaptured § 1250 gain is that portion of any long-term capital gain that would be treated as ordinary income if § 1250 applied to *all* depreciation instead of to depreciation in excess of straight line. The amount of gain subject to a tax detriment, in this case a higher tax rate, is computed in a manner similar to that discussed above for § 1245 recapture.

> **Example 18-6.** Alaina purchased depreciable real property for $500,000 before 1987. She deducted $490,000 of depreciation. If she had deducted straight line depreciation, she would have deducted only $450,000. If she sells the property for a $70,000 gain, she reports $40,000 as ordinary income. It represents the excess of the depreciation she took over the straight line amount. The remaining $30,000 is unrecaptured § 1250 gain.

Chapter 19 discusses capital gains and losses, including the treatment of § 1231 gains and losses. Real property subject to straight line depreciation is categorized according to the rules discussed in that chapter. If the net result of those computations is long-term capital gain treatment for depreciable real estate, the taxpayer computes how much of the net gain is unrecaptured § 1250 gain.

The formula for taxing unrecaptured § 1250 gain includes adjustments other than prior depreciation. I.R.C. § 1(h)(6). This chapter focuses on prior depreciation and ignores the other adjustments.

Example 18-7. Avery purchased a building for $100,000 and used it in his business for several years. He deducted straight line depreciation of $27,000, which reduced his adjusted basis to $73,000. He sold the building for $80,000 and realized a gain of $7,000. He netted all his § 1231 transactions and determined that his $7,000 gain should be treated as long-term capital gain. Because the $7,000 gain was less than his prior depreciation, it is all unrecaptured § 1250 gain.

Example 18-8. If Avery had instead sold the building for $112,000, he would have realized a gain of $39,000. That gain has two components: $27,000 is unrecaptured § 1250 gain; the remaining $12,000 may qualify for taxation at a lower capital gain rate.

The examples above illustrate a useful rule for determining how much gain is unrecaptured § 1250 gain for property with a basis that reflects only post-1986 depreciation. Unrecaptured § 1250 gain is the lesser of actual gain or prior straight line depreciation deductions. It may qualify for long-term capital gain treatment but not for the lowest capital gain rates. Any additional gain may qualify for the lowest capital gain rates.

The maximum tax rate applied to net capital gain is usually 0%, 15%, or 20%. I.R.C. § 1(h)(1)(B)–(D). The maximum tax rate applied to unrecaptured § 1250 gain is 25%. I.R.C. § 1(h)(1)(E). Although this rate is higher than the normal maximum capital gain rate, it is lower than the maximum 37% rate applied to ordinary income. Even if gain is unrecaptured § 1250 gain, it counts as capital gain for purposes of computing the taxpayer's allowable deduction for capital losses.

b. Other Section 1250 Issues

A taxpayer who sells his principal residence usually can exclude up to $250,000 ($500,000 for a married couple filing a joint return) of gain. I.R.C. § 121. He may have taken depreciation deductions if he ever used the home in a business or income-producing activity. Those deductions affect how much of his gain qualifies for the exclusion.

Section 121(d)(6) provides that the exclusion applies only to the portion of the gain that exceeds depreciation taken for periods after May 6, 1997. Reg. § 1.121-1(d), (e) provides examples for allocating gain and determining the effect of prior depreciation. Chapter 6 discusses how business or income-producing use and depreciation affect the exclusion.

As was true for § 1245 property, depreciation is not recaptured when the taxpayer converts the property to personal use but does not sell it. Section 1250 taint follows property to a donee. It also follows property transferred to a spouse or to a former spouse incident to a divorce. If a taxpayer who owned § 1250 property disposes of it in a like-kind exchange or involuntary conversion, the recapture potential is transferred to her new property. If her depreciation deductions were less than the amount allowable, she uses the lower amount in her computations. I.R.C. § 1250(b)(3).

C. Section 1239

Section 1239 transforms potential capital gain or § 1231 gain into ordinary income. It applies to recognized gain if the parties are related and the transferee can depreciate the property. In determining whether property is depreciable, we consider only the taxpayer who acquires the property. It does not matter whether the seller could have deducted depreciation. We treat patent applications as depreciable property. I.R.C. § 1239(e).

> **Example 18-9.** August sold his vacation home to his controlled cor-
> poration, which will use it as a conference center. His gain attributable
> to the building is ordinary income even though he could not depreciate
> it because he held it for personal use. Gain attributable to the land is
> long-term capital gain because land is not depreciable.

Section 1239 differs from depreciation recapture in several ways. First, it makes the transferor's entire gain ordinary. It does not matter how much, if any, depreciation he took. Second, it applies only to transfers to a related party. Depreciation recapture is not limited by the identity of the transferee. Third, it applies only if the transferee can depreciate the property. Depreciation recapture can apply even if the transferee's use of the property prevents her from deducting depreciation.

Section 1239(b) applies to a person and all entities that person is treated as controlling. There are three relevant groups of controlled entities. The first is a corporation and a person that directly or indirectly owns more than 50% of the value of its stock. I.R.C. § 1239(c)(1)(A). The second is a partnership and a person that directly or indirectly owns more than 50% of the partnership's capital interest *or* profits interest. I.R.C. § 1239(c)(1)(B). The third covers entities described in § 267(b)(3), (10), (11), or (12): two corporations that are part of the same controlled group; a corporation and a partnership if more than 50% of the corporation's stock value and more than 50% of the partnership's capital or income interests are owned by the same persons; and two S corporations or an S corporation and a C corporation if more than 50%

of the value of each is owned by the same persons. I.R.C. § 1239(c)(1)(C). When a category is based on the value of the interest owned, remember to consider characteristics (*e.g.*, voting rights) that affect value.

Most of the § 267(c) constructive ownership rules apply in determining controlled entity status. These rules attribute ownership from one person to another. For example, a person is deemed to own interests that are owned by members of his family or by entities in which he has an ownership interest (or of which he is a beneficiary). I.R.C. § 1239(c)(2). Thus, if a mother owns stock in a corporation, her son constructively owns that stock. If he actually and constructively owns more than 50% of the stock value, the corporation is a controlled entity. The constructive ownership rules are discussed in Chapter 14.

Section 1239 also applies to a trust and a beneficiary and to the executor of an estate and a beneficiary. A taxpayer is related to a trust if he (or his spouse) is a beneficiary unless he has only a remote contingent beneficial interest. I.R.C. § 1239(b)(2). A contingent interest is remote if it is worth 5% or less of the value of the trust property. Valuation reflects the trustee's maximum power to benefit that beneficiary. I.R.C. § 318(a)(3)(B)(i). If the interest is vested, § 1239 applies no matter how little that interest is worth.

Sales or exchanges involving estate executors and beneficiaries have different outcomes depending on the what type of bequest is being satisfied. Bequests may cover a fractional share of the estate, a specific item of property, or a specified sum of money (pecuniary bequest). Pecuniary bequests are usually satisfied by transferring money to the beneficiary. But, if the estate has insufficient liquid funds, the executor may transfer estate property. Section 1239 does not apply to transfers made to satisfy pecuniary bequests even if the beneficiary can depreciate the property she receives. I.R.C. § 1239(b)(3).

Checkpoints

- Depreciation recapture prevents taxpayers from converting ordinary deductions taken in prior years into long-term capital gain in a later year.

- The recapture rules operate more harshly for § 1245 property than for § 1250 property. All prior depreciation taken on § 1245 property is subject to the recapture rules. Depreciation on § 1250 property placed in service after 1986 is subject to higher capital gain rates rather than to recapture at even higher ordinary income rates.

- A taxpayer who receives § 1245 or § 1250 property by inter vivos gift is subject to recapture if he sells the property. This rule applies even if the recipient never deducted depreciation.

- If § 1245 or § 1250 property is acquired as part of a nonrecognition transaction, such as an involuntary conversion, the replacement property is subject to recapture of depreciation taken on the original property as well as depreciation taken on the replacement property.

- Section 1239 treats gains on sales to certain related persons as ordinary if the acquiring taxpayer can depreciate the property.

- Sections 1239, 1245, and 1250 do not apply to losses.

- Sections 1245 and 1250 do not apply merely because a taxpayer converts business-use property to personal use. However, § 179 or § 280F may cause immediate ordinary income recapture if a taxpayer prematurely converts business property to personal use (or reduces his business use to 50% or less).

- Status as capital gain or loss depends on the type of property and the type of disposition.

- Some dispositions always result in capital gain or loss; some always result in ordinary gain or loss; and some result in one or the other depending on other factors.

- Except to the extent the taxpayer has net capital gain, his taxable income is ordinary income.

Chapter 19

Capital Gains and Losses

Roadmap

- Critique of rate preference
- Preliminary steps
- Significance of holding period
- Section 1231 transactions
- Categorizing other dispositions
- Capital gains and losses
- Categorizing capital gains and losses
- Determining the tax rate on net capital gain
- Limitations on capital loss deductions
- Sale of more than one asset
- Coordination with Section 170

A. Critique of Rate Preference

This chapter discusses the treatment of capital gains and losses. As the discussion indicates, the complexities associated with this topic can seem daunting. Given that taxpayers prefer to pay less rather than more tax, they may prefer dealing with those complexities rather than having their gains taxed at the higher rates applied to ordinary taxable income.

Supporters offer various justifications for the treatment of capital gains. One is promoting long-term investment. Another is relieving the adverse effects of taxing in one year a gain attributable to multiple years. Critics argue that "more than one year" is hardly long-term. They respond to the bunching argument by noting that there is no requirement that gains exceed a minimum amount, place the taxpayer in a higher rate bracket, or cause any other hardship. The current rules let taxpayers decide when (if ever) to realize capital gains but let them deduct capital losses against ordinary income when they sell loss property. By realizing gains and losses in separate years, they benefit even more.

B. Preliminary Steps

Working through a capital gain or loss problem involves several steps, some of which we cover in other chapters. Follow the steps below for each transaction during the year. The order in which you follow them, and which ones you can ignore, will vary based on the facts presented. The previous chapter addressed gains that are treated as ordinary because of depreciation recapture or § 1239 (item 4 below). In this chapter, you are determining which other gains and losses will (or will not) be treated as capital gains and losses and the relevant type of capital gain and loss.

1. Determine if the taxpayer has a realized gain or loss because there was a sale or other disposition.
2. Determine if any gain realized is included in gross income, and if any loss realized is deductible.
3. Determine if this year is the appropriate year for recognizing the gain or loss. If a nonrecognition provision applies to any part of the gain or loss, delete that amount from your computations.
4. Determine if any gain (or portion thereof) must be treated as ordinary because of depreciation recapture, § 1239, or one of the provisions discussed in this chapter. If so, delete that amount from your computations.
5. Determine if the asset is a capital asset or a § 1231 asset. Remember that holding period is relevant to § 1231 status.
6. Work through the § 1231 computations to determine if there is a net gain before considering gains and losses from capital assets.
7. Before treating a net § 1231 gain as capital, adjust for any ordinary § 1231 losses taken in the preceding five years.
8. Determine if the asset was sold or exchanged as opposed to compulsorily or involuntarily converted or determined to be worthless. This determination may have different significance for personal-use assets versus § 1231 assets.
9. Determine if the Code treats the gain or loss as capital even though the asset *was not* sold or exchanged or *was not* a capital asset.
10. Determine if the Code treats the loss as ordinary even though the asset *was* sold or exchanged and *was* a capital asset.
11. Determine the asset's holding period if the gain or loss will be capital or treated as capital.

12. Determine if capital gains exceed capital losses or if the reverse is true (or if the gains and losses are equal).
13. Determine if any capital gains are unrecaptured § 1250 gains and if any capital gains and losses are from sales of 28-percent gain property.
14. Determine the relevant tax rates applied to the taxpayer's ordinary taxable income and to his net capital gains, if any.
15. Be sure to tax any qualified dividends at the net capital gain rates even if the taxpayer does not have a net capital gain.
16. Determine how much of the loss is currently deductible and how much is carried forward to future years if capital losses exceed the capital gains.
17. Determine the short- or long-term character of any loss carried over from a prior year or to be carried to a future year.

C. Significance of Holding Period

As you work through capital and § 1231 gain and loss problems, remember that the relevant Code sections refer to holding period rather than ownership period. Although the two periods are often identical, holding period might exceed ownership period for a variety of reasons. First, the taxpayer may be able to add a prior owner's holding period to her own ownership period. Second, she may be able to add her holding period for an asset she previously owned to her ownership period. Third, a Code provision may lengthen her holding period by ignoring her actual disposition date. Alternatively, holding period may be shorter than her actual ownership period because a Code provision treats an item as short-term.

Although capital gain and loss provisions apply to both short-term and long-term holding periods, that is not the case for property that might be covered by § 1231. In addition, holding period is relevant to determining the appropriate tax rate applied to a taxpayer's gains.

If none of the rules discussed below applies, ownership period and holding period will be the same. The IRS has ruled that holding period excludes the day of purchase and includes the day of sale. Rev. Rul. 70-598, 1970-2 C.B. 168. A taxpayer who purchases property on January 3 and sells it on March 3 has a holding period that begins January 4 and ends March 3.

1. Section 1223 Holding Periods

If § 1223 applies, holding period usually exceeds the taxpayer's actual ownership period because he has a substituted basis. His basis for the property is computed with reference to his basis for some other piece of property or with reference to another taxpayer's basis for the property.

Section 1223(1) applies to property received in a nonrecognition transaction. If the taxpayer's basis is computed with reference to his basis for the property he exchanged, and that property was either a capital or § 1231 asset, his holding period for the new property includes his holding period for the property he exchanged.

> **Example 19-1.** On March 10, 2020, Armando made a § 1031 like-kind exchange of investment land worth $200,000, which he had purchased for $160,000 on November 1, 2017. He received investment land worth $200,000. He recognizes none of his $40,000 realized gain, and his $160,000 basis for his new land reflects the basis of the land he purchased on November 1, 2017. His holding period for his new land includes his holding period for his original land.

Section 1223(1) also covers replacement property acquired following a § 1033 involuntary conversion. It applies even if he received only cash, which he used to acquire the replacement property. If he was temporarily disinvested because of a gap between the date property was converted and the date he acquired replacement property, that gap period is not included in his holding period.

Section 1223(2) applies to property that the taxpayer acquired from another person if his basis is computed with reference to the other person's basis for the property. For example, if he received a gift of property from his mother, he takes her § 1015(a) basis for the property. His holding period includes her holding period. Section 1223(2) also applies to the holding period for property transferred between spouses and property transferred between former spouses incident to a divorce. The transferee takes the transferor's basis and includes the transferor's holding period in computing her holding period for the property received.

Section 1223(9) applies to property acquired from a decedent, whether by devise, intestacy, or other method of transmission at death. If § 1014 governs the taxpayer's basis, a sale of that property is treated as long-term even if it takes place within one year after the decedent's death.

Section 1223 includes several other holding period rules. One of them, § 1223(3), applies to stock or securities acquired in a § 1091 wash sale. Although most of the § 1223 rules provide for a longer holding period, § 1223(5) does not do so. If a taxpayer exercised rights to acquire stock or securities, his holding period begins when he exercises the rights. It does not begin when he acquires the rights.

2. Holding Periods Governed by Other Code Sections

An employee who receives property that is subject to a substantial risk of forfeiture can report the property's value in the year of receipt or wait until it is substantially vested. I.R.C. §83(a)–(b). Her holding period begins when she reports the property's value as gross income. I.R.C. §83(f); Reg. §1.83-4(a).

Taxpayers who own shares of stock or other securities that become worthless during the year do not use the exact date of worthlessness as the date of disposition. Instead, their holding period is deemed to end on the last day of the year. I.R.C. §165(g)(1). A taxpayer who suffers a nonbusiness bad debt loss is deemed to have a holding period of not more than one year; that makes his loss short-term. It does not matter how long the debt was outstanding. I.R.C. §166(d).

Section 1233 applies to a taxpayer who makes a short sale, which often involves selling a security he does not own. He acquires the security in time to deliver it and close the transaction. This section applies if the property used to close the transaction is a capital asset. He may own substantially identical property when he makes the short sale. If so, his gain on closing the short sale is short-term if he held the substantially identical property for less than a year on the date of the short sale. I.R.C. §1233(b)(1). If he sustained a loss on closing the short sale, that loss is long-term if he held the substantially identical property for more than one year on the date of the short sale. I.R.C. §1233(d).

D. Section 1231 Transactions

1. Property Covered by Section 1231

Section 1231 covers three combinations of property and events. First, it covers sales or exchanges of property used in a trade or business. I.R.C. §1231(a)(3)(A)(i). Second, it covers compulsory or involuntary conversions of property used in a trade or business. I.R.C. §1231(a)(3)(A)(ii)(I). Third, it covers compulsory or involuntary conversions of capital assets held more than one year that are held in connection with a trade or business or a transaction entered into for profit. I.R.C. §1231(a)(3)(A)(ii)(II). Section 1231(a)(3)(A) defines transactions that give rise to §1231 gains; §1231(a)(3)(B) applies the same definitions to losses.

The definition above requires that capital assets be held more than one year to be included in the §1231 computations. Although §1231(a)(3) doesn't mention a holding period for property used in a trade or business, most trade or business property is also subject to a more than one-year holding period requirement. The holding period requirements are discussed below.

The definition of capital asset used for § 1231 is the same as the § 1221 definition described later in this chapter. The asset failed to qualify for capital gain or loss treatment because it was compulsorily or involuntarily converted, not because it wasn't a capital asset. The definition of property used in a trade or business in § 1231 reflects the § 1221(a)(2) definition of property excluded from capital asset status, but § 1231 does not apply if the property was not held long enough. Section 1231(b)(1) begins with a broad definition: it is property used in a trade or business that is held more than one year and that is either subject to the allowance for depreciation or is real property. This category covers machinery, equipment, buildings, and land used in the trade or business.

Section 1231(b)(1)(A)–(D) lists four types of property that are not covered by § 1231(b)(1): (1) property of a kind that would properly be includible in the taxpayer's inventory if on hand at the end of the year; (2) property primarily held for sale to customers in the ordinary course of the taxpayer's trade or business; (3) a patent, invention, model or design, secret formula or process, copyright, literary, musical, or artistic composition, letter, memorandum, or similar property held by a taxpayer described in § 1221(a)(3); and (4) a publication of the U.S. government that a taxpayer described in § 1221(a)(5) received from the government other than by purchase at the price offered for sale to the public. These four categories are largely the same as those excluded from capital asset status by § 1221(a)(1), (3), and (5).

Taxpayers who hold property for more than one purpose might categorize it as inventory or as § 1231 property. The "primarily" language presents problems similar to those raised in § 1221(a)(1) for potential capital assets. For example, in *International Shoe Machine Corp. v. United States*, 491 F.2d 157 (1st Cir. 1974), the court held that "primarily" referred to sales in the ordinary course of business rather than to liquidating sales. The taxpayer had argued that the term should be applied to its reason for holding the property, which was to produce rental income. It derived most of its income from leasing equipment and sold equipment only if the customer insisted. Sales revenue accounted for less than 10% of its income in each year at issue. The court noted that the equipment sold still had rental value, so the taxpayer was not liquidating its investment; that meant the sales were in the ordinary course of its business.

Section 1231(b)(2)–(4) adds three categories of property used in a trade or business. First, timber, coal, and domestic iron ore covered by § 631 qualify. Section 631 includes a more than one-year holding period. Second, livestock other than poultry may qualify. Cattle and horses held for 24 months or more, or other livestock held for 12 months or more, qualify if they are held for draft, breeding, dairy, or sporting purposes. Note the difference in language — instead of *more than* 24 (or 12) months, the required holding period is 24 (or 12) months *or more*. Third, unharvested crops qualify if disposed of at the same time, and to the same person, as the land on which they stand. The land must be held more than one year and be used in the taxpayer's trade or business. No holding period requirement applies to the crops, which arguably should be treated as inventory and thus taxed as ordinary income.

2. Section 1231 Computations

Section 1231 gains and losses are often called quasi-capital gains and losses. When § 1231 applies, the tax consequences are generally as favorable as — and sometimes more favorable than — they would be if the transaction was treated directly as either capital or ordinary. As is true for capital gains and losses, § 1231 applies only to gains that are included in gross income and only to losses that are deductible in computing taxable income. I.R.C. § 1231(a)(4)(A). Before applying § 1231, we also eliminate any taxable gain that represents depreciation recapture or § 1239 gain.

If § 1231 transactions result in a net gain, the taxpayer treats them as long-term capital gains and losses. I.R.C. § 1231(a)(1). He aggregates his actual capital gains and losses, the § 1231 gains and losses, and any other gains and losses that the Code treats as capital gains and losses in making the computations discussed in this chapter. If his § 1231 transactions result in a net loss (or equal gains and losses), those gains and losses are treated as ordinary. I.R.C. § 1231(a)(2).

Section 1211 limits a taxpayer's ability to deduct capital losses that exceed capital gains. Because a taxpayer whose § 1231 losses equal or exceed his gains treats both gains and losses as ordinary, a net § 1231 loss avoids the limit that applies to capital losses.

Before determining whether we have a net gain or a loss from these transactions, we separate our potential § 1231 gains and losses into two groups. We consider transactions in the "preliminary hotchpot" first. We then move to the general hotchpot.

a. Preliminary Hotchpot

Section 1231 transactions are initially categorized by type of transaction: gains and losses from involuntary conversions versus all other § 1231 gains and losses. Only the first type goes into the preliminary hotchpot. The gains and losses in the preliminary hotchpot are either eliminated from § 1231 or included in the general hotchpot with all other § 1231 transactions.

The preliminary hotchpot includes gains and losses attributable to involuntary conversions arising from fire, storm, shipwreck, or other casualty, or from theft. I.R.C. § 1231(a)(4)(C). These are the events that § 165(c)(3) looks to in determining personal casualty gains and losses, but § 165(c)(3) is not relevant here. Section 1231 does not apply to personal-use property.

If the net losses from preliminary hotchpot events exceed the net gains, the gains and losses drop out of § 1231 and are treated as ordinary gains and losses. If the net gains exceed the net losses (or gains and losses are equal), the transactions are considered in the general hotchpot.

Note that § 1231(a)(4)(C) applies only to *involuntary* conversions. Compulsory conversions caused by government seizure, requisition, or condemnation are not part of the preliminary hotchpot. They are always part of the general hotchpot.

> **Example 19-2.** Abel's factory was destroyed by lightning. His delivery truck was destroyed in a collision. The factory was insured for its $800,000 value; His adjusted basis (after deducting $200,000 of straight-line depreciation) was $550,000. The truck was not insured; his adjusted basis for it was $15,000. If he spends at least $800,000 to replace the factory, and elects § 1033 nonrecognition for his gain, the $250,000 gain realized is not included in any § 1231 computation. The preliminary hotchpot results in a $15,000 net loss from involuntary conversions of property used in a trade or business. That loss is excluded from § 1231; he deducts it as an ordinary loss.

> **Example 19-3.** If Abel does not replace the factory, his $250,000 gain is gross income. As a result, he has a net $235,000 gain from involuntary conversions. Because he does not have a net loss in the preliminary hotchpot, we include both involuntary conversions in the general hotchpot.

b. General Hotchpot

After working through the preliminary hotchpot, the taxpayer nets all transactions covered by § 1231 in the general hotchpot. If she has a net gain, all gains and losses are treated as long-term capital gains and losses. If she does not, all gains and losses are treated as ordinary.

> **Example 19-4.** Biddy realized a $200,000 gain from selling land she used for five years as a business parking lot. She realized a $350,000

loss on land she held for investment for two years; the city took the land in an eminent domain proceeding. The two transactions result in a $150,000 net loss in the general hotchpot. Because she does not have a net gain, her gain and loss are both treated as ordinary.

Example 19-5. Biddy also realized a $180,000 gain when her fully insured factory (on which she had taken only straight-line depreciation) was destroyed by a tornado. If she does not replace the factory, her $180,000 gain is gross income from an *involuntary* conversion; it first goes into the preliminary hotchpot. Because the preliminary hotchpot does not result in a net loss, the $180,000 gain is included in the general hotchpot. She now has a $30,000 net gain in the general hotchpot. She reports both gains as long-term capital gains; she reports the loss as a long-term capital loss.

3. Loss Recapture

A taxpayer who realizes a net § 1231 loss in one year and a net § 1231 gain in a different year benefits more than a taxpayer who realizes the gain and loss in the same year. The net loss is an ordinary loss; it does not reduce gain eligible for the net capital gain rates. The net gain qualifies for those lower rates.

Example 19-6. Brandy sold § 1231 property and realized a $6,000 gain and a $5,000 loss in Year 1. Because she has a net § 1231 gain, she reports her $6,000 gain as long-term capital gain and her $5,000 loss as long-term capital loss. Her $1,000 net gain can qualify for the lower net capital gain rates.

Example 19-7. Arvin sold § 1231 property and realized a $6,000 gain in Year 1 and a $5,000 loss in Year 2. In Year 1, he reports a $6,000 gain that can be taxed at the lower net capital gain rates. In Year 2, he deducts a $5,000 ordinary loss, which offsets income taxed at the higher rates applied to ordinary income. He probably saves more taxes deducting his $5,000 loss than he pays because of his $6,000 gain.

Section 1231(c) limits a taxpayer's ability to benefit from realizing net § 1231 gains and losses in different years. He must treat a net § 1231 gain as ordinary if he has non-recaptured net § 1231 losses from the five preceding taxable years. Section 1231(c) does not apply if the net gain year precedes the net loss year. Net losses in the preliminary hotchpot do not adversely affect gains realized in a later year. I.R.C. § 1231(c)(5).

Example 19-8. Angus sold § 1231 property and realized a net $5,000 loss in Year 1 and a net $6,000 gain in Year 2. He deducted a $5,000 ordinary loss in Year 1. He can treat only $1,000 of his Year 2 gain as long-term capital gain. The first $5,000 is treated as ordinary income because he had a $5,000 non-recaptured net § 1231 loss in Year 1.

Example 19-9. Angus also realized an $800 loss from a theft of § 1231 property in Year 1. Because the preliminary hotchpot for Year 1 resulted in a net loss, he did not include his $800 loss in the general hotchpot. Although Angus deducted that loss as an ordinary loss in Year 1, he does not have to report an additional $800 of his Year 2 gain as ordinary.

Angus realized only one gain. If a taxpayer realizes more than one § 1231 gain, he must determine which gain is recaptured as ordinary. This matters if he has net § 1231 gains attributable to unrecaptured § 1250 gain or collectibles gain, which are potentially subject to the 25% and 28% rates. Section 1(h)(8) authorizes the IRS to prescribe an allocation in that situation. Notice 97-59, 1997-2 C.B. 309, provides that recapture is applied first to gains that would be taxed at 28%, next to gains that would be taxed at 25%, and last to gains taxed at the lower rates in effect for other net capital gains. This allocation method benefits the taxpayer; his potentially lowest taxed gains are the last to be offset by non-recaptured losses.

Example 19-10. In Year 1, Amos realized a $5,000 loss from selling land used in his business. Because he had no other § 1231 transactions, he deducted an ordinary loss. In Year 2, he realized a $4,000 gain from selling a business building; the entire gain was unrecaptured § 1250 gain. He also realized a $4,000 gain from a theft of an insured coin collection that he held as an investment. Those were his only § 1231 transactions that year. We tax the $4,000 gain attributable to the coin collection and $1,000 of the gain attributable to the building's unre-captured § 1250 gain as ordinary income in Year 2. We treat the remaining $3,000 gain attributable to the unrecaptured § 1250 gain as long-term capital gain. It retains its status as unrecaptured § 1250 gain for purposes of computing the relevant tax rate.

E. Categorizing Other Dispositions

The taxpayer's deduction for net investment interest is affected by her treatment of net capital gain and qualified dividends. She cannot treat net capital gain or dividend income as investment income if she computes her tax on those gains and dividends using the § 1(h) rates. I.R.C. §§ 1(h)(2), (11)(D)(i), 163(d)(4)(B). If she wants to offset those gains and dividends against investment expenses, she must treat them as ordinary income.

Section 165(h) applies to casualty or theft gains and losses involving property held for personal use. Although the casualty or theft is not a sale or exchange, the gains and losses are treated as capital gains and losses if the taxpayer has a net gain from these events. He still reduces his losses by $100 per casualty or theft, but he does not reduce them by 10% of his AGI. If the casualties or thefts do not result in a net gain, the gains and losses are treated as ordinary (and the net loss is reduced by 10% of AGI in addition to the reduction of $100 per casualty or theft). I.R.C. § 165(h)(2). We illustrate these computations, including the situations in which a federally declared disaster is required, in Chapter 14.

Keep two points in mind with respect to personal casualty or theft gains and losses. First, only recognized gains and losses are relevant. If the taxpayer elects § 1033 nonrecognition with respect to a gain, it does not count in determining whether personal casualty or theft gains exceed personal casualty or theft losses. Second, these rules apply to both short-term and long-term gain and loss property. The compulsory or involuntary conversions of business and investment property discussed in the preceding section require a long-term holding period for § 1231 status.

Losses from nonbusiness bad debts are capital losses even if there is no sale or exchange. I.R.C. § 166(d). They are always short-term losses no matter how long the taxpayer held the obligation.

Section 1234(a) provides that purchase options generally take the same character as the property the taxpayer will acquire on exercising the option. If the option is inventory, it is not a capital asset even if the property to be acquired will be a capital asset. If the purchaser lets the option lapse, the option is treated as sold or exchanged on its expiration date. The taxpayer who granted an option to transfer stocks, securities, or commodities may also qualify for capital gain or loss status; her gain or loss will be treated as short-term. I.R.C. § 1234(b). Similar rules apply to other rights to acquire property and to securities futures contracts. I.R.C. §§ 1234A, 1234B.

Section 1241 provides that amounts a lessee receives for cancelation of a lease are treated as if they were received in exchange for the lease. This section also applies to amounts received by a distributor of goods for cancellation of a distributor's agreement, but only if he has a substantial capital investment in the distributorship.

Even though corporate stock is a capital asset, a loss on its sale or exchange is treated as ordinary if the stock is qualifying small business stock. I.R.C.

§ 1244. Similar rules apply to losses from small business investment company stock and certain losses of small business investment companies. I.R.C. §§ 1242, 1243. Because § 1244(b) limits the taxpayer to $50,000 of ordinary loss per year (doubled on a joint return), a taxpayer with a larger loss treats the excess loss as a capital loss.

Depreciation recapture may apply to a capital asset that is sold or exchanged; the gain attributable to excess depreciation is taxed as ordinary income even if the remaining gain qualifies for capital gain treatment (either directly or through § 1231). If a taxpayer sells a capital asset or § 1231 property to a related person who can depreciate it, § 1239 treats his gain as ordinary. If he sells the asset to an unrelated person, § 1239 does not apply.

As discussed in Chapter 16, when debt obligations are issued with original issue discount, the taxpayer allocates part of the issue price to interest. This reduces the amount that can qualify for capital gain (or potentially increases a capital loss) on a subsequent disposition of the bond.

Section 1252 applies to sales of certain farmland held less than 10 years. When it applies, part of the gain is treated as ordinary. This section applies to taxpayers who have deducted § 175 soil and water conservation expenditures.

Section 1253 applies to sales or exchanges of franchises, trademarks, and trade names. If the taxpayer retains any significant power, right, or continuing interest in the subject matter of the asset, the transfer cannot qualify as a sale or exchange. Prohibited retained rights include the right to disapprove an assignment of the interest, a right to terminate at will, and a right to make the transferee sell only the transferor's products. Gains and losses are ordinary if the taxpayer retained the prohibited rights.

F. Capital Gains and Losses

The taxpayer's capital gains and losses come from two sources: transactions that satisfy the definition of capital gain or loss discussed in this section and dispositions described in the preceding sections that are treated as capital gains or losses.

Taxpayers realize gain or loss when they make a sale or other disposition of any type of property. The capital gain and loss provisions are more limited. They initially apply only to sales or exchanges of a capital asset. I.R.C. § 1222. In other words, the taxpayer must make the required type of disposition (sale or exchange) of the required type of property (capital asset) before doing any capital gain and loss computations involving those gains and losses and any gains and losses treated as capital. The taxpayer must also remove any potential ordinary gain when the transaction results in gain that is partially ordinary and partially treated as capital.

1. Sale or Exchange

Sale or exchange is a narrower concept than sale or other disposition. For example, casualties, thefts, and bad debt losses are not sales or exchanges. But some forced transfers do qualify. For example, a foreclosure is treated as a sale.

Even if the taxpayer sold or exchanged a capital asset, we ignore her gain if it is excluded from gross income or she is subject to a nonrecognition provision. We also ignore any nondeductible losses (*e.g.*, losses on sales to related persons or losses on sales of personal use property) and losses subject to nonrecognition provisions.

2. Capital Asset

The Code defines the term capital asset using negative phrasing: all property, even property associated with a trade or business, is a capital asset unless it is excluded by § 1221. As discussed below, there are both statutory and judicially recognized exclusions from capital asset status.

a. Statutory Exclusions in Section 1221(a) and Exceptions

(1) Inventory

Section 1221(a)(1) excludes three types of property: (1) stock in trade; (2) other property of a kind that would properly be includible in inventory if on hand at year-end; and (3) property held primarily for sale to customers in the ordinary course of business. This exclusion puts taxpayers who earn their living from manufacturing or selling on the same footing as taxpayers who earn their living by performing services. Each taxpayer reports ordinary income.

The terms used in § 1221(a)(1) are not simply three ways of saying the same thing. Consider, for example, a taxpayer who manufactures goods. Raw materials and work-in-process are components of his inventory but are not held for sale to customers. Only his finished goods are held for sale.

The term "primarily for sale to customers" is relevant if the taxpayer holds property for both sale and rent or sells property previously acquired for investment. If he does not hold the property primarily for sale to customers in the ordinary course of his trade or business, he may qualify for § 1231 treatment on selling rental property or capital gain treatment on selling investment property. Courts often begin their analysis with the holding in *Malat v. Riddell*, 383 U.S. 569 (1966). That case involved a taxpayer who sold property acquired for either development or sale. The government argued that "primarily" could be satisfied if the sale motive was substantial. The Court held that "primarily" meant principally.

Real property presents problems because taxpayers who own investment property may take steps that make it more saleable. They may subdivide it, make improvements, or advertise that the property is available. Congress enacted § 1237 to provide a safe harbor for taxpayers in this situation, but that section is not exclusive. Taxpayers may still establish capital asset status even if § 1237 does not apply.

Section 1237(a) provides that subdividing the property does not alone transform it into property held primarily for sale to customers. Property is covered by this section if the taxpayer did not previously hold it for sale to customers and does not own other real property for sale to customers in the current year. She cannot have made substantial improvements to the property, and she generally must have held it at least five years. Even if she meets these requirements, gain realized from the sixth and subsequent sales of lots in the tract is treated as gain from property held primarily for sale to customers. Section § 1237(b) limits the amount so treated to 5% of the selling price.

Judicial opinions involving sales of real property include *Bynum v. Commissioner*, 46 T.C. 295 (1966), and *Biedenharn Realty Co. v. United States*, 526 F.2d 409, 423 (5th Cir. 1976). Each held against the taxpayer based on the substantial nature of the activities involved. The *Biedenharn Realty* court noted: "The frequency and substantiality of sales over an extended time, the significant improvement of the basic subdivisions, the acquisition of additional properties, the use of brokers, and other less important factors persuasively combine to doom taxpayer's cause."

In *Rice v. Commissioner*, T.C. Memo. 2009-142, the Tax Court listed nine relevant factors: (1) the taxpayer's purpose in acquiring the property; (2) the purpose for which the property was subsequently held; (3) the taxpayer's everyday business and the relationship of the income from the property to total income; (4) the frequency, continuity, and substantiality of sales; (5) the extent of developing and improving the property to increase the sales; (6) the extent to which the taxpayer used advertising, promotion, or other activities to increase sales; (7) the use of a business office for the sale of property; (8) the character and degree of supervision or control the taxpayer exercised over any representative selling the property; and (9) the time and effort the taxpayer habitually devoted to the sales. Because any appeal in *Rice* would be to the Fifth Circuit, which decided *Biedenharn Realty*, the Tax Court opinion noted that frequency and substantiality of sales were among the most important factors. It determined that the taxpayers made relatively few sales, that they had no choice but to purchase the larger tract as the seller did not offer a smaller portion, and that many of the improvements would have been necessary even if they followed their original plan and built only their own home on the property.

Dealers in securities are another group that could be disadvantaged by a strict reading of § 1221(a)(1). Even if they hold stocks and bonds for investment, those assets are property of a type that would be included in their inventory. Section 1236(a) lets them qualify for capital asset status if they clearly identify the security as held for investment by the end of the day on which it is acquired and do not hold it for sale to customers at any time thereafter.

(2) Property Used in a Trade or Business

Section 1221(a)(2) excludes property used in the taxpayer's business if it is subject to the allowance for depreciation or is real property. As discussed earlier in this chapter, § 1231 generally applies to this property if it has been held for more than 12 months. The § 1231 netting may result in taxing gains and losses as if they were long-term capital gains and losses. Section 1221(a)(2) does not exclude depreciable property that is held for the production of income and not used in a trade or business. Reg. § 1.1221-1(b). Although that property is not excluded from capital asset status, it is subject to the depreciation recapture computations discussed in Chapter 18.

(3) Certain Intellectual Property

Section 1221(a)(3) excludes the following intellectual property: patent, invention, model or design, secret formula or process, copyright, literary, musical, or artistic composition, letter or memorandum, or similar property held by the taxpayer whose personal efforts created it. If the property is a letter, memorandum, or similar property, it also excludes it in the hands of the person for whom it was prepared or produced. Finally, it excludes all the listed items if the owner computes his basis with reference to the basis of the person covered by the first two exclusions. Section 1221(a)(3) applies whether or not the property's creator held it for sale or regularly produced similar items.

> **Example 19-11.** Adam painted a portrait of his dog. Many years later, he sold it for $1,000. His gain is ordinary income. If he gave the portrait to his daughter Bea, and she sold it, her gain is ordinary income because she took Adam's basis for it. If Bea instead inherited the portrait

when Adam died, she would not use his basis. In that case the portrait is a capital asset in her hands unless she is a dealer holding it for sale to customers.

An important exception applies. Taxpayers can elect to treat gain and loss from the sale of musical compositions (or copyrights in such compositions) as capital gain and loss. Section 1221(b)(3) is an exception to the rule that a taxpayer who produces a literary, musical, or artistic composition cannot treat it as a capital asset. It is also an exception for situations in which the creator's efforts would result in the asset being treated as § 1221(a)(1) inventory. The election is available to the composition's creator and to transferees who take his basis. Reg. § 1.1221-3(a). This provision applies individually to each musical composition or copyright covering a musical composition.

Section 1221(a)(3) did not exclude patents from capital asset status until the Tax Cuts and Jobs Creation Act of 2017. That act did not repeal § 1235, which let a taxpayer whose efforts led to the creation of a patent treat its transfer as the sale or exchange of a capital asset held more than one year. Section 1235 required her to transfer all substantial rights to the patent or an undivided interest in such rights. A license for a few years would not have qualified but a 25% interest in all rights associated with the patent would have qualified. The transfer could not have been by gift, inheritance or devise or made to a related person. Payments contingent on the patent's productivity or use could have qualified. IRS guidance (or further legislation) is needed to reconcile the language of revised § 1221(a)(3) with that of § 1235, at least with respect to the patent's creator and anyone whose basis reflects the creator's basis.

(4) Other Section 1221(a) Exclusions

Section 1221(a)(4) is similar in its effect to § 1221(a)(1) — it prevents the taxpayer from reporting income attributable to his normal earning activities as capital gains. It excludes accounts and notes receivable the taxpayer acquires in the ordinary course of business for services rendered or for the sale of property covered by § 1221(a)(1).

> **Example 19-12.** Abe sold inventory for $1,000 to Bunny. She promised to pay the $1,000 in two years, plus interest, and gave Abe an IOU. Because his inventory was not a capital asset, the IOU is not a capital asset.

Section 1221(a)(5) excludes a government publication that the taxpayer acquired from the U.S. government for less than the price at which it is available to the general public. It also applies to anyone who uses his basis for the publication. This provision effectively reversed the holding of Rev. Rul. 75-342, 1975-2 C.B. 341. The IRS had ruled that a member of Congress did not have to treat bound volumes of the Congressional Record as a literary composition, letter, or memorandum.

Section 1221(a)(6)–(7) excludes certain derivatives and hedging transactions. Section 1221(a)(8) excludes supplies that the taxpayer regularly uses or consumes in the ordinary course of his trade or business. Normally he would deduct those supplies and reduce his ordinary taxable income. If he sells surplus supplies, he cannot treat them as capital assets.

b. Judicially Recognized Exclusions

The Supreme Court denied capital gain treatment in *Hort v. Commissioner*, 313 U.S. 28 (1941), for amounts a landlord received for canceling a lease. It held likewise in *Commissioner v. P. G. Lake, Inc.*, 356 U.S. 260 (1958), when the taxpayer sold the right to future income from oil payments. Taxpayers have unsuccessfully argued for capital gain treatment for a variety of similar payments. These include *qui tam* awards, *Alderson v. United States*, 686 F.3d 791 (9th Cir. 2012); rights to future lottery payments, *Prebola v. Commissioner*, 482 F.3d 610 (2d Cir. 2007); and lost profits, *Freda v. Commissioner*, T.C. Memo. 2009-191. The *Freda* decision focused on the language of the settlement agreement, which did not sufficiently support the taxpayer's claim that the payment was for injury to (or destruction of) a trade secret.

The Supreme Court treated the gain from selling contracts for future delivery of corn as ordinary income in *Corn Products Refining Co. v. Commissioner*, 350 U.S. 46, 52 (1955). The taxpayer purchased the contracts to protect itself from increases in the price of corn, which it used in manufacturing, but the contracts were not inventory. The Court determined that these were profits "arising from the everyday operation of a business." It noted that Congress had never overruled the IRS's longstanding treatment of hedging transactions as insurance rather than as dealings in capital assets and that both lower courts considered the hedging transactions to be an integral part of the taxpayer's business.

Corn Products led to many years of uncertainty, particularly if taxpayers could assert multiple motives for their property acquisitions. Corporate stock was particularly troublesome. Most individuals purchase stock as an investment, but a taxpayer might purchase a large block of a corporation's stock to secure a business relationship with a supplier or customer; there might also be an investment motive for the purchase. In *W.W. Windle Co. v. Commissioner*, 65 T.C. 694 (1976), the Tax Court held that stock was a capital asset if the taxpayer had a substantial investment motive. A more substantial business motive for the purchase did not matter. The Supreme Court went further in *Arkansas Best Corp. v. Commissioner*, 485 U.S. 212 (1988), and held that stock was a capital asset irrespective of motive. This holding prevented taxpayers who sold stock from asserting a substantial investment motive if they had gains and no substantial investment motive if they had losses. Although *Corn Products* was not overruled, its holding may be limited to acquisitions of inventory-related assets.

Transactions often involve several taxable years. Taxpayers may have to repay amounts they previously received, or they may receive a repayment. Chapter 16 focused on when and how to report the later event. It did not cover the character of any amounts received or repaid. The *Arrowsmith* doctrine uses the character reported in the earlier year in characterizing the later amount. In *Arrowsmith v. Commissioner*, 344 U.S. 6, 8 (1952), the taxpayer reported a liquidating distribution as a capital gain. Because he had transferee liability, he had to pay a judgment to the liquidated corporation's creditors. The Court held the repayment was a capital loss even though paying his creditors was not a sale or exchange: "And it is plain that their liability as transferees was not based on any ordinary business transaction of theirs apart from the liquidation proceedings. It is not even denied that had this judgment been paid after liquidation, but during the year 1940, the losses would have been properly treated as capital ones."

Relation-back to the earlier transaction may also occur when the earlier transaction resulted in ordinary gain or loss. For example, in *Bresler v. Commissioner*, 65 T.C. 182 (1975), the earlier transaction resulted in a § 1231 ordinary loss. When the taxpayers recovered a judgment against a competitor who allegedly caused the loss, they could not report it as capital gain. If they had received the damages in the year of the original loss, the damages would have reduced the loss subject to § 1231.

G. Categorizing Capital Gains and Losses

We categorize capital gains and losses (and gains and losses treated as capital gains and losses) in two ways: holding period and type of asset.

1. Holding Period

a. Short-Term and Long-Term

Section 1222(1)–(4) divides capital gains and losses into four holding period categories: short-term capital gains; short-term capital losses; long-term capital gains; and long-term capital losses. We refer to them by initials: STCG, STCL, LTCG, and LTCL.

Gains are covered by § 1222(1) and (3) only to the extent they are included in gross income. We ignore any excluded gain from a sale of a principal residence. We also ignore any gain that is not currently recognized because a nonrecognition provision applies. Losses are covered by § 1222(2) and (4) only to the extent they are deducted in computing taxable income. Because the capital loss provisions do not provide an independent basis for deducting a loss, we ignore losses sustained on selling personal-use assets, losses sustained on selling business or investment property to a related person, and losses covered by non-recognition provisions.

Capital gains and losses are short-term if their holding period is one year or less. They are long-term if their holding period exceeds one year. Taxpayers categorize gains and losses by holding period before beginning the tax computations described in this chapter. They then net gains and losses within each holding period group.

There is net STCG if total STCG exceeds total STCL. I.R.C. § 1222(5). There is net STCL if total STCL exceeds total STCG. I.R.C. § 1222(6). There is net LTCG if total LTCG exceeds total LTCL. I.R.C. § 1222(7). There is net LTCL if total LTCL exceeds total LTCG. I.R.C. § 1222(8). Unless gains and losses are equal, there is either net STCG *or* net STCL. There is either net LTCG *or* net LTCL. You cannot have both net gain *and* net loss in the same holding period category. There is no requirement that you have gain or loss in any every category.

b. Overall Net Result

We determine overall net gain or loss by netting the short-term result against the long-term result. If the taxpayer has each type of gain or loss and none of them nets to zero, he has six possible outcomes: (1) net STCG *and* net LTCG; (2) net STCL *and* net LTCL; (3) net STCG that exceeds net LTCL; (4) net STCL that exceeds net LTCG; (5) net LTCG that exceeds net STCL; and (6) net LTCL that exceeds net STCG. If a category has no transactions, we simply ignore it; it does not affect the computations.

An overall net gain is called capital gain net income. I.R.C. § 1222(9). Taxpayers qualify for the lower § 1(h) tax rates only if they have *net* capital gain. Net LTCG must exceed net STCL, or there must be net LTCG and no net STCL. I.R.C. § 1222(11). Taxpayers who have net capital gain *always* have capital gain net income. Taxpayers who have capital gain net income do not necessarily have net capital gain.

> **Example 19-13.** Angie realized an $8,000 net STCG and a $6,000 net LTCG. She thus had both capital gain net income and net capital gain.

> **Example 19-14.** Arnold realized an $11,000 net STCL and a $17,000 net LTCG. He thus had both capital gain net income and net capital gain.

> **Example 19-15.** Amelia realized a $15,000 net STCG and a $4,000 net LTCL. She thus had capital gain net income. Because she did not have a net LTCG, she did not have net capital gain.

Section I discusses the annual limit on deducting an overall net loss. A loss that exceeds that limit is a net capital loss. I.R.C. § 1222(10). Taxpayers who have net capital loss always have an overall net loss. Taxpayers who have an overall net loss do not necessarily exceed the deduction limit required to have a net capital loss.

> **Example 19-16.** Ben realized a $7,000 net STCL and a $12,000 net LTCL. Because his overall net loss exceeded the maximum amount he could deduct against ordinary income ($3,000), he also had a net capital loss.

> **Example 19-17.** Barb realized a $22,000 net STCG and a $30,000 net LTCL. Because her overall net loss exceeded the maximum amount she could deduct against ordinary income ($3,000), she also had a net capital loss.

> **Example 19-18.** Bob realized a $10,000 net STCL and a $9,000 net LTCG. He thus had an overall net loss. Because that overall net loss did not exceed the annual deduction limit, he did not have a net capital loss.

Although we net capital gains and losses to determine net gain or loss, we do not net them in computing gross income, adjusted gross income (AGI), or taxable income. Capital gains are gross income; capital losses are deducted in computing AGI.

2. Type of Asset

We also categorize capital gains and losses based on the type of asset. There are three categories: (1) property subject to the lowest capital gain rates (0%, 15%, and 20%); (2) unrecaptured § 1250 gain; and (3) 28-percent rate gain. Property falls into category (1) unless it is described in one of the other two categories. Qualified dividends, discussed later in this chapter, also fall into category (1).

a. Unrecaptured Section 1250 Gain

Gain realized on selling depreciable property is at least partly attributable to prior depreciation deductions rather than to actual appreciation. Those deductions reduced taxable income subject to the rates applied to ordinary income. To prevent taxpayers from converting those ordinary deductions into capital gains, Congress enacted §§ 1245 (generally for personal property) and 1250 (generally for real property). Chapter 18 illustrates the mechanics of those sections.

Unrecaptured § 1250 gain is the portion of a taxpayer's gain attributable to straight-line depreciation taken on real property held more than one year. If the real property qualifies for capital gain treatment, the gain attributable to that depreciation also qualifies. The tax rate applied to that gain is the lower of the rate applied to her ordinary income or 25%. If the property involved is § 1231 property (discussed in Section D) and she does not have a net § 1231 gain, her § 1231 gains and losses are treated as ordinary. We ignore unrecaptured § 1250 gain on those assets. Even if she has a net § 1231 gain, the amount treated as unrecaptured § 1250 gain on that property cannot exceed her net § 1231 gain. I.R.C. § 1(h)(6)(B).

> **Example 19-19.** Angela sold a building used for several years in her business. She realized a gain of $175,000. Of that gain, $75,000 is unrecaptured § 1250 gain. Because she realized a net § 1231 gain, the $175,000 gain qualifies as LTCG. The tax rate for the $100,000 gain that is not allocable to prior depreciation does not exceed 20%. Only the $75,000 unrecaptured § 1250 gain can be taxed at the 25% rate.

> **Example 19-20.** Brent sold two items of business real property. He realized a loss of $15,000 from selling land and a gain of $65,000 from selling a building. Of that gain, $62,000 is unrecaptured § 1250 gain.

Because his gains exceed his losses, his § 1231 transactions are treated as long-term capital gains and losses. Although $62,000 of his gain is potentially unrecaptured § 1250 gain, his net § 1231 gain is only $50,000. Only $50,000 of the gain attributable to depreciation on the building can be taxed at the 25% rate.

b. 28-Percent Rate Gain

Section 1(h)(4)(A) treats two types of property as 28-percent rate gain property: gain from selling stock covered by § 1202 and collectibles. Because the current version of § 1202 excludes 100% of the taxpayer's gain from gross income, we limit our discussion of 28-percent rate gain property to collectibles.

The 28-percent rate gain category covers gains and losses from the sale or exchange of collectibles held more than one year. The following assets are collectibles: works of art; rugs and antiques; metals and gems; stamps and coins; and alcoholic beverages. I.R.C. § 408(m). The computation of collectibles gains and losses includes only amounts that otherwise would be included in gross income or allowed as a deduction. I.R.C. § 1(h)(5)(A). For example, a taxpayer may sustain a loss on selling a rug held for purely personal use. His loss does not become deductible merely because rugs are collectibles.

H. Determining the Tax Rate on Net Capital Gain

1. Net Short-Term Capital Gain

If a taxpayer has no long-term gains, and his short-term gains exceed his capital losses, the computation is simple. No special rates apply to his taxable income because he does not have a net capital gain. As discussed above, net capital gain requires net long-term capital gain. If he receives qualified dividends, which are discussed below, those dividends are taxed at the lower capital gain rates.

2. Net Long-Term Capital Gain

If a taxpayer has a long-term capital gain, he might qualify for lower rates, but only if he also has net capital gain. That requires that his long-term gains exceed his long-term losses. In addition, if he has a net short-term loss, his net long-term gain must exceed that loss. The taxpayers in Examples 19-13 and 19-14 above had net capital gain; the taxpayer in Example 19-15 did not.

Even if the taxpayer does not have net capital gain, his qualified dividends are taxed at the lower capital gain rates.

If we determine that the taxpayer qualifies for the lower rates, we then determine her maximum rate. That depends on the type of gain and her other taxable income. The current tax rates applied to ordinary income range from 10% to 37%. I.R.C. § 1(j). The capital gain rates vary depending on which of the three categories are represented in her net capital gain. The computations provided in § 1(h) (with the gloss added by § 1(j)(5)) have two outcomes. First, they ensure that the tax rate applied to net capital gains is the lesser of the rate applied to ordinary taxable income or the relevant capital gain rate. Second, they define how we determine the portion of net capital gain attributable to unrecaptured § 1250 gain or 28-percent rate gain. The latter outcome is relevant if the taxpayer has both capital gains and capital losses.

> **Example 19-21.** Barbara's taxable income exceeds $1 million this year; her marginal tax rate is 37%. Her taxable income includes the following capital gains and losses: (1) LTCG of $24,000 on selling shares of stock; (2) LTCG of $10,000 on selling antique jewelry; (3) STCL of $5,000 on selling investment land. She has a net capital gain of $29,000. If we offset her gain on selling stock by her loss on selling land, she would have net gain of $19,000 taxed at 20% and net gain of $10,000 taxed at 28%. If we instead offset her gain on selling the jewelry by her loss on selling land, she would have net gain of $24,000 taxed at 20% and net gain of $5,000 taxed at 28%. As explained in the discussion below, § 1(h)(4)(B) gives the latter result.

3. Terminology

Section 1(h) appears daunting in part because of its length and in part because of the terminology used. The terminology can be confusing because the Code provides two meanings for the term net capital gain and then adds another term, adjusted net capital gain. In addition, its definitions of gain potentially taxed at the 25% and 28% rates includes certain losses that are not from property normally subject to those rates. Finally, it includes qualified dividends in the mix.

Net capital gain is defined in § 1222(11) as the excess of net LTCG over net STCL. A taxpayer who does not receive qualified dividends does not qualify for capital gain rates unless he satisfies that definition.

Net capital gain is defined in § 1(h)(11) as net capital gain plus qualified dividend income. That definition applies only for purposes of § 1(h). Qualified dividends are dividends received from most taxable domestic corporations and certain dividends received from qualified foreign corporations. For purposes of this chapter, we assume that all dividends are qualified.

Adjusted net capital gain is defined in § 1(h)(3) as net capital gain (using the § 1222(11) definition) reduced by unrecaptured § 1250 gain and by 28-percent rate gain and then increased by qualified dividends. This definition is designed to provide the lower capital gain rates for qualified dividends even if the taxpayer does not have a net capital gain. It is also designed to exclude gains that might be taxed at the 25% and 28% rates from taxation at the 0%, 15%, and 20% capital gain rates.

> **Example 19-22.** Albert's taxable income places him in the 12% tax rate bracket this year. His taxable income is below the maximum 0% capital gain amount. He has no capital gains, a $1,000 capital loss, and $250 of qualified dividends. Although he does not have a net capital gain, he has an adjusted net capital gain of $250. The $250 will be taxed at 0% instead of at 12%.

> **Example 19-23.** Amelia's taxable income places her in the 37% tax rate bracket this year. It exceeds the maximum amount to qualify for the 15% capital gains rate. Her taxable income includes a $10,000 LTCG from selling an antique rug and a $250 dividend. Although she has a net capital gain of $10,000, that gain is not included in her adjusted net capital gain. Her adjusted net capital gain is $250; that amount will be taxed at 20% instead of at 37%. Her gain on selling the rug will be taxed at 28%.

Section 1(h)(4) defines 28-percent rate gain as the sum of collectibles gain and § 1202 gain, reduced by the sum of collectibles loss, net STCL, and any LTCL loss carried over to the taxable year. Note that collectibles gain and loss require a long-term holding period. I.R.C. § 1(h)(5)(A). But short-term gains and losses attributable to collectibles remain relevant. They are netted along with the taxpayer's other short-term gains and losses to determine if he has a net STCG gain (taxed at ordinary rates or used to increase his ability to deduct a net LTCL) or a net STCL (applied against any net LTCG and subject to the capital loss deduction limits if net STCL exceeds net LTCG).

Section 1(h)(6) defines unrecaptured § 1250 gain as the gain that would have been ordinary if § 1250(b)(1) had applied to all depreciation, reduced by the sum of any collectibles loss, net STCL, and LTCL carryovers that exceeded collectibles gain.

> **Example 19-24.** Adam's taxable income exceeds the maximum amount to qualify for the 15% capital gains rate. This year, he had a $25,000

LTCG from selling an antique rug and a $10,000 LTCG from selling a building; $2,000 of the gain on selling the building was unrecaptured § 1250 gain. Adam also had a $4,000 STCL from selling shares of stock. His overall net capital gain is $31,000. When Adam computes his tax, he will report $21,000 of 28-percent rate gain, $2,000 of unrecaptured § 1250 gain taxed at 25%, and $8,000 of adjusted net capital gain taxed at 20%.

Example 19-25. Adam instead had a $25,000 LTCG from selling an antique rug and a $10,000 LTCG from selling a building; $2,000 of the gain on selling the building was unrecaptured § 1250 gain. Adam also had a $26,300 STCL from selling shares of stock. His overall net capital gain is $8,700. When Adam computes his tax, he will report no 28-percent rate gain, $700 of unrecaptured § 1250 gain taxed at 25%, and $8,000 of adjusted net capital gain taxed at 20%.

4. Computing the Tax

a. Taxable Income Within a Single Maximum Rate Category

To determine the taxpayer's potential capital gain rate, we use the definition I.R.C. §1(j)(5) applies to the terms in I.R.C. §1(h). Section 1(h), as in effect before the Tax Cuts and Jobs Act of 2017, applied the 0%, 15%, and 20% capital gain rates based on the taxpayer's marginal tax bracket. Taxpayers who were subject to tax at rates below 25% had a 0% rate on their net capital gains; taxpayers who were subject to rates above 25% and below 39.6% had a 15% rate on their net capital gains. Taxpayers subject to the 39.6% rate had a 20% rate on their net capital gains. The 2017 legislation eliminated that rate structure.

Instead of changing the ordinary income rate brackets that applied to each capital gains rate, Section 1(j)(5) substituted dollar amounts for the § 1(h) tax rate percentages and provided for adjusting those amounts, beginning in 2019, to reflect inflation. In 2020, the maximum 0% rate amount is $80,000 for married taxpayers filing a joint return and a surviving spouse, $53,600 for a head of household, and $40,000 for all other individual taxpayers. The maximum 15% rate amount is $496,600 for married taxpayers filing a joint return and a surviving spouse, $469,050 for a head of household, $441,450 for other unmarried taxpayers, and $248,300 for married taxpayers filing separately.

We determine the tax using two computations. The first computation applies the § 1(j) rates to the taxpayer's entire taxable income. The second computation, which comprises up to six categories, recomputes the tax using separate rates for ordinary taxable income and net capital gains. The taxpayer pays whichever of these computations produces the smaller tax.

The discussion and examples below use an unmarried taxpayer who is not a surviving spouse or a head of household.

Category 1: a tax computed the greater of (1) taxable income reduced by net capital gain or (2) the lesser of taxable income below the maximum 0% rate amount or taxable income minus adjusted net capital gain. I.R.C. § 1(h)(1)(A). This computation yields the portion of taxable income taxed at the rates applied to ordinary income.

Category 2: a tax imposed at 0% on the lesser of (1) adjusted net capital gain or (2) taxable income that does not exceed the excess of taxable income that would be taxed at the maximum 0% rate amount over taxable income reduced by adjusted net capital gain. I.R.C. § 1(h)(1)(B). This is the tax imposed on adjusted net capital gain eligible for a 0% tax rate.

Category 3: a tax imposed at 15% on the lesser of two amounts. The first amount is the lesser of adjusted net capital gain or taxable income that exceeds the amount taxed in Category 2. The second amount is the excess of taxable income that does not exceed the maximum 15% rate amount over the sum of the amounts taxed in Categories 1 and 2. I.R.C. § 1(h)(1)(C). This is the tax imposed on adjusted net capital gain eligible for a 15% rate.

Category 4: a tax imposed at 20% on the amount by which the lesser of adjusted net capital gain or taxable income exceeds the amounts taxed in Categories 2 and 3. I.R.C. § 1(h)(1)(D).

Category 5: a tax imposed at 25% on the excess of unrecaptured § 1250 gain over any excess of the amount taxed in Category 1 plus net capital gain over taxable income. I.R.C. § 1(h)(1)(E).

Category 6: a tax imposed at 28% on the excess of taxable income over amounts taxed in Categories 1, 2, 3, 4, and 5. This is the tax imposed on collectibles gain. I.R.C. § 1(h)(1)(F).

Example 19-26. Beryl has ordinary taxable income of $19,000 in 2020; her marginal tax rate is 10% and her income tax is $1,900.

Example 19-27. Beryl's 2020 taxable income is instead all long-term capital gain from selling shares of stock. Her taxable income is all net capital gain; it is also adjusted net capital gain.

Category 1: Beryl's taxable income reduced by net capital gain is $0. Her taxable income below the 0% maximum rate amount is $19,000. Her taxable income minus adjusted net capital gain is $0. None of her income falls into Category 1.

Category 2: Beryl's adjusted net capital gain is $19,000. Her taxable income that would be taxed at the maximum 0% rate is $19,000; it exceeds her taxable income reduced by adjusted net capital gain ($0) by $19,000. Both segments of this computation give us $19,000 that is taxed at the 0% rate. Beryl owes no tax for 2020.

Example 19-28. Beryl's 2020 taxable income is instead all long-term capital gain from selling a collectible. Her taxable income is all net capital gain; none of it is adjusted net capital gain.

Category 1: Beryl's taxable income reduced by net capital gain is $0. Her taxable income below the 0% maximum rate amount is $19,000. Her taxable income minus adjusted net capital gain is $19,000. All of Beryl's taxable income is taxed in Category 1 because $19,000 exceeds $0. It is taxed at her normal 10% tax rate. Her $1,900 tax is the same as the tax she would pay if she had only ordinary taxable income.

Example 19-29. Beryl's 2020 taxable income is instead comprised of $2,000 of ordinary income, $6,000 of long-term capital gain from selling shares of stock, and $11,000 of long-term capital gain from selling a collectible. She has net capital gain of $17,000 and adjusted net capital gain of $6,000.

Category 1: Beryl's taxable income reduced by net capital gain is $2,000. Her taxable income below the 0% maximum rate amount is $19,000. Her taxable income minus adjusted net capital gain is $13,000. Because $13,000 is greater than $2,000, we tax $13,000 at her normal 10% tax rate. Her Category 1 tax is $1,300.

Category 2: Beryl's adjusted net capital gain is $6,000. Her taxable income that would be taxed at the maximum 0% rate is $19,000; it exceeds her taxable income reduced by adjusted net capital gain ($13,000) by $6,000. Both segments of this computation give us $6,000 that is taxed at the 0% rate. All of her taxable income has been taxed: $13,000 at 10% in Category 1 and $6,000 at 0% in Category 2.

Taxpayers with larger amounts of taxable income continue the computation through categories 3 through 6. Keep in mind that only adjusted net capital gain (which includes qualified dividends) qualifies for the 0%, 15%, and 20% rates in Categories 2 through 4.

b. Taxable Income That Straddles Maximum Rate Categories

The examples above featured a taxpayer who qualified for only one of the three lowest capital gain rates. The example below illustrates a taxpayer whose 2020 net capital gain is taxed at more than one rate.

> **Example 19-30.** Amanda has taxable income of $50,000. It includes $15,000 of LTCG from selling shares of stock. Her taxable income reduced by net capital gain is $35,000. That is less than the $40,000 maximum 0% capital gain amount. Amanda's taxable income in Category 1 is $35,000. That income is taxed at the rates applied to ordinary income. The first $5,000 of her LTCG falls into Category 2; it is taxed at 0%. The remaining $10,000 LTCG falls into Category 3; it is taxed at 15%.

c. The Effect of Current-Year Capital Losses

The computations illustrated above featured taxpayers who realized capital gains but no capital losses. Capital losses have two potential effects. First, they reduce the amount of capital gain that qualifies for the lower capital gain rates. Second, if capital losses exceed capital gains, they are deductible only to the extent allowed by § 1211(b).

If capital gains exceed capital losses, we must determine how much of the taxpayer's capital gain qualifies for the reduced tax rates. As we discussed earlier in this chapter, we initially net gains and losses based on holding period; a taxpayer qualifies for the capital gain tax rates only if she has net LTCG that exceeds net STCL (and thus has net capital gain). If she does not have net capital gain, no special tax rates apply.

If the taxpayer does have net capital gain, and some of it is attributable to unrecaptured § 1250 gain or 28-percent rate gain, we allocate her losses against her gains to determine the proper tax rates for her net gain. As indicated above, short-term losses initially offset short-term gains; long-term losses initially offset long-term gains. If short-term losses exceed short-term gains, we must appropriately allocate the excess loss against long-term gains. (If long-term losses exceed long-term gains, we cannot have net capital gain.)

We allocate current-year net STCL as follows. If there is any 28-percent gain, we allocate net STCL to that gain. If there is no 28-percent gain (or if net STCL exceeds the 28-percent gain), we allocate the unused net STLC to unrecaptured § 1250 gain. We allocate net STCL against other components of net capital gain only to the extent it is not needed to offset 28-percent gain and unrecaptured § 1250 gain.

Example 19-31. Angie had the following capital gains and losses: $10,000 STCL from selling shares of stock; $3,000 STCG from selling investment land; $15,000 LTCG from selling her vacation home; $1,000 LTCL from selling a painting held for investment; and $7,000 LTCG from selling an antique rug. Angie had a $7,000 net STCL; she had a $21,000 net LTCG. Because her net LTCG exceeded her net STCL, she had net capital gain of $14,000. To determine if any of her net capital gain is potentially taxed at 28%, begin with her $7,000 collectibles gain and reduce it by her $1,000 collectibles loss and by $6,000 of her net STCL. That eliminates any gain that could be subject to tax at 28%. Her $1,000 remaining net STCL offsets the gain that could be taxed at 0%, 15%, or 20%.

d. The Effect of Capital Loss Carryovers

We initially allocate capital losses carried over from an earlier year using our normal rules. Long-term loss carryovers first offset long-term gains; they offset short-term gains only to the extent the carried over loss exceeded the short-term gains. Short-term loss carryovers first offset short-term gains; they offset long-term gains only to the extent the carried over loss exceeded the long-term gains. If any current-year gain is 28-percent gain, we allocate long-term loss carryovers to that gain before we allocate it against any other long-term gain. I.R.C. § 1(h)(4). We allocate any unused long-term loss carryover against unrecaptured § 1250 gain before we allocate it against any gain that might be taxed at 0%, 15%, or 20%. I.R.C. § 1(h)(6).

I. Limitations on Capital Loss Deductions

Deduction limits apply when total capital losses exceed total capital gains. In addition to deducting capital losses to the extent of capital gains, a taxpayer also deducts the lesser of the excess loss or $3,000 ($1,500 for a married taxpayer who files a separate return). I.R.C. § 1211(b). Although qualified dividends are taxed at the lower rates applied to net capital gains, they do not increase the loss deduction. Noncorporate taxpayers carry excess capital losses (the net capital loss) forward indefinitely. I.R.C. § 1212(b).

Example 19-32. Allison received salary of $100,000 in 2019. She also realized LTCG of $15,000 and LTCL of $25,000. She reported $115,000 of gross income. She deducted $18,000 of her loss (total gain plus

$3,000) in computing AGI. She carried her $7,000 net capital loss to 2020. She takes it into account along with any 2020 gains and losses in 2020. If necessary, she carries any remaining amount to 2021 and later years.

As discussed below, only LTCG qualifies for the lower capital tax rates. Because short-term losses initially offset short-term gains, and long-term losses initially offset long-term gains, we must properly characterize any loss carryover.

Example 19-33. Ashton realized a net STCG of $5,000 and a net LTCG of $7,000 in 2019. He has a $2,000 capital loss carryover from 2018. If the carryover is short-term, he has $3,000 net STCG and $7,000 net LTCG for 2019. If it is long-term, he has $5,000 net STCG and $5,000 net LTCG for 2019. He prefers the first possibility because the lower § 1(h) rates apply only to net LTCG.

We categorize the carryover based on events in the year the loss was realized. If the taxpayer realized only one type of loss, the excess loss keeps that character in the later year. I.R.C. § 1212(b)(1). Section 1212(b)(2) governs when he realized net losses from both short-term and long-term transactions. As a general rule, it treats any loss deducted against ordinary income as offsetting a hypothetical STCG. It reaches this result using the following language: "there shall be treated as a short-term capital gain in the [earlier] taxable year an amount equal to" the excess loss deducted in the earlier year. (This discussion ignores an additional computation, adjusted taxable income, which adds back personal exemptions, as they are not deductible in 2018 through 2025.) Because we are pretending that an amount (up to $3,000) of ordinary income was actually STCG in the earlier year, we make it more likely that the loss carried over will be long-term instead of short-term.

Example 19-34. In addition to salary, Al realized net STCL of $4,000 and net LTCL of $1,000 in 2019. He deducted $3,000 of his $5,000 total capital losses. When he carried the $2,000 net capital loss to 2020, he had to determine if it was short-term or long-term. Because we pretend that Al realized STCG of $3,000 in 2019, he is deemed to have deducted $3,000 of his STCL in 2019. His carryover to 2020 consists of the remaining $1,000 of his net STCL and all $1,000 of his net LTCL.

J. Sale of More Than One Asset

In Chapter 9, we discuss unallocated verdicts and settlements in situations involving damages. The recipient obviously prefers to allocate his receipts to items that are excluded from gross income. The payor may not care about the allocation, particularly if all payments she makes are either deductible or nondeductible (or if insurance covers her full outlay). The IRS reserves the right to challenge an allocation that was not made by a disinterested party (*e.g.*, a judge or a jury).

Similar issues arise when a taxpayer sells an entire business. An unincorporated business is not a single asset; it is comprised of various tangible and intangible properties, only some of which may be capital or § 1231 assets. The seller would prefer to allocate the sales price in a way that maximizes capital gain and minimizes ordinary income (and that maximizes capital gain that is not taxed at the 25% or 28% rate). The buyer would prefer to allocate the sales price in a way that maximizes and accelerates her deductions. For example, she would prefer to allocate as much as possible to depreciable machinery and as little as possible to nondepreciable land. Section 1060 requires the parties to use the same allocation, thus limiting the seller's ability to maximize capital gains and the buyer's ability to maximize ordinary income deductions for the same transaction.

Section 1060 applies to transactions defined as applicable asset acquisitions. The definition covers any transfer (whether directly or indirectly) of assets that constitute a trade or business if the transferee's basis is determined by reference to the consideration she paid for the assets. I.R.C. § 1060(c). That would be the case if the transaction was a sale in which the transferor recognized gain or loss.

Reg. § 1.1060-1(b)(2)(i) defines trade or business as a group of assets the use of which would constitute an active trade or business under § 355 (covered in business tax courses). It also defines a trade or business as a group of assets to which goodwill or going concern value could attach. Reg. § 1.1060-1(b)(1) provides that an applicable asset acquisition is any transfer, whether direct or indirect, of a group of assets if the assets transferred constitute a trade or business in the hands of either the seller or the purchaser.

Section 1060 provides rules to determine the transferee's basis for assets he receives and the transferor's gain or loss. The § 1060(a) flush language provides for allocating the consideration received in the same manner as amounts are allocated to assets under § 338(b)(5). It also lets the parties agree on, and be bound by, a written allocation of the consideration or the fair market value of the assets. The IRS is not bound by that agreement. Reg. § 1.1060-1(c)(4).

The allocation generally reflects each asset's fair market value, but certain assets (such as money on hand or in a bank) take priority. This result makes sense because, if the business has a bank account, the transferee would not pay a higher or lower amount for the account. And, although some assets could have been sold separately, assets such as goodwill may have no value outside the business.

Reg. § 1.338-6(b) allocates the selling price, in the following order:

Class 1: cash and bank accounts other than certificates of deposit;
Class 2: certain actively traded personal property and certificates of deposit;
Class 3: assets that are marked to market at least annually and debt instruments;
Class 4: inventory assets;
Class 5: all assets not assigned to another class;
Class 6: section 197 intangibles other than goodwill and going concern value; and
Class 7: goodwill and going concern value.

Reg. § 1.1060-1(d), Example 2, illustrates an agreement between the parties that assigns value to various asset classes. That example also illustrates the effect of an IRS redetermination.

K. Coordination with Section 170

Capital asset status affects the amount treated as a charitable contribution deduction. If property is appreciated, the amount of the gift is its appreciated value if a sale of the property would result in long-term capital gain or § 1231 gain. The property must be either (1) real property; (2) intangible property; or (3) tangible personal property that the charity will use in its exempt function. I.R.C. § 170(e)(1). Because that section applies even if the asset is a collectible, the interaction of §§ 1(h) and 170(e)(1) offers tax-saving opportunities.

Example 19-35. April is in the 37% tax rate bracket. She plans to sell a capital asset and donate a different capital asset to an art museum. Each asset is worth $100,000, has a basis of $80,000, and has been held more than one year. Asset 1 is a painting; Asset 2 is investment land. The museum would display the painting; it would add the land to its endowment. Her charitable gift is $100,000 no matter which asset she donates. If she sells the painting, her $20,000 gain is taxed at a flat 28% rate because it is a collectible; if she sells the land, the tax rate will not exceed 20%. By selling the land and donating the painting, she pays $1,600 less tax than if she sells the painting and donates the land.

Checkpoints

- Long-term capital gains are taxed at lower rates than ordinary income. The tax rate depends on the taxpayer's taxable income and type of capital asset; it can be as low as 0% and as high as 28%.

- Deduction limits apply to capital losses that exceed capital gains. Taxpayers can carry excess losses to future years.

- An asset's holding period often exceeds the taxpayer's actual ownership period.

- As a general rule, capital gain or loss results from selling or exchanging a capital asset. Qualified dividends also qualify for the lower capital gains rates.

- Most personal-use and investment assets are capital assets.

- Many productive assets used in a trade or business, and even some investment assets, are subject to a separate computation to determine if they have net gains or losses. If § 1231 applies, a taxpayer who has net gains reports gains and losses as capital. Otherwise, he reports them as ordinary and avoids the capital loss limitations.

- The Code contains numerous rules treating gains and losses as capital even though they do not qualify as sales or exchanges of capital assets. It also has rules that convert some otherwise qualifying capital gains and losses into ordinary gains and losses.

- Section 1060 applies allocation rules from the regulations for § 338(b)(5) to an applicable asset acquisition. As a result, the buyer and seller of a business assign the same values to the assets being transferred. This prevents the seller from allocating the price to capital gain assets while the buyer allocates it to items that are currently deductible or depreciable.

Chapter 20

Filing Status and Allocating Income

Roadmap

· Introduction

· Status

· Income from services

· Income from property

· Income in respect of a decedent

· Kiddie tax

A. Introduction

This chapter addresses two intertwined concepts. We first address the taxpayer's status. Status affects the appropriate tax rate schedule, limitations on various tax benefits, and liability for underpayment of tax. We then discuss rules used to determine who should report income. Not surprisingly, the income recipient is not necessarily the appropriate taxpayer. The taxpayer who rendered services or owned income-producing property may try to assign the tax consequences to a person who is taxed at a lower rate. Attempted assignments of income are likely to occur within a family group, but that is not always the case. Because taxpayers may use entities to allocate income, the discussion of entity taxation in the next chapter is also relevant. We conclude with the so-called kiddie tax. Taxpayers to whom it applies may be taxed at their parent's tax rate on unearned income even if they received that income through their own efforts.

B. Status

1. Taxpayers Who Are Not Dependents

Taxpayers fall into one of four tax rate categories: (1) married individuals filing joint returns and surviving spouses; (2) heads of households; (3) unmarried individuals (other than surviving spouses and heads of households); and (4) married individuals filing separate returns. I.R.C. § 1(j)(2)(A)–(D). These categories affect the amount of certain deductions and the tax rate schedule used. Based on the inflation-adjusted rates in effect for 2020, unmarried individuals and married individuals filing separately each owe income tax of $47,367.50 on taxable income of $207,350; heads of households with that amount of taxable income owe income tax of $45,926; married individuals filing a joint return and surviving spouses owe income tax of $94,735 on taxable income of $414,700 (twice the amounts for unmarried individuals and married individuals filing separately). In 2020, married individuals filing joint returns and surviving spouses reach the 37% marginal bracket for taxable income greater than $622,050 ($311,025 if they file separate returns). Heads of household and other unmarried taxpayers reach that bracket when their taxable income exceeds $518,400.

Married taxpayers. If married individuals file a joint return, their tax rates are based on each spouse earning half of the total income. A couple whose income is derived $800,000/$800,000 is treated the same as a couple whose income is derived $0/$1,600,000. Some married couples pay more income tax than they would if they were unmarried. A "marriage penalty" may result if the spouses have relatively equal amounts of income. Other couples pay less income tax than they would if they were unmarried. A "marriage bonus" may result if the spouses have significantly different incomes. The bottom five tax brackets for single individuals and married individuals filing separately are currently the same.

Joint returns carry the risk of joint and several liability. I.R.C. § 6013(d)(3). It may be imposed even if any wrongdoing—underreporting income, overstating deductions, or failing to file or pay—is primarily that of one spouse. Section 6015 offers full or partial relief from joint and several liability to taxpayers who meet its requirements. Spouses who file separately, other than those living in community property jurisdictions, report only their separate income and deductions. They avoid joint and several liability, but they are ineligible for tax benefits that require married taxpayers to file a joint return.

Taxpayers can file a joint return only if they are eligible. Spouses who are legally separated under a decree of divorce or separate maintenance are not eligible. I.R.C. §§ 7703(a)(2), 6013(d)(2). Although married individuals who live apart but are not legally separated are eligible, one or both may qualify for treatment as a head of household, as discussed later in this section. I.R.C. § 7703(b). Married taxpayers are not eligible if either spouse is a nonresident alien during any part of the taxable year or if they have different taxable years. I.R.C. § 6013(a).

Taxpayers may try to avoid being treated as married by obtaining a year-end divorce (which ends their marital status) and remarrying early the next year. The IRS has ignored year-end divorces (followed by year-beginning remarriages) when the taxpayers intended only to take advantage of the rate structure or other benefits available to unmarried taxpayers. Rev. Rul. 76-255, 1976-2 C.B. 40. One appellate court remanded a dispute to the Tax Court to determine if the IRS could ignore such a divorce as a sham when it was unclear if state law would ignore it. *Boyter v. Commissioner*, 668 F.2d 1382 (4th Cir. 1981).

Surviving spouses. If a taxpayer was widowed in a previous year, and did not remarry, § 2(a) lets her qualify for the tax rate schedule used by married taxpayers filing jointly. She is not filing a joint return; she is simply using the joint return rates. She can qualify for surviving spouse status for up to two years following her spouse's death. She must maintain as her home a household that is the principal place of abode of her child or stepchild for whom she would be entitled to a dependency exemption. In addition, she must have been eligible to file a joint return with the deceased spouse for the year of his death.

Heads of households. An unmarried individual may also qualify for head of household status. The rate structure for heads of households is slightly more favorable than that used by other unmarried taxpayers (other than surviving spouses). This reflects the fact that a head of household is often a single parent.

The taxpayer must satisfy three requirements to be a head of household: (1) he must be unmarried or treated as unmarried; (2) he must not be a surviving spouse; and (3) he must provide a household for a qualified individual. I.R.C. § 2(b). In addition, he cannot have been a nonresident alien at any time during the year. He is unmarried if he has never been married, is divorced or legally separated, or is widowed and does not qualify as a surviving spouse. He also qualifies as unmarried if his spouse is a nonresident alien at any time during the taxable year or if he satisfies the conditions in § 7703(b). That section treats him as unmarried if he does not file a joint return, he maintains a household that is the principal place of abode of his dependent child for more than half of the year, and the other spouse is not a member of that household during the last six months of the year. A child can qualify as his dependent for this purpose even if the child's other parent is entitled to treat the child as a dependent because of the rules in § 152(e) (Chapter 13).

Example 20-1. Annie and Barry are married but have not lived together since Barry moved out in February. Annie paid more than half the costs of maintaining the home in which she lives with their dependent daughter Callie. If they do not file a joint return, Annie files as a head of household, and Barry files as married, filing a separate return.

A taxpayer satisfies the "providing a household" requirement by maintaining as his home a household that constitutes the principal place of abode, for more than half of the year, of an unmarried qualifying child or of a person for whom he would be entitled to a dependency exemption. He can also satisfy the requirement by maintaining a household that constitutes the principal place of abode of his parent for whom he is entitled to a dependency exemption. The parent does not have to be a member of his household, but the parent's gross income must be less than the exemption amount. I.R.C. § 152(d)(1)(B). Although the exemption deduction is disallowed for 2018 through 2025, the IRS annually announces an inflation-adjusted amount that taxpayers can use as a surrogate for the exemption amount. That amount is $4,300 in 2020.

In most cases the taxpayer qualifies as a head of household because the other person is a member of the taxpayer's household for the requisite period. If the other person is a qualifying child, the taxpayer does not have to provide more than half of the child's support. Instead, the child must satisfy the tests described in Chapter 13. If the other person is not a qualifying child, the taxpayer must provide more than half of his support and be entitled to a dependency exemption for him.

2. Significance of Dependent Status

Before Congress enacted the Tax Cuts and Jobs Act of 2017, taxpayers who had dependents could deduct an inflation-adjusted exemption for each dependent in addition to deducting exemptions for themselves and their spouses. We used the rules in §§ 151 and 152 for that purpose. For 2018 through 2025, however, taxpayers cannot deduct personal exemptions. But an individual's status as a dependent remains important for both himself and for the parent or other individual who could have claimed him as a dependent.

A taxpayer who is the dependent of another taxpayer does not qualify for the standard deduction taken by taxpayers who don't itemize. Instead of deducting the inflation-adjusted amount provided in § 63(c), he deducts an amount based on a formula that favors earned income over unearned income. That formula is described in Chapter 13. A taxpayer who is a dependent is also ineligible for various other benefits. For example, he can't claim that someone else is his dependent (§ 152(b)(1)). Depending on his age and other factors, he may be subject to the kiddie tax.

An employee who has a dependent can exclude from gross income any fringe benefit (Chapter 3) available to the dependent if the Code section authorizing the exclusion includes dependents in its definition of employee. Taxpayers with dependents can include medical expenses they pay for the dependent in computing their § 213 medical expense deduction. An unmarried taxpayer who has a dependent may qualify as a head of household.

Code sections providing tax benefits to taxpayers with dependents vary in their application. Some simply require the dependent to be a qualifying child or a qualifying relative (Chapter 13); others impose a maximum age requirement, which is not necessarily uniform throughout the Code. Still others are available only to the custodial parent even if that parent has assigned the dependency exemption to the noncustodial parent. Focus on the Code section's definition of dependent when dealing with these provisions.

3. Status Based on Other Factors

Taxpayers who are at least 65 qualify for an additional standard deduction. I.R.C. § 63(c)(1)(B), (3), (f). (That benefit is also available to taxpayers who are legally blind.) Taxpayers who are at least age 59.5 can withdraw retirement funds without being subject to a 10% tax on early withdrawals. I.R.C. § 72(t)(2)(A)(i); some withdrawals may escape the penalty for taxpayers who are at least 55. I.R.C. § 72(t)(2)(A)(v). The amount a taxpayer can treat as a medical expense for long-term care insurance premiums varies based on the taxpayer's age. I.R.C. § 213(d)(10). Taxpayers with no dependents can take an earned income tax credit only if they are at least 25 and are less than age 65. I.R.C. § 32(c)(1)(A)(ii)(II). This list is not all-inclusive. As with provisions based on status as a dependent, these provisions do not have a uniform age.

A nonresident alien who has gross income that is not excluded by a treaty is subject to the income tax. We do not cover provisions treating nonresident alien taxpayers differently from citizens and resident aliens in this book.

C. Income from Services

1. Code Rules

Section 73 taxes compensation income to the minor who earned it even if his parents have a right to it under state law. But § 73 does not make a salary reasonable. If the employer is related to the minor, she has an incentive to pay excessive compensation if she is in a higher marginal tax bracket than the minor. Each dollar treated as salary is taxed at the minor's lower marginal rate instead of at her higher marginal rate. The result does not change if she incorporates her business; a related person is paying the compensation.

> Example 20-2. Arnold earns $8 per hour working as a part-time cashier in an auto parts store owned by an unrelated party. Even if state law gives his parents ownership of the income, Arnold is taxed on it.

> Example 20-3. Assume that Arnold's mother, who owns a coffee shop, hires him as a part-time cashier for $20 per hour. Because he earned only $8 per hour at the auto parts store, the IRS should succeed if it challenges the salary as unreasonable. Arnold is taxed on the amount treated as reasonable. His mother can deduct only the amount determined to be reasonable.

Section 66 applies to residents of community property states. In those states, earnings of each spouse are treated as earnings of the community. Each spouse has an undivided one-half interest in those earnings. Because joint returns using a separate rate schedule have been allowed since 1948, much of the advantage previously enjoyed by residents of community property states has ended. Residents of both community property and common law states can report all their income on a joint return.

If they do not file a joint return, spouses in common law states report only their actual income on the separate returns. Each spouse in a community property state reports one-half of the community income if they file separately. The different reporting rules reflect the different property regimes. The Supreme Court upheld this difference in *Poe v. Seaborn*, 282 U.S. 101 (1930). But these rules could cause hardship in a troubled marriage. The spouses may no longer share their income or even share information about that income. Section 66(a) applies to earned income that is treated as community income by spouses who do not file a joint return. The income is allocated to the spouse who actually earned it, and not equally to each spouse, if they live apart at all times during the year and no earned income is transferred between them.

2. Judicial and IRS Decisions

Two factors are important in determining whether income is taxed to the person who earned it: (1) whether the service provider voluntarily relinquished a right to the income; and (2) whether she had the ability to direct who would receive it.

a. Contractual Assignments

An early decision on this topic is *Lucas v. Earl*, 281 U.S. 111, 114–15 (1930). The Earls entered into a contract in 1901 to treat income earned by either of them as owned one-half by each. There was no income tax then. The Supreme Court did not consider their motive the determining factor. The Court's opinion includes two terms — "anticipatory arrangements" and "fruit [and] tree" — that are regularly cited in decisions regarding assignment of income.

> There is no doubt that the statute could tax salaries to those who earned them and provide that the tax could not be escaped by antic-ipatory arrangements and contracts however skilfully [sic] devised to prevent the salary when paid from vesting even for a second in the man who earned it. That seems to us the import of the statute before us and we think that no distinction can be taken according to the motives leading to the arrangement by which the fruits are attributed to a different tree from that on which they grew.

The split allowed in *Poe v. Seaborn, supra,* arose by operation of the state's community property law and not by contract. Although the joint return regime enacted in 1948 limits the importance of this issue in an intact marriage, the holding in *Lucas v. Earl* remains viable for assignments in other contexts.

b. Directing Payment to Another Person

Lucas v. Earl involved a contract. But a service provider might assign income to another person without being required to do so by contract. In those situations, courts focus on his right to determine who receives the income. If he tells his employer to pay fees or salary to a third party, he must still report the income.

A direction of payment to another person may be taxed to the service provider even if the assignment is required by a divorce decree. *Kochansky v. Commissioner*, 92 F.3d 957, 959 (9th Cir. 1996), involved a divorce settlement that allocated a portion of a contingent fee to the taxpayer's former spouse. In holding for the government, the court cited to *Lucas v. Earl*.

> In the present case, Kochansky did not own, and could not transfer, the McNarys' claim that was producing the contingency. Nor did he transfer himself or his law practice. He continued to render and control the personal services that produced the fee. He transferred only the

right to receive the income. In terms of the tree-fruit analogy, "there was no tree other than [the taxpayer] himself."

c. Refusal to Accept Income

If the service provider refuses to accept compensation, and does not direct that compensation to another person, she generally avoids taxation. For example, an individual who volunteers her services to charity is not taxed on the hypothetical value of her services.

The refusal to accept principle has also been applied when the taxpayer was entitled to compensation but refused to accept it. *Commissioner v. Giannini*, 129 F.2d 638, 641 (9th Cir. 1942), is often cited for this rule. Mr. Giannini was entitled to 5% of the corporation's net profits. After being credited with more than $400,000 for the first half of the year, he informed the directors that he would not accept any additional compensation that year. The corporation donated the remaining salary to a university to establish a foundation in his honor. The Ninth Circuit distinguished *Giannini* from *Lucas v. Earl*. It noted that the lower court's findings were "to the effect that the taxpayer did not receive the money, and that he did not direct its disposition. All that he did was to unqualifiedly refuse to accept any further compensation for his services with the suggestion that the money be used for some worth while purpose. So far as the taxpayer was concerned, the corporation could have kept the money."

The IRS respected a waiver of fees by the executor of an estate in Rev. Rul. 66-167, 1966-1 C.B. 20. The executor was the decedent's surviving spouse and was entitled to half of her estate pursuant to the will. The ruling held he did not have gross income with respect to the waived fees, half of which he then received as a tax-free devise. The fees do not have to be waived before any services are rendered but the waiver must primarily evidence intent to render a gratuitous service.

d. Registered Domestic Partners

Several states authorize civil unions or let their residents register their domestic partnerships. Some of these states are common law; others are community property. Even before the Supreme Court held that states could not outlaw same-sex marriage, the IRS had recognized income-splitting (or other aspects of the relationship) outside so-called traditional marriage. For example, CCA 201021050 stated that registered domestic partners in California should report one-half of their income on each of their returns but file as unmarried individuals. The ruling applied to income from services and from property. Under California law, as amended in 2007, registered domestic partners had full community property treatment unless they signed an agreement opting out of it.

e. Service Provider Acting as Agent

A service provider may be required to transfer income paid by a third party to his employer. To determine if he has gross income, we apply agency principles. If he was acting as his employer's agent, he does not have gross income. Instead, it is his employer's gross income.

An IRS ruling discussing agency principles involved faculty members who worked in a law school's clinical program. Their contract required them to turn over fees received for clinic representation of indigent clients. Representation was part of their duties, for which they already received a law school salary. The clerk of the court involved had taken the position that fees could not be made payable to the law school or its clinic. After citing the general rule regarding anticipatory assignment of income, the ruling stated: "However, the Internal Revenue Service has recognized that amounts that would otherwise be deemed income are not, in certain unique factual situations, subject to the broad rule of inclusion provided by section 61(a) of the Code." Rev. Rul. 74-581, 1974-2 C.B. 25, 26. A similar ruling covered fees received by physicians working on behalf of a hospital's medical research and education foundation. Rev. Rul. 76-479, 1976-2 C.B. 20.

Other rulings involve members of a religious order who remit their earnings to the order. The IRS applied the agency principle when a member was directed to perform services for another agency of the supervising church or an associated institution. Rev. Rul. 77-290, 1977-2 C.B. 26. It reached a different result in Rev. Rul. 84-13, 1984-1 C.B. 21. The member had received permission to establish a private practice. Because he had taken vows of poverty and obedience, he remitted his net earnings to the order. He did not limit his practice to members of the order or even to members of any religious order, and he was free to accept or reject potential clients. The IRS cited to language in Rev. Rul. 79-132, 1979-1 C.B. 62, 63: "The vow of poverty itself does not cause the member to be considered an agent...."

Liddy v. Commissioner, T.C. Memo. 1985-107, illustrates how the agency principle applies when a taxpayer receives funds as a conduit. Mr. Liddy participated in activities related to intelligence gathering regarding potential opponents that President Nixon might face in running for reelection in 1972. He received funds, disbursed them to other persons, and did not report them as gross income. He was taxed only on amounts for which he could not provide an accurate accounting. The Tax Court noted that "amounts received over which a taxpayer is acting as a mere agent or conduit are not required to be reported as income."

D. Income from Property

1. Fruit and Tree Doctrine

Helvering v. Horst, 311 U.S. 112 (1940), is frequently cited for its statement that the fruit-income cannot be attributed to a different tree-taxpayer than the one on which it grew. That case involved bonds to which interest coupons were attached. Shortly before the interest was payable, the father detached the coupons and gave them to his son. The father retained the underlying bonds and remaining coupons. He could have avoided this result by giving his son both the bonds and the coupons that were not yet due. He could also have transferred all his ownership rights to a trust of which his son was the income beneficiary and his daughter was the remainder taker.

Bonds issued without coupons are subject to the same rules if the issuer makes regular interest payments. Some bonds are issued without either coupons or regular interest payments. Many U.S. government bonds are issued this way. The discount from face value represents the interest that the purchaser will receive when the bond matures. Section 454(a) provides options for taxpayers who own non-interest-bearing obligations issued at a discount and redeemable for fixed amounts that increase at stated intervals. The bond owner does not report gross income until he disposes of the bond unless he elects to report the increase in value on a current basis. If he dies without having reported the interest, the increase in value that occurred before his death is generally treated as § 691 income in respect of a decedent. It is taxed to the recipient rather than to the decedent. *See* Rev. Rul. 64-104, 1964-1 C.B. 223. If he gratuitously transfers the bond before he dies, Rev. Rul. 55-278, 1955-1 C.B. 471, requires him to report the increase in redemption amount as gross income. That 1939 Code ruling cites to *Helvering v. Horst*.

In a ruling citing Rev. Rul. 55-278, the IRS indicated that the assignment of income principle applied even to transfers between spouses (or between former spouses incident to a divorce) that would normally not involve recognition of gain. *See* Rev. Rul. 87-112, 1987-2 C.B. 207, which involved bonds issued at a discount. In Rev. Rul. 2002-22, 2002-1 C.B. 849, the IRS changed its reasoning and indicated it would not assert assignment of income principles. Instead, it would have taxed the transferor spouse in Rev. Rul. 87-112 based on § 454 and its regulations.

Income that does not accrue over time is treated differently. When a corporation declares a dividend, for example, several dates are involved. The declaration date is the date on which the board of directors declares that it will pay a dividend and sets the amount per share. The record date determines who is entitled to receive the dividend on the payment date. A shareholder who sells her stock before the record date is not entitled to the dividend. A shareholder who sells her stock after the record date is entitled to it even though the sale occurs before the dividend payment date. The same rules apply if the shareholder transfers the stock gratuitously. *See Bishop v. Shaughnessy*, 195 F.2d 683 (2d Cir. 1952).

Assignments of contingent income rights are more likely to succeed. For example, in PLR 201232024, the IRS determined that the assignor would not be taxed on the proceeds of a lawsuit he assigned while an appeal was pending. The ruling discusses several judicial opinions comparing rights to income that is certain to occur with claims that are doubtful or contingent at the time of the transfer. It stated that "a transferor who makes an effective transfer of a claim in litigation to a third person before the time of the expiration of appeals in the case is not required to include the proceeds of the judgment in income under the assignment of income doctrine because such claims are contingent and doubtful in nature."

Potential problems arise when a taxpayer gratuitously transfers an intangible asset that is attributable to his own efforts. For example, he might have obtained a patent or a copyright. If he transfers it to a donee, should the royalties be taxed to the new owner instead of the person whose efforts produced it? The issues discussed below regarding the relevance of title apply here. If the original taxpayer had negotiated the royalty contract before making the transfer, he probably will be taxed on the royalties. If the donee negotiated the contract, the donee is likely to be the appropriate taxpayer.

2. Relevance of Title to Property

Income from property does not necessarily follow title if that does not accurately reflect economic reality. The title holder may be accommodating a different taxpayer for reasons other than tax evasion. For example, in *Monk v. Commissioner*, T.C. Memo. 2008-64, the income of a bar was not taxed to the person whose name was on the liquor license and checking account. He did not bear any risk of ownership or share in the bar's profits. He had placed his name on the relevant documents because the actual owner had a felony conviction and feared he would be denied a license. The court treated the arrangement as a lease from which the nominal owner received rental income.

Likewise, in *Salvatore v. Commissioner*, T.C. Memo. 1970-30, a mother was taxed on the gain from selling a service station even though she had transferred an interest in the station to her children. The transfer occurred after she had entered into a contract to sell the property. If she had transferred the interest before negotiating the sale, the outcome would likely have been different.

The next chapter considers another aspect of property ownership, the transfer of interests in a partnership from one family member to another. The kiddie tax discussed below has reduced the family's ability to benefit from transfers to younger beneficiaries, but family partnerships continue to offer a means for splitting income among multiple taxpayers.

3. Sale of Future Income Rights

A taxpayer who sells a future right to income and receives its value may be able to report gross income currently instead of waiting until the buyer receives the income. This technique, which was upheld in *Estate of Stranahan v. Commissioner*, 472 F.2d 867 (6th Cir. 1973), can be used to increase current-year income. For example, a taxpayer may have an expiring deduction carryover that he can offset against current income, or he may expect tax rates to increase in future years. In *Estate of Stranahan*, the taxpayer sold his rights to future dividends declared by a corporation; his son was the buyer. Both were shareholders and employees of the corporation. In fact, the father was a founding shareholder and his son succeeded him as an officer. None of these relationships appeared to have affected the court's decision.

E. Income in Respect of a Decedent

A decedent's estate (and ultimately his beneficiaries) receives his property and the right to income he did not receive before he died. A beneficiary who inherits property generally takes a fair market value basis, so she avoids being taxed on appreciation that occurred during the decedent's life. I.R.C. § 1014. A different rule applies to income rights. If the decedent used the cash method, his final tax return does not include items of income paid after his death. Those items are income in respect of a decedent. They do not qualify for the § 102(a) exclusion for gifts, bequests, devises, or inheritances. The person who receives them includes them in gross income. I.R.C. § 691(a)(1). The recipient looks to the decedent in determining the character of that income. I.R.C. § 691(a)(3).

The decedent may also owe deductible amounts that he did not pay before dying. These could include personal expenses, such as mortgage interest and state and local taxes, or business or income-producing expenses. The deduction is taken by the estate when it pays the item. If the estate is not liable for payment, the deduction is taken by a person who acquires an interest in property from the decedent if that interest is subject to the obligation. I.R.C. § 691(b).

Income in respect of a decedent is considered in calculating the decedent's estate tax. Section 691(c) lets any person who reports income in respect of a decedent deduct the estate tax attributable to that item.

F. Kiddie Tax

Students who work generally have part-time school year and full-time summer jobs with relatively low per-hour rates. If they could compute their taxable income and income tax the same way as other unmarried individuals, they would likely be taxed at the lowest rates.

Parents and other relatives who are taxed at higher rates might try to transfer income to a child or grandchild by transferring income-producing property to him. In the most egregious cases, the transfer might be even more suspect. A parent or other relative might transfer income-producing property but retain the ability to retake the property. He might report the income as the child's and count on not being audited.

Section 1(g) reduces a family's ability to shift the tax consequences of property income to a younger family member. It does so by taxing an affected individual at her parent's rate on most of her unearned income. It does not apply to her earned income.

The rules governing the kiddie tax initially changed for 2018 and later years as a result of the Tax Cuts and Jobs Act or 2017. Those changes, which applied the tax rate schedule used for trusts and estates, had unexpected, and adverse, tax consequences for many moderate-income families. Congress restored the pre-2018 rules at the end of 2020 and let taxpayers select the set of rules they preferred for 2018 and 2019. The discussion below covers the now-restored original rules.

The kiddie tax applies to any child who has not attained age 18 by the end of the taxable year. It also applies to any child who has attained age 18 but who has not attained age 19 by the end of the taxable year and qualifies as a dependent using the definitions in § 152(c)(3)(A). Finally, it applies to any child who has not attained age 24, is a full-time student, and qualifies as a dependent using the same definitions. Children who are at least age 18 are exempt if their earned income exceeds one-half of their support for the year. A child who has no living parent or who is married and files a joint return is also exempt. I.R.C. § 1(g)(2).

Section 1(g) uses the §911(d)(2) definition of earned income: "wages, salaries, or professional fees, and other amounts received as compensation for personal services actually rendered...." In addition to interest, dividends, and other investment income, the child's gross income from taxable scholarships, prizes, and punitive damages received on account of personal injury are categorized as unearned income. Section 1(g)(4)(C) provides only one exception: gross income from a qualified disability trust is treated as earned income.

When the kiddie tax applies, the child's earned income and a portion of her unearned income are taxed at her rates. The remainder of her unearned income is taxed at her parents' rates and is called net unearned income. The portion of her unearned income taxed at her own rates is equal to her standard deduction plus the greater of her standard deduction or her itemized deductions attributable to unearned income. In most cases, she does not itemize deductions, so the relevant amount is usually twice her standard deduction. Note that the standard deduction for purposes of the kiddie tax categories is a flat amount. It is not computed the same way as the standard deduction used in computing taxable income.

The child first computes her taxable income without regard to the kiddie tax. She then computes an amount equal to the sum of (1) the tax that would be due on her taxable income after subtracting her net unearned income and (2) the tax due on her share of the allocable parental tax. Her tax is whichever computation yields the larger amount. I.R.C. § 1(g)(1).

The computation above introduces two terms: net unearned income and allocable parental tax. The net unearned income is computed by starting with the child's adjusted gross income that is not attributable to earned income and subtracting her standard deduction and the greater of her standard deduction or her itemized deductions. I.R.C. § 1(g)(4). The standard deduction provided by § 63(c)(5)(A) is inflation-adjusted.

The allocable parental tax is her share of the amount by which her parent's tax would be increased if the parent's taxable income included the net unearned income of all children subject to the kiddie tax. If there is only one such child, the computation is relatively simple. We add the child's net unearned income to the parent's taxable income and then recompute the parent's tax. If there is more than one child subject to the kiddie tax, the total allocable parental tax is allocated among the children based on each child's share of the total net unearned income. I.R.C. § 1(g)(3)(B). The parent does not recompute any exclusions, deductions, or credits as part of the computation. I.R.C. § 1(g)(3)(A). If the parent is in a higher tax bracket than the child, the child's net unearned income is taxed at the parent's highest tax rate. If the child is in a higher tax bracket than the parent, she pays tax on all her income using her own rate schedule.

If the parents do not file a joint return, the parents' marital status is relevant. If they are not married, the custodial parent's tax computation is used. If they are married and file separate returns, the computation is based on the income of the parent with the greater taxable income. I.R.C. § 1(g)(5).

If the child itemizes deductions, she computes the unearned income that is not subject to the kiddie tax by adding two amounts. The first amount is the § 63(c)(5)(A) standard deduction. The second amount is the greater of the § 63(c)(5)(A) standard deduction or her itemized deductions attributable to adjusted gross income that is not earned income.

Checkpoints

- Married taxpayers can file jointly or file separate returns.

- Joint returns are required for certain tax benefits. Separate returns avoid joint and several liability.

- Unmarried taxpayers qualify for lower tax rates if they are surviving spouses or heads of households than if they are neither.

- Eligibility for certain tax benefits can be affected by the taxpayer's age, citizenship or residency, or status as a dependent.

- Income from services is generally taxed to the person who rendered the services.

- Compensatory arrangements are more likely to be scrutinized if the parties are related.

- Income from property is generally taxed to the person who owns the property.

- A taxpayer who transfers the right to income but retains the income-producing property remains taxable on the income.

- A taxpayer who receives income in respect of a decedent includes it in gross income even though it was received gratuitously.

- The kiddie tax limits the tax saved by transferring income-producing property to a child described in § 1(g).

Chapter 21

Income-Producing Entities

Roadmap
• Introduction
• Corporations
• Partnerships
• Limited liability companies
• Trusts and estates

A. Introduction

This chapter introduces entities that report gross income and expenses. Although tax attributes are important, their shareholders, partners, and beneficiaries may care more about centralization of management, business continuity, or asset protection. The entity's tax consequences—and those of its owners—reflect the type of entity and the distributions, if any, that it makes. These topics are covered in greater detail in specialized tax courses.

Transactions between a closely held entity and an owner or beneficiary may be affected by Code sections limiting deductions for expenses or losses. Even if no formal disallowance provision applies, the IRS scrutinizes these transactions closely because the parties are not acting at arm's-length.

B. Corporations

Unless a corporation elects S corporation status, it is a C corporation. The letters C and S describe the location of many of the relevant Code sections—Subtitle A (Income Taxes), Chapter 1 (Normal Taxes and Surtaxes), Subchapters C and S.

C and S corporations share the corporate characteristics covered in a business entities course. They issue shares of stock to shareholders, who can transfer their shares to third parties without affecting the corporation's existence. Shareholders' liability for corporate actions is generally limited. Status as a shareholder does not confer a right to participate in management. Closely held corporations often vary from the norm. To maintain control by family members, they may issue shares that are subject to transfer or voting restrictions.

Although the term corporation implies an entity that has incorporated pursuant to a statute, incorporation may not be required for tax purposes. The regulations let an unincorporated entity, such as a limited liability company, elect to be taxed as a corporation. Reg. § 301.7701-3. If it does not make an election, a single-owner unincorporated entity is disregarded as an entity separate from its owner; it is called a "disregarded entity" or a "tax nothing," and an entity with more than one owner is taxed as a partnership. The regulations governing this election are the "check the box" regulations. For purposes of this chapter, the term corporation means an incorporated entity.

1. C Corporations and S Corporations

C corporations. A C corporation pays tax on its taxable income at the flat rate of 21%. I.R.C. § 11(b). Before 2018, most C corporations were taxed at graduated rates, which ranged from 15% to 35%. So-called qualified personal service corporations were taxed at a flat rate of 35%; although they now use the flat 21% rate, different accounting methods apply to them. These entities, which are defined in § 448(d)(2), primarily provide services in the fields of health, law, engineering, architecture, accounting, actuarial science, performing arts, or consulting. Substantially all the value of their stock is owned by employees (including categories treated as employees) performing such services.

Shareholders are taxed on corporate profits only if they receive a dividend, which is a distribution of the corporation's earnings and profits (E&P). I.R.C. §§ 301(c)(1), 316. E&P is a concept used in determining if a distribution is a taxable dividend. It differs from taxable income. For example, a corporation can deduct federal income tax in computing E&P but not in computing taxable income. E&P also differs from accounting income. Because the corporation cannot deduct the dividends it pays, distributed earnings are taxed to both the C corporation and its shareholders. That aspect of dividends is often referred to as the double taxation of corporate profits.

> **Example 21-1.** ABC Corporation had taxable income of $100,000 in 2019 and paid federal income tax of $21,000. ABC distributed $10,000 of its after-tax profits to its shareholders. They report $10,000 of gross income.

S corporations. A corporation must elect S corporation status to avoid being taxed as a C corporation. The rules governing eligibility appear in § 1361(b). To qualify for S status, a corporation can have no more than 100 shareholders, although members of a family are treated as one shareholder for this purpose. I.R.C. § 1361(c)(1). It cannot have nonresident aliens as shareholders, there are limitations on the types of entities that can be shareholders, and it can issue only one class of stock. The rules governing the election, to which all shareholders must consent, appear in § 1362.

An S corporation generally pays no tax. Instead, its shareholders are taxed on their pro rata share of the entity's taxable income. If it sustains a loss for the year, they deduct their pro rata share of that loss. Items that would be treated differently at the shareholder level are reported separately from the corporation's other taxable income. For example, a corporation with ordinary taxable income of $100,000 and long-term capital gain income of $7,000 reports those as separate items to its shareholders; it does not simply report taxable income of $107,000. Section 1366 provides the rules for reporting income and deductions on the shareholders' returns.

Because S corporations are pass-through entities, distributions to shareholders avoid double taxation. Shareholders report their share of both distributed and undistributed taxable income. They adjust their basis in the corporation's stock to reflect their share of corporate income, loss, and actual distributions. Their basis for debt owed them by the corporation may also be affected.

> **Example 21-2.** S Corporation had taxable income of $120,000 in Year 1 but made no distributions to its two 50% shareholders. Each shareholder reports $60,000 of gross income and increases his basis for his stock by $60,000. If the corporation had not elected S status, its shareholders would report no gross income, they would not increase their stock basis, and the corporation would be taxed on $120,000.

> **Example 21-3.** In Year 2, S Corporation had neither taxable income nor loss. It distributed $4,000 to each shareholder. They report no gross income in Year 2 because they reported that income in Year 1. Each shareholder reduces his basis for his stock by $4,000.

2. Using Corporations to Reduce Taxes

Because the top individual rate exceeds the top corporate rate, shareholders of a closely held C corporation might prefer retaining earnings in the corporation rather than distributing them. This is particularly true if they plan to sell their shares in the near future. They may also prefer that the corporation raise funds by borrowing and paying deductible interest instead of selling more shares, paying nondeductible dividends, and potentially diluting their ownership percentage. If the shareholders are also employees, they might have the corporation pay higher salaries and hope the IRS does not challenge those salaries as disguised dividends.

The lower tax rate applied to dividends by § 1(h) reduces somewhat the double taxation associated with paying dividends. In addition, the Code includes various anti-abuse provisions designed to prevent using a corporation to avoid taxes. Those provisions are covered in courses focusing on corporate taxation.

Although even undistributed income is taxed to its shareholders, the S corporation still offers potential tax savings if its shareholders are also its employees. Amounts they receive as salary are subject to both income and employment taxes, while their share of the corporation's taxable income is subject only to income taxes. The corporation and its shareholder-employees are not acting at arm's-length in setting salaries, and the IRS has succeeded in increasing the amount allocated to salary. This ability to allocate is analogous to the assignment of income issues discussed in an earlier chapter. Instead of trying to allocate income to a different taxpayer, the parties are trying to characterize it in a way that reduces the amount subject to employment tax.

The reasonable compensation issue is illustrated by *David E. Watson, PC v. United States*, 668 F.3d 1008 (8th Cir. 2012). The S corporation paid its sole shareholder a $24,000 salary and a $203,651 profit distribution in 2002 and similarly disparate amounts in 2003. He was a CPA with a master's degree in taxation. Because the court accepted the government expert's testimony that $91,431 would be reasonable compensation, the corporation owed employment tax on the amount it should have treated as salary.

C. Partnerships

Partnerships generally do not pay tax. Instead, they compute taxable income or loss and report those items to their partners. I.R.C. § 701. As is true for S corporations, partners are taxed on their share of partnership income even if there are no distributions. They increase their basis for their partnership interests by their share of partnership income; they reduce it by their share of partnership loss and by actual distributions. Partnership items that would be treated differently at the partner level (*e.g.*, capital gains) are reported separately from other items. I.R.C. § 702. When a partner renders services to his partnership or engages in other transactions with it, the tax consequences are affected by whether he is acting in his capacity as a partner. I.R.C. § 707.

Partnerships are not subject to limitations on the number of owners, types of owners, or types of ownership interest they can have. Thus, a partnership with 150 unrelated partners is possible, as is a partnership in which some partners own interests in partnership profits but not in partnership capital. A partnership can have general partners with management rights and unlimited liability for partnership debts and limited partners with neither characteristic. These possibilities necessitate complicated rules governing partnership tax allocations.

The partnership agreement generally governs the allocation of income and deductions. Section 704(b)(2) provides for reallocation for tax purposes if the allocation in the agreement does not have substantial economic effect. If the agreement has substantial economic effect, a family partnership offers an opportunity for reducing taxes. A parent who does not need her share of partnership profits for her own living expenses might transfer a partnership interest to her children. This technique is more promising if partnership profits are attributable to capital rather than to services performed by the partners.

By transferring a partnership capital interest, the parent also transfers the tax consequences of income produced by that interest. Two provisions limit this income-shifting technique. The first is the § 1(g) kiddie tax. When it applies, children who are younger than 19 (and children who are students and younger than 24) may be taxed at their parents' rate on their net unearned income. The second is § 704(e)(1). It provides for reallocating the distributive share back to the donor partner, even if capital is a material income-producing factor. Section 704(e)(1) applies if the donee's share of income is determined without allowance for reasonable compensation for services the donor renders or if the income allocated to the donated capital is proportionately greater than the amount allocated to the donor's capital. Unlike the kiddie tax, this provision does not have an age cut-off.

The regulations include guidelines for determining whether the transfer of the partnership interest will be recognized and whether capital is a material income-producing factor. The transferee must have acquired his interest "in a bona fide transaction, not a mere sham for tax avoidance or evasion purposes, and ... [be] the real owner of such interest." Reg. § 1.704-1(e)(1)(iii). The transfer must vest dominion and control of the partnership interest in the donee. Transactions between family members will be closely scrutinized, and a partnership may be recognized for some income tax purposes but not for others. Capital is a material income-producing factor if a substantial portion of the gross income is attributable to the employment of capital. Substantial inventories or substantial investment in plant, machinery, or equipment will ordinarily qualify. Reg. § 1.704-1(e)(1)(iv).

In *Commissioner v. Culbertson*, 337 U.S. 733, 742 (1949), the taxpayer entered into an oral partnership agreement with his four sons. They paid for their shares using gifts from him and their share of a loan that was repaid through partnership operations. The Court held that many factors were relevant in determining whether the parties "in good faith and acting with a business purpose intended to join together in the present conduct of the enterprise." These factors included the agreement, the conduct of the parties, their statements, testimony of disinterested persons, the relationship of the parties, their respective abilities and capital contributions, the actual control of income and the purpose for which it is used, and any other relevant facts.

A partnership might not involve a traditional business enterprise. In *Estate of Winkler v. Commissioner*, T.C. Memo. 1997-4, the court treated a family activity of purchasing lottery tickets as a partnership. But in *Dickerson v. Commissioner*, T.C. Memo. 2012-60, it refused to do so and held that mere joint ownership did not involve sufficient business activity to constitute a partnership. The court distinguished the facts in the two cases, including whether there was a consistent family practice of making ticket purchases.

The compensation versus share of profits allocation discussed for S corporations also applies to limited partners. If a partner receives compensation, both income tax and employment tax apply. If he receives a share of profits, only income tax applies. Section 1402(a)(13) excludes from the definition of net earnings from self-employment "the distributive share of any item of income or loss of a limited partner, as such, other than guaranteed payments ... to that partner for services actually rendered to or on behalf of the partnership to the extent that those payments are established to be in the nature of remuneration for those services." The Tax Court imposed employment tax on a limited partner in *Renkemeyer, Campbell & Weaver, LLP v. Commissioner*, 136 T.C. 137 (2011). The partnership treated none of its revenues from its law practice as net earnings from self-employment. It allocated the bulk of its profits to a partner that was an S corporation that generated only a small amount of revenue. The court held that a limited liability partnership (LLP) such as that in *Renkemeyer* was different from a traditional limited partnership, so § 1402(a)(13) did not prevent this treatment. Limited partners in an LLP may have management powers even though they are not subject to partnership debt.

D. Limited Liability Companies

Although limited liability companies (LLCs) have several corporate characteristics—the members can centralize management, and they enjoy limited liability—they are taxed as corporations only if they elect that treatment as allowed by Reg. § 301.7701-3. Otherwise, they are taxed as partnerships if they have more than one member and as disregarded entities if they have only one. No matter which tax regime governs, LLCs are not sole proprietorships, partnerships, or corporations. Courts must determine which rules governing other entities apply to them. For example, in *Walker v. Commissioner*, T.C. Memo. 2012-5, a dentist who previously had operated his practice as an S corporation formed an LLC to operate it. The LLC was taxed as a partnership. Dr. Walker held 1% of the LLC ownership; the remaining 99% was held by another LLC. The second LLC had no assets other than income allocated to it by the first LLC; it had no business activities. Its interests were owned by Dr. Walker, his wife, and their children. The second LLC did not distribute income; the doctor paid his children's taxes on undistributed income. The court rejected his attempts to avoid employment taxes and assign income to his children. The taxpayers in *Hardy v. Commissioner*, T.C. Memo. 2017-16, avoided this treatment for income from an LLC for which they had no management power.

E. Trusts and Estates

Trustees invest trust property and distribute income or principal either currently or in the future. A settlor may use a trust to pass wealth to future generations with more privacy than is provided by a will, provide for management of assets, or split her wealth over time between family members and charities. For tax purposes, a trust may be a simple trust or a complex trust. As a general rule, a simple trust must distribute all its income currently, and a complex trust can accumulate income for distribution at a later date. Estates are generally short-lived entities, established to collect the decedent's assets, pay her debts, and distribute the net assets (and income accumulated during the probate process) to the beneficiaries named in her will or to her intestate heirs.

Trusts and estates are entities separate from their beneficiaries, and the income tax rules that apply to these entities and their beneficiaries are complicated. Beneficiaries of complex trusts usually report income when they receive distributions; the trust is taxed on accumulated income. Beneficiaries of simple trusts may be taxed on trust income they have not yet received. Trust and estate income retains its character when it is reported to beneficiaries.

Example 21-4. The XYZ Trust received dividends of $5,000 and rents and interest of $6,000 and distributed all $11,000 to its only beneficiary, Andrew. Because the tax rates applied to dividends are lower than the rates applied to rents and interest, XYZ reports the dividends separately on the form it sends Andrew for use in preparing his tax return.

Some trusts are deemed controlled by their settlors, who may have retained a power to revoke or a reversionary interest. Income of a grantor trust is taxed to the settlor even if it is not distributed (or is distributed to a different person). The tax rules governing trusts and estates begin at § 641. Rules governing grantor trusts begin at § 671. Section 1398 governs taxation of an individual's bankruptcy estate.

Unless the trust is a grantor trust, it is a separate taxable entity. Thus, income that would be taxed to one person if owned outright can be split between the trust and its beneficiary. If the rates applied to trusts were similar to the rates applied to individuals, income-splitting would allow more income to be taxed at the lowest rates.

> **Example 21-5.** The Amy Trust can accumulate income or pay it to Amy. The trust had $50,000 of taxable income this year. If it accumulates the income, it is taxed on that income. If it distributes the income, Amy is taxed. If it distributes half the income and retains the rest, the trust and Amy are each taxed on half of the income. If the trust is a grantor trust, Amy is taxed on its income even if she receives no distributions.

Retaining income provides few tax benefits because of the rate structure applied to trusts. The tax rate structure for 2018 through 2025 has four marginal tax rates compared to seven for individuals. I.R.C. § 1(j)(2)(E). Perhaps more important, trusts and estates reach the 37% top rate at a low level of taxable income (taxable income greater than $12,950 in 2020). Because the entity is likely to be in a higher tax rate bracket than many of its beneficiaries, there are often no tax benefits for retaining income in the entity.

Checkpoints

- Corporations, partnerships, LLCs, trusts, and estates compute taxable income. Some of these entities are separate taxpayers; others are conduits for income and deductions reported by their owners.

- Owner-employees may be interested in using the entity to reduce both income and employment taxes.

- The check the box regulations let unincorporated entities such as LLCs elect to be taxed as corporations.

- C corporation shareholders report income only if they receive a dividend distribution. Because the corporation cannot deduct that dividend, distributed profits are subject to double taxation.

- S corporation shareholders report their pro rata share of corporate profits whether or not they receive a distribution. The S corporation does not pay tax on its profits. Shareholders also deduct their share of corporate losses.

- Partners report their pro rata share of partnership profits whether or not they receive a distribution. The partnership does not pay tax on its profits. Partners also deduct their share of partnership losses.

- Owner-employees of closely held pass-through entities may try to allocate their share of earnings to profits instead of salary so that they can avoid employment taxes.

- Taxable income of a trust or estate is generally taxed to the entity, if retained, or to the beneficiary, if distributed. In some cases, trust income is taxed to the trust's settlor.

Mastering Income Tax
Master Checklist

Chapter 1 • Introduction

❑ Income tax is imposed on taxable income, which is gross income minus deductions.

❑ Tax rates vary based on marital status, amount of taxable income, and types of taxable income.

❑ The alternative minimum tax increases the likelihood that taxpayers who extensively utilize various tax benefits pay a minimum amount of tax.

❑ Some Code sections have expiration dates, which can be extended; some Code sections are subject to inflation adjustments.

❑ The taxpayer can litigate without paying a deficiency proposed by the IRS if he petitions the Tax Court. He can litigate in district court or the Court of Federal Claims only if he first pays the disputed amount.

Chapter 2 • Overview of Gross Income

❑ Gross income is broadly defined to include accessions to wealth over which the taxpayer has dominion.

❑ Gross income does not include loans, because the taxpayer's obligation to repay offsets the value of the amount he borrows.

❑ Noncash items are gross income based on their value when received.

❑ The realization principle lets taxpayers defer reporting gains until they dispose of the property.

❑ Bargain purchases are not gross income; found property is gross income.

❑ The value of performing services for oneself or using one's own property is not gross income.

Chapter 3 • Income from Performing Services

❏ Although gross income includes compensation in any form, several fringe benefits are excluded by specific Code sections.

❏ If an employee receives property that is subject to a substantial risk of forfeiture, she can elect to be taxed immediately or postpone taxation until the property is substantially vested.

❏ Property is subject to a substantial risk of forfeiture if the employee's right to keep or transfer it is subject to forfeiture if he fails to render required services or if other conditions are not satisfied.

❏ Employee achievement awards received for length of service or safety achievement can be excluded. These awards are subject to dollar limits, as are the employer's deductions for these awards.

❏ Exclusions apply to benefits for health care, group-term life insurance, education expenses, adoption expenses, meals and lodging on the employer's business premises, and housing benefits provided by religious organizations and educational institutions.

❏ Generic benefits are provided by § 132, including benefits for which the employer incurs no substantial additional cost, discounts to employees for purchasing employer products or services, payments of an employee's business-related expenses, and benefits that are de minimis.

❏ Many fringe benefits are subject to nondiscrimination rules or dollar limitations.

❏ An employee can use a salary reduction agreement to pay for certain qualified benefits with pre-tax dollars.

Chapter 4 • Gratuitous Transfers; Transfers Between Spouses and Former Spouses

❏ Gross income does not include money or the value of other items the taxpayer receives as a gift, bequest, devise, or inheritance.

❏ The donor's motive generally determines if there was a compensatory motive, which prevents the exclusion from applying.

❏ The exclusion is based on the donor's detached, disinterested motives of generosity or similar donative motives.

❏ The exclusion is not available for gifts of income or for the income attributable to property received as a gift.

❏ The exclusion applies only to the receipt of the item. If the donee later sells the property, she may realize a gain or loss.

❑ The donee of an inter vivos gift generally takes the donor's basis for both gain and loss.

❑ The donee uses a lower basis for loss if the donor's basis exceeded the property's value on the date of the gift.

❑ The donee takes a fair market value basis for property received from a decedent.

❑ A spouse, or a former spouse who receives property incident to a divorce, treats the receipt as a gift and takes the transferor spouse's basis for the property.

❑ In a part gift/part sale transaction, the donee's basis is the greater of the donor's adjusted basis or the consideration paid by the donee.

Chapter 5 • Gain and Loss: Basis and Amount Realized

❑ Taxpayers realize gain if the amount realized exceeds their adjusted basis for gain. They realize loss if their adjusted basis for loss exceeds their amount realized.

❑ Amount realized equals the money and the value of any other consideration received, including debt the transferee agrees to pay.

❑ Adjusted basis is original basis—usually cost—increased by improvements and decreased by depreciation. Taxpayers who receive property as a prize or as compensation take a "tax cost" basis for the property.

❑ Taxpayers generally recognize gains or losses in the year they realize them, but exceptions apply to donative transfers and to nonrecognition transactions.

❑ Debt incurred to purchase the property is included in the purchaser's basis. Debt assumed by the buyer is included in the seller's amount realized.

❑ When a nonrecognition transaction occurs, either the transferor's basis shifts to replacement property he receives or his basis shifts to the person who receives the property.

Chapter 6 • Excluded Gains

❑ Taxpayers who sell a principal residence may exclude up to $250,000 of their gain; the maximum is doubled for married taxpayers who file a joint return.

❑ Taxpayers must own the property and use it as a principal residence for at least two years out of the five years preceding the sale. The exclusion is generally available only once in any two-year period.

❑ Relief provisions apply if taxpayers cannot meet the qualification rules because of job change, health, or unexpected circumstances. Additional relief provisions apply based on changes in marital status or certain types of employment.

❏ Anti-abuse rules prevent taxpayers from converting depreciation recapture into excluded gain or from excluding gain that is not attributable to using the property as a principal residence.

❏ Shareholders who own qualified small business corporation stock may be allowed to exclude gains from selling their stock.

Chapter 7 • Life Insurance and Annuities

❏ The proceeds of a life insurance policy are generally excluded from gross income if they are received by reason of the death of the insured.

❏ The exclusion for proceeds can apply to benefits paid before death if the insured is terminally or chronically ill.

❏ The exclusion does not apply, or is limited, if the policy is transferred for a valuable consideration, if it is company-owned life insurance, or if proceeds are payable in installments after the insured's death.

❏ The exclusion applies even if the insured's employer paid the premiums as a fringe benefit.

❏ An annuity is a series of periodic payments made over a fixed term or over a variable term, such as for the annuitant's life.

❏ The taxpayer uses the exclusion ratio to compute the portion of each payment he can exclude from gross income.

❏ Payments received after he has recovered his investment tax-free are gross income. His final tax return includes his unrecovered cost if he dies before recovering his investment tax-free.

Chapter 8 • Discharge of Indebtedness

❏ A taxpayer who does not repay amounts he owes has gross income unless an exclusion provision applies.

❏ Exclusions apply to discharges of indebtedness that occur in a bankruptcy proceeding, when the taxpayer is insolvent, and in situations involving farms, business real property, and principal residences.

❏ The insolvency exclusion is limited to the amount by which the debtor was insolvent before the discharge.

❏ Taxpayers reduce various tax attributes—including basis of their property—if they exclude income from discharge of indebtedness. That results in increased future income.

❏ There are also exclusions for amounts the debtor could have deducted, certain discharged student loans, and debt reductions made by a creditor-seller.

❏ Section 108 includes anti-abuse rules, including one that applies if a related party acquires the debt.

❑   If a debtor surrenders property to the creditor, nonrecourse debt is treated as an amount realized even if it exceeds the value of the property.
❑   If the debt is recourse, the amount realized is limited to the property's value; any additional discharged debt is treated as debt discharge.

Chapter 9 • Compensation for Injuries or Sickness

❑   Damages to property are gross income to the extent they exceed the taxpayer's basis.
❑   Damages for lost business profits are gross income.
❑   Damages for personal physical injury or physical sickness are excluded unless they represent punitive damages or compensate for previously deducted medical expenses.
❑   Emotional distress is not a physical injury or sickness.
❑   Accident and health benefits from the taxpayer's own plan are excluded even if they exceed actual medical expenses or replace salary.
❑   Accident and health benefits from an employer-funded plan are gross income except to the extent they cover actual medical expenses or are payments for grievous injury and aren't based on time away from work.

Chapter 10 • Miscellaneous Inclusions and Exclusions

❑   Most prizes and awards are gross income whether or not the recipient entered a contest.
❑   If an award is made in property other than cash, the value of the property received is generally more relevant than the amount paid by the person making the award.
❑   Prizes are excluded if they are received for certain types of meritorious achievement. The recipient must not have entered the contest, must not have to render substantial future services, and must designate a qualifying government or tax-exempt organization to receive the prize.
❑   Gross income does not include scholarship and fellowship awards for tuition, fees, books, and equipment that are required for enrollment in the educational institution or for enrollment in a particular course.
❑   Exclusions are available for various educational savings plans, such as prepaid tuition programs.
❑   Interest on obligations of state and local governments is generally excluded from gross income.
❑   Income earned from U.S. government bonds and education savings programs is excluded if the funds are used for qualifying education expenses.

❏ Taxpayers who live and work in other countries can exclude limited amounts of foreign-source compensation income and employer-provided housing allowances.

❏ Additional exclusions appear in the Internal Revenue Code, in other statutes, and occasionally in administrative guidance.

❏ Alimony received under a post-2018 divorce or separation instrument is not included in the recipient's gross income. Alimony received under an earlier instrument may be included, depending on the terms of the instrument.

❏ Child support payments are not included in the recipient's gross income.

Chapter 11 • Overview of Deductions and Credits

❏ Deductions can be characterized by the type of activity in which the taxpayer is engaged or by where they appear on the tax return.

❏ Taxpayers take either itemized deductions or the standard deduction. In addition, they can take deductions listed in § 62.

❏ Some deductions are computed using formulas based on AGI.

❏ The appropriate year for taking a deduction is generally based on the taxpayer's accounting method.

❏ Credits are a direct offset against the tax otherwise due. A refundable credit can result in a refund even if it exceeds the tax otherwise due.

Chapter 12 • Business and Income-Producing Expenses

❏ Taxpayers can deduct ordinary and necessary expenses paid or incurred in carrying on a trade or business, for the production or collection of income, or for the management or preservation of property held for the production of income.

❏ In determining if an expense is ordinary and necessary, we consider whether similarly situated taxpayers make the outlay. We also look for public policy limitations that deny the deduction.

❏ An amount paid to purchase or improve an asset is a capital expenditure and is generally not currently deductible. This rule also covers rental payments that are really disguised purchases.

❏ Taxpayers recover the cost of capital expenditures through depreciation or amortization. Land is not depreciable because it is not subject to wear, tear, or obsolescence.

❏ Depreciation is computed using a formula for allocating basis over the property's useful life. Some property qualifies for 100% bonus depreciation or first-year expensing.

❑ Reasonable salaries are deductible. The Code includes limits applied to certain executives of publicly traded companies.

❑ Business travel expenses are deductible only if they are not lavish. Only 50% of reasonable meal expenses are deductible.

❑ The deductibility of transportation expenses (other than commuting) depends on whether the trip was primarily for business or pleasure. Additional limitations apply to foreign travel expenses.

❑ Commuting expenses are generally not deductible.

❑ Education expenses are not deductible if they qualify the taxpayer for a new trade or business.

❑ Expenses for business gifts and travel are subject to substantiation rules and other conditions.

❑ Clothing is deductible only if it is required by the job, is not suited for everyday wear, and is not so worn.

❑ Section 199A allows a limited deduction for qualified business income.

❑ Most unreimbursed employee business expenses are not deductible in 2018 through 2025.

❑ In determining if a former residence is "held for the production of income," courts consider the taxpayer's use of the property, attempts to rent it, and attempts to realize post-conversion appreciation.

Chapter 13 • Personal Expenses

❑ Personal outlays are deductible only if a specific Code section authorizes the deduction.

❑ Most personal deductions are allowed only if the taxpayer itemizes.

❑ Taxpayers can deduct alimony (for pre-2019 divorce or separation instruments), qualified education interest, qualified tuition, contributions to health savings accounts, and up to $300 of cash charitable contributions (2020 only) in computing AGI.

❑ The deduction for qualified residence interest is limited to loans covering no more than two qualified residences. The limits on acquisition indebtedness and home equity indebtedness vary based on when the debt was incurred.

❑ The deduction for state, local, and foreign taxes allowable with no business or income-producing connection is limited to real property taxes, personal property taxes, sales and use taxes, and income taxes. The deduction is capped at $10,000 in 2018 through 2025.

❑ The maximum deduction for gifts to charity is usually 50% of AGI, with a five-year carryover allowed for excess contributions. Gifts of cash may qualify for a 60% of AGI deduction limit (further increased for gifts in 2020).

❑ The charitable deduction varies depending on whether the gift was outright or in trust, whether the gift was cash or other property, and whether the charity was publicly supported or not.

❑ The deduction for unreimbursed medical care expenses is limited to amounts exceeding 10% of AGI (7.5% in 2020).

❑ Most taxpayers can take the standard deduction instead of deducting itemized deductions. The standard deduction amount is adjusted for inflation each year and varies based on filing status.

❑ Taxpayers could deduct personal exemptions for themselves, their spouses, and their qualifying dependents but not in 2018 through 2025. Different tests apply in determining whether a potential dependent is a qualifying child or a qualifying relative.

❑ Many personal deductions are subject to phase-outs based on the taxpayer's AGI.

Chapter 14 • Losses from Discrete Events

❑ Taxpayers who are engaged in a trade or business (or who hold property acquired in a transaction entered into for profit) deduct realized losses from both voluntary and involuntary dispositions.

❑ They use adjusted basis for loss to compute a total loss of business or for-profit property. They use the lesser of adjusted basis or decline in value for a partial loss.

❑ The deduction for casualty and theft losses of personal-use property is based on the lesser of the taxpayer's basis or the decline in value caused by the event for both total and partial losses. The amount computed by this formula is reduced by $100 per event and by any compensation received.

❑ To be a casualty loss, the loss must be sudden, unexpected, and unusual in nature.

❑ Personal casualty and theft losses are itemized deductions to the extent that they exceed personal casualty and theft gains. Only the amount of the net loss that exceeds 10% of AGI is deductible.

❑ In 2018 through 2025, personal casualty and theft losses that are not incurred in a federally declared disaster area are not deductible except to the extent the taxpayer has personal casualty gains that are not used to offset personal casualty and theft losses incurred in a disaster area.

❑ Losses from worthless securities that are capital assets are capital losses occurring on the last day of the taxable year. They are not treated as bad debts.

❑ Taxpayers can deduct bad debt losses if the debt is bona fide and uncollectible.

❑ Business bad debts are deductible as ordinary losses. Nonbusiness bad debts are treated as short-term capital losses.

❑ Although § 165 does not contain public policy limitations, courts may disallow a loss based on public policy grounds.

❑ A taxpayer cannot deduct a realized loss if the purchaser is a family member or related entity. Constructive ownership rules apply in determining if a corporation is a related entity.

❑ Section 267 applies a bright-line test. The taxpayer's motive for selling to the related person does not matter.

❑ Section 267 applies to both direct and indirect sales. Using a third-party as an intermediary does not avoid the disallowance if the sale is indirectly made to a related person.

❑ If the related person who acquired property later sells it at a gain, he reduces his gross income by the seller's previously disallowed loss.

Chapter 15 • Losses from Activities

❑ Section 280A limits the deductions a taxpayer may take if he makes both business or income-producing use and personal use of a residence. The uses can be concurrent (*e.g.*, a home office) or separate in time (*e.g.*, rental of personal-use property for part of the year).

❑ Section 183 disallows deductions that would normally be taken by a business or income-producing activity if the taxpayer does not engage in the activity for profit.

❑ Section 465 disallows deductions when a taxpayer is not at risk with respect to an activity. This may occur if the loss reported by the venture exceeds his contributions and he is not at risk because of nonrecourse financing.

❑ Section 469 disallows deductions for losses from activities in which the taxpayer's participation is too passive. The definition of a passive activity varies based on the type of activity.

❑ Section 461(l) disallows business losses that exceed the sum of business income plus an inflation-adjusted safe harbor amount.

❑ Wagering losses are not deductible to the extent they exceed wagering gains. This rule also applies to wagering expenses in 2018 through 2025.

❑ Several disallowance provisions provide for carrying disallowed items to future years.

Chapter 16 • Taxable Year and Accounting Methods

❏ Taxpayers report gross income and deductions for a single taxable year. Individuals usually use a calendar year. Entities often use a fiscal year ending in a month other than December.

❏ Strict adherence to annual accounting may not accurately reflect the economic consequences of transactions that affect multiple years.

❏ The tax benefit rule, claim of right provisions, and the net operating loss deduction provide relief from annual accounting.

❏ A cash-method taxpayer reports income when it is actually or constructively received. Income is constructively received when it is made available to her without restriction.

❏ An accrual-method taxpayer reports income when it is earned. He reports expenses when all events fixing the liability have occurred and the amount of the liability can be ascertained with reasonable accuracy. Economic performance may also be required.

❏ Businesses generally use the accrual method for inventory. If a business does not track the specific items it sells, it reports inventory using an assumption about the order in which it sells its inventory. The most likely assumptions are FIFO and LIFO.

❏ The installment method allocates the taxpayer's gain to each installment she receives. Exceptions apply to sales involving debt, sales of property subject to depreciation recapture, and sales to related persons.

❏ Taxpayers who perform long-term contracts generally report their profits using the percentage of completion method instead of the completed contract method.

❏ If a debt instrument does not provide for adequate interest, the original issue discount (OID) rules treat the discount from redemption price as interest instead of capital gain. The interest is included in gross income over the life of the instrument.

❏ Section 483 applies to sales that are not covered by the OID rules but that also fail to provide for adequate interest.

❏ Section 7872 applies to loans that do not provide for adequate interest. The computations reflect whether the loan is payable on demand or has a fixed term.

❏ If the loan is compensation-related, the borrower may also have gross income from compensation, for which the lender receives a business expense deduction. If the loan is a gift loan, the lender may have made a gift that is subject to gift tax.

Chapter 17 • Gain and Loss: Nonrecognition Provisions

❑ Nonrecognition provisions postpone taxation of gain or deduction of loss until a later disposition occurs.

❑ The postponed gain or loss is built into the basis of replacement property (or is used by the recipient in the case of transfers to a spouse or to a former spouse incident to a divorce).

❑ Partial gain recognition is possible if the taxpayer disinvests by receiving some nonqualifying property or keeping part of the proceeds of an involuntary conversion.

❑ The holding period for the property disposed of is usually added to the taxpayer's holding period for the replacement property.

❑ Some nonrecognition provisions apply only to gain; others apply only to loss. Some apply to both. Some nonrecognition provisions are mandatory; others are elective.

❑ Section 1031 is a mandatory provision governing exchanges of like-kind real property held for productive use in a trade or business or for investment. It applies to both gains and losses.

❑ Section 1033 covers gains from compulsory or involuntary conversions of any type of property. The replacement property must usually be similar or related in service or use to the property converted. Section 1033 is generally elective.

❑ Section 1091 is a mandatory provision covering losses from sales of stock or securities. It applies when the taxpayer acquires substantially identical stock or securities within 30 days before or after the loss disposition.

❑ Section 1041 is a mandatory provision covering gain or loss when a taxpayer transfers property to a spouse or to a former spouse. The section applies to transfers to a former spouse only if they are incident to their divorce.

❑ Section 1038 is a mandatory provision covering gain or loss when a taxpayer who sold real property reacquires it in full or partial satisfaction of debt secured by the property.

❑ Section 1400Z-2 is an elective provision covering gain when a taxpayer sells appreciated property and invests at least some of his gain in a qualified opportunity fund. The taxpayer does not have to use his entire sales proceeds to obtain nonrecognition.

Chapter 18 • Character of Gain and Loss; Depreciation Recapture; Section 1239

❏ Taxpayers who deduct depreciation reduce taxable income subject to the tax rates on ordinary income.

❏ Sections 1245 and 1250 limit their ability to report gain on that property as long-term capital gain.

❏ Section 1245 applies to all prior depreciation. Section 1250 usually applies only to depreciation in excess of the straight line amount.

❏ Unrecaptured § 1250 depreciation can qualify for capital gain treatment at a 25% tax rate instead of the lower rates applied to other capital gains.

❏ Section 1239 treats a taxpayer's gain as ordinary if he sells property to a related taxpayer that can depreciate it.

Chapter 19 • Capital Gains and Losses

❏ Long-term capital gains are taxed at lower rates than ordinary income. Dividends also qualify for these lower rates.

❏ The tax rates applied to collectibles and unrecaptured section 1250 gain are higher than the rates normally applied to net capital gains.

❏ Deduction limits apply to capital losses that exceed capital gains. Individual taxpayers can carry excess losses to future years.

❏ The taxpayer's holding period may reflect the time she held a different asset or the time her asset was held by another taxpayer.

❏ As a general rule, capital gain or loss results from selling or exchanging a capital asset.

❏ Most personal use and investment assets are capital assets.

❏ Code provisions may result in treating gains and losses as capital even though they are not from sales or exchanges of capital assets.

❏ Many business and investment assets are subject to a separate computation to determine if they have net gains or net losses. If § 1231 applies, a taxpayer who has net gains reports gains and losses as capital. Otherwise, he reports gains and losses as ordinary and avoids the capital loss limitations.

❏ Some Code provisions may convert potential capital gains and losses into ordinary gains and losses.

Chapter 20 • Filing Status and Allocating Income

❏ Income is generally taxed to the person who rendered the services or owned the income-producing property even if another person received it.

❏ Arrangements between related parties are more likely to be scrutinized than arrangements negotiated at arm's-length.

❏ Married taxpayers who file joint returns may pay more (or less) tax than if they were single. Benefit or detriment reflects whether their incomes are similar or disparate.

❏ The kiddie tax reduces the tax savings available from transferring income-producing property to a child. Only a limited amount of unearned income escapes taxation at the parent's marginal tax rate.

❏ When a cash-method taxpayer dies before receiving salary, fees, interest, or other items of income, his final tax return does not report them as gross income. Income in respect of a decedent items are gross income of the estate or of the beneficiary who receives them.

Chapter 21 • Income-Producing Entities

❏ An individual can operate a business directly as a sole proprietor, but she can also operate it indirectly through a corporation, partnership, LLC, or other entity.

❏ If the business operates as a C corporation, its shareholders report income when the corporation pays a dividend from its after-tax earnings. The corporation and its shareholders both are taxed on distributed earnings.

❏ If the business operates as an S corporation or partnership, shareholders and partners report their share of entity income even if it is not distributed. S corporations and partnerships are "pass-through" entities.

❏ An LLC can take advantage of "check the box" regulations and be taxed as a corporation instead of as a pass-through entity.

❏ If owners and entities are taxed separately, the allocation of income between them (and among owners) may provide tax-reduction opportunities.

❏ When an owner is also an employee, a pass-through entity may designate minimal amounts as salary in an attempt to reduce employment taxes. A C corporation, on the other hand, may designate payments as salary instead of dividends so that it can deduct them.

❏ Trusts and estates reach the highest tax rate at very low levels of taxable income.

Index